T0375459

Lecture Notes in Computer Science

Lecture Notes in Artificial Intelligence   **15170**

Founding Editor

Jörg Siekmann

Series Editors

Randy Goebel, *University of Alberta, Edmonton, Canada*
Wolfgang Wahlster, *DFKI, Berlin, Germany*
Zhi-Hua Zhou, *Nanjing University, Nanjing, China*

The series Lecture Notes in Artificial Intelligence (LNAI) was established in 1988 as a topical subseries of LNCS devoted to artificial intelligence.

The series publishes state-of-the-art research results at a high level. As with the LNCS mother series, the mission of the series is to serve the international R & D community by providing an invaluable service, mainly focused on the publication of conference and workshop proceedings and postproceedings.

Haizhou Li · Tanja Schultz · Yalei Bi · Jian Zhu ·
Hongsheng He · Jun Ma · Siqi Cai ·
Wanyue Jiang · Shuzhi Sam Ge
Editors

Social Robotics

16th International Conference, ICSR + InnoBiz 2024
Shenzhen, China, September 25–28, 2024
Proceedings

Springer

Editors
Haizhou Li 🆔
The Chinese University of Hong Kong
Shenzhen, China

Tanja Schultz 🆔
University of Bremen
Bremen, Germany

Yalei Bi
Shenzhen Institute of Advanced Technology
Shenzhen, China

Jian Zhu
The Chinese University of Hong Kong
Shenzhen, China

Hongsheng He 🆔
The University of Alabama
Tuscaloosa, AL, USA

Jun Ma
The Hong Kong University of Science
Guangzhou, China

Siqi Cai 🆔
National University of Singapore
Singapore, Singapore

Wanyue Jiang 🆔
Qingdao University
Qingdao, China

Shuzhi Sam Ge 🆔
National University of Singapore
Singapore, Singapore

ISSN 0302-9743 ISSN 1611-3349 (electronic)
Lecture Notes in Artificial Intelligence
ISBN 978-981-96-1150-8 ISBN 978-981-96-1151-5 (eBook)
https://doi.org/10.1007/978-981-96-1151-5

LNCS Sublibrary: SL7 – Artificial Intelligence

This Springer imprint is published by the registered company Springer Nature Singapore Pte Ltd.
The registered company address is: 152 Beach Road, #21-01/04 Gateway East, Singapore 189721, Singapore

If disposing of this product, please recycle the paper.

Preface

The 16th International Conference on Social Robotics (ICSR) + InnoBiz 2024 was held in Shenzhen, 25–28 September 2024. It was an exciting journey preparing for the event because it was the first time the conference came to Shenzhen, the robotics manufacturing hub in China. Shenzhen designates artificial intelligence, robotics, and intelligent robotics as part of its strategic and future industry clusters. It aspires to become a leading innovation center of global influence for robotics. Shenzhen was proud to host the conference with the theme of Innovation for Business - InnoBiz 2024.

The Chinese University of Hong Kong, Shenzhen was founded in 2014, with AI and Robotics as one of its core competences. At its 10th anniversary, CUHK-Shenzhen was pleased to be the local organization of the conference, in collaboration with Global Robotics, Arts, and Science Synergies (GRASS), Shenzhen Institute of Artificial Intelligence and Robotics for Society, Shenzhen Research Institute of Big Data, Shenzhen Robotics Association, and the Chinese and Oriental Languages Information Processing Society. This book comprises the peer-reviewed proceedings of the conference. Out of 82 submitted manuscripts, an international team of Senior Program Committee and Program Committee members rigorously reviewed and selected 36 regular papers for inclusion in the proceedings.

The conference featured 3 keynote speeches, 36 regular presentations, 26 invited presentations, 10 industry exhibitions, one expert panel, and one robotics design competition. Along the way, the local organization was helped greatly by Shuzhi Sam Ge, John-John Cabibihan, and the ICSR Steering Committee, to whom we are extremely thankful.

We would like to take this opportunity to thank CUHK-Shenzhen, COLIPS council, and the local volunteers for their efforts and dedication, in particular, Jian Zhu, Hongsheng He, and Jun Ma for chairing the technical committee, Siqi Cai and Wanyue Jiang for taking care of the publicity, Xinyuan Qian for organizing the special sessions, Rachel Tan for coordinating the industry track and exhibitions, Amit Kumar Pandey for organizing the design competition, and Wen Wu for leading the secretariat. Finally, we are immensely grateful for the continued support from the authors, participants, and sponsors, without whom ICSR + InnoBiz 2024 would not have been possible.

September 2024   Haizhou Li
Tanja Schultz
Yalei Bi
Jian Zhu
Hongsheng He
Jun Ma
Siqi Cai
Wanyue Jiang
Shuzhi Sam Ge

Organization

General Chair

Li, Haizhou   Chinese University of Hong Kong, China

General Co-chairs

Schultz, Tanja   Universität Bremen, Germany
Bi, Yalei   Shenzhen Institute of Advanced Technology,
     Chinese Academy of Sciences, China

Program Committee Chairs

Zhu, Jian   Chinese University of Hong Kong, Shenzhen,
     China
He, Hongsheng   University of Alabama, USA
Ma, Jun   Hong Kong University of Science and
     Technology (Guangzhou), China

Industry Chairs

Huang, Dongyuan   UBTECH Robotics, China
Dong, Minghui   Chinese and Oriental Languages Information
     Processing Society, Singapore

Local Arrangement Chair

Pan, Chunlei   National University of Singapore, Singapore

Workshop Chairs

Qian, Xinyuan   University of Science and Technology Beijing,
     China
Vollmer, Anna-Lisa Britta   Universität Bielefeld, Germany

Finance Chair

Cabibihan, John-John   Qatar University, Qatar

Competitions Chair

Pandey, Amit Kumar   Rovial Space, France

Publication Chairs

Cai, Siqi   National University of Singapore, Singapore
Jiang, Wanyue   Qingdao University, China

Publicity Chair

Zhang, Yuxin   Tsinghua University, China

Young Leader Chair

Bao, Dan   Tsinghua University, China

Sponsorships/Exhibitions Chairs

Wu, Yan   A-Star, Singapore
Wang, Lei   Chinese and Oriental Languages Information
                                      Processing Society, Singapore
Rachel Tan   SRA, China

Standing Committee Chair

Ge, Shuzhi Sam   National University of Singapore, Singapore

Standing Committee

Khatib, Oussama   Stanford University, USA
Mataric, Maja   University of Southern California, USA

Li, Haizhou	Chinese University of Hong Kong, Shenzhen, China
Dario, Paolo	Scuola Superiore Sant'Anna, Italy
Kheddar, Abderrahmane	LIRMM Montpellier, France and CNRS-AIST, Japan
Wang, Tianmiao	Beihang University, China

Contents

xiv   Contents

Diverse Gaussian Sampling for Human Motion Prediction

Jiefu Luo[1,2,3], Jiansheng Wang[4], Zhenfei Liu[1,2,3], and Jun Cheng[1,3(✉)]

[1] Guangdong Provincial Key Laboratory of Robotics and Intelligent System,
Shenzhen Institute of Advanced Technology, Chinese Academy of Sciences,
Shenzhen, China
jun.cheng@siat.ac.cn
[2] University of Chinese Academy of Sciences, Beijing, China
[3] The Chinese University of Hong Kong, Hong Kong, China
[4] Department of Pediatric Orthopedics, Shenzhen Children's Hospital, Shenzhen
518000, Guangdong, People's Republic of China

Abstract. In many industrial applications, it is necessary to obtain accurate human motion prediction. The prediction of human movement based on a 3D skeleton, which forecasts future postures using the human skeletal structure, significantly aids in enabling machines to understand human behavior and react more intelligently. Additionally, by predicting human actions, potential dangers can be perceived, especially in safety-related issues, necessitating a broader range of predictions. In this paper, considering the greater diversity generated by Variational Autoencoders (VAEs), we employ VAEs for prediction. In contrast to other studies, our primary focus is on obtaining more diverse samples. Extensive experiments demonstrate that our proposed model performs well on the Human 3.6M [35] and HumanEva-I [36] datasets.

Keywords: Human motion prediction · Diversity Prediction ·
Sampling method

1 Introduction

Human motion prediction plays a pivotal role in various domains, including human-computer interaction and autonomous driving [40–45]. However, predicting a person's future actions can be challenging due to the subjectivity of human intent, leading to diverse potential outcomes. In many safety-critical applications, the ability to generate diverse predictive results is essential.In recent work, Variational Autoencoders (VAEs) [23] have been widely used for diverse predictions. Additionally, some studies have employed Denoising Diffusion Probabilistic Models (DDPMs) [25] as part of diffusion models to generate diverse outcomes. In the context of VAEs, the DLow method [11], which employs a diverse latent flow approach, has achieved noteworthy results. This paper builds upon this foundation and focuses on enhancing feature extraction.

H. Li et al. (Eds.): ICSR + InnoBiz 2024, LNAI 15170, pp. 1–12, 2025.
https://doi.org/10.1007/978-981-96-1151-5_1

Considering traditional resampling methods, the randomness of Gaussian samples is primarily influenced by the randomly assigned ϵ. As ϵ approaches zero, sample values tend towards zero, and the positions of larger values become relatively fixed. We hypothesize that by employing affine transformations, it is possible to generate samples that traverse the primary feature space. In this approach, randomness is derived not only from ϵ but also from the coefficients of the affine transformation. Therefore, we propose our sampling method for this process. To validate the effectiveness of our model, we conducted extensive experiments using two large-scale datasets: Human 3.6M and HumanEva-I. Our results demonstrate that our model surpasses most existing methods in terms of diversity prediction and accuracy. The main contributions of this paper can be summarized as follows:

- Variational Autoencoders (VAEs) were utilized for diverse prediction, and remarkable results were achieved, even with a relatively simple RNN-based VAE.
- A diversity sampling method was introduced, resulting in richer samples through trainable networks.

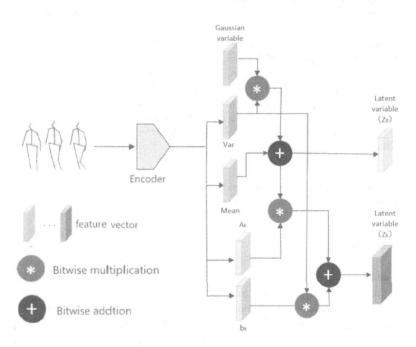

Fig. 1. Illustration of the sampling methods of the proposed DGVAE. The DGVAE reintroduces Gaussian variables for resampling and affine transformation. By resampling, we get the first latent variable Z_0, and on the basis of Z_0, affine transformations are performed to get other different latent variables Z_k, k stands of the number of latent variables

2   Related Work

2.1   Human Motion Prediction

In past works on human motion prediction, machine learning algorithms have been widely used to analyze human motion data. Techniques such as Functional Principal Component Analysis (FPCA) [3], wavelet decomposition [4], and more commonly, Markov models [1,2,5,6] and their variants have been utilized for prediction. However, with the continuous development of deep learning in recent years, an increasing number of deep learning networks have been applied to this task, including RNNs [18–20], CNNs [21,22], Transformers [35], VAEs [23], GANs [24], DDPMs [25].

2.2   Diversity Prediction

Due to the variability in human subjective intent and other factors, human movements exhibit certain uncertainties. Therefore, generating a good range of future predictions is an important consideration. A good diversity prediction requires the generated futures to be as diverse as possible while conforming to the laws of the physical world. Most models based on VAEs [7–17], DDPMs [26–30], and some based on GANs [31,32,36] have explored stochastic prediction. For example, DLow [11] based on VAEs proposes a diversity latent flow, generating latent variables Z of different distributions to achieve both accuracy and diversity in generation. Emad et al. [31] proposed the HP-GAN based on GANs, which combines a random vector with the embedding state at test time to simulate diversity, producing a diverse range of generative results. Similarly, methods based on DDPMs can also produce diverse outcomes, generally by introducing different initial noises to generate diverse results, as seen in HumanMAC [26].

3   Methodology

As depicted in Fig. 2, our model employs a simplistic RNN-based architecture as the backbone for both the Encoder and Decoder. This model utilizes diverse affine transformations to derive novel latent variables, with the coefficients of these transformations being generated by neural networks. Subsequently, these latent variables are decoded by the Decoder to produce the final output. We call our model DGVAE(Diverse Gaussian-sampling VAE).

We employ the traditional encoder-decoder model, where we need to extract a feature value $c = e_\theta\{x_0, x_1, \ldots, x_h\}$ from the historical sequence. This feature value c is then used to generate the future posture sequence $\{x_{h+1}, x_{h+2}, \ldots, x_{h+f}\} = d_\theta(c)$, where f represents the length of the future sequence, e_θ represents the encoder network, and d_θ represents the decoder network, achieving end-to-end generation of future postures.

Furthermore, for diversity prediction, we need to generate K different future posture sequences, denoted as $\{x_{h+1}, x_{h+2}, \ldots, x_{h+f}\}^i = d_\theta(c)$, $i = 1, 2, \ldots, k$.

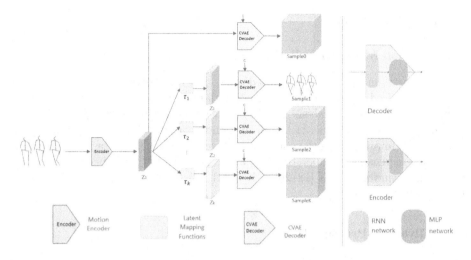

Fig. 2. Basic structure of the model. The historical sequence is encoded into latent variables, which are then transformed through different mapping functions $\tau_k(\cdot)$ to produce varied latent variables. These are used by RNNbased VAE to generate the predicted sequence Sample$K$.

3.1 Diverse Gaussian Sampling

In light of these issues, we propose a new sampling method. Similar to a standard VAE encoder, we have a known historical sequence $X_h = \{x_0, \ldots, x_h\}$, where $X_h \in \mathbb{R}^{B \cdot h \cdot d}$, B represents batch size, h represents input time length, and d represents feature dimension. X_h is input into the encoder, and its distribution is trained to align with the normal distribution, along with using reconstruction error to make our encoder compatible with our pretrained VAE decoder. Then, through our affine transformation τ_{ϕ_k}, we transform the original latent variables.

Our method takes full account of the 68-95-99.7 rule of Gaussian distribution; The entire sampling process is shown in Fig. 1. Initially, we obtain a random Gaussian sample ϵ, and through resampling, we acquire the corresponding latent variable $z_0 = E_\mu(X_h) + E_{\text{var}}(X_h) \cdot \epsilon$. Here, E_μ represents the process in the Encoder for obtaining the distribution mean from the historical sequence X_h, and E_{var} represents obtaining the distribution variance from X_h. This process is similar to the traditional resampling method. Then, we use our mapping function τ_{ϕ_k} to obtain the new latent variable $z_k = \tau_{\phi_k}(z_0)$.

For the new mapping function, we also use an affine transformation, i.e., $z_k = \tau_k(z_0) = A_k \cdot z_0 + b_k \cdot E_{\text{var}}(X_h)$. To better cover the latent space, we impose a simple constraint on $-1 \leq b_k \leq 1$, aiming to keep each element of b_k between -1 and 1. For values exceeding this range, i.e., $-2 \leq b_k \leq 2$, we apply a larger coefficient for penalization. The primary role of A_k is to change the sign of the original sample while maintaining a certain linearity with it. b_k expands the search range, allowing each value to have a greater chance of reaching high standard deviation positions, thereby enriching our latent variables.

For the coefficients of A_k and b_k:

$$L_{\text{size}} = \alpha \sum_m |(|A_k^m| - 1)| + \beta \sum_i |(|b_k^i| - 1)| + \gamma \sum_j |(|b_k^j| - 2)| \qquad (1)$$

For $|A_k^m| - 1$, where m represents the positions in matrix A_k greater than 1, that means m is the position index of the three-dimensional (batchsize, future length, feature dimension) matrix, A_k^m is the value at the corresponding position of A_k, for each A_k^m, $|A_k^m| > 1$, and $||$ represents the absolute value operation. $|b_k^i| - 1$ and $|b_k^j| - 2$ are similar. In this function, γ is set to a relatively large value as a penalizing term.

3.2   Other Loss Function Design

In terms of the diversity loss function, we also adopt an energy-based formula:

$$E_d(X) = \frac{1}{K(K-1)} \sum_{i=1}^{K} \sum_{j \neq i}^{K} \exp\left(-\frac{D^2(x^i, x^j)}{\sigma_d}\right) \qquad (2)$$

In our approach, we utilize the Euclidean distance D to estimate the distance between different samples and employ a Radial Basis Function (RBF) kernel with scale σ_d. x^i and x^j stand for different future sequences of predictions, By minimizing the energy function, samples tend to align with low-energy distributions, corresponding to high diversity scenarios. This function acts as the primary constraint for training A_k and b_k.

Given the considerable randomness in our sampling method, we have designed several loss functions to constrain the results. For reconstruction loss, we use two types of reconstruction. Firstly, an ℓ_1 loss is used for the sample that differs the least from the true value among all generated samples. Finally, an ℓ_1 loss is applied to all samples and the true value. This is done to prevent mode collapse; in the absence of this last reconstruction loss, results often exhibit uncharacteristic behaviors. Our reconstruction loss function is expressed as:

$$L_{\text{recon}} = \beta \cdot \min\left(\frac{1}{N} \sum_{n=1}^{N} |(x_{h+1:h+f})_n - (x_{h+1:h+f}^k)_n|_1\right)$$
$$+ \gamma \cdot \frac{1}{K} \cdot \frac{1}{N} \sum_{k=1}^{K} \sum_{n=1}^{N} ||(x_{h+1:h+f})_n - (x_{h+1:h+f}^k)_n||_1 \qquad (3)$$

Therefore, the total training loss function during the sampling process is:

$$L_{\text{total}} = L_{\text{size}} + L_{\text{recon}} + E_d(X) \qquad (4)$$

For our method, the overall training process can be outlined as follows, B stands for batchsize, H stands for historical sequence length, K stands for Number of total output samples, k stands for the number of sample, D stands for feature dimension, t and d stands for Intermediate feature dimension. F stands for future sequence length. KL stands for KL divergence:

Algorithm 1. Training DGVAE

Require: x: Input vector (B, H, D)
Ensure: y: Output vector (K, B, F, D)
1: $\mu \leftarrow Encoder(x)$, $\quad \sigma \leftarrow Encoder(x)$ $\quad A \leftarrow Encoder(x)$ $\quad b \leftarrow Encoder(x)$ $\quad \mu$
    and σ size is (B, t, d) $\quad A$ and b size is (K, B, t, d)
2: $noise \leftarrow (B, t, d)$ $\quad$ Random noise generated
3: $Z_0 = \mu + noise * \sigma$
4: $y_0 = Decoder(Z_0)$
5: **while** $0 < k < N$ **do**
6: $\quad\quad Z_k = A[k] * Z_0 + b[k] * \sigma$
7: $\quad\quad y_k = Decoder(Z_k)$
8: **end while**
9: $y = concat(y_0...y_k)$
10: **loss** $= KL(N(\mu, \sigma^2)||N(0,1)) + L_{\text{total}}$

---

4 Experiments

In this section, we introduce the datasets and evaluation metrics. Subsequently, we will provide a detailed presentation that includes quantitative analysis, qualitative analysis, and ablation studies.

4.1 Dataset

Human3.6M Dataset: [33] This dataset includes 11 subjects and 3.6 million frames of video, featuring 15 types of actions per subject. Human actions are recorded at 50 frames per second. In our work, we use a skeleton representation with 17 joints. We train and test our model on five subjects (S1, S5, S6, S7, S8) and test on two additional subjects (S9 and S11). The future motion prediction window is set to 2 s (100 time steps), with a historical motion window of 0.5 s (25 time steps).

HumanEva-I Dataset: [34] It comprises three subjects, with human motions recorded at 60 Hz. For comparison purposes, we follow the settings of previous works, using a 15-joint skeleton representation. Our model predicts future motion for 1 s (60 time steps), observing an interval of 0.25 s (15 time steps).

For quantitative comparison, we benchmark our method against several state-of-the-art works, including DeLiGAN [36], MT-VAE [10], DLow [11], GSPS [37], MOJO [13], BeLFusion [39], DivSamp [38], MotionDiff [29].

In line with prior research, we employ five metrics to assess the performance of our model:

- **Average Pairwise Distance (APD):** This metric quantifies the L2 distance between all pairs of predicted of the same input, this metric measures the diversity of the results. The formula is:

$$APD = \frac{1}{K(K-1)} \sum_{i \neq j} ||\hat{X}^i_{h+1:h+f} - \hat{X}^j_{h+1:h+f}|| \tag{5}$$

Here, K stands for Number of total output samples, i and j stands for the different number of sample, f stands for future sequence length, h stands for history sequence length. $\hat{X}^i_{h+1:h+f}$ and $\hat{X}^j_{h+1:h+f}$ stands for the ith and jth sample of predicted future sequence.

- **Average Displacement Error (ADE):** ADE computes the Average Displacement Error between the ground truth and the result most similar to the ground truth, offering an assessment of overall accuracy. The formula is:

$$ADE = \min_i \frac{1}{f} \sum_{j=1}^{f} ||\hat{X}^i_{h+j} - X_{h+j}|| \qquad (6)$$

f stands for future sequence length, h stands for history sequence length, i stands for the ith sample, j stands for the number of future sequence length. X_{h+j} stands for jth frame of ground truth, $\hat{X}^i_{h+j}$ stands for jth frame of ith sample.

- **Final Displacement Error (FDE):** stands for Final Displacement Error, only calculates the distance between the last pose of the ground truth and the last pose of the most similar result to the ground truth. The formula is:

$$FDE = \min_i ||\hat{X}^i_{h+f} - X_{h+f}|| \qquad (7)$$

- **Multi-Modal Average ADE (MMADE):** MMADE is a multi-modal extension of ADE, we use his to stand for the input history sequence, future stand for the ground truth of his, P stands for the total number posture of the dataset that is sililar to his, his_p and $future_p$ stand for history sequence and future sequence of the pth posture. Considering the diversity of predictions. For a set of $\{(his_p, future_p)\}_{p=1}^{P}$, where the past motion his_p is similar enough to his, we take their future motion $\{future_p\}_{p=1}^{P}$ as the pseudo ground truths of his. The formula is:

$$\text{MMADE} = \frac{1}{P} \sum_{p=1}^{P} \min_{i \in \{1,...,K\}} ||\tilde{future}_i - future_p||^2 \qquad (8)$$

i stands for the ith sample, K stands for the total number of samples. $||\tilde{future}_i - future_p||^2$ denotes the squared Euclidean distance between the predicted trajectory $\tilde{future}_i$ and the true (or pseudo-true) future motion $future_p$.

- **Multi-Modal Final Displacement Error (MMFDE):** Similar to FDE, MMFDE assesses the final predicted frame's accuracy across multiple predictions similar as MMADE.

4.2 Comparison with the State-of-the-Arts

Quantitative Results: The experimental outcomes, as illustrated in Table 1, demonstrate that our method achieves state-of-the-art results in the Final Displacement Error (FDE), Multi-Modal Average Displacement Error (MMADE), and Multi-Modal Final Displacement Error (MMFDE) metrics for the Human3.6M [33] dataset. For the HumanEva-I [36] dataset, our method similarly exhibits superior performance in ADE, FDE. In metrics where our method does not attain the top position, it nevertheless maintains robust competitiveness.

Table 1. Quantitative Experimental Results. The numbers in bold indicate the state-of-the-art results achieved. The symbol '–' signifies that the results for those particular metrics or models were not reported in the baseline studies. The models with the best performance across the evaluated metrics are highlighted in bold.

Method	Human3.6M					HumanEva-I				
	APD↑	ADE↓	FDE↓	MMADE↓	MMFDE↓	APD↑	ADE↓	FDE↓	MMADE↓	MMFDE↓
DeliGAN [36]	6.509	0.483	0.534	0.520	0.545	2.177	0.306	0.322	0.385	0.371
MT-VAE [10]	0.403	0.457	0.595	0.716	0.883	0.021	0.345	0.403	0.518	0.577
DLow [11]	11.741	0.425	0.518	0.495	0.531	4.855	0.251	0.268	0.362	0.339
GSPS [37]	14.757	0.389	0.496	0.476	0.525	5.825	0.233	0.244	0.343	0.331
MOJO [13]	12.579	0.412	0.514	0.497	0.538	4.181	0.234	0.244	0.369	0.347
BeLFusion [39]	7.602	0.372	0.474	0.473	0.507	–	–	–	–	–
DivSamp [38]	15.310	**0.370**	0.485	0.475	0.516	**6.109**	0.220	0.234	**0.342**	**0.316**
MotionDiff [29]	**15.353**	0.411	0.509	0.508	0.536	5.931	0.232	0.236	0.352	0.320
Ours (DGVAE)	10.194	0.396	**0.479**	**0.469**	**0.495**	4.473	**0.217**	**0.225**	0.359	0.317

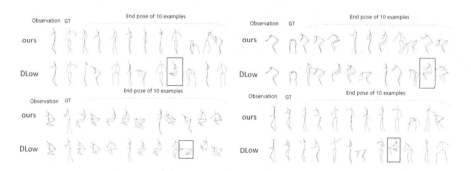

Fig. 3. Presents the visualization results. The red-black skeletons and green-purple skeletons denote the observed and predicted motions, respectively. The first row illustrates the visualization of our model, while the second row displays the visualization results of the DLow model. (Color figure online)

Qualitative Analysis: We conducted a visual comparative analysis between the DLow model and our model on the h3.6 m dataset. As illustrated in Fig. 3, Observation represents the last frame of the observed historical sequence, GT represents the last frame of the real future sequence, and End pose of 10 examples represents the last frame results of the predicted 10 samples. The results indicate that the DLow model exhibits some drift and unreasonable limb movements, Some unreasonable results have been marked with black boxes. The two upper figures and the right bottom one mainly exhibit unreasonable drifting and deviation from the ground, while the left bottom figure mainly displays some inverse kinematics. In contrast, our method mitigates these issues to a certain extent.

4.3   Ablation Study

Reconstruction Constraint. Considering the interplay between diversity and accuracy in our model, we conducted an ablation study focusing on the reconstruction loss component. In particular, we fixed $\beta = 1$ to examine the influence of varying the coefficient γ in the L_{recon}. As shown in Table 2, we present the impact of varying γ on the performance of the model. A smaller value of γ tends to enhance the diversity of the generated results. Initially, an increase in γ can improve the overall performance of the model. However, beyond a certain point, further increases in γ start to deteriorate the model's performance. we posit, lies in the fact that an absence or a relatively small γ value affords the model a larger search space, thereby enhancing the Average Prediction Diversity (APD). As the γ value decreases, the model's search space diminishes until it reaches a critical threshold. Conversely, as the γ value continues to increase, the search space dwindles below this critical range, rendering the model unable to capture the entire target distribution space, subsequently leading to a decline in its fitting capability. Thus, it is crucial to calibrate the value of γ appropriately.

Table 2. Ablation Study Results for γ on DGVAE. The best-performing models are highlighted in bold.

Method	Human3.6M					HumanEva-I				
	APD↑	ADE↓	FDE↓	MMADE↓	MMFDE↓	APD↑	ADE↓	FDE↓	MMADE↓	MMFDE↓
Ours (DGVAE, $\gamma = 1$)	–	–	–	–	–	2.698	0.225	0.234	0.382	0.352
Ours (DGVAE, $\gamma = 0.2$)	4.675	0.397	0.486	0.475	0.502	4.473	**0.217**	**0.225**	**0.359**	**0.317**
Ours (DGVAE, $\gamma = 0.1$)	5.501	**0.394**	**0.479**	0.471	0.499	5.688	0.218	0.228	**0.359**	0.326
Ours (DGVAE, $\gamma = 0.01$)	10.194	0.396	**0.479**	**0.469**	**0.495**	8.404	0.226	0.242	0.374	0.352
Ours (DGVAE, $\gamma = 0.001$)	**14.831**	0.401	0.489	0.474	0.505	**8.985**	0.227	0.247	0.376	0.360

Size Constraint. In our study, we scrutinized the impact of applying constraints $-1 \leq A_k \leq 1$, $-1 \leq b_k \leq 1$, and $-2 \leq b_k \leq 2$ within the context of the transformation $z_k = \tau_k(z_0) = A_k \cdot z_0 + b_k$, as shown in Table 3, In the absence of these constraints, the outcomes of our model are delineated in Table 3. Evaluations were performed under scenarios where constraints $-1 \leq A_k \leq 1$ and $-1 \leq b_k \leq 1$ were exclusively enforced, alongside a condition devoid of any constraints, with findings elucidated in the preceding table. It was discerned that minimizing the constraints on size facilitated enhanced diversity; conversely, this had an adverse effect on other metrics, notably precision.

Table 3. Ablation Study Results for size constraints. The best-performing models under the same γ are highlighted in bold.

Method	Use $-1 \leq A_k \leq 1$ and $-1 \leq b_k \leq 1$	Use $-2 \leq b_k \leq 2$	Human3.6M				
			APD↑	ADE↓	FDE↓	MMADE↓	MMFDE↓
Ours (DGVAE, $\gamma = 0.01$)	✓	✓	10.194	**0.396**	**0.479**	**0.469**	**0.495**
Ours (DGVAE, $\gamma = 0.01$)	✓	✗	10.666	0.397	0.481	0.470	0.497
Ours (DGVAE, $\gamma = 0.01$)	✗	✗	**11.478**	0.399	0.486	0.474	0.504

5 Conclusion

In this paper, a novel sampling methods for latent variables in Variational Autoencoders (VAEs) used for prediction tasks are proposed. State-of-the-art results have been achieved by utilizing a simple RNN-based network structure. It is hoped that these methods will serve as an inspiration for future work in this field, potentially leading to further advancements and innovations.

Acknowledgement. Guangdong Major Project of Basic and Applied Basic Research (2023B0303000016), National Natural Science Foundation of China (U21A20487), Shenzhen Technology Project (JCYJ2022081 8101206014, JCYJ20220818101211025), Guangdong Technology Project(2022B1515120067), Yunnan Science & Technology Project (202305AF150152), CAS Key Technology Talent Program.

References

1. Lehrmann, A.M., Gehler, P.V., Nowozin, S.: Efficient nonlinear Markov models for human motion. In: Proceedings of the IEEE Conference on Computer Vision and Pattern Recognition, pp. 1314–1321 (2014)
2. Wang, J., Hertzmann, A., Fleet, D.J.: Gaussian process dynamical models. In: Advances in Neural Information Processing Systems, vol. 18 (2005)
3. Ormoneit, D., Sidenbladh, H., Black, M., et al.: Learning and tracking cyclic human motion. In: Advances in Neural Information Processing Systems, vol. 13 (2000)
4. Pullen, K., Bregler, C.: Animating by multi-level sampling. In: Proceedings Computer Animation 2000, pp. 36–42. IEEE (2000)
5. Taylor, G.W., Hinton, G.E., Roweis S.: Modeling human motion using binary latent variables. In: Advances in Neural Information Processing Systems, vol. 19 (2006)
6. Taylor, G.W., Sigal, L., Fleet, D.J., et al.: Dynamical binary latent variable models for 3D human pose tracking. In: 2010 IEEE Computer Society Conference on Computer Vision and Pattern Recognition, pp. 631–638. IEEE (2010)
7. Bourached, A., Griffiths, R.R., Gray, R., et al.: Generative model-enhanced human motion prediction. Appl. AI Lett. **3**(2), e63 (2022)
8. Bie, X., Guo, W., Leglaive, S., et al.: HiT-DVAE: Human motion generation via hierarchical transformer dynamical VAE. arXiv preprint arXiv:2204.01565 (2022)
9. Bütepage, J., Kjellström, H., Kragic, D.: Anticipating many futures: online human motion prediction and generation for human-robot interaction. In: 2018 IEEE International Conference on Robotics and Automation (ICRA), pp. 4563–4570. IEEE (2018)

10. Yan, X., Rastogi, A., Villegas, R., et al.: MT-VAE: learning motion transformations to generate multimodal human dynamics. In: Proceedings of the European conference on computer vision (ECCV), pp. 265–281 (2018)
11. Yuan, Y., Kitani, K.: DLow: diversifying latent flows for diverse human motion prediction. In: Computer Vision–ECCV 2020: 16th European Conference, Glasgow, UK, 23–28 August 2020, Proceedings, Part IX, pp. 346–364. Springer (2020)
12. Zhang, Y., Black, M.J., Tang, S.: Perpetual motion: generating unbounded human motion. arXiv preprint arXiv:2007.13886 (2020)
13. Zhang, Y., Black, M.J., Tang, S.: We are more than our joints: Predicting how 3D bodies move. In: Proceedings of the IEEE/CVF Conference on Computer Vision and Pattern Recognition, pp. 3372–3382 (2021)
14. Ling, H.Y., Zinno, F., Cheng, G., et al.: Character controllers using motion VAEs. ACM Trans. Graphics (TOG) **39**(4), 40:1–40:12 (2020)
15. Ma, H., Li, J., Hosseini, R., et al.: Multi-objective diverse human motion prediction with knowledge distillation. In: Proceedings of the IEEE/CVF Conference on Computer Vision and Pattern Recognition, pp. 8161–8171 (2022)
16. Mao, W., Liu, M., Salzmann, M.: Weakly-supervised action transition learning for stochastic human motion prediction. In: Proceedings of the IEEE/CVF Conference on Computer Vision and Pattern Recognition (2022)
17. Salzmann, T., Pavone, M., Ryll, M.: Motron: Multimodal probabilistic human motion forecasting. In: Proceedings of the IEEE/CVF Conference on Computer Vision and Pattern Recognition, pp. 6457–6466 (2022)
18. Elman, J.L.: Finding structure in time. Cogn. Sci. **14**(2), 179–211 (1990)
19. Graves, A., Graves, A.: Long short-term memory. In: Supervised Sequence Labelling with Recurrent Neural Networks, pp. 37–45 (2012)
20. Cho, K., Van Merriënboer, B., Gulcehre, C., et al.: Learning phrase representations using RNN encoder-decoder for statistical machine translation. arXiv preprint arXiv:1406.1078 (2014)
21. LeCun, Y., Bottou, L., Bengio, Y., et al.: Gradient-based learning applied to document recognition. Proc. IEEE **86**(11), 2278–2324 (1998)
22. Krizhevsky, A., Sutskever, I., Hinton, G.E.: ImageNet classification with deep convolutional neural networks. In: Advances in Neural Information Processing Systems, vol. 25 (2012)
23. Kingma, D.P., Welling, M.: Auto-encoding variational bayes. arXiv preprint arXiv:1312.6114 (2013)
24. Goodfellow, I., Pouget-Abadie, J., Mirza, M., et al.: Generative adversarial nets. In: Advances in Neural Information Processing Systems, vol. 27 (2014)
25. Ho, J., Jain, A., Abbeel, P.: Denoising diffusion probabilistic models. In: Advances in Neural Information Processing Systems, vol. 33, pp. 6840–6851 (2020)
26. Chen, L.H., Zhang, J., Li, Y., et al.: HumanMAC: masked motion completion for human motion prediction. arXiv preprint arXiv:2302.03665 (2023)
27. Ahn, H., Mascaro, E.V., Lee, D.: Can we use diffusion probabilistic models for 3D motion prediction?. arXiv preprint arXiv:2302.14503 (2023)
28. Wei, D., Sun, H., Li, B., et al.: Human joint kinematics diffusion-refinement for stochastic motion prediction. In: Proceedings of the AAAI Conference on Artificial Intelligence, vol. 37, no. 5, pp. 6110–6118 (2023)
29. Tevet, G., Raab, S., Gordon, B., et al.: Human motion diffusion model. arXiv preprint arXiv:2209.14916 (2022)
30. Tian, S., Zheng, M., Liang, X.: TransFusion: a practical and effective transformer-based diffusion model for 3D human motion prediction. arXiv preprint arXiv:2307.16106 (2023)

31. Barsoum, E., Kender, J., Liu, Z.: HP-GAN: probabilistic 3D human motion prediction via GAN. In: Proceedings of the IEEE Conference on Computer Vision and Pattern Recognition Workshops, pp. 1418–1427 (2018)
32. Kundu, J.N., Gor, M., Babu, R.V.: BiHMP-GAN: bidirectional 3D human motion prediction GAN. In: Proceedings of the AAAI Conference on Artificial Intelligence, vol. 33, no. 01, pp. 8553–8560 (2019)
33. Ionescu, C., Papava, D., Olaru, V., et al.: Human3.6m: large scale datasets and predictive methods for 3d human sensing in natural environments. IEEE Trans. Pattern Anal. Mach. Intell. **36**(7), 1325–1339 (2013)
34. Sigal, L., Balan, A.O., Black, M.J.: HumanEva: synchronized video and motion capture dataset and baseline algorithm for evaluation of articulated human motion. Int. J. Comput. Vision **87**(1–2), 4–27 (2010)
35. Li, Z., Zhou, Y., Xiao, S., et al.: Auto-conditioned recurrent networks for extended complex human motion synthesis. arXiv preprint arXiv:1707.05363 (2017)
36. Gurumurthy, S., Kiran Sarvadevabhatla, R., Venkatesh Babu, R.: DeliGAN: generative adversarial networks for diverse and limited data. In: Proceedings of the IEEE Conference on Computer Vision and Pattern Recognition, pp. 166–174 (2017)
37. Mao, W., Liu, M., Salzmann, M.: Generating smooth pose sequences for diverse human motion prediction. In: Proceedings of the IEEE/CVF International Conference on Computer Vision, pp. 13309–13318 (2021)
38. Dang, L., Nie, Y., Long, C., et al.: Diverse human motion prediction via gumbel-softmax sampling from an auxiliary space. In: Proceedings of the 30th ACM International Conference on Multimedia, pp. 5162–5171 (2022)
39. Barquero, G., Escalera, S., Palmero, C.: BelFusion: latent diffusion for behavior-driven human motion prediction. In: Proceedings of the IEEE/CVF International Conference on Computer Vision, pp. 2317–2327 (2023)
40. Kooij, J.F., Flohr, F., Pool, E.A., et al.: Context-based path prediction for targets with switching dynamics. Int. J. Comput. Vision **127**(3), 239–262 (2019)
41. Sotelo, M.Á.: Advanced motion prediction for self-driving cars. In: 2021 IEEE International Conference on Autonomous Robot Systems and Competitions (ICARSC), pp. 1–2. IEEE (2021)
42. Sidiropoulos, A., Karayiannidis, Y., Doulgeri, Z.: Human-robot collaborative object transfer using human motion prediction based on cartesian pose dynamic movement primitives. In: 2021 IEEE International Conference on Robotics and Automation (ICRA), pp. 3758–3764. IEEE (2021)
43. Kong, Y., Wei, Z., Huang, S.: Automatic analysis of complex athlete techniques in broadcast taekwondo video. Multimed. Tools Appl. **77**(11), 13643–13660 (2018)
44. Zhou, C., Pei, C.: The future training of sports intelligent robot technology. System **3**(13), 7–13 (2021)
45. Xie, J., Chen, G., Liu, S.: Intelligent badminton training robot in athlete injury prevention under machine learning. Front. Neurorobot. **15**, 18 (2021)

Multi-scale Separable Convolution and Dilated Attention for Machinery Fault Diagnosis

Lijun Zhang[1,2,3], Dong Qiu[1,2,3], Peng Cui[1,2,3], and Jinjia Wang[1,2,3]([envelope])[ORCID]

[1] College of Information Science and Engineering, Yanshan University, Qinhuangdao 066000, China
wjj@ysu.edu.cn
[2] Hubei Key Laboratory of Intelligent Robot (Wuhan Institute of Technology)), Wuhan 430205, China
[3] Anhui Province Key Laboratory of Machine Vision Inspection, Wuhu 241000, China

Abstract. CNNs have promoted the development of intelligent fault diagnosis and improved the diagnostic ability of models. However, due to the widespread existence of complex noise in actual industrial production environments, these noises may make it impossible to fully extract fault information by relying solely on CNN. Therefore, in order to meet this challenge, this paper proposes a new mechanical fault diagnosis framework that combines multi-scale separable convolution and dilated attention mechanisms (MSCDA). This method combines the advantages of CNN in local feature extraction and the ability of Transformer to capture global information, improving the diagnostic ability of the model under noise interference. The model first uses multi-scale separable convolution (MSC) to extract detailed local features from vibration signals. Secondly, the multi-scale dilated attention (MSDA) mechanism is used to capture more and more extensive feature information. Experimental results show that, compared with existing diagnosis framework based on CNN and transformer, this methodology has higher accuracy and anti-noise capability, and can be better applied in practice.

Keywords: Machinery Fault diagnosis · MSC · MSDA

1 Introduction

Bearings and gears, as key components of mechanical systems, in the industrial field, play an indispensable role [1,2]. Intelligent fault diagnosis is able to automatically analyse signal features and classify faults [3–5]. Among these, CNN-based fault diagnosis is particularly noteworthy [6,7]. While CNNs excel at extracting local features from vibration signals, they struggle to classify faults in noisy environments due to their reliance on local features alone.

© The Author(s), under exclusive license to Springer Nature Singapore Pte Ltd. 2025
H. Li et al. (Eds.): ICSR + InnoBiz 2024, LNAI 15170, pp. 13–23, 2025.
https://doi.org/10.1007/978-981-96-1151-5_2

Recent advances in transformers have demonstrated strong feature extraction and modelling capabilities for long sequences, making them popular in CV and NLP [8,9]. Some researchers have also explored their application in fault diagnosis [10,11]. Due to the continuous nature of vibration signals, local features remain important and transformers often fall short in this area compared to CNNs. It is therefore possible to enhance diagnostic performance by combining the strengths of both models to jointly extract local and global features from vibration signals [12,13]. Han et al. [14] improved diagnosis capability under noise interference by modifying the Convformer and the SE attention mechanism.

The integration of CNN and Transformer models has proven effective for fault diagnosis in rotating machinery. However, CNNs often compress feature information in the convolutional embedding stage, resulting in some loss. In addition, the global application of self-attention mechanisms can significantly increase the computational cost. To address these issues, Howard et al. [15] proposed MobileNets, an efficient network module that employs separable convolution to more effectively extract feature information and reduce loss. Zheng et al. [16] analysed global attention and found that shallow attention has properties of locality and sparsity that improve performance in tasks such as image classification.

Building on the foundations of previous research, this paper introduces a novel fault diagnosis framework that integrates multi-scale separable convolution with dilated attention mechanisms. The key contributions include the following:

(1) Multi-Scale Separable Convolution Module: This module extracts multiple local features from vibration signals with precision, preserving local structural information.
(2) Multi-Scale Dilated Attention Module: This module is used in the shallow stage of attention. It learns representations at different scales, efficiently aggregates multi-scale semantic information, and reduces computational redundancy by using varying dilation rates.
(3) Enhanced accuracy and robustness. In comparison to alternative CNN and transformer-based fault diagnosis methodologies, the proposed approach demonstrates enhanced accuracy and robustness.

2   Related Work

A typical CNN model consists of alternating layers, such as activation, fully connected, and convolutional layers. By adjusting the number of layers and the convolution kernel size, features from various receptive fields can be extracted, aiding intelligent fault diagnosis. Pang et al. [6] proposed a vibration bispectrum-based CNN approach that enhances nonlinear features from signals. However, these methods often overlook the significant noise interference in real industrial environments, which disrupts the periodic frequency characteristics of vibration signals and hampers accurate feature extraction, ultimately reducing diagnostic accuracy.

A typical Transformer module consists of four main components: a positional feedforward module, a multi-head self-attention mechanism, a layer normalization module, and a multi-layer perceptron. The calculation process is described in detail in [14]. However, Transformers are typically used with large datasets, and fault diagnosis data is often insufficient to support Transformer training compared to these larger datasets. It is not feasible to rely solely on Transformers for fault diagnosis. The latest research proves that combining the respective properties of CNNs and Transformers significantly improves diagnostic performance.

3 Proposed Methodology

3.1 Multi-scale Separable Convolutional Module

Multi-Scale Convolutional module utilizes cross-channel convolution to integrate feature information across different channel dimensions. Inspired by depth-wise separable convolution [15], we designed the MSC module, illustrated in the MSC Block in Fig. 2. This design captures features from multiple receptive fields, preserving fine-grained details and maintaining local structural information in the signals.

First, cross-channel convolution integrates the input features. Then, separable convolutions with different kernel sizes efficiently extract different local features. Finally, the features are merged and refined through BN and GELU layers, yielding final embeddings with multiple local features. The specific procedure is as follows:

$$w = Concat_{j=1}^{C_2} \left(\sum_{i=1}^{C_1} u_{i,j}^1 * x_i \right) \tag{1}$$

$$y = Concat_{j=1}^{C_2} \left(Conv \left(v_j^{k_t} * w_j \right) \right) \tag{2}$$

where the input is $x \in R^{C_1 \times N_1}$ and the output is $y \in R^{C_2 \times N_2}$. The feature map after cross-channel convolution is $w \in R^{C_2 \times N_1}$. The convolution kernel weights of size 1 are represented by $u^1 \in R^{C_2 \times C_1}$, while the depth convolution with kernel size k_l is represented by $v^{k_t} \in R^{C_2 \times k_t}$. Finally, $Conv(\cdot)$ denotes a pointwise convolution with a 1×1 kernel.

3.2 Multi-scale Dilated Attention

Due to patches at the far end of the shallow attention stage are mostly irrelevant, indicating that shallow attention does not require a global field of view. Based on this analysis, we propose a Window Sliding Delayed Attention (WSDA) method. This method sparsely selects points around the center of a given dot to compute self-attention. The calculation formula is:

$$Y = WSDA(Q, K, V, r) \tag{3}$$

$$y_j = Attention\,(q_j, K_r, V_r) = Softmax\left(\frac{q_j K_r^T}{\sqrt{d_k}}\right) V_r \qquad (4)$$

where the dilation rate is $r > 0$. The output of WSDA for the input message is denoted as y_j, while K_r and V_r refer to the selected keys and values from the feature maps. WSDA uses a sliding window to apply self-attention to query patches, using zero-padding at the edges to preserve the size of the feature map. It establishes long-range dependencies by sparsely selecting keys and values around the query center.

In order to better attend to the perceptual domain of vibration signals and obtain more information, we propose a MSDA method. In this method, different dilation rates are set for different heads in order to learn multiple scale representations simultaneously. First, the feature mappings corresponding to Q, K are obtained by linear projection. Then, the feature mapping channel is divided into m different heads and different expansion rates are set for different heads as follows:

$$h_j = WSDA\,(Q_j, K_j, V_j, r_j) \qquad (5)$$

$$Y = Linear\,(Concat\,[h_1, h_2, \cdots, h_m]) \qquad (6)$$

where h_j is the j-th head and r_j is the dilation rate of the j-th head. The resulting $\{h_j\}_{j=1}^m$ are fused by performing WSDA on the feature mappings of the different heads. The feature fusion is then performed using a linear layer. By setting different expansion rates for each head, the self-attention mechanism captures vibration information from different receptive fields.

$$Y = CPE(\hat{Y}) + \hat{Y} = DwConv(\hat{Y}) + \hat{Y} \qquad (7)$$

$$Z = \begin{cases} MSDA(Norm(Y)) + Y \\ GSA(Norm(Y)) + Y \end{cases} \qquad (8)$$

where $\hat{Y}$ is the input to the current module, and $DwConv(\cdot)$ represent deep convolution with a 3×3 kernel. MSDA is applied in the first two layers, while global self-attention (GSA) is used in the last four layers. The complete MSDA process is illustrated in Fig. 1.

Fig. 1. Multi-Scale Dilated Attention block.

Figure 2 demonstrates the proposed fault diagnosis framework, which contains three phases: data collection and segmentation, model training and testing, and result presentation. The model comprises three layers: an input layer, a feature extraction layer and an output layer.

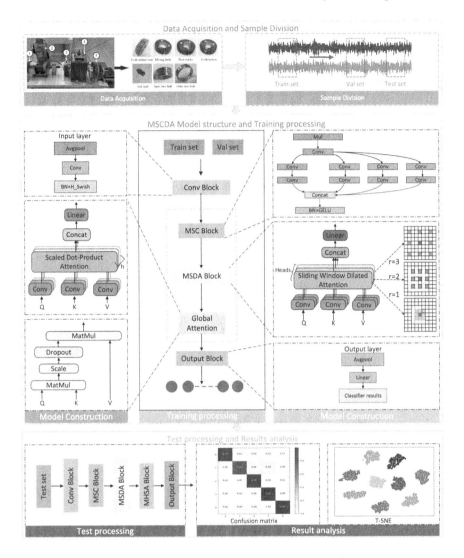

Fig. 2. Proposed fault diagnosis framework.

4 Case Study

In order to ascertain the efficacy of the proposed methodology in the presence of elevated noise levels, two distinct types of noise were incorporated into the test set, thereby emulating the conditions that may be anticipated in a genuine operational setting.

$$Random\ Gaussian : n_i = n_i + \gamma \tag{9}$$

$$Random\ Scale : n_i = \omega \times n_i \tag{10}$$

where $\omega \sim N(0, \mu)$ is gaussian white noise, $\gamma \sim N(1, \mu)$ is the scaling factor, and n_i is the i-th sample point. The noise is added with a probability of 50% to better simulate real engineering conditions. The variance μ serves to regulate the discrepancy between the training, validation, and test sets; an increase in μ will result in a corresponding increase in these differences.

We selected three fault diagnosis methods that combine CNN and Transformer architectures: CLFormer [12], ConvformerNSE [14] and Mcswin-T [13]. We also included two CNN-based methods, MobileNetV2 [17] and ResNet18 [18]. To minimise random error, each experiment was repeated five times, with 100 iterations per session. The loss function used was cross-entropy loss. The initial learning rate was 0.001, the batch size was 32, and an adaptive decay mode was used. The experiments were conducted using PyTorch 1.7.1 on an i7-7700K CPU and GTX1080Ti GPU.

4.1   Case 1 Fault Diagnosis of Gearbox

The dataset from Xi'an Jiaotong University [19] comprises vibration signals recorded at 1800 rpm with a sampling frequency of 20,480 Hz. It includes nine types of faults: four bearing faults, four gear faults and one mixed fault. The vibration signals are segmented into samples of 1024 data points using a sliding window. For each health condition, 1200 samples are collected and divided into training, validation, and test sets in a ratio of 5:3:4. Two levels of random noise, as described in Eq. (9) and Eq. (10), are added to the test set.

Table 1. Average diagnostic accuracy for each method.

Methods	Accuracy (%)			
	$\mu = 0.0$	$\mu = 0.2$	$\mu = 0.4$	$\mu = 0.6$
MSCDA	99.56	**97.66**	**83.62**	**72.71**
MCSwin-T [13]	**99.92**	96.34	81.24	71.70
CLFormer [12]	89.47	82.68	73.41	64.93
Convformer-NSE [14]	91.41	77.74	67.83	62.54
MobileNet-V2 [17]	98.44	91.23	73.72	67.51
ResNet18 [18]	99.63	94.64	80.43	69.54

Table 1 shows the classification accuracies of all methods at different noise levels μ. The highest accuracy under each condition is highlighted in bold. As μ increases, the proposed method consistently shows superior robustness compared to others. At $\mu = 0$, ResNet18 and MCSwin-T perform comparably to the proposed method. However, as μ increases, their robustness decreases. At $\mu = 0.2$, the average accuracies of ResNet18 and MCSwin-T are 1.32% and 3.02% lower, respectively, compared to the proposed method. At $\mu = 0.4$ their accuracies are

2.38% and 3.19% lower, respectively. For $\mu = 0.6$ the reductions are 1.01% and 3.17% respectively.

To illustrate the feature extraction capability, we used Distributed Stochastic Neighbor Embedding (T-SNE) for visualization, as shown in Fig. 3. Our method effectively distinguishes different fault types, forming clear clusters and boundaries. In contrast, other methods show varying degrees of sample overlap, particularly for defect types like broken teeth and missing teeth, indicating some similarity in characteristics.

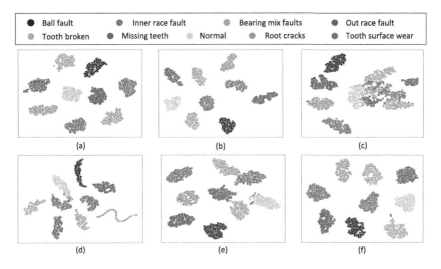

Fig. 3. Visualization of the extracted features: (a) MSCDA (b) MCSwin-T (c) CLFormer (d) Convformer-NSE (e) MobileNet-V2 (f) ResNet18.

4.2   Case 2 Fault Diagnosis of Bearing

The dataset from the University of Ottawa's SpectraQuest [20]. It recorded outer ring defects, inner ring defects, spherical defects, and a mixture of all three, as well as the health status, for a total of five different data samples. The data samples were sampled at a frequency of 200kHz, with 600, 300 and 300 samples selected for each defect. Each sample contains 1024 data points. Two different sizes of random noise Eq.(9) and Eq.(10) are added to the test set.

Table 2 displays the classification accuracies of each method at various noise levels μ. At $\mu = 0$, the accuracy of the proposed method is comparable to that of MCSwin-T and ResNet18. However, as the noise levels increase, these methods show reduced noise immunity compared to the proposed method. Specifically, at $\mu = 0.2$, CLFormer is 7.8% less accurate than the proposed method. At $\mu = 0.4$ and $\mu = 0.6$, both CLFormer and ResNet18 exhibit significantly lower accuracy. This performance degradation is attributed to the increased impact of noise on

Table 2. Average diagnostic accuracy for each method.

Methods	Accuracy (%)			
	$\mu = 0.0$	$\mu = 0.2$	$\mu = 0.4$	$\mu = 0.6$
MSCDA	97.51	**95.77**	**90.35**	**81.52**
MCSwin-T [13]	**97.77**	75.79	64.83	62.31
CLFormer [12]	91.60	87.97	78.25	64.69
Convformer-NSE [14]	94.01	65.21	59.68	57.93
MobileNet-V2 [17]	95.03	73.95	64.04	61.21
ResNet18 [18]	97.60	84.17	72.23	69.67

local feature extraction, making it challenging to obtain complete and accurate feature signals.

To compare the feature extraction capabilities of each method under noise interference, Fig. 4 shows the confusion matrix at $\mu = 0.2$. The horizontal coordinates (0–4) represent five defect types. The proposed method accurately identifies most defect types, achieving over 97% accuracy for four of the five types, with 100% accuracy for fault types 3 and 4. CLFormer achieves 97% accuracy for fault type 0 but less than 65% for several other types. Overall, the proposed method demonstrates superior accuracy compared to all other methods across all defect types.

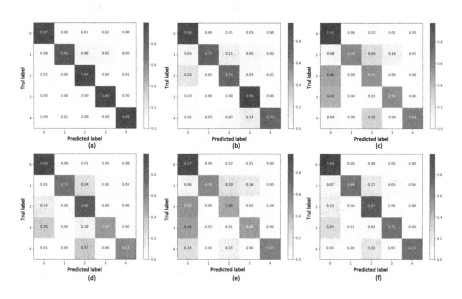

Fig. 4. Confusion matrix for each method: (a) MSCDA (b) MCSwin-T (c) CLFormer (d) Convformer-NSE (e) MobileNet-V2 (f) ResNet18

4.3   Ablation Study

To assess the impact of the multi-scale separable convolutional block and multi-scale dilation attention block, we conducted ablation experiments by individually removing each module. This created two new models: one without the convolutional embedding module and another without the multi-scale dilation attention module. The results, shown in Table 3, indicate that using both modules together improves model performance. The convolutional embedding module effectively enhances local feature extraction and preserves crucial local information. Specifically, including the convolutional embedding module before self-attention computation results in a classification accuracy improvement of approximately 2.0% on the OU-Bearing dataset.

The MSDA module significantly improves model performance. Without MSDA, using only the global attention mechanism leads to a performance drop of approximately 1.5% as noise levels increase. This decline highlights the importance of MSDA in capturing multiple representations across different scales and aggregating multiscale semantic information, which enhances classification performance. Comparing these results with those of our proposed model confirms the superior performance of the MSDA module.

Table 3. Average diagnostic accuracy for each method.

Methods	Accuracy (%)			
	$\mu = 0.0$	$\mu = 0.2$	$\mu = 0.4$	$\mu = 0.6$
MSCDA	**97.51**	**95.77**	**90.35**	**81.52**
-Multi_Conv_Embedding	97.48	93.93	87.45	80.76
-Multi_Scale_Dilated_Att	96.40	94.44	87.41	80.48

5   Conclusions

To address feature information loss in traditional CNNs, this paper introduces a fault diagnosis model framework that combines multi-scale separable convolution (MSC) and dilated attention (MSDA). The MSC module extracts local perceptual features from vibration signals while maintaining structural integrity, while the MSDA module captures and aggregates multiscale semantic information. Compared to existing CNN-based and transformer diagnostic methods, our approach offers superior accuracy and robust noise immunity. Future research will focus on developing fault diagnosis methods for scenarios with limited samples, aiming to further enhance accuracy and applicability.

Acknowledgments. This work was supported in part by Hebei Natural Science Foundation (F2024203081), S&T Program of Hebei (236Z0101G), the Open Research Fund of Anhui Province Key Laboratory of Machine Vision Inspection (KLMVI-2023-HIT-13), and the Open Research Fund of Hubei Key Laboratory of Intelligent Robot (Wuhan Institute of Technology) (HBIR202208).

References

1. Wu, Y., Tang, B., Deng, L., Li, Q.: Distillation-enhanced fast neural architecture search method for edge-side fault diagnosis of wind turbine gearboxes. Expert Syst. Appl. **208**, 118049 (2022)
2. Hilbert, M., Smith, W.A., Randall, R.B.: The effect of signal propagation delay on the measured vibration in planetary gearboxes. J. Dyn. Monit. Diagn. **1**(1), 9–18 (2022)
3. Chen, X., Shao, H., Xiao, Y., Yan, S., Cai, B., Liu, B.: Collaborative fault diagnosis of rotating machinery via dual adversarial guided unsupervised multi-domain adaptation network. Mech. Syst. Signal Process. **198**, 110427 (2023)
4. Xiao, Y., Shao, H., Feng, M., Han, T., Wan, J., Liu, B.: Towards trustworthy rotating machinery fault diagnosis via attention uncertainty in transformer. J. Manuf. Syst. **70**, 186–201 (2023)
5. Shao, H., Li, W., Cai, B., Wan, J., Xiao, Y., Yan, S.: Dual-threshold attention-guided GAN and limited infrared thermal images for rotating machinery fault diagnosis under speed fluctuation. IEEE Trans. Industr. Inform. (2023)
6. Pang, X., Xue, X., Jiang, W., Lu, K.: An investigation into fault diagnosis of planetary gearboxes using a bispectrum convolutional neural network. IEEE/ASME Trans. Mechatron. **26**(4), 2027–2037 (2020)
7. Tang, S., Zhu, Y., Yuan, S.: Intelligent fault identification of hydraulic pump using deep adaptive normalized CNN and synchrosqueezed wavelet transform. Reliabil. Eng. Syst. Saf. **224**, 108560 (2022)
8. Dosovitskiy, A., et al.: An image is worth 16×16 words: transformers for image recognition at scale. arXiv preprint arXiv:2010.11929 (2020)
9. Xiong, R., et al.: On layer normalization in the transformer architecture. In: International Conference on Machine Learning, pp. 10524–10533. PMLR (2020)
10. Ding, Y., Jia, M., Miao, Q., Cao, Y.: A novel time-frequency transformer based on self-attention mechanism and its application in fault diagnosis of rolling bearings. Mech. Syst. Signal Process. **168**, 108616 (2022)
11. Li, Y., Zhou, Z., Sun, C., Chen, X., Yan, R.: Variational attention-based interpretable transformer network for rotary machine fault diagnosis. IEEE Trans. Neural Netw. Learn. Syst. (2022)
12. Fang, H., et al.: CLFormer: a lightweight transformer based on convolutional embedding and linear self-attention with strong robustness for bearing fault diagnosis under limited sample conditions. IEEE Trans. Instrum. Meas. **71**, 1–8 (2021)
13. Chen, Z., Chen, J., Liu, S., Feng, Y., He, S., Xu, E.: Multi-channel calibrated transformer with shifted windows for few-shot fault diagnosis under sharp speed variation. ISA Trans. **131**, 501–515 (2022)
14. Han, S., Shao, H., Cheng, J., Yang, X., Cai, B.: Convformer-NSE: a novel end-to-end gearbox fault diagnosis framework under heavy noise using joint global and local information. IEEE/ASME Trans. Mechatron. **28**(1), 340–349 (2022)
15. Howard, A., et al.: Searching for MobileNetV3. In: Proceedings of the IEEE/CVF International Conference on Computer Vision, pp. 1314–1324 (2019)
16. Jiao, J., et al.: DilateFormer: multi-scale dilated transformer for visual recognition. IEEE Trans. Multimed. (2023)

17. Sandler, M., Howard, A., Zhu, M., Zhmoginov, A., Chen, L.C.: MobileNetV2: inverted residuals and linear bottlenecks. In: Proceedings of the IEEE Conference on Computer Vision and Pattern Recognition, pp. 4510–4520 (2018)

18. He, K., Zhang, X., Ren, S., Sun, J.: Deep residual learning for image recognition. In: Proceedings of the IEEE Conference on Computer Vision and Pattern Recognition, pp. 770–778 (2016)

19. Li, T., Zhou, Z., Li, S., Sun, C., Yan, R., Chen, X.: The emerging graph neural networks for intelligent fault diagnostics and prognostics: a guideline and a benchmark study. Mech. Syst. Signal Process. **168**, 108653 (2022)

20. Huang, H., Baddour, N.: Bearing vibration data collected under time-varying rotational speed conditions. Data Brief **21**, 1745–1749 (2018)

SegmentAnything-Based Approach to Scene Understanding and Grasp Generation

Songting Liu[1], Zhezhi Lei[2], Haiyue Zhu[3]($^{(\boxtimes)}$), Jun Ma[4], and Zhiping Lin[1]

[1] School of Electrical and Electronic Engineering, Nanyang Technological University
(NTU), Singapore 639798, Singapore
{lius0081,ezplin}@ntu.edu.sg

[2] School of Electrical and Computer Engineering, National University of Singapore
(NUS), Singapore 117583, Singapore
lei_zhezhi@u.nus.edu

[3] Singapore Institute of Manufacturing Technology (SIMTech), Agency for Science,
Technology and Research (A*STAR), 2 Fusionopolis Way, Singapore 138634,
Singapore
zhu_haiyue@simtech.a-star.edu.sg

[4] Robotics and Autonomous Systems Thrust, The Hong Kong University of Science
and Technology (Guangzhou), Guangzhou 511453, China
jun.ma@ust.hk

Abstract. Autonomous robot grasping in multi-object scenarios poses significant challenges, requiring precise grasp candidate detection, determination of object-grasp affiliations. To solve these challenges, this research presents a novel approach to address these challenges by developing a dedicated grasp detection model called GraspAnything, which is extended from SegmentAnything model. The GraspAnything model, based on SegmentAnything (SAM) model, receives bounding boxes as prompts and simultaneously outputs the mask of objects and all possible grasp poses for parallel jaw gripper. A grasp decoder module is added to the SAM model to enable grasp detection functionality. Experiment results have demonstrate the effectiveness of our model in grasp detection tasks. The implications of this research extend to various industrial applications, such as object picking and sorting, where intelligent robot grasping can significantly enhance efficiency and automation. The developed models and approaches contribute to the advancement of autonomous robot grasping in complex, multi-object environments.

Keywords: Autonomous Robot Grasping · Grasp Detection · Multi-Object Environments

1   Introduction

Robot grasping has been a fundamental challenge in the field of robotics and automation. The ability to accurately detect and grasp objects is crucial for

S. Liu and Z. Lei—The first two authors contributed equally to this work.

H. Li et al. (Eds.): ICSR + InnoBiz 2024, LNAI 15170, pp. 24–30, 2025.
https://doi.org/10.1007/978-981-96-1151-5_3

various applications, such as manufacturing, warehousing, and home assistance. Traditional approaches to robot grasping often rely on predefined object models and carefully engineered features, limiting their flexibility and adaptability to new objects and environments.

Recent advancements in deep learning and computer vision have paved the way for more intelligent and versatile robot grasping systems. Models like GG-CNN [2], Dex-Net [3] and GR-ConvNet [4] have demonstrated remarkable capabilities in grasp pose detections based on RGB and depth map, enabling operations on unseen objects with high success rate. However, the task of autonomous robot grasping in multi-object scenarios remains a significant challenge, as it requires not only precise grasp candidate detection but also an understanding of object-grasp affiliations.

The motivation behind this research stems from the need to develop intelligent robot grasping systems that can operate effectively in complex, multi-object environments. Existing robot grasping methods are only trained to predict all possible grasp poses but ignoring objects, hence requiring a separate object detection model to detect the location of target object. This limitation hinders their practical applicability in dynamic environments where novel objects may be encountered. Therefore, there is a strong motivation to develop an open-vocabulary grasping system that can adapt to new objects without the need for retraining [5–7].

In this research, we focus on grasp detection task and propose a grasp detection model called GraspAnything which can recognize the pose of objects, especially in complex environments.

2   Related Work

Robot grasping detection is a crucial component in the development of autonomous robotic systems capable of manipulating objects in various environments. The goal of grasp detection is to identify suitable grasping points or regions on an object that allow a robot to securely and stably hold the object for manipulation tasks.

Traditionally, grasp detection methods relied on analytical approaches based on geometric and physical models of objects and robot grippers. These methods often required precise knowledge of object shapes, sizes, and material properties, limiting their applicability in dynamic and unstructured environments. With the advent of deep learning, data-driven approaches have emerged as a prominent solution for grasp detection. These methods leverage large datasets of grasping examples to learn generalizable models that can predict suitable grasping points or regions on novel objects [8,9].

Both the 2D rectangle grasping and 6-DoF pose grasping have been extensively explored. To address the multi-object scenarios, both 2D heatmaps and 3D equivalents are proposed to localize the graspness as the first stage, and then for corresponding pose regression in the second stage. The grasp detection is also treated as a special formation of object detection problem, and most works

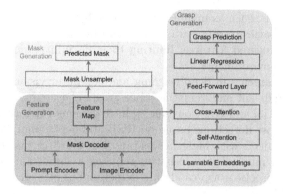

Fig. 1. The architecture of the GraspAnything model

build the grasp detectors based on two-stages object detection models such as Faster-RCNN [10].

Various sensor formats are explored as the input for the prediction network, such as RGB image, depth map, RGB-D image and point cloud. Many methods take depth image as input for grasp inference, but they rely on additional sensors and their accuracy is highly dependent on the quality of the input depth image [11,12]. In this work, we only focus on 2D rectangle grasping detection based on RGB image input.

3   Method

3.1   Feature Generation

The GraspAnything model's segmentation function is built upon Meta's SegmentAnything (SAM) model [1], which has demonstrated remarkable performance in instance segmentation tasks. The SAM model is designed to generate high-quality instance masks from simple prompts, such as bounding boxes or points, making it a powerful tool for object segmentation.

Figure 1 shows the architecture of our GraspAnything model. The segmentation branch of the model consists of four main components: an image encoder, a prompt encoder, a mask decoder, and a mask upsampler. The image encoder is a vision transformer (ViT) that extracts features from the input image. The prompt encoder processes the input prompts, such as bounding boxes or points, and generates corresponding embeddings. The mask decoder takes the image features and prompt embeddings as input and produces mask latent in high dimension but low resolution. The mask upsampler is to upsample the mask latent to the final mask output which is of the same size of input image.

During training, we set all model parameters to be trainable. To prevent model from forgetting mask prediction ability, we also apply mask prediction loss during training:

$$L_{BCE} = -\frac{1}{N} \sum_{i=1}^{N} [y_i \log(\widehat{y_i}) + (1 - y_i) \log(1 - \widehat{y_i})]$$

$$L_{Dice} = 1 - \frac{2 \times \sum_{i=1}^{N} y_i \widehat{y_i}}{\sum_{i=1}^{N} y_i^2 + \sum_{i=1}^{N} \widehat{y_i}^2}$$

$$L_{mask} = \lambda_{BCE} L_{BCE} + \lambda_{Dice} L_{Dice}$$

where y_i is the ground truth mask value for each pixel, $\widehat{y_i}$ is the predicted mask value for each pixel, N is the total number of pixels (in our case is always 1024×1024), λ_{BCE} and λ_{Dice} are loss coefficients for binary cross-entropy loss and dice loss, respectively.

3.2 Grasp Generation

We extend the functionality of SAM to grasp detection by adding a grasp detection branch. A detailed breakdown of the grasp detection branch is in Fig. 1. Given the mask decoder output F_m, we use it as the context for cross attention blocks in the grasp decoder. To be specific, given the learnable embeddings $E_0 \in R^{N_q \times 256}$:

$$E_i = FF_i(CA_i(SA_i(E_{i-1}), F_m, F_m)), \; i \in [1, N_{layers}]$$

where N_q is a hyperparameter denoting the maximum number of grasp boxes to detect, N_{layers} is the number of transformer blocks in the grasp decoder, SA stands for self-attention module, CA stands for cross-attention module, and FF stands for the feed-forward layer. With the final output $E_{N_{layers}}$, grasp predictions are calculated as:

$$\left[\widehat{\mathbf{x}}, \widehat{\mathbf{y}}, \widehat{\mathbf{o}}, \widehat{\mathbf{w}}, \widehat{\theta}, \widehat{\mathbf{c}}\right] = \sigma(Linear(E_{N_{layers}})), \; [\widehat{\mathbf{x}}, \widehat{\mathbf{y}}, \widehat{\mathbf{o}}, \widehat{\mathbf{w}}, \widehat{\theta}, \widehat{\mathbf{c}}] \in \mathbf{R}^{6 \times N_q}$$

where $\widehat{\mathbf{x}}$, $\widehat{\mathbf{y}}$ are the center coordinates of the grasp boxes, $\widehat{\mathbf{o}}$ is the predicted gripper opening distance, $\widehat{\mathbf{w}}$ is the allowed range for the gripper to shift, $\widehat{\theta}$ is the predicted rotation angle of the gripper regarding to horizontal axis, $\widehat{\mathbf{c}}$ is the predicted confidence scores, σ stands for the sigmoid activation function, $Linear$ is the final regression layer.

To calculate loss, we create a 1-to-1 matching between ground truth grasp boxes and the predicted ones. Following DETR, we use Hungarian Match for this matching problem. First, we construct a cost matrix C, $C \in R^{N_q \times n}$, where n is the number of ground truth grasp annotations. Each element C_{ij} of the matrix represents the cost of assigning the i-th prediction to the j-th ground truth object. We form the cost matrix as follows:

$$C_{ij} = \lambda_c \times \text{CrossEntropyLoss}(\widehat{c_i}, c_j)$$
$$+ \lambda_{bbox} \times \text{L1Loss}\left(\left[\widehat{x_i}, \widehat{y_i}, \widehat{o_i}, \widehat{w_i}, \widehat{\theta_i}\right], [x_j, y_j, o_j, w_j, \theta_j]\right)$$
$$+ \lambda_{giou} \times \text{GIOULoss}([\widehat{x_i}, \widehat{y_i}, \widehat{o_i}, \widehat{w_i}], [x_j, y_j, o_j, w_j])$$

After the cost matrix is obtained, we use the Hungarian algorithm to find the assignment of predictions to ground truth objects that minimizes the total cost. Formally, we seek to find a bijection $f : P \rightarrow G$ that minimizes the total cost: $\min_f \sum_{i=1}^{N} C_{i, f(i)}$, where P is the set of predictions, G is the set of ground truth objects, and $f(i)$ gives the ground truth object assigned to the i-th prediction. Once the optimal assignment is found, compute the loss for the model based on this assignment:

$$
\begin{aligned}
L_{grasp} = \ &\lambda_c \times \text{CrossEntropyLoss}\,(\widehat{\mathbf{c}}, \mathbf{c}) \\
&+ \lambda_{bbox} \times \text{L1Loss}\left(\left[\widehat{\mathbf{x}}, \widehat{\mathbf{y}}, \widehat{\mathbf{o}}, \widehat{\mathbf{w}}, \widehat{\theta}\right], [\mathbf{x}, \mathbf{y}, \mathbf{o}, \mathbf{w}, \theta]\right) \\
&+ \lambda_{bbox} \times \text{GIOULoss}\left([\widehat{\mathbf{x}}, \widehat{\mathbf{y}}, \widehat{\mathbf{o}}, \widehat{\mathbf{w}}], [\mathbf{x}, \mathbf{y}, \mathbf{o}, \mathbf{w}]\right)
\end{aligned}
$$

4   Results

We built GraspAnything upon SegmentAnything ViT-B with 12-layered, 768-dimensional image encoder. The additional grasp decoder is a 6-layered, 256-dimensional transformer decoder.

The GraspAnything model was trained on combined dataset of OCID-grasp [14], VMRD [13], Jacquard [13] and MetaGraspNet [16] for 500k steps, with batch size of 16. Learning rate of the grasp decoder extension is set to 1×10^{-4} and the pretrained SegmentAnything modules to 1×10^{-5}. For evaluations, we further finetune the model on each single dataset for 100k steps to improve performance on the dataset domain and fit to the dataset distribution.

We evaluate the performance of our system on OCID-grasp and Jacquard using grasp success rate which measures the ability of the model to predict accurate grasp boxes for a given object.

The results are presented in Table 1. Figure 2 shows various detection results on images from these two datasets. With completely different structure from previous models which mostly based on heatmap prediction or anchor-based prediction, our model achieves grasp success rates that are nearly equal to the state-of-the-art (SOTA) models on both datasets, while keeping the flexibility in object selection and minimizing the misallocation from predicted grasps to the

Fig. 2. Example predictions on the OCID-grasp and Jacquard dataset. Left of each pair: original images and box prompts for desired object to grasp. Right of each pair: Top-3 grasps and instance masks predicted by the model.

desired object. This demonstrates the effectiveness of our approach in accurately predicting grasp boxes for objects in cluttered environments.

Table 1. Evaluation of grasping performance

Dataset	Methods	Grasp Success Rate
OCID-grasp	GG-CNN	63.4
	GR-ConvNet	74.1
	EfficientGrasp RGB-D [17]	76.4
	Det-Seg-Refine [14]	89.02
	GSMR-CNN [18]	**91.9**
	GraspAnything (Ours)	87.3
Jacquard	Zhou [19]	81.95
	Depierre [15]	85.74
	Song [20]	91.5
	Det-Seg-Refine	**92.65**
	GraspAnything (Ours)	89.4

5 Conclusion

This research successfully tackles the complexities inherent in autonomous robot grasping within multi-object environments. By extending the SegmentAnything model to create the novel GraspAnything model, we have developed a dedicated solution that excels in identifying precise grasp candidates. Experimental results have demonstrated effectiveness of GraspAnything in grasp detection tasks, thereby affirming its potential for broad application in robotic grasping systems. This advancement represents a step forward in enhancing the efficiency and reliability of autonomous robotic interactions in complex scenarios.

References

1. Kirillov, A., et al.: Segment anything. In: Proceedings of the IEEE/CVF International Conference on Computer Vision, pp. 4015–4026 (2023)
2. Morrison, D., Corke, P., Leitner, J.: Closing the loop for robotic grasping: a real-time, generative grasp synthesis approach. arXiv preprint arXiv:1804.05172 (2018)
3. Mahler, J., Matl, M., Liu, X., Li, A., Gealy, D., Goldberg, K.: Dex-net 3.0: computing robust vacuum suction grasp targets in point clouds using a new analytic model and deep learning. In: 2018 IEEE International Conference on robotics and automation (ICRA), pp. 5620–5627. IEEE (2018)
4. Kumra, S., Joshi, S., Sahin, F.: GR-ConvNet v2: a real-time multi-grasp detection network for robotic grasping. Sensors **22**(16), 6208 (2022)

5. Morgan, A.S., Wen, B., Liang, J., et al.: Vision-driven compliant manipulation for reliable, high-precision assembly tasks. arXiv preprint arXiv:2106.14070 (2021)
6. Di Lillo, P., Arrichiello, F., Di Vito, D., Antonelli, G.: BCI-controlled assistive manipulator: developed architecture and experimental results. IEEE Trans. Cogn. Dev. Syst. **13**(1), 91–104 (2020)
7. Zhang, H., Lan, X., Bai, S., et al.: A multi-task convolutional neural network for autonomous robotic grasping in object stacking scenes. In: Proceedings of the 2019 IEEE/RSJ International Conference on Intelligent Robots and Systems (IROS), pp. 6435–6442. IEEE (2019)
8. Dong, M., Zhang, J.: A review of robotic grasp detection technology. Robotica **2023**, 1–40 (2023)
9. Caldera, S., Rassau, A., Chai, D.: Review of deep learning methods in robotic grasp detection. Multimodal Technol. Interact. **2**(3), 57 (2018)
10. Ren, S., He, K., Girshick, R., Sun, J.: Faster R-CNN: Towards real-time object detection with region proposal networks. Adv. Neural. Inf. Process. Syst. **28**, 91–99 (2015)
11. Ainetter, S., Böhm, C., Dhakate, R., et al.: Depth-aware object segmentation and grasp detection for robotic picking tasks. arXiv preprint arXiv:2111.11114 (2021)
12. Redmon, J., Angelova, A.: Real-time grasp detection using convolutional neural networks. In: Proceedings of the 2015 IEEE International Conference on Robotics and Automation (ICRA), pp. 1316–1322. IEEE (2015)
13. Zhang, H., Lan, X., Zhou, X., Tian, Z., Zhang, Y., Zheng, N.: Visual manipulation relationship network for autonomous robotics. In: 2018 IEEE-RAS 18th International Conference on Humanoid Robots (Humanoids), pp. 118–125. IEEE (2018)
14. Ainetter, S., Fraundorfer, F.: End-to-end trainable deep neural network for robotic grasp detection and semantic segmentation from RGB. In: 2021 IEEE International Conference on Robotics and Automation (ICRA), pp. 13452–13458. IEEE (2021)
15. Depierre, A., Dellandréa, E., Chen, L.: Jacquard: a large scale dataset for robotic grasp detection. In: 2018 IEEE/RSJ International Conference on Intelligent Robots and Systems (IROS), pp. 3511–3516. IEEE (2018)
16. Gilles, M., et al.: MetaGraspNetV2: all-in-one dataset enabling fast and reliable robotic bin picking via object relationship reasoning and dexterous grasping. IEEE Trans. Autom. Sci. Eng. (2023)
17. Cao, H., Chen, G., Li, Z., Feng, Q., Lin, J., Knoll, A.: Efficient grasp detection network with Gaussian-based grasp representation for robotic manipulation. IEEE/ASME Trans. Mechatron. (2022)
18. Holomjova, V., Starkey, A.J., Meißner, P.: GSMR-CNN: an end-to-end trainable architecture for grasping target objects from multi-object scenes. In: 2023 IEEE International Conference on Robotics and Automation (ICRA), pp. 3808–3814. IEEE (2023)
19. Zhou, X., Lan, X., Zhang, H., Tian, Z., Zhang, Y., Zheng, N.: Fully convolutional grasp detection network with oriented anchor box. In: 2018 IEEE/RSJ International Conference on Intelligent Robots and Systems (IROS), pp. 7223–7230. IEEE (2018)
20. Song, Y., Gao, L., Li, X., Shen, W.: A novel robotic grasp detection method based on region proposal networks. Robot. Comput.-Integr. Manuf. **65**, 101963 (2020)

Content-Aware Efficient Learner
for Audio-Visual Emotion Recognition

Guanjie Huang, Weilin Lin, and Li Liu$^{(\boxtimes)}$

The Hong Kong University of Science and Technology (Guangzhou), Guangzhou, China
avrillliu@hkust-gz.edu.cn

Abstract. Audio-Visual Emotion Recognition (AVER) is essential in various real-world applications. Many methods try to extract and fuse the audio and visual modalities to comprehend better and classify the underlying emotion. Recently, large pre-trained models brought powerful modality-fusion ability in general datasets and significantly outperformed traditional small-scale models. However, they are less effective in complementing some specialized scenarios due to the conflict of meanings between the two modalities. This paper proposes a parameter-efficient fine-tuning method, *Content-Aware Efficient Learner (CAEL)*, to solve this problem with subtle computational consumption. Specifically, we propose an adapter network based on the pre-trained audio and visual transformers for modality fusion. To better fuse the two modalities, propose content-aware attention, in which the audio and visual information align and fuse under the guidance of the speech content. Extensive experiments on the CREMA-D dataset verify the effectiveness and efficiency of our proposed framework.

Keywords: Emotion Recognition · Multimodal Learning · Transfer Learning

1 Introduction

Emotion recognition (ER) has garnered widespread interest and research attention due to its numerous potential applications. For example, introducing the emotion-aware recommender system to promote the user-friendly advertisement [21] and the tone-aware chatbot to enhance user experience [15]. With the explosive growth of multi-modal information in social media, such as audio and visual data, extracting and fusing them has become the mainstream solution for emotion recognition [11,29,35]. Notably, the consistency and complementarity characteristic of audio-visual information enables their cooperation in emotion recognition, such as a calm face with a calm voice indicating consistency, while a raising voice can reveal potential anger, indicating complementarity. Therefore, the key challenges to fully utilizing audio-visual information for ER lie in

---

G. Huang and W. Lin—These authors contributed equally.

© The Author(s), under exclusive license to Springer Nature Singapore Pte Ltd. 2025
H. Li et al. (Eds.): ICSR + InnoBiz 2024, LNAI 15170, pp. 31–40, 2025.
https://doi.org/10.1007/978-981-96-1151-5_4

the general modality-fusion ability for consistency and the specialized modality-alignment ability for complementarity. Large pre-trained models have proven effective with impressive general ability toward various tasks [6,22,31]. Recently, a similar paradigm has also been utilized in Audio-Visual Emotion Recognition (AVER) [29], which exhibits a significant general modality-fusion ability while less effective on complementarity due to the conflict of meanings among different modalities. On the contrary, the traditional supervised small model trained from scratch performs less effective modality consistency than the large pre-trained models and easily over-align with the specific dataset, where the complementarity may be a bias to mislead the modality fusion. To leverage strengths and mitigate limitations as mentioned above, we focus on conducting efficient fine-tuning based on the AVER pre-trained model for both utilizing the general modality-fusion ability on it and improving the specialized modality-alignment ability on the specific dataset.

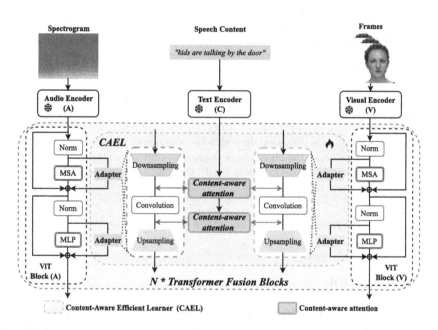

Fig. 1. Overview of Content-Aware Efficient Learner. "CAEL", "MSA", and "MLP" are short for Content-Aware Efficient Learner, multi-head self-attention, and multi-layer perceptron.

To this end, we propose *Content-Aware Efficient Learner* (**CAEL**). Specifically, it is an efficient learner structure based on a trainable adapter based on the pre-trained transformers. We propose *content-aware attention* to effectively align audio and visual modalities via content guidance. The experimental results on CREMA-D [2] show that our CAEL can achieve a great performance and efficiency trade-off. Our contributions can be summarized as three-fold:

1) We innovatively formulate the AVER problem into an efficient fine-tuning problem considering both consistency and complementarity by utilizing the powerful pre-trained models in this field.
2) We emphasize the essential of aligning the audio-visual modalities using additional content. And further proposed a novel approach, CAEL.
3) The extensive experiments validate the effectiveness and efficiency of our proposed CAEL.

2   Related Work

The majority of research on AVER focuses on two aspects: unimodal feature extraction and audio-visual feature fusion.

In the realm of unimodal feature extraction, some seminal methods have been developed over the past two decades [36–39]. Early studies focused on hand-crafted features for both modalities, exemplified by IS13 [24] and eGeMAPS [10] for audio, as well as LBP-TOP [41] and HOG [8] for video. As deep learning has become the major research trend in the past few years, using deep neural networks for feature extraction offers a promising and powerful solution. They are trained on extensive audio and image/video datasets to serve as audio-visual feature extractors, such as PANNs [17] and VGGish [12] for audio, and VGGFace [3] and C3D [32] for video. Recently, large self-supervised pre-trained models have achieved significant success in emotion recognition for both audios (*e.g.*, Wav2vec2.0 [1] and HuBERT [14]) and video (*e.g.*, SVFAP [28] and MAE-DFER [27]).

Except for unimodal feature extraction, the fusion of audio-visual features is also vital for accurate emotion recognition, which can be categorized into three primary strategies: early, late, and model-level fusion [18,19,37,38]. Early fusion typically involves the integration of audio-visual features at the input level [5,20], whereas late fusion amalgamates audio-visual predictions at the decision level [25,30]. The most prevalent approach is model-level fusion. For instance, MulT [33] employs cross-modal attention to capture intricate interactions within unaligned audio-visual feature sequences. EMT [26] enhances MulT by incorporating the global multimodal context, which interacts with local unimodal features to facilitate efficient cross-modal information exchange. The recent T-MEP [40] adopts a similar approach to MulT, utilizing self-attention and cross-attention mechanisms in an interleaving manner to fuse fine-grained audio-visual tokens.

Although plenty of methods are proposed for better utilizing or fusing different modalities, they are mostly designed for training from scratch, where the trainable parameters are usually substantial, especially the large pre-trained models with great general ability and deficient accuracy on some specific datasets. We consider the great potential of efficient fine-tuning techniques for AVER. Furthermore, we attach importance to the content when aligning the two modalities, which is normally overlooked by the previous fusing methods.

3   Methods

3.1   Problem Setup

AVER takes audio and visual as input and conducts emotion classification. We denote each audio-visual paired data sample as $\mathcal{X} = \{\mathcal{V}, \mathcal{A}, \mathcal{C}, \mathcal{Y}\}$. For the input of visual modality, we uniformly sample a temporal sequence of F frames $\mathcal{V} = \{\mathbf{V}_1, \mathbf{V}_2, ..., \mathbf{V}_F\}$ from the given video. For the j-th frame in $\mathcal{V}$, $\mathbf{V}_j \in \mathbb{R}^{H \times W \times 3}$ has height H and width W. For audio input, it is transferred into a spectrogram $\mathcal{A} \in \mathbb{R}^{M \times D}$, where M and D are frequency and time. $\mathcal{Y}$ is the annotation label of the speaker's emotion. In most cases, the samples also provide the corresponding content $\mathcal{C}$ of the speech. In some datasets, text content is highly correlated with emotional information. To make the model reflect the emotion recognition ability in a wider range of scenarios, we conducted experiments on more challenging datasets. These contents are selected from a fixed number of sentences, meaning emotions cannot be judged from content alone. Models conduct inference on the test set after finetuning on the training set. Modality Fusion operations can occur before, during, or after encoding. The decision head then processes the outcomes to generate the final emotion prediction.

3.2   Overview of Audio-Visual Learning Process for AVER

As illustrated in Fig. 1, Our CAEL for AVER forms a dual-stream structure built on ViT [9]. Visual frames and the audio spectrogram are first fed into fixed unimodal encoders for feature extraction, followed by several fusion blocks for cross-modal learning. The CAEL is incorporated into each fusion block as a multi-layer perception (MLP) and multi-head self-attention (MSA) layers' parallel module to achieve efficient finetuning of the AVER task. The content of each sample is processed and introduced into CAEL by designed content-aware attention. After the last fusion block, the visual tokens and audio tokens are put into the head for the final prediction and compute the cross-entropy loss.

3.3   Content-Aware Efficient Learner

CAEL is built on adapters [13,16], which is one of the parameter-efficient transfer learning methods. To perform effective multimodal learning with significantly reduced trainable parameters. We leverage speech content in the original video as the key part of the alignment and guidance of the audio and visual modalities.

Contents are Compact Aligners. In common AVER tasks, the model is expected to accurately identify the emotion of the current task through the changes in the speaker's facial expressions and intonation. Although the speaker's content can provide a key hint for the current emotion in some tasks, the same text content may correspond to different emotions in real situations. Current datasets often require speakers to follow fixed sentence patterns to record multiple emotional videos. This results in the content not being able to benefit emotional cognition directly. This is also why current algorithms rarely use content.

Although content does not contain direct semantic information for emotional judgment, its compact token structure processed by text encoder has become an excellent medium for aligning complex audio-visual modalities. Specifically, by taking advantage of the natural consistency of the temporal structure of these three modalities, using content tokens allows the model to focus more on the important information in the remaining two modalities, thereby achieving efficient learning with only a few parameters.

Content-Aware Attention. The fusion strategy plays an important role in multimodal learning, which targets efficiently fusing multiple modalities to promote joint decision-making. In this paper, with content tokens extracted from the corresponding content, specially designed content-aware attention is executed between adapters of the audio and video streams for effective fusion.

In each CAEL, audio, video, and content tokens all go through the downsampling layers first, which are single-layer feed-forward layers. We denote the tokens after downsampling in a transformer layer as $\mathcal{T} = \{\mathbf{T}^v, \mathbf{T}^a, \mathbf{T}^c\}$ with $\mathbf{T}^v$, $\mathbf{T}^a$ and $\mathbf{T}^c$ as video, audio and content tokens, respectively. Content-aware attention is directed before and after the convolution layer and consists of three steps:

Selection. With the incorporated content tokens, the purpose of this step is to guide the model to focus on important audio tokens and video tokens and ignore others, which also compresses tokens into a small set. This is implemented with the following attention functions:

$$
\begin{aligned}
\mathbf{T}^{c,v} &= \mathrm{CMA}(\mathbf{T}^c, \mathbf{T}^v, \mathbf{T}^v), \\
\mathbf{T}^{c,a} &= \mathrm{CMA}(\mathbf{T}^c, \mathbf{T}^a, \mathbf{T}^a),
\end{aligned}
\tag{1}
$$

where CMA means cross-modal attention [34] and is defined as

$$
\mathrm{CMA}(\mathbf{Q}, \mathbf{K}, \mathbf{V}) = Softmax(\frac{\mathbf{Q}\mathbf{K}^{trans}}{\sqrt{d}})\mathbf{V},
\tag{2}
$$

where $\mathbf{Q}$, $\mathbf{K}$, and $\mathbf{V}$ denote query, key, and value tokens, respectively. trans is the transpose operation and $\frac{1}{\sqrt{d}}$ is the scaling factor with d as the dimension of keys.

Fusion. This step contains two cross-modal attention operations:

$$
\begin{aligned}
\mathbf{T}^{v,c,a} &= \mathrm{CMA}(\mathbf{T}^v, \mathbf{T}^{c,a}, \mathbf{T}^{c,a}), \\
\mathbf{T}^{a,c,v} &= \mathrm{CMA}(\mathbf{T}^a, \mathbf{T}^{c,v}, \mathbf{T}^{c,v}),
\end{aligned}
\tag{3}
$$

The fusion across three modalities generates the new tokens by considering their importance from different perspectives.

Summation. The summation step sums the corresponding tokens for each modality to form new modality tokens. The calculations are presented as follows:

$$\overline{\mathbf{T}}^v = \lambda^v \mathbf{T}^{v,t,a} + \mathbf{T}^v,$$
$$\overline{\mathbf{T}}^a = \lambda^a \mathbf{T}^{a,t,v} + \mathbf{T}^a, \tag{4}$$

where λ^v and λ^a are learnable parameters. The new tokens gather information from different attention levels. After this step, residual connections return new tokens to individual modal streams.

4 Experiments and Results

In this section, we introduce the benchmark dataset and implementation details. Then, we present the comparative and ablation study results.

4.1 Dataset

CREMA-D [2] (Crowd-sourced Emotional Multimodal Actors Dataset) is a high-quality audio-visual dataset, containing 7442 video clips from 91 actors (including 48 male and 43 female). It consists of totally six different emotions as the label, *i.e.*, anger, disgust, fear, happy, neutral, and sad. Specifically, each actor selected one of the 12 sentences and presented it using one of the six emotions and four different emotion levels (low, medium, high, and unspecified).

We follow the data preprocessing and data splitting scheme in [29]. For each visual clip, we extract the human face by using OpenFace[1]. And no further preprocess is needed on the audios, since their sampling rate is already 16k in the origin. After that, we split the dataset under the setting of 5-fold cross-validation in a *subject-independent* manner[2], *e.g.*, 18 actors per split.

4.2 Implementation Details

We used the audio and visual encoders from [29] as the backbone and loaded the model pretrained on VoxCeleb2 [7]. The audio and visual encoders contain 12 transformer blocks each, and we set the last 8 of them as fusion blocks. The dimension of the tokens is 512. During training, we froze the parameters of the pretrained model. A pretrained CLIP text encoder (also 12 transformer blocks but with 768-dimension tokens) is used to obtain the content tokens from the original samples In CAEL, the dimension of tokens is downsampling to 16 first. Then, after two content-aware attentions and convolutional layers for audio and visual individually, tokens are restored to the original dimension and added to the transformer block. Our framework was implemented using Pytorch, and all experiments were conducted on NVIDIA RTX A6000 GPU.

---

[1] https://github.com/TadasBaltrusaitis/OpenFace.git.
[2] Split the training and test sets according to different actors.

4.3 Comparative Studies

Performance on CREMA-D. In Table 1, we show the comparative results on the CREMA-D dataset. CAEL, using less than one-tenth of the trainable parameters of other methods, achieves the second-best performance. In particular, the performance of CAEL is significantly better than all unimodal models, even though their parameters are dozens of times larger. This shows that CAEL effectively utilizes the complementary information in the audio-visual modalities and achieves efficient multimodal learning.

It is particularly noteworthy that compared to the base model [29], our method achieves comparable performance with less than one-fortieth of trainable parameters. It cannot be denied that full parameter fine-tuning brings better results, but CAEL still achieves a trade-off between performance and efficiency.

4.4 Ablation Study

Table 1. Comparison with state-of-the-art methods on CREMA-D. Modality: A (Audio), V (Visual), A+V (Audio + Visual). WAR: weighted average recall.

Method	Modality	#Params (M)	WAR
Wav2Vec2.0 [1]	A	95	72.41
HuBERT [14]	A	95	72.57
WavLM-Plus [4]	A	95	73.39
SVFAP [28]	V	78	77.37
MAE-DFER [27]	V	85	77.38
MulT Base [33]	A+V	38	68.87
MulT Large [33]	A+V	89	70.22
VQ-MAE-AV+ Attn. Pooling [23]	A+V	30	78.40
VQ-MAE-AV+ Query2Emo [23]	A+V	30	80.40
HiCMAE-B [29]	A+V	81	**84.89**
CAEL	A+V	**1.7**	81.09

In Table 2, we show ablation study results on CREMA-D. Note that the base model indicates the backbone without adapters. EL stands for the basic efficient learner, which did not use the content for guidance. The performance gap proves that the content information and efficient learner design in our proposed framework effectively improve the model's performance.

Table 2. Ablation study.

Method	WAR
Base model	73.69
+ EL	77.16
+ **CAEL**	**81.09**

5   Conclusion

In this work, we propose the Content-Aware Efficient Learner (CAEL), an efficient fine-tuning method for Audio-Visual Emotion Recognition. This method adopts adapters with content-aware attention to fuse and align different modalities under the guidance of speech content, thereby achieving both consistency and complementarity between the two modalities. Further, the few updating parameters make it a potential solution for broader applications. The experimental results on CREMA-D validate the effectiveness of CAEL.

Acknowledgments. This work was supported by the National Natural Science Foundation of China (No. 62101351), Guangzhou Municipal Science and Technology Project: Basic and Applied Basic research projects (No. 2024A04J4232).

References

1. Baevski, A., Zhou, Y., et al.: wav2vec 2.0: a framework for self-supervised learning of speech representations (2020)
2. Cao, H., Cooper, D.G., et al.: CREMA-D: crowd-sourced emotional multimodal actors dataset. IEEE Trans. Affect. Comput. **5**(4), 377–390 (2014)
3. Cao, Q., Shen, L., et al.: VggFace2: a dataset for recognising faces across pose and age. In: FG 2018 (2018)
4. Chen, S., Wang, C., et al.: WavLM: large-scale self-supervised pre-training for full stack speech processing. IEEE J. Sel. Top. Signal Process. **16**(6), 1505–1518 (2022)
5. Chen, S., Jin, Q., et al.: Multimodal multi-task learning for dimensional and continuous emotion recognition. In: Proceedings of the 7th Annual Workshop on Audio/Visual Emotion Challenge (2017)
6. Chen, Y., et al.: USCL: pretraining deep ultrasound image diagnosis model through video contrastive representation learning. In: de Bruijne, M., et al. (eds.) MICCAI 2021, Part VIII. LNCS, vol. 12908, pp. 627–637. Springer, Cham (2021). https://doi.org/10.1007/978-3-030-87237-3_60
7. Chung, J.S., Nagrani, A., Zisserman, A.: Voxceleb2: deep speaker recognition. arXiv (2018)
8. Dalal, N., Triggs, B.: Histograms of oriented gradients for human detection. In: CVPR (2005)
9. Dosovitskiy, A., Beyer, L., et al.: An image is worth 16×16 words: transformers for image recognitfion at scale. In: ICLR (2020)
10. Eyben, F., Scherer, K.R., et al.: The Geneva minimalistic acoustic parameter set (GeMAPS) for voice research and affective computing. IEEE Trans. Affect. Comput. **7**(2), 190–202 (2015)
11. Fan, R., Liu, H., et al.: AttA-NET: attention aggregation network for audio-visual emotion recognition. In: ICASSP (2024)
12. Hershey, S., Chaudhuri, S., et al.: CNN architectures for large-scale audio classification. In: ICASSP (2017)
13. Houlsby, N., Giurgiu, A., et al.: Parameter-efficient transfer learning for NLP. In: ICML (2019)
14. Hsu, W.N., Bolte, B., et al.: HuBERT: self-supervised speech representation learning by masked prediction of hidden units. TASLP **29**, 3451–3460 (2021)

15. Hu, T., Xu, A., et al.: Touch your heart: a tone-aware chatbot for customer care on social media. In: Proceedings of the 2018 CHI Conference on Human Factors in Computing Systems (2018)
16. Jie, S., Deng, Z.H.: Convolutional bypasses are better vision transformer adapters. arXiv (2022)
17. Kong, Q., Cao, Y., et al.: PANNs: large-scale pretrained audio neural networks for audio pattern recognition. IEEE/ACM Trans. Audio Speech Lang. Process. **28**, 2880–2894 (2020)
18. Liu, L., Feng, G., Beautemps, D., Zhang, X.P.: Re-synchronization using the hand preceding model for multi-modal fusion in automatic continuous cued speech recognition. IEEE Trans. Multimed. **23**, 292–305 (2020)
19. Liu, L., Hueber, T., Feng, G., Beautemps, D.: Visual recognition of continuous cued speech using a tandem CNN-HMM approach. In: Interspeech, pp. 2643–2647 (2018)
20. Meng, L., Liu, Y., et al.: Valence and arousal estimation based on multimodal temporal-aware features for videos in the wild. In: CVPR (2022)
21. Polignano, M., Narducci, F., et al.: Towards emotion-aware recommender systems: an affective coherence model based on emotion-driven behaviors. Expert Syst. Appl. **170**, 114382 (2021)
22. Radford, A., Kim, J.W., et al.: Learning transferable visual models from natural language supervision. In: ICML (2021)
23. Sadok, S., Leglaive, S., Séguier, R.: A vector quantized masked autoencoder for audiovisual speech emotion recognition. arXiv (2023)
24. Schuller, B., Steidl, S., et al.: The interspeech 2013 computational paralinguistics challenge: social signals, conflict, emotion, autism. In: INTERSPEECH (2013)
25. Sun, L., Lian, Z., et al.: Multi-modal continuous dimensional emotion recognition using recurrent neural network and self-attention mechanism. In: Proceedings of the 1st International on Multimodal Sentiment Analysis in Real-Life Media Challenge and Workshop (2020)
26. Sun, L., Lian, Z., et al.: Efficient multimodal transformer with dual-level feature restoration for robust multimodal sentiment analysis (2023)
27. Sun, L., Lian, Z., et al.: MAE-DFER: efficient masked autoencoder for self-supervised dynamic facial expression recognition. In: ACM Multimedia (2023)
28. Sun, L., Lian, Z., et al.: SVFAP: self-supervised video facial affect perceiver. arXiv (2023)
29. Sun, L., Lian, Z., et al.: HiCMAE: hierarchical contrastive masked autoencoder for self-supervised audio-visual emotion recognition. arXiv (2024)
30. Sun, L., Xu, M., et al.: Multimodal emotion recognition and sentiment analysis via attention enhanced recurrent model. In: MSAC (2021)
31. Touvron, H., Martin, L., et al.: Llama 2: open foundation and fine-tuned chat models. arXiv (2023)
32. Tran, D., Bourdev, L., et al.: Learning spatiotemporal features with 3D convolutional networks. In: ICCV (2015)
33. Tsai, Y.H.H., Bai, S., et al.: Multimodal transformer for unaligned multimodal language sequences. In: ACL (2019)
34. Vaswani, A., Shazeer, N., et al.: Attention is all you need. In: NeurIPS (2017)
35. Verbitskiy, S., Berikov, V., Vyshegorodtsev, V.: ERANNs: efficient residual audio neural networks for audio pattern recognition. Pattern Recogn. Lett. **161**, 38–44 (2022)
36. Wang, J., Zhao, Y., Liu, L., Xu, T., Li, Q., Li, S.: Emotional talking head generation based on memory-sharing and attention-augmented networks (2023)

37. Wu, C.H., Lin, J.C., Wei, W.L.: Survey on audiovisual emotion recognition: databases, features, and data fusion strategies. APSIPA Trans. Signal Inf. Process. **3**, e12 (2014)
38. Zeng, Z., Pantic, M., et al.: A survey of affect recognition methods: audio, visual and spontaneous expressions. In: ICMI (2007)
39. Zhang, S., Yang, Y., et al.: Deep learning-based multimodal emotion recognition from audio, visual, and text modalities: a systematic review of recent advancements and future prospects. Expert Syst. Appl. 121692 (2023)
40. Zhang, X., Li, M., et al.: Transformer-based multimodal emotional perception for dynamic facial expression recognition in the wild. IEEE Trans. Circuits Syst. Video Technol. (2023)
41. Zhao, G., Pietikainen, M.: Dynamic texture recognition using local binary patterns with an application to facial expressions. IEEE Trans. Pattern Anal. Mach. Intell. **29**(6), 915–928 (2007)

The Impact of Synchronized Visual and Auditory Attention on Human Perception

Lichuan Jiang[1,2], Jiani Zhong[1], Muqing Jian[1], Xuanzhuo Liu[1], Siqi Cai[1,3(✉)], and Haizhou Li[1,3]

[1] School of Data Science, The Chinese University of Hong Kong, Shenzhen 518172, Guangdong, People's Republic of China
`elesiqi@nus.edu.sg`
[2] TUM School of Computation, Information and Technology, Department of Electrical Engineering, Technical University of Munich, Munich, Germany
[3] Machine Learning Lab (MLL), University of Bremen, Bremen, Germany

Abstract. The cocktail party problem shows the remarkable human ability to selectively attend to and recognize one source of auditory input in a noisy environment. However, individuals may struggle to identify a speaker's voice when they are unfamiliar with the speakers and don't have a clear visual focus, which results in less visual information. This raises the question: How can visual information aid in extracting information from a speaker's voice? This study explores how synchronized visual and auditory attention impact human perception in scenarios involving two speakers. Using Tobii Glasses 3 to track participants' eye movements and pupil diameters, combined with questionnaire responses, we explore how these factors influence speech comprehension. Our results demonstrate that participants achieve higher accuracy in speech comprehension when they focus their gaze on the speaker they are listening to, compared to scenarios where visual attention is divided between speakers or where they rely solely on auditory cues. These findings highlight the effectiveness of synchronizing visual and auditory attention in improving the acquisition and processing of information.

Keywords: Multi-modal · Audiovisual Attention · Human Perception · Speech Comprehension · Pupil Diameter

1 Introduction

In a cocktail party, individuals with normal hearing abilities possess the remarkable capacity to separate and focus on specific speech to gather relevant information [1]. However, even individuals with normal hearing find it increasingly

---

L. Jiang and J. Zhong—These authors contributed equally to this work as co-first authors.

M. Jian and X. Liu—These authors contributed equally to this work as co-second authors.

© The Author(s), under exclusive license to Springer Nature Singapore Pte Ltd. 2025
H. Li et al. (Eds.): ICSR + InnoBiz 2024, LNAI 15170, pp. 41–50, 2025.
https://doi.org/10.1007/978-981-96-1151-5_5

difficult to recognize a speaker's voice when they are unfamiliar with the speakers and don't have a clear visual focus, which results in less visual information. In these scenarios, the potential role of visual cues remains relatively unexplored. This raises the question of how visual information can aid in extracting the target speaker's voice, particularly in complex auditory environments.

The integration of multiple sensory modalities within the human perceptual system, particularly the synchronization of visual and auditory attention, is essential for enhancing information processing capabilities [2,3]. This synergy is particularly valuable where auditory cues alone may be insufficient. Understanding how visual attention compensates for auditory limitations or enhances overall perception holds profound implications for communication strategies, multimedia design, and educational settings [4,5].

Previous studies in visual and auditory modalities have significantly advanced our understanding of attentional processes [6,7]. Perspectives vary, with some emphasizing constraints in concurrent attentional capacities [8], while others highlight potential synergies among sensory modalities [9]. Recent studies have investigated attention's role in "cross-modal correspondences" [10,11], the dynamic interaction between eye movements and linguistic stimuli [12], and the influence of gaze behavior on multisensory integration [2]. Recent research [12] has provided new insights into eye movements related to attended and unattended natural speech sentences. By integrating simultaneously recorded eye-tracking and magnetoencephalographic data with temporal response functions, the study reveals that eye gaze aligns with attended speech.

Despite these advancements, gaps remain in understanding how attention operates across different modalities, especially in complex auditory environments. Quantitatively measuring attention levels and synchronizing visual and auditory attention are crucial for advancing this field. This study aims to bridge these gaps by integrating eye-tracking and facial recognition technologies to explore individual and interactive sensory processing mechanisms. Specifically, we employ Tobii Glasses 3 to precisely collect eye movement and pupil diameter data, alongside facial recognition through video recordings, ensuring accurate and efficient measurement of participants' attention. Using AI-generated materials, we achieve rigorous control and precision in experimental design, thereby enabling sophisticated investigations into multi-modal attention. The contribution of this paper can be mainly summarized as:

1. Development of a comprehensive dataset that includes audiovisual stimuli, eye movement, and pupil diameter data, along with questionnaires to enhance research in visual and auditory attention.
2. Quantitative analysis exploring the effects of synchronized visual and auditory attention on human perception.
3. Contributing linguistic and cultural diversity through research conducted in Chinese, thereby enriching understanding across different cultural contexts.

2   Methods and Materials

2.1   Hypothesis

We hypothesize that the alignment of visual information plays a pivotal role in human auditory attention and speech Comprehension. To validate this hypothesis, we have designed the following experiment.

2.2   Experiment Setup

As illustrated in Fig. 1, we developed a multi-talker speech perception system to evaluate the impact of synchronized visual and auditory attention. The experiment consisted of six groups, each with four video clips, featuring two AI digital avatars simultaneously speaking different dates in Mandarin Chinese from left and right sections. A continuous period during which a participant watches a video clip is referred to as a "trial", with each participant completing a total of 24 trials.

(a) Experiment Configuration

| LL = Look LEFT & Listen LEFT 4 Clips (MF, FM FF, MM) | RR = Look RIGHT & Listen RIGHT 4 Clips (MF, FM FF, MM) | LR = Look LEFT & Listen RIGHT 4 Clips (MF, FM FF, MM) | RL = Look RIGHT & Listen LEFT 4 Clips (MF, FM FF, MM) | 4 NL: Listen LEFT + 4 NR: Listen RIGHT (MF, FM FF, MM) = 8 Clips |

(b) Tobii Glasses 3   **(d) Experiment Setup**

(c) Data Analysis

Visual attention calculation

*Head to computer: 60cm; Floor to head: 130cm; Floor to desk: 90cm; Desk to the top of the computer: 45cm

Fig. 1. Experiment overview. (a) Experiment configuration: Two dates are spoken simultaneously by two speakers in the video. Participants are instructed to listen and look toward specified directions. M = Male, F = Female, MF = Male (Left) Female (Right), and others in a similar fashion. (b) Tobii Glasses 3 used for monitoring visual parameters. (c) Data analysis: Visualization of the visual attention calculation procedure. (d) Experiment setup.

To ensure consistent sound input and provide spatial cues, the Head Related Transfer Function (HRTF) [13] was employed. Participants were seated in a soundproof chamber with earphones and eye-tracking glasses. They were instructed to fixate their gaze and listen to the voice according to different condition setups as described below. Subsequently, they recorded the dates they perceived in a questionnaire following each clip.

The experiment was conducted under three conditions: SameSide, DifferSide, and OnlyListen. In the SameSide condition, subjects were instructed to focus their gaze on one side while listening to speech from the same side. In the Differ-Side condition, subjects focused their gaze on one side while listening to speech from the opposite side (see 1). The OnlyListen group involved participants listening to speech without any visual cues. Both the SameSide and DifferSide conditions were further categorized into four sub-conditions: RR (both stimuli on the right), LL (both on the left), RL (listening on the right, looking left), and LR (listening on the left, looking right). Participants' gaze directions were monitored using Tobii Pro Glasses 3 [14].

Participants. 16 healthy participants aged between 18 and 22 were recruited from the university. The participant group comprised 6 males and 10 females, including 3 individuals (1 male and 2 females) from Indonesia who were non-native Mandarin speakers. Despite not being native speakers, these three participants exhibited exceptional speech comprehension of the Chinese dates used in our experiment. It should be noted that data from two participants were excluded from the analyses due to failure to follow the experimental instructions.

2.3   Data Acquisition

Eye Movements and Pupil Diameter. Eye movements indicate where visual attention is directed and for how long, showing which speaker captures interest. Meanwhile, changes in pupil diameter reflect the mental effort, offering insights into the cognitive load of tasks [15]. To investigate both visual attention and cognitive effort, we utilized the Tobii Pro Glasses 3 [14], an advanced wearable eye-tracking device that captures real-world visual data while allowing for natural user interactions. This device records visual data from a first-person perspective at a sampling rate of 100 Hz. Specifically, the device records detailed eye movements, pupil diameter changes, and gaze point locations at a sampling rate of 100 Hz. Analysis of these metrics provides valuable insights into the dynamics of visual attention and cognitive workload among participants.

Questionnaire Design. The questionnaire comprises six groups (see Sect. 2.2 for details). Each group contains four questions, where participants are asked to record the dates of the target speaker in each audio clip. The sequence of clips within each group is designed to test the accuracy of identifying males and females under different conditions. The clips are organized as follows:

- One male on the left and one female on the right (MF)
- One female on the left and one male on the right (FM)
- Two males, one on the left and one on the right (FF)
- Two females, one on the left and one on the right (MM)

At the end of each section, participants are asked to provide a subjective rating of their visual attention to the target person, as well as of the attention level of listening (rated from "not focused" 0 to "very focused" 6).

3 Data Analysis and Results

We quantify the visual and audio attention across multiple dimensions:

- Audio Attention: Accuracy of questionnaire responses serves as an indicator.
- Visual Attention: Eye movement and gaze point locations were analyzed to measure visual attention.
- Cognitive workload: Pupil diameter serves as a metric for measuring cognitive workload.

3.1 Analysis of Eye-Tracking Signals

Gaze Point Analysis. Using the face recognition function of OpenCV [16], we calculate the period where video frames occur, in addition to utilizing the timestamp event markers sent by E-Prime. This ensures us a more exact period in which subjects see two faces on the screen. After subtracting the target faces in the video, we compare the location of the faces with the gaze points locations and calculate the level of visual attention V_a using the formula

$$V_a = \frac{number\ of\ 'in-box'\ frames}{total\ number\ of\ speaker\ frames}$$

Here, the 'box' denotes the region around the target speaker's face determined by computer vision methods [16]. Correct fixation is determined by counting the frames where the gaze point falls within this specified region in each trial. The ratio of correct fixation frames to total frames with faces is computed to provide a measure of attention time proportion.

Pupil Diameter Analysis. Pupil diameter is a significant indicator of a subject's attention level and cognitive load [17–19]. Larger pupil dilations are generally associated with higher cognitive load and concentration [20]. Furthermore, pupil dilation patterns can index information processing and attentional states, with systematic variations corresponding to engagement levels [21]. In this study, we analyzed pupil diameter variability to assess attentional states across different experimental conditions. Specifically, we compared pupil size variability between the SameSide condition (RR and LL) and the DifferSide condition (RL and LR). Pupil size variability, measured as the variance in pupil diameter, serves as an indicator of cognitive load [22]. Larger variability typically reflects greater pupil dilation.

As shown in Fig. 2(a), the average variability was lower in the SameSide condition compared to the DifferSide condition, with the DifferSide condition exhibiting greater variability. Figure (2(b) provides a detailed view of pupil size variability across participants in different conditions. Although there are individual differences in pupil size variability, the DifferSide condition generally exhibited higher variability across participants. This finding suggests that the synchronized visual and auditory information influences pupil size variability. Specifically, the DifferSide condition likely induces higher cognitive load, emphasizing the critical role of synchronized visual information from the attended speaker's face in optimizing attentional focus and enhancing speech comprehension.

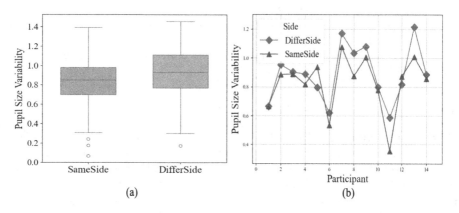

(a)   (b)

Fig. 2. (a) Comparison of pupil size variability between SameSide and DifferSide conditions. (b) Pupil Size variability across participants in SameSide and DifferSide conditions.

3.2   Analysis of Questionnaire Data

To ensure that participants adhered to the experimental instructions, particularly regarding their attention to the target speaker, we evaluated the accuracy of their responses to questions pertaining to each clip [23]. To achieve this, we employed a partial scoring system based on the Partial Credit Model, a robust framework commonly used in auditory identification tasks [24]. This model enables us to assess varying degrees of correctness in participants' responses.

Our scoring system is categorized as follows:
1. Completely incorrect (0 points): The participant didn't identify any aspect of the target information.
2. Partially correct (0.5 points): The participant correctly identifies either the month or the date.
3. Fully correct (1 point): The participant accurately identifies both the month and the date.

Data Preprocessing. Data recorded from the SameSide and DifferSide groups were analyzed for comparison. To ensure the reliability of the analyzed answers, we excluded 33 out of 192 responses (16 trials × 12 participants) where participants did not look at the requested face for at least half of the trial time (i.e., visual attention below 50%). For the OnlyListen group, 5 responses were excluded out of 112 (8 trials × 14 participants) responses where the participants opened their eyes. After data processing, we evaluate the null hypothesis (H0): there is no difference between the groups of answers.

Statistical Analysis. The questionnaire data is independent across groups and sufficiently large to support robust statistical analysis. A normality test (Shapiro-Wilk test) was conducted within each group, indicating that the data follow a non-normal distribution. Given that the data is categorical (with values of 0, 0.5, and 1), non-parametric statistical methods were applied. Specifically, the Mann-Whitney U test and Chi-square test were employed to evaluate the differences across different groups. Both tests showed similar results.

As shown in Table 1, the within-group tests reveal no significant differences, suggesting that these data exhibit comparable levels of accuracy. Consequently, there is insufficient evidence to reject the null hypothesis within groups, leading to the combination of these conditions for subsequent between-group analyses.

Results indicate significant differences in answer accuracy between groups. Specifically, the SameSide condition significantly rejects the null hypothesis compared to the OnlyListen group, suggesting that the SameSide condition results in better accuracy than the OnlyListen group. Similarly, the comparison between SameSide and DifferSide also rejects the null hypothesis. However, no statistically significant difference is found between the "DifferSide" and "OnlyListen" groups, thus failing to reject the null hypothesis in this comparison. These findings highlight the importance of synchronized visual and auditory attention in enhancing information comprehension, particularly emphasizing the contribution of visual cues to speech perception.

The accuracy of the questionnaire responses shows a notable decline across the SameSide, DifferSide, and OnlyListen groups for 10 out of 12 participants. Specifically, the average accuracy declines from 69% in the SameSide group to 56% in the DifferSide group, and 54% in the OnlyListen group. These results indicate that synchronized visual and auditory attention, along with visual cues,

Table 1. Statistical significance test results of questionnaire data within and between groups

Group Type	Within Groups			Between Groups		
	SameSide (LL&RR)	Differside (LR&RL)	OnlyListen (NR&NL)	SameSide & OnlyListen	SameSide & DifferSide	DifferSide & OnlyListen
Significance	n.s.	n.s.	n.s.	p < 0.001	p < 0.05	n.s.

[a] LL, RR, LR, RL, SameSide, Differside, and OnlyListem represent conditions as detailed in Sect. 2.2.

[b] n.s.: $p > 0.05$, not statistically significant

significantly help the participants to process auditory information, while mismatching visual cues help no more than the OnlyListen setting.

4 Discussion

Our study explored auditory and visual attention mechanisms through various experimental conditions: SameSide, DifferSide, and OnlyListen. The findings reveal that task difficulty significantly influenced participant performance in speech comprehension. Specifically, accuracy was notably higher in the less complex SameSide condition, where visual and auditory information were synchronized, compared to the more challenging DifferSide and OnlyListen conditions.

In the DifferSide condition, where participants had to process auditory stimuli with mismatched facial expressions, they faced significant challenges compared to the SameSide condition with synchronized cues. This condition highlighted the crucial role of matching facial cues in aiding comprehension in complex auditory environments. On the other hand, the OnlyListen condition, which removed visual input, revealed the difficulties participants had in perceiving spatial direction. This condition further underscored the essential role of visual cues in accurately interpreting auditory stimuli.

We also examined the relationship between objective measures of auditory attention and subjective evaluations. Linear regression analysis revealed Pearson correlation coefficients of −0.52, 0.13, and −0.10 for the SameSide, DifferSide, and OnlyListen conditions, respectively. These discrepancies highlight the need for objective standards in evaluating auditory attention, as relying solely on subjective assessments may not fully capture the complexities of auditory processing.

Overall, our findings provide valuable insights into how visual and auditory attention interact, emphasizing the importance of synchronized audiovisual information for effective speech comprehension. These results have significant implications for designing multimodal interfaces and educational strategies, suggesting that incorporating visual cues can enhance auditory attention.

5 Conclusion

The use of AI-generated materials and eye-tracking technology in this study has enhanced our understanding of the interaction between visual and auditory modalities in cognitive processes. Our findings emphasize the crucial role of visual information in auditory attention tasks. Specifically, the increased difficulty observed in the DifferSide condition, where visual and auditory cues were mismatched, underscores the importance of synchronizing visual and auditory attention for effective speech comprehension. Similarly, the OnlyListen condition revealed significant challenges in identifying speakers without visual cues, highlighting the necessity of visual information for accurate speech perception. Future research could investigate diverse populations, such as individuals with hearing impairments, to offer valuable insights into the role of visual and auditory cues under various conditions. Understanding these differences can contribute to the development of more inclusive and accessible multimodal systems.

Acknowledgments. The research is supported by Internal Project of Shenzhen Research Institute of Big Data (Grant No. T00120220002); Undergraduate Research Award of The Chinese University of Hong Kong, Shenzhen; Shenzhen Science and Technology Research Fund, Fundamental Research Key Project Grant No. JCYJ20220818103001002, and Shenzhen Science and Technology Program Grant No. ZDSYS20230626091302006.

Disclosure of Interests. The authors have no competing interests to declare that are relevant to the content of this article.

References

1. McDermott, J.H.: The cocktail party problem. Curr. Biol. **19**(22), R1024–R1027 (2009)
2. Ahmed, F., Nidiffer, A.R., Lalor, E.C.: The effect of gaze on EEG measures of multisensory integration in a cocktail party scenario. Front. Hum. Neurosci. **17** (2023)
3. Cai, S., Zhu, H., Schultz, T., Li, H.: EEG-based auditory attention detection in cocktail party environment. APSIPA Trans. Signal Inf. Process. **12**(3) (2023)
4. Marsh, J.E., Campbell, T.A., Vachon, F., Taylor, P.J., Hughes, R.W.: How the deployment of visual attention modulates auditory distraction. Atten. Percept. Psychophys. **82**(1), 350–362 (2020)
5. Kolarik, A.J., Pardhan, S., Moore, B.C.J.: A framework to account for the effects of visual loss on human auditory abilities. Psychol. Rev. **128**(5), 913–935 (2021)
6. Hutmacher, F.: Why is there so much more research on vision than on any other sensory modality? Front. Psychol. **10**, 2246 (2019)
7. Schwartz, J.L., Berthommier, F., Savariaux, C.: Seeing to hear better: evidence for early audio-visual interactions in speech identification. Cognition **93**(2), B69–B78 (2004)
8. Oberauer, K.: Working memory and attention—a conceptual analysis and review. J. Cogn. **2**(1), Article 36 (2019)

9. Duncan, J., Martens, S., Ward, R.: Restricted attentional capacity within but not between sensory modalities. Nature **387**(6635), 808–810 (1997)
10. Evans, K.K.: The role of selective attention in cross-modal interactions between auditory and visual features. Cognition **196**, 104119 (2020)
11. Tiippana, K.: What is the McGurk effect? Front. Psychol. **5**, 725 (2014)
12. Gehmacher, Q., et al.: Eye movements track prioritized auditory features in selective attention to natural speech. Nat. Commun. **15**, 3692 (2024)
13. Algazi, V., Duda, R., Thompson, D., Avendano, C.: The CIPIC HRTF database. In: Proceedings of the 2001 IEEE Workshop on the Applications of Signal Processing to Audio and Acoustics (Cat. No.01TH8575), pp. 99–102 (2001)
14. Tobii AB: Tobii Pro Glasses 3 User Manual (2022). https://go.tobii.com/tobii-pro-glasses-3-user-manual
15. Parthasarathy, A., Hancock, K.E., Bennett, K., DeGruttola, V., Polley, D.B.: Bottom-up and top-down neural signatures of disordered multi-talker speech perception in adults with normal hearing. eLife **9**, e51419 (2020)
16. Bradski, G.: The OpenCV library. Dr. Dobb's J. Softw. Tools (2000)
17. Pedrotti, M., et al.: Automatic stress classification with pupil diameter analysis. Int. J. Hum.-Comput. Interact. **30**(3), 220–236 (2014). https://doi.org/10.1080/10447318.2013.848320
18. Kang, O.E., Huffer, K.E., Wheatley, T.P.: Pupil dilation dynamics track attention to high-level information. PLoS ONE **9**(8), e102463 (2014)
19. Minadakis, G., Lohan, K.: Using pupil diameter to measure cognitive load (2018)
20. Krejtz, K., Duchowski, A.T., Niedzielska, A., Biele, C., Krejtz, I.: Eye tracking cognitive load using pupil diameter and microsaccades with fixed gaze. PLoS ONE **13**(9), e0203629 (2018)
21. Smallwood, J., et al.: Pupillometric evidence for the decoupling of attention from perceptual input during offline thought. PloS One **6**(3), e18298 (2011)
22. Beatty, J.: Task-evoked pupillary responses, processing load, and the structure of processing resources. Psychol. Bull. **91 2**, 276–92 (1982). https://api.semanticscholar.org/CorpusID:38397659
23. O'Sullivan, J.A., et al.: Attentional selection in a cocktail party environment can be decoded from single-trial EEG. Cereb. Cortex **25**(7), 1697–1706 (2015)
24. Alain, C., Arnott, S., Picton, T.: Bottom-up and top-down influences on auditory scene analysis: Evidence from event-related brain potentials. J. Exp. Psychol.: Hum. Percept. Perform. **27**, 1072–1089 (2001)

CollectiveSFT: Scaling Large Language Models for Chinese Medical Benchmark with Collective Instructions in Healthcare

Jingwei Zhu[1,2] , Minghuan Tan[2(✉)] , Min Yang[2] , Ruixue Li[3] ,
and Hamid Alinejad-Rokny[4]

[1] University of Science and Technology of China, Hefei, China
`jingweizhu@mail.ustc.edu.cn`
[2] Shenzhen Institute of Advanced Technology, Chinese Academy of Sciences,
Shenzhen, China
`{mh.tan,min.yang}@siat.ac.cn`
[3] Xiangshui County Party School, Yancheng, China
[4] School of Computer Science and Engineering, The University of New South Wales,
Sydney, Australia
`Hamid.AlinejadRokny@UoN.edu.au`

Abstract. The rapid progress in Large Language Models (LLMs) has prompted the creation of numerous benchmarks to evaluate their capabilities. This study focuses on the Comprehensive Medical Benchmark in Chinese (CMB) [25], showcasing how dataset diversity and distribution in supervised fine-tuning (SFT) may enhance LLM performance. Remarkably, We successfully trained a smaller base model to achieve scores comparable to larger models, indicating that a diverse and well-distributed dataset can optimize performance regardless of model size. This study suggests that even smaller models may reach high performance levels with carefully curated and varied datasets. By integrating a wide range of instructional content, our approach addresses potential issues such as data quality inconsistencies. Our results imply that a broader spectrum of training data may enhance a model's ability to generalize and perform effectively across different medical scenarios, highlighting the importance of dataset quality and diversity in fine-tuning processes (https://github.com/CAS-SIAT-XinHai/CollectiveSFT).

Keywords: Large Language Models · Fine-Tuning Methodologies · Medical Applications · Dataset Diversity · Benchmarking Performance

1 Introduction

With the rapid development of Large Language Models (LLMs), there is increasing interest in applying LLMs to the physical health domain. Due to the specialized nature of physical health, LLMs need to acquire extensive medical knowledge, ensure accuracy, and exhibit patience when interacting with patients. To

H. Li et al. (Eds.): ICSR + InnoBiz 2024, LNAI 15170, pp. 51–60, 2025.
https://doi.org/10.1007/978-981-96-1151-5_6

evaluate the knowledge and accuracy of LLMs in this domain, various medical benchmarks have been established. Some models have achieved impressive scores, demonstrating their potential as basic doctor assistants for daily use.

Despite these advancements, several major concerns remain regarding the instructions used for fine-tuning these models. Firstly, the diversity and distribution of instructions may still be limited. As highlighted by Zheng et al. [31], the effectiveness of fine-tuning is heavily influenced by the variety and richness of the instruction sets used.

To address this issue, we propose integrating a diverse array of instruction types and related domains into our fine-tuning dataset. Our approach involves collecting instructions from multiple question types and ensuring a comprehensive representation of different domains. Specifically, we focus on creating a dataset that includes real-world dialogue reconstructions, consultation records from medical forums, and various other sources. This comprehensive approach aims to enhance the model's performance across different medical scenarios.

In this work, we explore the potential of supervised fine-tuning (SFT) in improving the performance of a smaller model in the medical domain. By utilizing a diverse and well-distributed dataset, we aim to demonstrate that even a smaller model can achieve competitive performance in specialized tasks. Our experiments highlight the importance of dataset quality in fine-tuning processes and show that a well-curated dataset can significantly enhance a model's capabilities, even with limited parameters.

2   Related Work

2.1   Instruction Tuning

Instruction tuning is a highly effective approach for improving the performance of language models on unseen tasks in zero-shot or few-shot scenarios [27]. This method involves training models with a variety of instructions, enabling them to better understand and execute tasks they have not been explicitly trained on.

Natural Instructions [18] represents an effort to create a comprehensive set of human-crafted instructions designed to enhance model performance across a wide range of tasks. These instructions serve as a valuable resource for fine-tuning models to perform well in diverse applications. Building on this concept, Super-NaturalInstructions [26] expands the scope by including even more detailed and varied instructions, further improving the robustness and adaptability of language models.

To address the issue of limited diversity in human-crafted instructions, Unnatural Instructions [11] introduces a vast dataset of imaginative and varied instructions collected with minimal human effort. This innovative approach leverages automated methods to generate a rich and diverse set of instructions, significantly enhancing the model's ability to handle a wider array of tasks with improved accuracy and efficiency.

2.2 Open-Source Medical Models

In the realm of medical LLMs, several notable open-source projects have emerged, such as HuatuoGPT [28] and BenTsao [24]. These models are designed to assist in medical consultations and diagnostics by leveraging large-scale medical dialogues and literature.

HuatuoGPT and BenTsao [7] have undertaken the task of collecting extensive medical dialogue datasets. They use advanced language models like GPT-4 to reconstruct these dialogues into question-answer pairs for model training. This method aims to improve the models' understanding of medical consultations and enhance their ability to provide accurate and relevant responses.

However, these models also come with notable limitations. One major concern is the risk of overfitting to specific datasets, which can limit their generalizability to new, unseen medical scenarios. The reliance on reconstructed dialogues might lead to inconsistencies in data quality, affecting the robustness of the models' responses.

These challenges highlight the need for ongoing refinement and evaluation of open-source medical models. A key area of focus should be the diversity and distribution of datasets used during fine-tuning. Ensuring a wide variety of instructions and data sources may enhance the model's ability to generalize and perform effectively across various medical tasks. By carefully curating and diversifying the datasets, it is possible to develop more robust and versatile medical LLMs, capable of providing reliable and comprehensive support in healthcare settings. Our work aims to address these issues, striving to improve the overall performance of medical LLMs through strategic dataset diversification.

3 Collective Instruction Set

3.1 Data Collection

The datasets we gather encompass various types, from conversations to question-answering pairs. While we primarily focus on English and Chinese datasets, we also acknowledge the availability of healthcare datasets in other languages, such as HeadQA [23] in Spanish and FrenchMedMCQA [14] in French.

Our review of publicly accessible datasets indicated that many formats are unsuitable for model fine-tuning due to inconsistencies in structure, detail levels, and annotation standards. To tackle these issues, we decided to standardize all datasets into the Alpaca format [22]. This format includes fields for instruction, input, and output, as well as optional fields for system prompts and history, tailored for specific use cases. By adopting a standardized format, we ensure consistent data processing, enhancing its effectiveness for training and fine-tuning models.

Reconstructing the datasets involves several steps. First, we extract relevant information from each dataset, preserving key details. Then, we reformat this information into the Alpaca structure, which entails defining clear instructions for the model, specifying inputs, and providing expected outputs. For conversational data, we include history fields to maintain context across dialogue turns.

Table 1 summarizes all collected data, detailing their language, style, topic size, and instruction size. By aligning diverse datasets into a single, coherent format, we facilitate more effective training processes and enhance the models' ability to generalize across different medical tasks.

In addition to reformatting existing datasets, we also aim to expand our collection with new data sources. This involves curating data from medical forums, academic publications, and other relevant repositories. This ongoing effort ensures our models remain relevant and effective in real-world medical applications.

Moreover, incorporating diverse datasets helps mitigate biases present in individual data sources. By integrating data from various origins and languages, we create a more balanced and comprehensive training environment. This diversity is essential for developing robust, reliable models capable of providing accurate medical advice across different contexts and populations.

Table 1. Public medical datasets used for fine-tuning our model. The table shows their size with original format and number of instructions constructed for this work.

Language	Dataset Name	Style	Topic Size	Instruction Size
English	PubMedQA [13]	QA	273,518	273,518
	MedMCQA [20]	MCQA	182,822	182,822
	HeadQA [23]	QA	2,657	2,657
	Total		458,997	458,997
Chinese	cMedQA2 [29]	QA	100,000	188,783
	cMedDialogue [1]	QA	792,099	792,099
	webMedQA [9]	QA	252,850	50,570
	MedicalDialog [10]	Dialogue	2,725,989	4,503,475
	CMID [6]	NER	12,254	11,786
	NLPEC [15]	MCQA	18,703	18,703
	CMB [25]	MCQA	269,359	269,359
	MLEC-QA [16]	MCQA	108,988	108,988
	DISCMed [4]	Dialogue	464,898	1,362,307
	Total		4,745,140	7,306,070

3.2 Instruction Set Construction

We construct instructions based on the data types of the collected datasets, ensuring that each type is processed into a unified format that the language models can effectively utilize. This standardization is crucial for maintaining consistency and clarity across different data sources, which is essential for optimizing the model's performance. The following sections detail the strategies used to process various formats of datasets into a standardized format.

Multiple-Choice Question Answering. For the MCQA format, we use a consistent method to process the data. The instruction field typically contains background information and descriptions about the source of the question, which helps the LLM understand the context better. The input field combines the original question with all the answer options. The output field provides the correct answer, along with an explanation if available in the dataset.

Question Answering. The QA format is simpler compared to other formats. We leave the input field blank and fill the instruction field with the original question and the output field with the corresponding answer.

Dialogue. The dialogue format differs slightly from others due to the nature of conversational data. In this case, we include an additional field named "history" that contains the entire chat history up to that point. The instruction field contains the current question, the input field is left blank, and the output field provides the response. This approach helps the LLM understand the context of the ongoing conversation.

Sequence Labeling. For sequence labeling, specifically in Named Entity Recognition (NER) tasks, we set the instruction field to request an analysis of specific noun entities and the intent of the description. The input field contains the original content, while the output field consolidates all identified noun entities into a new description that captures the intended meaning. This method aids the LLM in recognizing and understanding specialized terminology in the medical domain.

By standardizing these diverse data formats into a single instructional framework, we ensure consistency and clarity in training. This approach enhances the LLM's ability to generalize and perform effectively across various medical tasks, leading to more reliable and robust models.

4 Experiments

4.1 Hyperparameter Optimization

We employ advanced tools like LLaMA-Factory [30] to fine-tune our models, exploring various hyperparameters such as cut-off length, epoch count, and learning rate. These parameters are crucial for the models' performance and efficiency.

For our fine-tuning base model, we have selected the InternLM2.5-7B base model [12] due to its outstanding reasoning capabilities. This model stands out for its ability to handle complex tasks with high accuracy and efficiency. Additionally, the 7B parameter size is particularly advantageous as it strikes a balance between performance and resource requirements. This size is common for personal deployment because it does not demand extensive computational resources, making it accessible for a wider range of applications, including those with limited hardware. By choosing the InternLM2.5-7B base model, we aim to leverage its strengths in reasoning while maintaining feasibility for personal and small-scale deployments, ensuring that our fine-tuning processes are both effective and practical.

Our experiments indicate that cut-off length profoundly affects the model's performance. Specifically, a shorter cut-off length yields better results with the same dataset. This improvement is due to the dataset's average length; shorter cut-off lengths help the model capture essential information within each instance, enhancing output accuracy and relevance.

In benchmark scenarios, particularly with multiple-choice questions, a slightly shorter cut-off length proves beneficial. For instance, CMB Exam emphasizes accuracy in answering specific questions over conversational abilities. By aligning the cut-off length with the dataset's average length, we boost the model's efficiency and accuracy for these specialized tasks. Shorter cut-off lengths enable the model to concentrate on the core content of questions and options, improving its ability to select correct answers. Adjusting other hyperparameters like epoch count and learning rate in tandem with cut-off length further refines performance. A higher epoch count allows the model to learn more comprehensively from the training data, while a well-tuned learning rate ensures optimal convergence without overshooting or getting trapped in local minima.

Overall, our hyperparameter optimization strategy balances these parameters to achieve peak performance for specific applications. Through systematic experimentation with different settings, we fine-tune our models to excel in their tasks, ensuring reliable and effective performance in real-world medical applications.

4.2 Performance over CMB Benchmark

We achieve an outstanding score in the CMB using a remarkably small model as shown in Table 2, significantly smaller than any other model at the top of the benchmark. This achievement can be attributed to the diversity and distribution of our dataset. Our results demonstrate that the quality of the dataset is the most critical factor influencing the performance of model fine-tuning.

By using a wide variety of data formats and sources, we create a training set that is rich and representative of diverse medical scenarios. This strategy allows our smaller model to generalize better and perform effectively across different tasks within the CMB. The success of our fine-tuning process shows the importance of dataset diversity and demonstrates that even with fewer model parameters, top performance can be achieved through careful dataset selection and distribution.

Furthermore, our findings challenge the conventional belief that larger models are inherently superior. Instead, they emphasize that a well-curated and diverse dataset can significantly enhance a model's capabilities, enabling smaller models to compete with and even surpass larger ones. This has important implications for the development of efficient, resource-conserving models that do not compromise on performance.

Table 2. Performance Comparison of Some Open-source Medical Models focusing on specific exam scores and overall averages. (Only open-source models were selected, excluding closed-source models. Data retrieved from CMB leaderboard on July 24, 2024. (https://cmedbenchmark.llmzoo.com/static/leaderboard.html))

Model	Total Avg.	Training Grad.	Nursing Exam	Pharm. Exam	Med. Tech. Exam	Prof. Knowledge	Med. Postgrad.
CollectiveSFT-7B	**77.05**	83.00	**85.75**	**79.25**	**72.50**	90.25	**80.25**
InternLM2.5-7B [12]	71.40	75.80	78.13	68.28	70.92	65.00	72.19
HuatuoGPTII-34B [5]	76.80	82.50	75.50	73.25	68.75	87.75	77.00
Qwen-72B-Chat [21]	74.38	**88.00**	75.00	77.00	70.25	**94.25**	65.50
Yi-34B-Chat [2]	69.17	78.75	69.50	69.75	63.75	87.00	56.50
AntGLM-Med-10 [17]	64.09	81.75	62.00	63.75	60.25	82.50	64.50
GPT-4 [19]	59.46	64.50	60.75	39.50	57.00	77.50	61.25
HuatuoGPTII-7B [5]	59.00	70.75	64.75	60.00	57.75	70.25	53.75
Qwen-14B-Chat [21]	57.64	69.00	60.50	51.25	51.75	73.00	50.00
Baichuan2-13B-Chat [3]	48.87	56.50	47.75	44.50	45.50	63.25	39.25
Qwen-7B-Chat [21]	46.58	56.25	46.00	42.00	37.25	63.50	39.50
ChatGLM2-6B [8]	45.05	48.25	47.25	43.75	43.00	54.25	42.25

5 Discussion and Conclusion

In this article, we have highlighted the potential of using diverse datasets to improve model performance using SFT. Our findings suggest that incorporating a variety of data types is an effective way to enhance the capabilities of models, achieving better performance with fewer GPU resources.

Our study also uncovered some limitations associated with this method. One notable issue is that while the fine-tuned smaller models excel at answering multiple-choice questions accurately and effectively, they may lose some of their conversational abilities. This loss means that although the models perform well on specific tasks like MCQA, they struggle to maintain engaging and coherent conversations with users during interactive sessions. This trade-off between specialized task performance and general conversational ability is an important consideration for the application in real-world scenarios.

Additionally, we observed common problems associated with smaller models, such as hallucination. Hallucination refers to the generation of plausible but incorrect or nonsensical information by the model. This issue can undermine the reliability of the model's responses and poses a significant challenge for its deployment in sensitive domains like healthcare, where accuracy is paramount.

In conclusion, while the use of diverse datasets in supervised fine-tuning offers a promising pathway for quickly enhancing a model's knowledge base and task-specific performance, it also presents several challenges that need to be addressed. Future work should focus on developing strategies to preserve the conversational capabilities of fine-tuned models and reduce instances of hallucination. Overall, this method shows great potential for improving the efficiency and effectiveness of LLMs, but it requires careful consideration and further innovation to fully realize its benefits.

Acknowledgments. This work was partially supported by China Postdoctoral Science Foundation (2023M733654), Guangdong Basic and Applied Basic Research Foundation (2023A1515110496), Shenzhen Science and Technology Innovation Program (KQTD20190929172835662).

References

1. Chinese medical dialogue data 中文医疗问答数据集 (2019). https://github.com/Toyhom/Chinese-medical-dialogue-data
2. 01.AI:: Yi: Open foundation models by 01.AI (2024)
3. Baichuan: Baichuan 2: open large-scale language models. arXiv preprint arXiv:2309.10305 (2023). https://arxiv.org/abs/2309.10305
4. Bao, Z., et al.: DISC-MedLLM: bridging general large language models and real-world medical consultation (2023)
5. Chen, J., et al.: HuatuoGPT-II, one-stage training for medical adaption of LLMs (2023). https://arxiv.org/abs/2311.09774
6. Chen, N., Su, X., Liu, T., Hao, Q., Wei, M.: A benchmark dataset and case study for Chinese medical question intent classification. BMC Med. Inform. Decis. Mak. **20**(3), 125 (2020). https://doi.org/10.1186/s12911-020-1122-3
7. Du, Y., et al.: The calla dataset: probing LLMs' interactive knowledge acquisition from Chinese medical literature (2023)
8. Du, Z., et al.: GLM: general language model pretraining with autoregressive blank infilling (2022). https://arxiv.org/abs/2103.10360
9. He, J., Fu, M., Tu, M.: Applying deep matching networks to Chinese medical question answering: a study and a dataset. BMC Med. Inform. Decis. Mak. **19**(2), 52 (2019). https://doi.org/10.1186/s12911-019-0761-8
10. He, X., et al.: MedDialog: two large-scale medical dialogue datasets (2020)
11. Honovich, O., Scialom, T., Levy, O., Schick, T.: Unnatural instructions: tuning language models with (almost) no human labor. In: Rogers, A., Boyd-Graber, J., Okazaki, N. (eds.) Proceedings of the 61st Annual Meeting of the Association for Computational Linguistics (Volume 1: Long Papers), pp. 14409–14428. Association for Computational Linguistics, Toronto (2023). https://doi.org/10.18653/v1/2023.acl-long.806, https://aclanthology.org/2023.acl-long.806
12. InternLM:: InternLM2 technical report (2024)
13. Jin, Q., Dhingra, B., Liu, Z., Cohen, W., Lu, X.: PubMedQA: a dataset for biomedical research question answering. In: Inui, K., Jiang, J., Ng, V., Wan, X. (eds.) Proceedings of the 2019 Conference on Empirical Methods in Natural Language Processing and the 9th International Joint Conference on Natural Language Processing (EMNLP-IJCNLP), pp. 2567–2577. Association for Computational Linguistics, Hong Kong (2019). https://doi.org/10.18653/v1/D19-1259, https://aclanthology.org/D19-1259

14. Labrak, Y., et al.: FrenchMedMCQA: a French multiple-choice question answering dataset for medical domain. In: Lavelli, A., Holderness, E., Jimeno Yepes, A., Minard, A.L., Pustejovsky, J., Rinaldi, F. (eds.) Proceedings of the 13th International Workshop on Health Text Mining and Information Analysis (LOUHI), pp. 41–46. Association for Computational Linguistics, Abu Dhabi (2022). https://doi.org/10.18653/v1/2022.louhi-1.5, https://aclanthology.org/2022.louhi-1.5

15. Li, D., Hu, B., Chen, Q., Peng, W., Wang, A.: Towards medical machine reading comprehension with structural knowledge and plain text. In: Webber, B., Cohn, T., He, Y., Liu, Y. (eds.) Proceedings of the 2020 Conference on Empirical Methods in Natural Language Processing (EMNLP), pp. 1427–1438. Association for Computational Linguistics, Online (2020). https://doi.org/10.18653/v1/2020.emnlp-main.111, https://aclanthology.org/2020.emnlp-main.111

16. Li, J., Zhong, S., Chen, K.: MLEC-QA: a Chinese multi-choice biomedical question answering dataset. In: Moens, M.F., Huang, X., Specia, L., Yih, S.W.T. (eds.) Proceedings of the 2021 Conference on Empirical Methods in Natural Language Processing, pp. 8862–8874. Association for Computational Linguistics, Online and Punta Cana (2021). https://doi.org/10.18653/v1/2021.emnlp-main.698, https://aclanthology.org/2021.emnlp-main.698

17. Li, Q., et al.: From beginner to expert: modeling medical knowledge into general LLMs (2024). https://arxiv.org/abs/2312.01040

18. Mishra, S., Khashabi, D., Baral, C., Hajishirzi, H.: Cross-task generalization via natural language crowdsourcing instructions. In: Muresan, S., Nakov, P., Villavicencio, A. (eds.) Proceedings of the 60th Annual Meeting of the Association for Computational Linguistics (Volume 1: Long Papers), pp. 3470–3487. Association for Computational Linguistics, Dublin (2022). https://doi.org/10.18653/v1/2022.acl-long.244, https://aclanthology.org/2022.acl-long.244

19. OpenAI:: GPT-4 Technical report (2023)

20. Pal, A., Umapathi, L.K., Sankarasubbu, M.: MedMCQA: a large-scale multi-subject multi-choice dataset for medical domain question answering. In: Flores, G., Chen, G.H., Pollard, T., Ho, J.C., Naumann, T. (eds.) Proceedings of the Conference on Health, Inference, and Learning. Proceedings of Machine Learning Research, vol. 174, pp. 248–260. PMLR (2022). https://proceedings.mlr.press/v174/pal22a.html

21. QwenLM:: Qwen technical report. arXiv preprint arXiv:2309.16609 (2023)

22. Taori, R., Gulrajani, I., Zhang, T., Dubois, Y., Li, X., Guestrin, C., Liang, P., Hashimoto, T.B.: Stanford alpaca: an instruction-following llama model (2023). https://github.com/tatsu-lab/stanford_alpaca

23. Vilares, D., Gómez-Rodríguez, C.: HEAD-QA: a healthcare dataset for complex reasoning. In: Korhonen, A., Traum, D., Màrquez, L. (eds.) Proceedings of the 57th Annual Meeting of the Association for Computational Linguistics, pp. 960–966. Association for Computational Linguistics, Florence (2019). https://doi.org/10.18653/v1/P19-1092, https://aclanthology.org/P19-1092

24. Wang, H., et al.: HuaTuo: tuning llama model with Chinese medical knowledge (2023)

25. Wang, X., et al.: CMB: a comprehensive medical benchmark in Chinese. arXiv preprint arXiv:2308.08833 (2023)

26. Wang, Y., et al.: Super-NaturalInstructions: generalization via declarative instructions on 1600+ NLP tasks. In: Goldberg, Y., Kozareva, Z., Zhang, Y. (eds.) Proceedings of the 2022 Conference on Empirical Methods in Natural Language Processing, pp. 5085–5109. Association for Computational Linguistics, Abu Dhabi

(2022). https://doi.org/10.18653/v1/2022.emnlp-main.340, https://aclanthology.org/2022.emnlp-main.340

27. Wei, J., et al.: Finetuned language models are zero-shot learners. In: International Conference on Learning Representations (2022). https://openreview.net/forum?id=gEZrGCozdqR

28. Zhang, H., et al.: Huatuogpt, towards taming language models to be a doctor. arXiv preprint arXiv:2305.15075 (2023)

29. Zhang, S., Zhang, X., Wang, H., Guo, L., Liu, S.: Multi-scale attentive interaction networks for Chinese medical question answer selection. IEEE Access **6**, 74061–74071 (2018). https://doi.org/10.1109/ACCESS.2018.2883637

30. Zheng, Y., et al.: LLaMAFactory: unified efficient fine-tuning of 100+ language models. In: Proceedings of the 62nd Annual Meeting of the Association for Computational Linguistics (Volume 3: System Demonstrations). Association for Computational Linguistics, Bangkok (2024). http://arxiv.org/abs/2403.13372

31. Zheng, Z., Liao, L., Deng, Y., Nie, L.: Building emotional support chatbots in the era of LLMs (2023)

A New Multi-axis Force Sensor for Measuring the Wheel-Terrain Interaction Ahead of the Robotic Vehicles

Mujia Shi[1] , Lihang Feng[1,2(✉)] , Lixin Jia[1] , and Aiguo Song[2]

[1] Nanjing Tech University, Nanjing 211816, China
lfeng8@njtech.edu.cn
[2] Southeast University, Nanjing 210096, China
a.g.song@seu.edu.cn

Abstract. In extraterrestrial exploration missions, complex terrains affect the terrain traversability of planetary rovers, consequently impacting their mission completion rates. Existing methods that rely on visual perception for environmental sensing are unable to detect soft terrains, which may lead to issues such as wheel sinkage for planetary rovers. In this paper, a forward tactile perception wheel specifically for wheel-terrain contact forces detection is designed. Our approach includes mechanical structure design, decoupling methods, and component integration techniques to genuinely incorporate multi-axis sensors into the forward sensing wheel, achieving high-precision and high-reliability wheel-soil interaction detection. Experiments have demonstrated the effectiveness of the designed forward sensing wheel.

Keywords: wheel-terrain contact force · terrain tactile sensing · rover traversability · multi-axis force sensor · wheel-terrain interaction

1 Introduction

During extraterrestrial exploration and data collection missions, planetary rovers often encounter challenges such as wheel sinkage due to the complex terrain of the operating environment and unknown terrain types [1, 2]. These issues significantly degrade the rover's terrain traversal capability, consequently lowering the completion rate of extraterrestrial exploration tasks. Therefore, the demand for accurate terrain perception ahead of the rover is urgent.

Accurate measurement of the interaction between planetary rover wheels and the extraterrestrial surface terrain (WTI) is crucial for achieving precise terrain perception ahead of the rover [2]. Current research on WTI can be divided into traditional modeling methods and real-time detection methods. Traditional modeling methods such as the Bekker model [3], Janosi-Hanamoto model [4], and Wong-Reece [5] model can achieve WTI modeling but suffer from strict modeling conditions and difficulties in determining model parameters. In recent years, scholars have increasingly focused on real-time

© The Author(s), under exclusive license to Springer Nature Singapore Pte Ltd. 2025
H. Li et al. (Eds.): ICSR + InnoBiz 2024, LNAI 15170, pp. 61–71, 2025.
https://doi.org/10.1007/978-981-96-1151-5_7

detection methods by designing WTI real-time perception systems. And Ishigami developed an In-wheel Sensor System (ASPL) [6] integrating multidimensional force sensors for measuring wheel-terrain forces and optical sensors for measuring wheel sinkage on the wheel surface, aiming to achieve real-time precise WTI measurement. Nagatani et al. developed a Built-in Force Sensor Array (BFSA) wheel [7], integrating multiple Flexi-Force force sensor arrays on the wheel surface to measure normal and shear forces in real time. Higaa et al. developed a real-time wheel-terrain perception system [8], installing multidimensional force/torque sensors on the wheel axis in real time. Yao et al. developed an airborne sensor-transparent wheel integrating multiple multidimensional force sensors on the wheel axis [9], aiming to achieve precise terrain perception ahead of the rover. Additionally, Feng et al. [10] and Zhang et al. [11] designed a class of forward perception detectors located in front of the planetary rover to achieve real-time perception of the terrain ahead, mitigating issues such as wheel sinkage caused by geometric and non-geometric obstacles such as rocks and loose terrain (Fig. 1).

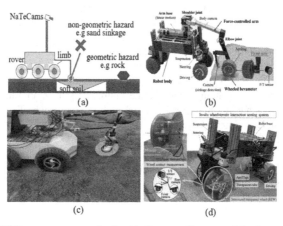

Fig. 1. Different WTI measurement wheels, (a) Concept diagram of the forward sensing system, (b)&(c) Front detection wheels, (d) WTI measurement wheels directly installed on the planet rover

While existing research has to some extent addressed the issue of rover mobility, however, the wheel forces measured by multi-axis force sensors installed at the wheel axle cannot fully reflect the actual wheel-terrain interactions i.e. the terrain tactile force sensing of the wheel. Coupling errors caused by force transmission components such as bearings and bolts exist, and these errors are difficult to eliminate. In response, we design a novel multi-axis sensor for sensing the Wheel-Terrain Interaction forces and torques. More concretely, the main contributions of this article are as follows:

(1) We have replaced the wheel hub with an 8-spoke elastomer, and sixteen strain gauges with the same temperature coefficient were arranged symmetrically on both sides of the 8-spoke elastomer elastic beam. We employ the Wheatstone bridge as the strain gauge bridge method for the forward sensing wheel.

(2) We have divided the strain of each elastic beam in the elastomer into tensile or compressive deformation and bending deformation. Moments of 10, 10 and 1 units

were applied on the x-, y-, and z-axes, respectively, and finite element analysis was performed on the strains of the elastic beams in each of these three cases.
(3) Finally, the effectiveness of the designed forward sensing wheel has been demonstrated through static experiments and dynamic experiments.

2 Design Requirement

2.1 The Forward Terrain Sensing System

When a planetary rover traverses the terrain ahead, it typically encounters geometric obstacles (such as rocks) and non-geometric obstacles (such as soft extraterrestrial soil). Usually, assessing the traversability of the terrain ahead relies on human experience and auxiliary visual systems. However, the harsh extraterrestrial environment limits the visual system's ability to identify non-geometric obstacles. Moreover, the presence of visual blind spots during the rover's movement significantly increases the difficulty of determining the traversability of the terrain ahead. As mentioned in the introduction, an effective solution to this problem is to design a forward terrain sensing system that can be mounted on the rover. The forward terrain sensing system consists of a forward mechanical arm and a forward sensing wheel. The forward mechanical arm enables the forward sensing wheel to follow the terrain, while the forward sensing wheel integrates a multi-axis force sensor to measure WTI (Wheel-Terrain Interaction) multi-axis forces and moments in real time. The accuracy and reliability of the forward sensing wheel in the forward terrain perception system determine the accuracy and reliability of the forward terrain perception. Collecting real-time WTI forces data through the forward sensing wheel provides a data basis for predicting dangerous terrain ahead of the planetary chariot.

2.2 The Basic Multi-axis Forces Decoupling

The forces and torques resulting from the wheel-terrain interaction (WTI) are measured by multi-axis force sensors deployed on the forward sensing wheel. Specifically, during the forward terrain detection task, the multi-axis force sensor deforms due to the WTI. This deformation is captured by sensing devices such as strain gauges and piezoelectric plates and is then converted into voltage signals for each dimension through a bridge circuit. Finally, through (1), structural decoupling is performed, where the voltage signals output by the multi-axis force sensor are converted into corresponding dimensional load signals.

$$V = CF \tag{1}$$

where $V(V_{F_x}, V_{F_z}, V_{M_y})$ represents the voltage signals output by the multi-axis force sensor for each dimension, and $F(F_x, F_z, M_y)$ represents the real-time load of the WTI. F_x denotes the shear force, typically generated by the friction between the rover's forward wheel and soft terrain. F_z represents the normal pressure, usually influenced by the rover's own weight and the carried load. M_y indicates the overturning moment, i.e., the torque on the forward sensing wheel in the axis direction perpendicular to the vehicle's forward motion. C represents the 3×3 transformation matrix, where the diagonal elements of this matrix indicate the sensitivity coefficients for each dimension, and the other elements represent the coupling errors between different dimensions. It is necessary to accurately design the multi-axis force sensor to minimize the coupling errors.

3 Design Implementation

3.1 Mechanical Design

The space inside the front sensing wheel is small, and the installation space for the multi-axis sensor is very limited. Most multi-axis force sensors are integrated into the forward sensing wheel axle or tire tread. Although this approach allows for the measurement of Wheel-Terrain Interaction (WTI) forces, the measurement points are often not centered on the wheel coordinate system, thereby introducing unnecessary measurement deviations. To address this issue, we have replaced the wheel hub with an 8-spoke elastomer, as shown in Fig. 2, while ensuring the performance of the forward sensing wheel remains unchanged.Sixteen strain gauges with the same temperature coefficient, R_i, are symmetrically deployed on both sides of the elastic beams of the 8-spoke elastomer. Symmetrical strain gauges are deployed in the middle regions of beams A, C, E, and G, and near the inner ring end regions of beams B, D, F, and H. T.

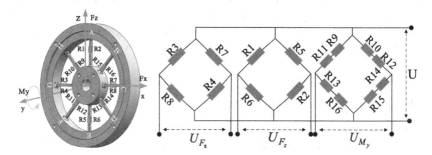

Fig. 2. Design drawing of 8-spoke elastomer and the Wheatstone bridge circuits

Once the elastomer design is completed, the strain gauges deployed on the elastomer convert the elastic strain values of the WTI on the elastic beams into corresponding resistance values. We employ the Wheatstone bridge with temperature compensation capability, high precision, high sensitivity, and high stability as the strain gauge bridge method for the forward sensing wheel. As shown in Fig. 2, it consists of three parts: U_{F_x} for the x-dimension, U_{F_z} for the z-dimension, and U_{M_y} for the y-dimension. The values of U_{F_x}, U_{F_z} and U_{M_y} are calculated using (2).

$$\begin{cases} U_{F_x} = 0.25UK(\sigma_7 + \sigma_8 - \sigma_3 - \sigma_4) \\ U_{F_z} = 0.25UK(\sigma_1 + \sigma_2 - \sigma_5 - \sigma_6) \\ U_{M_y} = 0.125UK(\sigma_{10} + \sigma_{12} + \sigma_{15} + \sigma_{14} - \sigma_9 - \sigma_{11} - \sigma_{13} - \sigma_{16}) \end{cases} \quad (2)$$

where U represents the power supply voltage, K represents the sensitivity coefficient of the strain gauge, and σ_i represents the real-time resistance change value of the i-th strain gauge. The value is calculated using (3), where ΔR_i represents the resistance change value of the i-th strain gauge under stress, and R_i represents the resistance value of the i-th strain gauge.

$$\sigma_i = \Delta R_i / R_i \tag{3}$$

3.2 Strain Analysis

When the forward sensing wheel conducts real-time terrain sensing, the strain conditions of each elastic beam in the elastomer can be categorized into tensile or compressive deformation and bending deformation. The Finite Element Analysis can be used to determine the strain-stress deformation. As shown in Fig. 3, assuming we apply a positive 10-unit force F_x to the x-axis, a positive 10-unit force F_z to the z-axis, and a positive 1-unit moment M_y to the z-axis.

- When a force F_x is applied to the x-dimension, the strain condition of the elastomer is shown in Fig. 3(a). At this time, beam C undergoes tensile deformation, and beam G undergoes compressive deformation. Since strain gauges of the same type are used, the sum of the absolute strain values of R_3 and R_4 is equal to the sum of the absolute strain values of R_7 and R_8. Beams A and E undergo bending deformation, and the strain values of R_1, R_2, R_3 and R_4 are approximately zero. Beams B and H undergo a combination of tensile and bending deformation, while beams D and F undergo a combination of compressive and bending deformation. At this time, the sum of the absolute strain values of R_1, R_2, R_9, R_{10}, R_{15} and R_{16} is equal to the sum of the absolute strain values of R_{11}, R_{12}, R_{13} and R_{14}. According to (2) and Table 1, F_z and M_y will equal to zero.
- When a force F_z is applied to the z-dimension, the strain condition of the elastomer is shown in Fig. 3(b). It is similar to the case where a force F_x is applied to the x-dimension. In this case, $F_x \approx 0N$ and $M_y \approx 0N \bullet mm$.
- When a moment M_y is applied to the y-dimension, the strain condition of the elastomer is shown in Fig. 3 (c). All elastic beams undergo bending deformation. At this time, the strain values on beams A, C, E, and G are approximately the same, and the strain values on beams B, D, F, and H are approximately the same. Combined with Table 1, it is found that the values of the symmetrical strain gauges on each beam are approximately the same and opposite in value. According to (2), we obtain $F_z \approx 0N$ and $F_x \approx 0N$.

3.3 System Integration

The forward sensing wheel consists of an encoder, a connecting shaft, a side bracket, a slip ring, a flange, and a multi-axis force sensor as shown in Fig. 4. The core components of the multi-axis force sensor are the elastomer and the circuit board. The encoder is used to detect real-time angle changes of the forward sensing wheel. The connecting shaft,

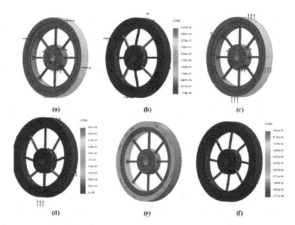

Fig. 3. Finite element analysis of the strain of each elastic beam under three conditions: (a)&(b) applying a positive force F_x; (c)&(d) applying a positive force F_z; (e)&(f) applying a positive moment M_y

Table 1. The applied force or torque in a single channel corresponds to the output of each strain gauge

	F_x	F_z	M_y
R1	$8.2742E-08$	$3.4090E-05$	$1.9834E-05$
R2	$8.2572E-08$	$3.4087E-05$	$-1.9836E-05$
R3	$-3.4085E-05$	$8.2228E-08$	$1.9842E-05$
R4	$-3.4084E-05$	$8.0633E-08$	$-1.9879E-05$
R5	$8.1358E-08$	$-3.4079E-05$	$1.9742E-05$
R6	$8.1503E-08$	$-3.4091E-05$	$-1.9734E-05$
R7	$3.4090E-05$	$8.1742E-08$	$1.9868E-05$
R8	$3.4080E-05$	$8.4572E-08$	$-1.9806E-05$
R9	$3.1491E-05$	$2.0786E-05$	$9.0361E-05$
R10	$2.0799E-05$	$3.1683E-05$	$-9.0350E-05$
R11	$2.0787E-05$	$3.1694E-05$	$9.0355E-05$
R12	$3.1489E-05$	$2.0759E-05$	$-9.0365E-05$
R13	$3.1485E-05$	$2.0760E-05$	$9.0354E-05$
R14	$2.0779E-05$	$3.1693E-05$	$-9.0353E-05$
R15	$2.0783E-05$	$3.1681E-05$	$9.0359E-05$
R16	$3.1493E-05$	$2.0790E-05$	$-9.0354E-05$

side bracket, and flange are fixed elements in the forward sensing wheel, ensuring its stability and establishing a rigid connection with the front exploration robotic arm. The slip ring is used to achieve electrical signal transmission between the various components of the forward sensing wheel and simultaneously provide power to each component.

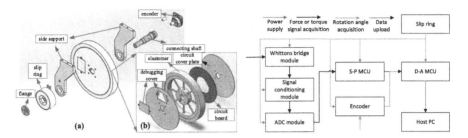

Fig. 4. The mechatronics integration of the sensing wheel

The data acquisition for the forward sensing wheel is also shown in Fig. 4. When WTI forces and moments are collected in real time, the strain signals in various dimensions collected by the strain gauges on the forward sensing wheel elastomer are transmitted through shielded coaxial cables to the signal conditioning module for noise reduction and amplification. The processed strain signals are transmitted through shielded coaxial cables to the ADC module for further conversion into digital signals. The digital signals are then transmitted via short-distance data lines to the Signal Processing MCU (S-P MCU) for further processing, including signal calibration, secondary filtering, and compensation, to ensure signal accuracy. The processed signals are transmitted through the CAN bus to the Data Acquisition MCU (D-A MCU). Simultaneously, the real-time rotation angle of the forward sensing wheel collected by the encoder is also transmitted to the Data Acquisition MCU module via SPI. The Data Acquisition MCU module aggregates the data collected at the same time and uploads it via RS232 serial line to the upper computer.

4 Calibration and Experiment

4.1 Static Calibration

The forward sensing wheel is calibrated using the experimental calibration platform shown in Fig. 5. The specific process involves applying and removing the 10 N load on the x-axis and z-axis, and applying and removing the 1 N * m moment arm on the y-axis. In Fig. 5, when the horizontal coordinate value is positive, it indicates that loading or unloading operations are performed along the positive direction of the main channel. Conversely, if the value is negative, it indicates that the forward sensing wheel performs loading or unloading operations after rotating 90 degrees clockwise. The vertical axis represents the AD-converted output values of each channel at a specific moment.

Adopting nonlinear error indicators, hysteresis error indicators, and repeatability error indicators to analyze the calibration result, the measurement result is shown in Table 2. It can be concluded that the designed forward sensing wheel exhibits high linearity, low hysteresis, and high consistency in data acquisition, meeting the quality requirements for force and torque data collection of the planetary rover WTI.

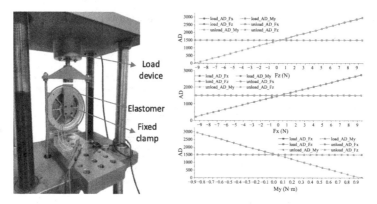

Fig. 5. Static calibration and its results of the forward sensing wheel

Table 2. Calibration result for evaluating static decoupling performance

	Non-linearity error (%)	Hysteresis error (%)	Repeatability error (%)
F_x	0.21	0.25	0.19
F_z	0.35	0.31	0.27
M_y	0.15	0.36	0.29

4.2 Dynamic Test

To further verify the real-time data collection performance of the designed forward sensing wheel, dynamic tests were conducted by installing the forward sensing wheel, which had been statically calibrated, in a soil tank test platform. As shown in Fig. 6, the test platform consists of a box structure with dimensions of 2 m * 1 m * 2 m. The inside of the test platform is evenly covered with a 20cm-thick layer of sand. A lead screw guide rail system is installed at the top of the test platform to drive the movement of the forward sensing wheel. The forward sensing wheel is connected to the lead screw guide rail via a retractable connecting rod. A laser rangefinder is attached to the back of the retractable connecting rod, which measures the depth of the wheel sinking into the sand. During the driving process, the WTI force and torque data collected are gathered by the STM32 microcontroller and transmitted to an upper computer for visualization via a Bluetooth module.

In the initial phase of the experiment, the forward sensing wheel was placed approximately 1 cm into the sand by adjusting the automatic link height. Subsequently, the forward sensing wheel was advanced at a constant power via the lead screw guide rail. After a period of movement, the forward sensing wheel was further pressed into the sand to about 4 cm using the automatic link, continuing its forward motion. As shown in Fig. 7, during the period from 113 s to 125 s, there were significant fluctuations in wheel force and torque. This was due to the complex interactions between the wheel and the sand during the sinking process. When the automatic link pressed down, it increased the

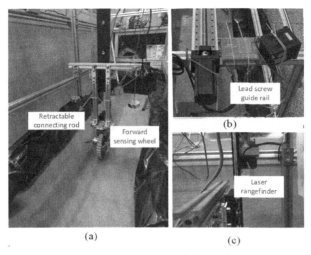

Fig. 6. Soil tank test platform: (a) Interior view of the platform; (b) Top view of the platform which includes the lead screw guide rail; (c) Radar rangefinder attached to the retractable connecting rod

pressure between the wheel and the sand, thereby causing an increase in F_z. Additionally, the sinking of the wheel increased the contact area between the wheel surface and the sand, resulting in increased friction force, which in turn led to an increase in F_x. Simultaneously, the wheel experienced asymmetric pressure from the soil on its sides during the sinking process, causing slight rotation and consequently leading to fluctuations in M_y.

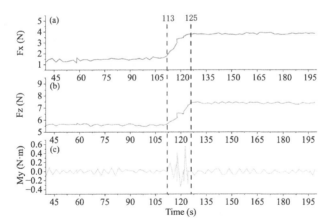

Fig. 7. Forward sensing wheel dynamic experiment results. (a) Real-time shear force F_x; (b) Real-time normal force F_z; (c) Real-time torque M_y

5 Conclusion

We have designed a novel forward sensing wheel for planetary rovers. Unlike previous studies where multi-axis force sensors were directly integrated into the wheel axle or tire surface, we have redesigned the multi-axis force sensors. The new forward sensing wheel design is completed from three aspects: mechanical structure, decoupling methods, and component integration. The focus in the mechanical structure is on how the multi-axis force sensors are truly "integrated" into the forward sensing wheel. Structural and rotational decoupling methods are employed to address coupling issues in various dimensions of the forward sensing wheel. The effectiveness of the designed forward sensing wheel has been demonstrated through static experiments and dynamic experiments.

Acknowledgement. This work was supported in part by Science and Technology Plan of Jiangsu Province (BZ2024057), Natural Science Foundation of China (62103184) and Jiangsu Province Postgraduate Research and Practice Innovation Plan Project (KYCX24_1599).

Disclosure of Interests. No potential conflict of interest was reported by the authors.

References

1. Basri, M., et al.: A hybrid deep learning approach for rover wheel slip prediction in off-road environments. In: 2022 IEEE International Symposium on Robotic and Sensors Environments (ROSE), pp. 1–7 (2022). Accessed 25 May 2024
2. Wang, Z., et al.: Linear prediction of high-slip sinkage for planetary rovers' lugged-wheels based on superposition principle. IEEE Robot. Autom. Lett. **8**(3), 1247–1254 (2023)
3. Salman, N.D., et al.: A modified pressure–sinkage model for studying the effect of a hard layer in sandy loam soil. Appl. Sci. **11**(12), Article no. 12 (2021). https://doi.org/10.3390/app11125499
4. He, G., et al.: Influence of hexapod robot foot shape on sinking considering multibody dynamics. J. Mech. Sci. Technol. **34**(9), 3823–3831 (2020). https://doi.org/10.1007/s12206-020-0833-9
5. Lim, Y., et al.: Development of a new pressure-sinkage model for rover wheel-lunar soil interaction based on dimensional analysis and bevameter tests. J. Astronomy Space Sci. **38**(4), 237–250 (2021). https://doi.org/10.5140/JASS.2021.38.4.237
6. Shirai, T., Ishigami, G.: Development of in-wheel sensor system for accurate measurement of wheel terrain interaction characteristics. J. Terrramech. **62**, 51–61 (2015)
7. Nagatani, K., et al.: Accurate estimation of drawbar pull of wheeled mobile robots traversing sandy terrain using built-in force sensor array wheel. In: 2009 IEEE/RSJ International Conference on Intelligent Robots and Systems, pp. 2373–2378 (2009). Accessed 22 May 2024
8. Higa, S., et al.: Reaction force/torque sensing wheel system for in-situ monitoring on loose soil. In: 19th International and 14th European-African Regional Conference of the ISTVS (2017). Accessed 22 May 2024
9. Yao, C., et al.: Wheel vision: wheel-terrain interaction measurement and analysis using a sensorized transparent wheel on deformable terrains. IEEE Robot. Autom. Lett. (2023). Accessed 22 May 2024

10. Feng, L., et al.: An instrumented wheel to measure the wheel–terrain interactions of planetary robotic wheel-on-limb system on sandy terrains. IEEE Trans. Instrum. Meas. **71**, 1–13 (2022)
11. Zhang, W., et al.: Predict the rover mobility over soft terrain using articulated wheeled bevameter. IEEE Robot. Autom. Lett. **7**(4), 12062–12069 (2022)

Potential-Field-Based Motion Planning for Social Robots by Adapting Social Conventions

Ziwei Yin[1](✉), Zhonghao Zhang[1], Wanyue Jiang[1], and Shuzhi Sam Ge[2]

[1] Qingdao University, Qingdao 266071, China
ziweiyin87@gmail.com , jwy@qdu.edu.cn
[2] National University of Singapore, Singapore 117576, Singapore
samge@nus.edu.sg

Abstract. Social robot behavior should conform to human social conventions. Social conventions concerning the social distance for interaction, the silence distance for non-disturbing, the safety distance for avoiding collision, the left-side passing-by preference, and the face-to-face communication rule are embedded in the motion planning procedure. Potential-field-based motion planning algorithms are designed in this paper, which not only considers the above-mentioned social conventions but also takes stationary obstacles and pedestrian avoidance into account. Simulations in different cases are conducted to verify both the effectiveness of the potential field and the compliance with the social conventions.

Keywords: Social Robots · Motion Planning · Potential Field

1 Introduction

With the rapid development of artificial intelligence, control technology, and computing science, robotics [5,7,13,21] has become one of the most popular fields in both scientific research and business marketing. Despite the industrial robot that has gained wide recognition, social robots that are socially evocative, socially situated, socially intelligent, or socially interactive, have shown their significance with promising potentials [6,14]. In the past few years, hundreds of social robots have been developed for research, service health care, education [2], entertainment, etc.

Many excellent studies have focused on the social aspects of human-robot interaction (HRI) [20]. Research based on Lakoff's politeness theory shows that using robotic manipulators and mobile robots can achieve different levels of enjoyment and trust [9]. Other studies indicate that people's perceptions of robots are influenced by their national culture and interaction experiences [12]. Nonverbal codes, including visual, auditory, haptic, olfactory, and gustatory elements, and their translation into design patterns, are believed to give robots

H. Li et al. (Eds.): ICSR + InnoBiz 2024, LNAI 15170, pp. 72–80, 2025.
https://doi.org/10.1007/978-981-96-1151-5_8

a sense of "aliveness" or "social agency" [19]. Since factors affecting trust are dynamic and evolving, a dynamic design approach is recommended for modeling human-robot trust [1]. For example, the airport service robot SPENCER plans appropriate actions by modeling human social behavior [18]. Social conventions vary across different cultures, but common rules, such as maintaining appropriate social distance, are universally present. Integrating these conventions into robot behavior design is crucial. Besides commonly developed social interaction capabilities such as speech, facial expression, and head movement, the motion of a social robot needs to be designed specifically to adapt to human social conventions. Various explorations have been conducted on social navigation [8,16,17]. For the motion among pedestrians, a real-time emotion-aware navigation algorithm is proposed, which formulates emotion-based proxemic constraints for navigation based on the facial expression and the human trajectory [3]. A combination of implicit HRI information (robot motion) and explicit HRI communication (visual/audio/haptic feedback) is developed to maximize the robot's transparency and efficiency during social navigation [4]. A planning framework named social momentum is proposed for legible robot motion generation in crowded environments [15]. These works use multiple sensors for human perception and conduct robot navigation based on the prediction of the human trajectory.

In this work, we focus on the motion planning and control of social robots. Human social conventions are helpful to improve the comfort of the human during this process, thus several typical social conventions are introduced. Considering the respect of personal space [10,11], various distances for collision avoidance, social interaction, and passing by without interruption, are defined and integrated into the design. Artificial potential fields are constructed for motion planning, where the situation that a robot approaches a human for interaction is considered. Potential fields for approaching a human from the front, approaching a human from the back are designed and their properties are analyzed. The motion control algorithm is presented based on the potential field. Numerical simulations were conducted using a typical differential wheel robot to validate the effectiveness of the proposed method.

2   Preliminaries

2.1   Overall Objective

Human social conventions, which should be conformed to for social robot behavior, include the social distance for interaction, the silence distance for non-disturbing, the safety distance for avoiding collision, the left-side passing-by preference, and the face-to-face communication rule. The overall objective is to design the potential-field-based motion planning algorithms, which not only consider the above-mentioned social conventions but also take stationary obstacles and pedestrian avoidance into account. In addition, it is necessary to verify the effectiveness of the proposed algorithms for the application of wheeled mobile robots by simulation or practice.

To effectively implement these social conventions in robot behavior, we define the following critical distances:

Definition 1. *Social Distance: the optimal distance for comfortable interaction between the robot and a human, allowing for effective communication without being intrusive.*

Definition 2. *Silence Distance: the minimum distance that ensures the robot's presence does not disturb nearby individuals, maintaining a sense of privacy and comfort.*

Definition 3. *Safety Distance: the minimum distance that the robot should maintain from humans or other obstacles to avoid collisions.*

These distances play a crucial role in ensuring the safety and politeness of the robot's interactions with humans. By clearly defining and adhering to these distances in motion planning algorithms, robots can better adapt to human social environments, follow societal etiquette norms, and enhance the overall quality and safety of human-robot interactions. This not only improves the effectiveness of robots in practical applications but also increases public acceptance and trust in social robots.

3   Potential Fields for Approaching a Human

In this section, the potential fields for approaching a human are designed. For social robots, approaching a human from the front and approaching a human from the back are treated differently. Safety distance d_{sf} is considered for safety issues, such as possible collisions between the robot and humans. Social distance d_{sc} refers to the distance between a robot and its interactive object. An appropriate social distance is maintained when a robot talks to a human.

3.1   Regular Design for Approaching a Destination

Conventionally, in artificial potential-field-based methods, an attractive potential field is designed to force the robot to the target. The attractive potential function is regularly defined as the distance between the robot and the target, which is fixed in space.

The potential field constructed by this method is unified in all directions. The attractive potential field and the corresponding virtual force are zero when the robot reaches the target, and become larger when the robot is further away from the target. The force is attractive since it always drives the robot to the target until it stops at the target position, which meets the requirement of approaching a regular destination.

When the target of the robot is a human, it is inappropriate to approach the target position directly. One intuitive way is to choose another position near the human to be socialized with and set it as the target position. In this way, the robot considers only the new target and ignores the feelings of the human, which is not the best solution for social objectives. In what follows, we consider two situations for a robot to approach a human, who is to be socialized with. Social rules will be embedded into the design of artificial potential fields so that social tasks can be conducted properly by the robot.

3.2   Approaching a Human from the Front

When the robot approaches a human from the front, the artificial potential field should drive the robot to a position that satisfies: 1) close enough to the human that they can interact with each other, 2) a certain distance should be kept so that the human does not feel offended. Here we use the *social distance* d_{sc} defined in Sect. 2 to accomplish this social goal.

In this part, an artificial potential field is designed according to social conventions. The robot is driven to stop at a certain area, in which the distance between the robot and the human is around the social distance, and the relative angle between them is inside a proper range.

The relative position between the robot and the human to be interacted with is shown in Fig. 1, where d_{hr} is the distance between the human and the robot. Hereinafter, the subscript r denotes the robot and h denotes the human. Let $\theta_{hr} = \psi_h - \psi_{hr}$, where ψ_h is the human facing direction, ψ_{hr} is the robot direction with respect to the human. The angular range θ_{hr} $in(-\pi/2, \pi/2)$ is considered to be proper for the robot to stop at.

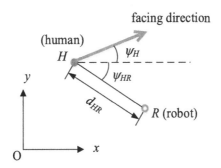

Fig. 1. The relative position between the robot and the human.

Figure 2 illustrates the 3D plot of the potential function, which is not simply attractive or repulsive. When the robot is away from the human to be interacted with, the potential field is attractive and decreases as the d_{hr} becomes smaller. When the distance between the robot and the human is around the social distance d_{sc}, the potential field is constant. When the robot is too close to the human, the potential field becomes repulsive and increases as the robot gets closer.

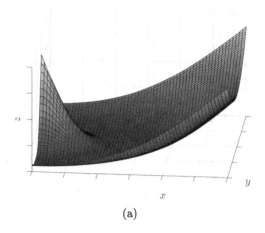

(a)

Fig. 2. Artificial Potential Field for a robot to approach a human from the front.

3.3 Approaching a Human from the Back

When the robot approaches a human from the back, it is quite different from coming from the front. The robot should stop in front of the human to catch his/her attention. Naturally, a side front position with a social distance to the human is proper for the target position.

Figure 3 illustrates the relative position between the robot and the human to be interacted with in this situation. The social interactive angle θ_{sc} is used here to describe the orientation of the target position with respect to the human. As in the figure, θ_{sc} is the angle between the facing of the human and the direction of the robot relative to the human. Denote ψ_h the facing of the human, $\psi_{hr} = \psi_h \pm \theta_{sc}$ indicates the direction from the human to the robot, where addition holds if the target position is on the left of the human and subtraction holds in the other case. Let d_{hr}, d_{ht} and d_{rt} denote the distance between the human and the robot, the human and the target, and the robot and the target, respectively. Figure 3(a) shows the case that the target is on the left of the human and Fig. 3(b) plots the other case. In Fig. 3(a), the robot is too offensive if it goes directly to the target position T from its current location since a part of the path RT is within the safety distance d_{sf} to the human, namely the yellow region, which is too close to be allowed. The solution is to bypass the human and go beyond the safety distance to the target position, whose corresponding trajectory is illustrated in the blue curve.

The artificial potential field in this case can be constructed as a couple of separate ones: an attractive field centered on the target position and a repulsive field centered on the human position. Since the robot goes to the target position to interact with the human, the distance between the human and the target is set as the social distance, namely $d_{ht} = d_{sc}$. The social distance d_{sc} is just a bit larger than the safety distance d_{sf}, which can easily lead to a too-large repulsive field to force the robot to go away from the target position. Elegant potential

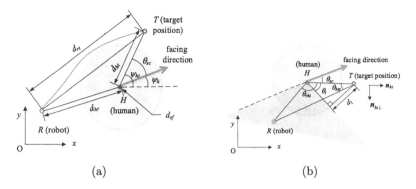

Fig. 3. The relative position between the robot and the human when the robot comes from the back: (a) the target position is set in the left front of the human; (b) the target position is set in the right front of the human. (Color figure online)

fields should be designed as a whole and capable of driving the robot to the target position without making the human uncomfortable.

The potential function of the attraction field is designed to guide the robot to the target position. This function diminishes as the robot approaches the target position, creating an attraction that prompts the robot to move toward the target. The potential function of the repulsion field is used to prevent the robot from getting too close to the human, and when the robot comes within a safe distance, the repulsion field will generate a repulsive force, forcing the robot away from the human. Specifically, when the robot is at a safe distance away, the attraction field plays a major role, guiding the robot to move towards the target position. When a robot approaches a human and comes within a safe distance, the exclusion field comes into play, forcing the robot to bypass the human and avoid direct contact. This design ensures that the robot will not be uncomfortable or startled by humans as it approaches its target location.

The potential field U_h, in this case, is plotted in Fig. 4, which is constructed by a repulsive field from the human and an attractive field from the target position. It can be observed that U_h is attractive to the target position in the whole region, except for the neighborhood around the human, which is repulsive and prevents possible collision.

4   Simulations

The effectiveness of the artificial potential field is verified by simulations on the differential wheel robot.

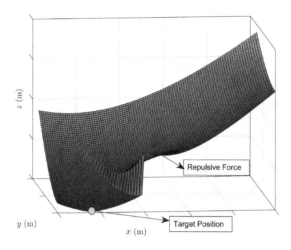

Fig. 4. Artificial Potential Field for a robot to approach a human from the back.

In this section, the social distance is set as $d_{sc} = 1\,\text{m}$, the safety distance to stationary obstacles is set to be $d_{sf} = 0.5\,\text{m}$, the silence distance to walking pedestrians is set to be $d_{sl} = 1.5\,\text{m}$, and the small distance parameter is set to be $\Delta d = 0.1\,\text{m}$. The numerical simulation is conducted on a differential wheel robot i, where $m = 5\,\text{kg}$ and the wheel distance $L = 0.5\,\text{m}$. The control parameters are chosen as $k_u = 1, k_o = 2, k_p = 0.2, k_1 = 0.6, k_2 = 0.01, k_3 = 1.6, k_4 = 0.6$.

Firstly, we test the effectiveness of the potential field in an obstacle-free environment. The case where the robot is designed to approach a human from the front is illustrated in the left two columns of Fig. 5. The human orientation is marked with the blue arrow, and the social distance and the safety distance are figured as the red circle and black circle, respectively. The first row shows the trajectory of the robot, moving directly to the human and stopping around the social distance. The speed of the robot and the virtual forces are illustrated in the second and third rows, respectively. The virtual force is the largest in the beginning and goes smaller when the robot approaches the human. Accordingly, the robot accelerates initially and slows as it nears the human. Due to the damping design, there is no position/speed overshoot. In the front-approaching case, the variation of virtual force is smooth. In the back approaching case, the virtual force has a distinct change of amplitude and direction when the robot goes to the human, which forces the robot to walk around the human without invading the safety distance. In both cases, the robot stops around the social distance in front of the human.

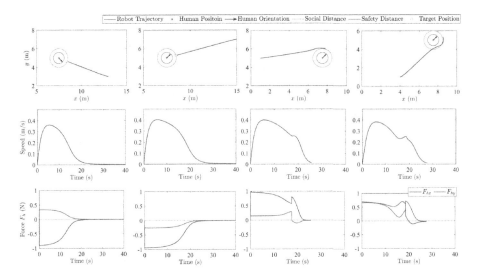

Fig. 5. Simulation results for a social robot to approach a human. (Color figure online)

5   Conclusion

The movement of a social robot is considered to conform to human social conventions. In this paper, sensors like vicon, camera, sonar, and imu, are adopted to distinguish between different people and robots and obtain their position and posture information. The social distance for interaction, the silence distance for non-disturbing, and the safety distance for avoiding collision are defined for the motion planning of social robots. Incorporated into the motion planning procedure are social conventions with respect to these distance regulations, the left-side passing-by preference, and the face-to-face communication rule. The designed potential-field-based motion planning algorithms not only consider the above-mentioned social conventions but also take stationary obstacle and pedestrian avoidance into account. And the motion control under the potential field is designed for the differential wheel robot. The simulations can demonstrate the performance of the potential field and the compliance with the social conventions.

References

1. Ahmad, M., Alzahrani, A., Robinson, S.: Exploring factors affecting user trust across different human-robot interaction settings and cultures. In: Proceedings of the 10th International Conference on Human-Agent Interaction, HAI 2022 (2022)
2. Belpaeme, T., Kennedy, J., Ramachandran, A., Scassellati, B., Tanaka, F.: Social robots for education: a review. Sci. Robot. **3**(21), eaat5954 (2018)
3. Bera, A., et al.: The emotionally intelligent robot: improving social navigation in crowded environments. arXiv preprint arXiv:1903.03217 (2019)

4. Che, Y., Okamura, A.M., Sadigh, D.: Efficient and trustworthy social navigation via explicit and implicit robot-human communication. IEEE Trans. Rob. **36**(3), 692–707 (2020)
5. Chi, W., Wang, J., Ding, Z., Chen, G., Sun, L.: A reusable generalized Voronoi diagram-based feature tree for fast robot motion planning in trapped environments. IEEE Sens. J. **22**(18), 17615–17624 (2022)
6. Dautenhahn, K.: Socially intelligent robots: dimensions of human-robot interaction. Philos. Trans. R. Soc. B: Biol. Sci. **362**(1480), 679–704 (2007)
7. Jiang, W., Ge, S.S., Hu, Q., Li, D.: Sliding-mode control for perturbed mimo systems with time-synchronized convergence. IEEE Trans. Cybern. 1–14 (2023). https://doi.org/10.1109/TCYB.2023.3330143
8. Kress-Gazit, H., Lahijanian, M., Raman, V.: Synthesis for robots: guarantees and feedback for robot behavior. Ann. Rev. Control Robot. Auton. Syst. **1**, 211–236 (2018)
9. Kumar, S., Itzhak, E., Edan, Y., Nimrod, G., Sarne-Fleischmann, V., Tractinsky, N.: Politeness in human-robot interaction: a multi-experiment study with non-humanoid robots. Int. J. Soc. Robot. **14**(8), 1805–1820 (2022)
10. Lasota, P.A., Fong, T., Shah, J.A.: A survey of methods for safe human-robot interaction. Found. Trends Robot. **5**(4), 261–349 (2017)
11. Lenz, K.: Behavior in public places. Notes on the social organization of gatherings. In: Goffman-Handbuch: Leben–Werk–Wirkung, pp. 291–297. Springer (2022)
12. Lim, V., Rooksby, M., Cross, E.S.: Social robots on a global stage: establishing a role for culture during human-robot interaction. Int. J. Soc. Robot. **13**(6), 1307–1333 (2021)
13. Liu, X., Li, Z., Zong, W., Su, H., Liu, P., Ge, S.S.: Graph representation learning and optimization for spherical emission source microscopy system. IEEE Trans. Autom. Sci. Eng. (2024)
14. Mahdi, H., Akgun, S.A., Saleh, S., Dautenhahn, K.: A survey on the design and evolution of social robots—past, present and future. Robot. Auton. Syst. 104193 (2022)
15. Mavrogiannis, C., Alves-Oliveira, P., Thomason, W., Knepper, R.A.: Social momentum: design and evaluation of a framework for socially competent robot navigation. ACM Trans. Hum.-Robot Interact. (THRI) **11**(2), 1–37 (2022)
16. Mavrogiannis, C., et al.: Core challenges of social robot navigation: a survey. ACM Trans. Hum.-Robot Interact. **12**(3), 1–39 (2023)
17. Möller, R., Furnari, A., Battiato, S., Härmä, A., Farinella, G.M.: A survey on human-aware robot navigation. Robot. Auton. Syst. **145**, 103837 (2021)
18. Triebel, R., et al.: Spencer: a socially aware service robot for passenger guidance and help in busy airports. In: Field and Service Robotics: Results of the 10th International Conference, pp. 607–622. Springer (2016)
19. Urakami, J., Seaborn, K.: Nonverbal cues in human-robot interaction: a communication studies perspective. ACM Trans. Hum.-Robot Interact. **12**(2), 1–21 (2023)
20. Wei, D., Chen, L., Zhao, L., Zhou, H., Huang, B.: A vision-based measure of environmental effects on inferring human intention during human robot interaction. IEEE Sens. J. **22**(5), 4246–4256 (2022)
21. Zu, L., Wang, Z., Liu, C., Ge, S.S.: Research on UAV path planning method based on improved HPO algorithm in multitask environment. IEEE Sens. J. **23**(17), 19881–19893 (2023)

Parametrically-Designed Artificial Hand with Multifunctional Grasps

John-John Cabibihan$^{(\boxtimes)}$ and Mohammed Mudassir

Department of Mechanical and Industrial Engineering, Qatar University, Doha, Qatar
john.cabibihan@qu.edu.qa

Abstract. The typical methods for developing artificial hands require long development time. It also takes assistance from specialists to fine-tune the details such as size, appearance, and fitting. Moreover, most highly-functional electric-powered prostheses are expensive, keeping them beyond the affordability of a large number of users. Sometimes the patients themselves need rehabilitative training to acquire skills in using these devices and accepting their new realities. To address some of these issues, a passive parametric 3D-printed artificial hand design is proposed in this work. The parameters are obtained from some anthropometric measurements from the non-injured hand. The technologies for rapid fabrication of custom designs are improving, making them more popular and affordable. The artificial hand model has been designed with parametric modeling techniques. The fabricated passive hand can perform up to 31 grasps out of the 33 grasps that the human hand can perform.

Keywords: Artificial hands · 3D printing · Passive prosthesis · Parametric design

1 Introduction

Our hands are prehensile organs through which not only can we sense our reality but also create, reshape, and live it. The loss of these significant limbs can be very traumatic for the victims regardless of whether it occurs due to accidents, diseases, or wars. Amputations and upper limb reductions not only prevent the patient from performing activities of daily living, socialization, and work, it can also cause social stigma, associated mental health problems, and loss of other socio-economic opportunities [5]. Many children are also born without limbs due to congenital defects. They need special care to accommodate them and support their education and development through alternative means. Furthermore, due to long-lasting wars in many parts of the world, people are losing their limbs. Many of these amputees suffer from trauma in addition to their physical disability. Prosthetic users, especially children and adolescents, need frequent adjustments as they grow. Adults need artificial hands with functionality that allow them to live with dignity and enable them to perform meaningful work.

H. Li et al. (Eds.): ICSR + InnoBiz 2024, LNAI 15170, pp. 81–92, 2025.
https://doi.org/10.1007/978-981-96-1151-5_9

To help them live fulfilling lives, affordable and functional artificial hand designs are needed. With the increased availability and popularity of low-cost additive manufacturing (also known as 3D printing), it is now possible to rapidly fabricate complex designs without requiring laborious processes from standard manufacturing such as casting and machining. Parametric artificial hand designs are especially suitable for patients who need frequent adjustments or replacements as in the case of children and adolescents. It can also be beneficial to patients living in remote regions where there might be a lack of expert designers or machining facilities. Thus, through this paper, we propose a parametric 3D-printed passive artificial hand based on anthropometric features.

The primary advantage of the parametric design is that it will require the end-user to measure a couple of features from the healthy hand and enter them into a program through a user-friendly graphical user interface (GUI). Thereupon, the program will automatically create the custom artificial hand design that can be sent to a 3D printer for fabrication. The ease, low-cost, and customized nature of the 3D printed artificial hand ensures that affordable prostheses are available and meet the need of individuals more accurately than what typical prosthesis development methods offer.

Upper-limb prostheses can be sorted into two categories based on their actuation: active and passive [18]. The active actuation prostheses are powered either electrically or by the body [9]. In contrast, passive artificial hands are usually used for cosmetic reasons; however, they can include mechanism that give them some functionality for grasping – making them dynamic passive as opposed to static passive prosthesis.

Electric-powered (EP) prostheses can offer many grasping features and functionalities but are often prohibitively expensive to buy and remain out of reach of many patients [2]. Currently, many open-source 3D-printed body-powered (BP) prostheses are available in the market; however, they offer limited functionality and have poor grasping performance [6]. Life-like passive prosthetics are worn by many users as they are affordable and can reduce social stigma [4, 22].

Prosthetics can also be classified based on functionality. Although many of the prosthetics are designed to be anthropomorphic, some prostheses are designed to serve special functions without adopting anthropomorphism. For example, the hook-type prosthesis does not look anthropomorphic, yet it can grasp and manipulate objects. Some prosthetics are designed to be used as specialized tools like forks, knives, or spoons. These can be categorized as static prosthetic tools. Other types of prosthetics can be adjustable depending on the tasks. All these static, dynamic, anthropomorphic, and non-anthropomorphic prosthetic devices and tools come under the broad umbrella of assistive technologies.

There are three main contributions of this work in terms of novelty, innovation, and methodology. Firstly, we have innovated on the familiar ball-and-socket joint and incorporated it into our design of a 3D artificial hand model. Secondly, we have demonstrated a parametric approach to designing passive artificial hand by using anthropometric features. Finally, we have produced a artificial hand by using 3D printing that can perform 31 grasps that is not reported elsewhere in the literature. Additionally, we have developed a code that can quickly generate this passive artificial hand model customized for each patient based on the given anthropometric features. We have innovated on the cosmetic passive artificial and made it dynamic and functional.

This paper is structured into several sections. Section 2 offers background on prostheses development and the state-of-the-art. Section 3 provides the rationale and the approach taken for this design. Section 4 demonstrates the results and discusses the different limitations of this design as well as highlighting the benefits. Finally, Sect. 5 offers a conclusion and recommendations for future work.

2 Background

Due to its dexterity and sophistication, the human hand can perform both precision and power grasps. Based on literature survey by Feix [13] the human hand grasps have been categorized into 33 distinct types. However, most commercially available artificial hands including electric and body-powered ones can only perform a limited number of grasps. It would be ideal to have an artificial hand that can perform all 33 grasps. Different approaches are taken to design anthropomorphic prostheses that may perform some selected grasps. For instance, the human hand grasps can be grouped by activities of daily living such as eating, or cleaning [20]. They can also be combined based on a specific routine like studying that requires activities such as typing or writing.

Although there is a lot of research for upper-limb prostheses, not a lot of attention has been paid to parametric designs. The problem with non-parametric designs is that they are hard to modify once finalized. The flexibility in fine-tuning to suit individual patients is very limited. Generally, scaling them up or down often results in the poor fitting. Through parametric design, the artificial hand can be fine-tuned based on a predetermined set of features. This can result in a better fit when scaling up or down and adjusting for different patients. Furthermore, parametric designs can consider other factors into accounts such as gender, race, age, or other relevant features. With parametric modeling, a pre-designed database of models can be used whereby the user only needs to give in the input parameters and immediately get a custom model as output and ready for 3D printing.

Pena Pitarch et al. [21] developed a kinematic model of the hand based with 25 degrees of freedom (DOFs). In their model, they considered the range of motion of the joints, workspace of the fingers, and the Denavit-Hartenberg parameters to describe the joint relations. They aimed to develop a comprehensive framework for the simulation of the hand for grasping and manipulating objects. They modeled the arching of the palm by considering 4 DOFs in the carpometacarpal (CMC) joints of the ring and little fingers - totaling 6 DOFs for each of these fingers. The thumb has 5 DOFs, and the index and middle fingers have 4 DOFs each. ElKoura and Singh [12] proposed a 27 DOFs kinematic model for the hand. They considered the thumb to have 5 DOFs, each of the other four fingers to have 4 DOFs, and the wrist to have 6 DOFs for translation and rotation.

With advances in computer graphics and processing capabilities, much artificial hand research and development can be done using simulation environments that can reduce the cost of development. For example, simulation software can provide a realistic environment by mimicking the effects of gravity, collision mechanics, friction, material properties, surface texture, sensors, and so on [10]. This can allow designers to change their concepts without resorting to fabrication for minor changes. Hauschild et al. [15] developed a virtual reality (VR) environment for testing and fitting neural prosthetic limbs. Through their environment, patients can use virtual limbs to manipulate virtual objects. It includes realistic modeling of the musculoskeletal and mechatronic systems that allow developers to build and test prosthetics before letting users try it out.

Furthermore, Phung and Perez [16] used Grasshopper with Rhinoceros 3D and Solidworks to design a parametric model for a 3D-printed prosthetic forearm considering the portion from elbow to the wrist. Users can input custom hand parameters using Grasshopper and quickly get a 3D model of the forearm that can then be fabricated using a 3D printer. Bustamante et al. [3] developed a parametric 3D-printed body-powered prosthetic hand using Rhinoceros and Autodesk Inventor. Moreo [19] developed a generalized parametric 3D-printed artificial hands for children in developing countries using Solidworks. They approached the problem from a product design perspective by starting with several different concepts and eliminating them based on different criteria such as comfort, cosmetics, controls, and functionality. Li and Tanaka [17] demonstrated through a feasibility study the suitability of using parametric designs for 3D-printed orthosis for fracture immobilization targeting upper limbs. They used Grasshopper with Rhinoceros 3D for modeling the orthosis. 5 nurses participated in a short training program where they learned to use the parametric program and were able to design 4 orthoses without any help within 20 min.

Cloutier and Yang [11] provides a review on the two types of control systems used for controlling electric-powered prostheses based on electromyographic (EMG) and electroneurographic (ENG) signals. In EMG control systems, the prostheses are controlled my electric signals generated during muscle contractions that are picked up by the sensors on the skin surface. This can allow the user finer control over the manipulation of the prosthetic hand grips. However, EMG methods have steep learning curve as the amputees have to control muscle groups that are not ordinarily used and may require extensive training for full control of the muscle-artificial hand coordination. It usually does not provide any sensory feedback to the user. In ENG method, the prosthesis is controlled by the peripheral nervous system (PNS) through a direct interface that is placed within the patient through an invasive procedure. This allows for greater control of the prosthesis with sensory feedback and can feel more natural to the user as the ENG signals are the same ones used for controlling regular motor functions in people with healthy limbs. Nevertheless, both of these methods are restricted by the limited capability of the prostheses such as limited grasping types, sensors, flexibility and so on.

Despite the popularity of electric-powered prosthetic hands in the market, they remain expensive, hard to maintain, and have limited grasp types. Many 3D-printed open-source prosthetic hand models are inexpensive and widely available. However, they usually do not offer many DOFs. They can be hard to control and have very few grasp poses. On the other hand, some users prefer passive prosthetic hands for affordability and cosmetic reasons even though they offer limited range of grasps and functionality.

3   Methods

To design and fabricate a 3D printed parametric passive prosthesis using anthropometric features, several steps have been taken. Firstly, interviews with patients were conducted to understand their needs. It helped in determining whether the passive artificial hands meet their requirements. Secondly, the data from the healthy hands of patients were collected using a low-cost rapid scanning technique using 3D scanners. The scans were post-processed and the anthropometric hand features have been extracted. A parametric 3D printed artificial hand model was developed. The 3D model was generated using a script written in Python programming language. The anthropometric features measured from the patient's hand were then entered into the parametric 3D model generator program. Upon receiving the input dimensions, it can generate a custom artificial hand model in real-time. It outputs a Standard Tessellation Language (STL) file that is sent to a 3D printer for rapid prototyping. Figure 1 shows an overview of the methodology.

Interview Patient   Anthropometric Data Collection   Parametric Prosthesis Hand Model   3D Printing

Fig. 1. The process for fabricating 3D printed passive parametric prosthesis includes understanding the patient's needs, collecting healthy hand scans, post-processing the data, generating the parametric 3D model, and 3D printing.

Several interviews were conducted with five patients in a refugee camp in Jordan in 2019. Their ages were between 8 to 22 years. Four of them were born with congenital upper limb reductions while the fifth one lost their hand and leg in the war. A patient named Nadia (not real name) said that she goes to school and wanted a prosthetic that could help her with lightweight activities such as holding a phone, mirror, or makeup box. She could then use her healthy hand to operate the phone or apply the makeup. She also said that she wants a prosthetic that looks realistic to facilitate social interactions without her disability or prosthesis bringing unwanted attention. She admitted that a cosmetic prosthetic would improve her self-esteem and body-image and help her feel better about herself and her body. It is to be noted that the interviews were rather experiential and focused more on the individual experiences as opposed to obtaining data with statistical significance. The procedures did not include invasive or potentially dangerous methods and were in accordance with the Code of Ethics of the World Medical Association (Declaration of Helsinki). Data were stored and analyzed anonymously. Consent was obtained from the legal guardians when interviewing the minors while the adult participants gave their consent themselves.

As the goal of a parametric prosthetic design is to make the prosthesis more attuned to the patient's hand features, the process begins by 3D scanning of the healthy hand of the patient. The 3D scanning is usually done with a structured light sensors camera. Alternatively, if X-rays or CT scans are used, then 3D imaging software such as Slicer 3D can be used to reconstruct a 3D model. The scans from the healthy hands are used for obtaining some anthropometric features such as hand length and hand width since the hands are mirror images of one another.

A depth camera was used for taking scans from the patients. The scanner was mounted on a tripod. The patient was seated during the scanning and rested their healthy hand on a stool. The healthy hand was oriented at an upright pose. The tripod was moved around the healthy hand, covering 270°. The tripod was fastened with a 1 m long cable to the stool to have a consistent distance from the hand during scanning. The whole scanning process takes less than ten 10 min. This scanning approach has been adopted from Gaballa et al. [14].

The 3D scanner captures the image of the hand as cloud points. There are several paid and free 3D cloud point scanning software available in the market. We used the 3D Scan software from Microsoft. A supported graphical processing unit (GPU) is required for scanning with this software. The cloud points were converted to mesh using a mesh editing program - MeshLab. After cleaning up the meshes, the model was exported as an STL file. Post-processing takes about 20 to 30 min by a proficient user.

The anthropometric relations between the fingers are obtained from [21]. They developed the relations between hand length and hand width with the length of the metacarpal and phalangeal bones. The hand length is defined as the sum of the length of the palms and middle finger. The hand width is the width of the metacarpal bones excluding the thumb.

The parametric modeling includes developing mathematical relations between the different anthropometric features of the hand as well as programming them in a way that enables creation of 3D models efficiently and exporting to STL format for 3D printing.

Some of the assumptions used for this passive prosthetic hand design include the following: i) The patient has a healthy hand that they can use for operating the prosthetic hand. ii) The prosthetic hand will be used for lightweight activities and social interactions. iii) A prosthetic glove would be worn over the passive prosthetic hand to increase the aesthetics.

Rhinoceros 3D (Rhino) is a commercial 3D modeling software developed by Robert McNeel & Associates. It runs on Windows (PC) and Macintosh (macOS) operating systems. The program supports parametric modeling using either polygonal meshes or splines. It supports non-uniform rational B-splines (NURBS) that can render mathematically accurate models. In other words, the polygonal mesh method would use tiny polygons to approximate the model whereas NURBS would render a model that is exactly defined mathematically. Mesh-based modeling and rendering are quite popular as it requires less computational resources. NURBS-based modeling and rendering are preferred where accurate representation is important.

Grasshopper 3D is a built-in plugin for Rhino that allows visual block-based programming for parametric designs. It can create novel shapes and patterns using generative algorithms with parametric relations. Generative algorithms are useful for designing shapes that can evolve in complexity, produce novel patterns, and are not hard coded for a selected range of values. Their evolution is guided by parameters instead of being restricted by them. This modeling approach suitable for designing a prosthetic hand as demonstrated by [17] and [3]. Figure 2 shows the Grasshopper interface with functional blocks. Grasshopper also supports Python 2.7 which allows for scripting and generating 3D models using the python libraries and APIs.

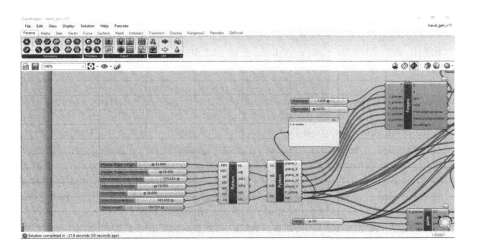

Fig. 2. Grasshopper with GUI allows the user to easily change the parameters to modify and create new prosthetic models.

After generating the prosthetic hand model on Rhino with Grasshopper, the model is exported as a standard tessellation language (STL) file. The STL file is prepared for 3D printing using the open-source slicing software Cura. Cura creates a G-code containing the instructions for printing based on the STL file. The G-code is a computer numerical control (CNC) programming language that is widely used in computer-aided manufacturing (CAM) for automated controlling of fabrication machines. The prosthetic hand is prototyped using a low-budget open-source 3D printer, Creality Ender-3 3D Printer.

4   Results and Discussion

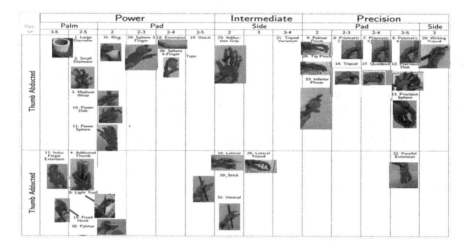

Fig. 3. All of the 31 grasps performed the fabricated passive prosthetic hand

The 3D printed parametric passive prosthesis is an alternative approach to designing and fabricating prosthetics that are patient-specific and offer some grasp functionality. The parametric model is versatile. Using the Python script in Grasshopper, the design can be quickly changed or adjusted for different patients. Some parametrically modified prosthetic hands are shown in Fig. 4. Notice that although the design looks similar, the joints, finger segments, palm, and overall features are different. These demonstrate how easily the hand can be tuned without requiring much effort from the designer.

The grasp results are shown in Fig. 3. The passive prosthetic hand can perform 31 out of the 33 grasps. The grasps that could not be achieved include the distal type and tripod variation which are like holding a pair of scissors and a pair of chopsticks, respectively.

The 3D printed hand is shown in Fig. 5. This is based on the hand dimensions of a patient's healthy hand. The palm and finger segments are printed separately. Ball and socket joints have been used for all the joints of the fingers and metacarpals. The ball and socket joints allow rotations along x, y, and z

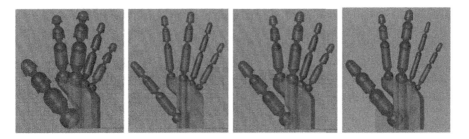

Fig. 4. Customized artificial hand models generated by changing a few parameters

axes. The ball is inserted into the socket by force. A low-tolerance (0.07 mm) value is used for the ball and socket joint so that there are a tight fit and enough friction to avoid the ball from slipping. Some of the limitations related to material include the use of polylactic acid (PLA) and acrylonitrile butadiene styrene (ABS) [1]. PLA deforms easily in the presence of heat, which can be a problem when using this prosthesis in high temperature environments.

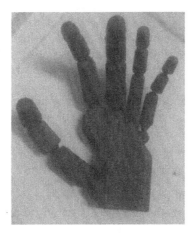

Fig. 5. 3D printed passive artificial hand

One of the main issues with this model is that the kinematics of the hand changes based on the hand features of the patients. For example, a hand with thicker finger segments and joints will affect the mobility and degree of freedom of the fingers. A thin finger segment will lead to increased mobility; however, it also increases the stresses at the neck of the finger segments leading to premature failure of the finger segments. Additionally, thinner segments caused excessive stress at the necks during the insertion of the ball into sockets.

Another challenge in using this model is that the quality of the hand depends on the printer and material. To mitigate this problem, we have devised a test to calibrate the printer settings to get an optimal print. For material variability, we made a baseline tolerance that works with mismatched materials. For example, if a component wears out and needs to be replaced, it can be easily replaced with another printed component made of a different material. The Python scripted model is suitable for the mass production of hands where it can produce a list of hands that can be provided via an Excel sheet. The hand can be switched by mirroring with a simple click of a toggle switch in Grasshopper. This will help solve the problem of the lack of available dimensions in either kind of amputees (left or right-handed).

Although a rigorous cost model for this design has not been developed, the cost of a prosthetic hand weighing about 40 g and printed using PLA would be about 1 USD. The price would vary depending on the size of the hand and as well as other associated costs like labor cost, energy cost, 3D printer cost, and so on.

5   Conclusion

In the conclusion, this paper addresses some of the problems that prosthetic users face in developing regions such as the lack of affordable prostheses, a passive cosmetic prosthesis for lightweight activities, and social interactions. The objectives of this paper have been met by demonstrating the feasibility of a parametric 3D prosthetic hand model developed using anthropometric features and fabricated using 3D printing. Furthermore, using a Python script the 3D model can be generated efficiently based on the features extracted from the patient hand scans. The fabricated prosthetic hand is tested for grasps. It was able to perform 31 grasps out of the 33 that the human hand can do. However, as it is a passive hand, the grasp forces are not strong enough to do any heavy load activity. Nevertheless, the cosmetic benefits it offers to the patients is one of the important considerations in designing passive prostheses.

Prostheses need to be designed taking into account the various needs of the patients. Younger patients would require frequent replacements or adjustments. Parametric approach would be enable quickly changing the design to suit this category of users. While the adult patients do not go through growth as much as the younger ones, they will still need adjustments as they age and their body changes with time.

In the future, the parametric modeling approach can be extended to include the forearm and the arm by determining the relations between the hand, forearm, and arm. Furthermore, this design approach can be extended to the body-powered and electric-powered prosthesis. Different materials can also be explored that have more desirable properties than PLA or ABS [7,8]. Different designs and types of joints can be explored to increase the grasp forces and mobility of the design. 3D-printing has made rapid-prototyping a relatively easy process. It is expected that we will see better prosthetic designs using this technology. Furthermore, usability and comfort for the prosthetic hand should be tested with patients. At the end of the day, the only good prosthetic design is the one the patient feels most comfortable with.

Acknowledgments. This work was supported by NPRP through Qatar National Research Fund (a member of Qatar Foundation) under Grant NPRP 11S-1229-170145. The statements made herein are solely the responsibility of the authors.

References

1. Alkhatib, F., Cabibihan, J.J., Mahdi, E.: Data for benchmarking low-cost, 3D printed prosthetic hands. Data Br. **25**, 104163 (2019)
2. Alkhatib, F., Mahdi, E., Cabibihan, J.J.: Design and analysis of flexible joints for a robust 3D printed prosthetic hand. In: IEEE International Conference on Rehabilitation Robotics, vol. pp. 784–789 (2019). https://doi.org/10.1109/ICORR.2019.8779372
3. Bustamante, M., Vega-Centeno, R., Sánchez, M., Mio, R.: A parametric 3D-printed body-powered hand prosthesis based on the four-bar linkage mechanism. In: Proceedings of the 2018 IEEE 18th International Conference on Bioinformatics and Bioengineering, BIBE 2018, pp. 79–85 (2018). https://doi.org/10.1109/BIBE.2018.00022
4. Cabibihan, J.J., Pattofatto, S., Jomâa, M., Benallal, A., Carrozza, M.C., Dario, P.: The conformance test for robotic/prosthetic fingertip skins. In: The First IEEE/RAS-EMBS International Conference on Biomedical Robotics and Biomechatronics, BioRob 2006, pp. 561–566. IEEE (2006)
5. Cabibihan, J.J.: Patient-specific prosthetic fingers by remote collaboration-a case study. PLoS ONE **6**(5), e19508 (2011). https://doi.org/10.1371/journal.pone.0019508
6. Cabibihan, J.J., et al.: Suitability of the openly accessible 3D printed prosthetic hands for war-wounded children. Front. Robot. AI **7**, 207 (2021)
7. Cabibihan, J.J., Carrozza, M.C., Dario, P., Pattofatto, S., Jomaa, M., Benallal, A.: The uncanny valley and the search for human skin-like materials for a prosthetic fingertip. In: 2006 6th IEEE-RAS International Conference on Humanoid Robots, pp. 474–477. IEEE (2006)
8. Cabibihan, J.-J., Pradipta, R., Chew, Y.Z., Ge, S.S.: Towards humanlike social touch for prosthetics and sociable robotics: handshake experiments and finger phalange indentations. In: Kim, J.-H., et al. (eds.) FIRA 2009. LNCS, vol. 5744, pp. 73–79. Springer, Heidelberg (2009). https://doi.org/10.1007/978-3-642-03983-6_11
9. Carey, S.L., Lura, D.J., Jason Highsmith, M.: Differences in myoelectric and body-powered upper-limb prostheses: systematic literature review. J. Rehabil. Res. Dev. **52**(3), 247–262 (2015). https://doi.org/10.1682/JRRD.2014.08.0192
10. Cavalcante, R., Gaballa, A., Cabibihan, J.J., Soares, A., Lamounier, E.: The importance of sensory feedback to enhance embodiment during virtual training of myoelectric prostheses users. In: 2021 IEEE Conference on Virtual Reality and 3D User Interfaces Abstracts and Workshops (VRW), pp. 770–771. IEEE (2021)
11. Cloutier, A., Yang, J.: Control of hand prostheses - a literature review. In: Proceedings of the Design Engineering Technical Conferences, vol. 6 A(March 2015) (2013). https://doi.org/10.1115/DETC2013-13349
12. ElKoura, G., Singh, K.: Handrix: animating the human hand. In: Proceedings of the 2003 ACM SIGGRAPH/Eurographics Symposium on Computer Animation, SCA 2003 (2003)

13. Feix, T., Romero, J., Schmiedmayer, H.B., Dollar, A.M., Kragic, D.: The GRASP taxonomy of human grasp types. IEEE Trans. Hum.-Mach. Syst. **46**(1), 66–77 (2016). https://doi.org/10.1109/THMS.2015.2470657

14. Gaballa, A., Lambert, L.A., Diab, K., Cabibihan, J.J.: Image processing of 3D scans for upper limb prosthesis of the war-wounded. In: 2020 IEEE 20th International Conference on Bioinformatics and Bioengineering (BIBE), pp. 596–601. IEEE (2020)

15. Hauschild, M., Davoodi, R., Loeb, G.E.: A virtual reality environment for designing and fitting neural prosthetic limbs. IEEE Trans. Neural Syst. Rehabil. Eng. **15**(1), 9–15 (2007)

16. Juarez Perez, A., Phung, L.: Development of software for digital manufacturing of children's prosthetic arms for 3D-printing (2020)

17. Li, J., Tanaka, H.: Feasibility study applying a parametric model as the design generator for 3D–printed orthosis for fracture immobilization. 3D Printing Med. **4**(1), 1–15 (2018). https://doi.org/10.1186/s41205-017-0024-1

18. Maat, B., Smit, G., Plettenburg, D., Breedveld, P.: Passive prosthetic hands and tools: a literature review. Prosthet. Orthot. Int. **42**(1), 66–74 (2018). https://doi.org/10.1177/0309364617691622

19. Moreo, M.: Parametric design of a 3D printable hand prosthesis for children in developing countries (2016)

20. Nasser, S., Rincon, D., Rodriguez, M.: Design of an anthropomorphic underactuated hand prosthesis with passive-adaptive grasping capabilities. In: Florida Conference on Recent Advances in Robotics and Robot Showcase, pp. 25–26 (2006)

21. Peña-Pitarch, E., Falguera, N.T., Yang, J.J.: Virtual human hand: model and kinematics. Comput. Methods Biomech. Biomed. Eng. **17**(5), 568–579 (2014). https://doi.org/10.1080/10255842.2012.702864

22. Truijen, S., et al.: The design of the paediatric prosthesis: assessment of stigma-inducing factors in primary school children, using a questionnaire. In: Ahram, T., Falcão, C. (eds.) AHFE 2019. AISC, vol. 972, pp. 869–881. Springer, Cham (2020). https://doi.org/10.1007/978-3-030-19135-1_85

Tolerant Tracking Control Protocol for PMSM Based on Policy Iteration Algorithm and Fault Compensation

Shuya Yan[1] , Xiaocong Li[4(✉)] , Huaming Qian[1] , Jun Ma[3] ,
and Abdullah Al Mamun[2]

[1] College of Intelligent Systems Science and Engineering, Harbin Engineering
University, Harbin 150001, China
{ya199367,qianhuaming}@hrbeu.edu.cn
[2] Department of Electrical and Computer Engineering, National University
of Singapore, Singapore 117583, Singapore
eleaam@nus.edu.sg
[3] Robotics and Autonomous Systems Thrust, The Hong Kong University of Science
and Technology (Guangzhou), Guangzhou, China
jun.ma@ust.hk
[4] Information Science and Technology, Eastern Institute of Technology,
Ningbo, China
xiaocongli@eitech.edu.cn

Abstract. In robotics applications, ensuring reliable performance in the presence of actuator faults is essential for maintaining system safety and reliability. This paper presents a tolerant tracking control method for permanent magnet synchronous motors (PMSMs) based on adaptive dynamic programming and fault compensation. The method simultaneously considers tracking accuracy and energy consumption through a policy iteration algorithm. In the optimality analysis of the algorithm, more relaxed conditions are provided to demonstrate that the performance function can converge to a near-optimal value within a finite number of iterations. In practical implementation, an actor-critic network is used to approximate the performance function and control protocol, alongside a fault detection mechanism based on an expanded time horizon, which achieves fault detection from arbitrary initial values. The effectiveness of the proposed algorithm is verified using a high-fidelity PMSM model in Simulink.

Keywords: Robot actuators · Tolerant tracking control · Motion control · Adaptive dynamic programming · Actuator faults · Fault compensation · Learning Control

1 Introduction

Reliable and high-precision control of actuators is a fundamental challenge in robotics. Traditional model-based motor control approaches depend heavily on

H. Li et al. (Eds.): ICSR + InnoBiz 2024, LNAI 15170, pp. 93–103, 2025.
https://doi.org/10.1007/978-981-96-1151-5_10

accurate mathematical models, and their performance can suffer if the model is not precise [1,2]. To address this, there is increasing interest in learning-based motor control. This approach utilizes data-driven techniques to enhance control without relying on precise models, offering the potential for more robust and adaptable actuator performance in dynamic environments.

Typically, traditional motor control methods such as PID control do not consider the optimal relationship between energy and motor tracking error. In order to ensure the optimal relationship between them, some researchers have applied optimal theory to motor tracking control [3,4]. Although the research on the optimal control of motor has been extensive, the existing research mainly focuses on the convergence analysis, and the optimization analysis is relatively rare [5,6]. In [7], convergence and optimality are analyzed by introducing gradient domination. Therefore, optimality analysis is one of the research contents of this paper. Considering that the actuator mechanism of the motor is prone to wear and tear, leading to faults and affecting the stability of the system. In recent decades, the study of actuator faults for motor has received widespread attention from scholars [2,8]. In [9,10], fault estimation values have been obtained by designing observers, and the accuracy of the estimation depends on the accuracy of system identification. To eliminate reliance on precise system models, subspace identification, model-free adaptive control, echo state networks and other methods have been developed. However, the above method does not consider the optimal control problem [11]. Therefore, in [12], reinforcement learning (RL) has been introduced into data-based tolerant tracking control. In [13,14], a data-based fault detection and estimation mechanism has been proposed. However, it is necessary to assume that the initial value of the system is 0 and the fault time is long enough. In [1], a detection mechanism that has no requirement for fault time and can detect arbitrary initial values has been proposed.

This article simultaneously considers the issues of energy and tracking accuracy, based on optimal control theory, to improve the control accuracy of the system and save energy consumption without relying on system identification. In optimality analysis, it is no longer assumed that the performance function is gradient domination, making the proof conditions more relaxed. Then the actuator fault detection mechanism with expanded time horizon is utilized, and the estimated value is compensated to the controller, so as to realize the tracking tolerance control of PMSM. This method can detect the system with arbitrary initial value, and the fault information can be obtained from the system data without designing any additional parameters. The forgetting factor is added to the method to reduce the influence of historical data on the current value and improve the compensation accuracy.

2   Problem Description

In field-oriented control, the velocity loop model of the motor in the $d - q$ frame is shown as follows:

$$\frac{d\omega}{dt} = -\frac{B}{J}\omega - \frac{1}{J}T_L + \frac{n\psi}{J}\left(i_q + i_q^a\right) \tag{1}$$

where ω and i_q stand for the angular velocity and current of q-axis, respectively, and are also system output and input signals. i_q^a is the actuator fault. B, J, T_L, n and ψ stand for the viscous frictional coefficient, rotor inertia, load torque, the number of pole pairs and the rotor flux linkage.

However, the control of the motor system is heavily dependent on the machine parameters. If the model parameters do not match the actual system, this will seriously affect the effect of control. Therefore, in order to achieve optimal control when the model is unknown, Nash equilibrium [15] is first introduced under the nominal system.

$$J\left(\tilde{\omega}\left(k\right), i_q\left(k\right)\right) = \sum_{\tau=k}^{\infty} D\left(\tilde{\omega}\left(\tau\right), i_q\left(\tau\right)\right) = D\left(\tilde{\omega}\left(k\right), i_q\left(k\right)\right) + J\left(\tilde{\omega}\left(k+1\right), i_q\left(k+1\right)\right)$$

(2)

where $\tilde{\omega}\left(k\right) = \omega_d\left(k\right) - \omega\left(k\right)$. ω_d stands for reference. Let $R > 0$ and $Q > 0$, representing positive matrices. $D\left(\tilde{\omega}\left(k\right), i_q\left(k\right)\right) = \tilde{\omega}^T\left(k\right) R\tilde{\omega}\left(k\right) + i_q^T\left(k\right) Qi_q\left(k\right)$.

In optimal control, in order to stabilize the control system (1) and ensure that the performance function (2) is bounded, control policy $i_q\left(k\right)$ must be admissible.

If $i_q\left(k\right)$ is admissible, the performance function is written as

$$V\left(\tilde{\omega}\left(k\right)\right) = \sum_{\tau=k}^{\infty} D\left(\tilde{\omega}\left(\tau\right), i_q\left(\tau\right)\right) = D\left(\tilde{\omega}\left(k\right), i_q\left(k\right)\right) + V\left(\tilde{\omega}\left(k+1\right)\right) \quad (3)$$

According to the Bellman optimality principle, the optimal performance function $V^*\left(\tilde{\omega}\left(k\right)\right)$ is

$$V^*\left(\tilde{\omega}\left(k\right)\right) = \min_{i_q(k)}\left\{D\left(\tilde{\omega}\left(k\right), i_q\left(k\right)\right) + V\left(\tilde{\omega}\left(k+1\right)\right)\right\} \quad (4)$$

The optimal control policy can be obtained as

$$i_q^*\left(k\right) = \arg\min_{i_q(k)} V^*\left(\tilde{\omega}\left(k\right)\right) \quad (5)$$

3   Policy Iteration Algorithm

In this section, the policy iteration algorithm process is presented. And provide proof of convergence for the algorithm and analysis of system stability.

Initialization: Any initial admissible policy $i_q^0\left(k\right)$, learning rate λ_a and the threshold ε.

Step 1: $t = t + 1$. Update the $V_{i^{t-1}}^t\left(\tilde{\omega}\left(k\right)\right)$.

$$V_{i^{t-1}}^t\left(\tilde{\omega}\left(k\right)\right) = D\left(\tilde{\omega}\left(k\right), i_q^{t-1}\left(k\right)\right) + V_{i^{t-1}}^t\left(\tilde{\omega}\left(k+1\right)\right) \quad (6)$$

Step 2: Update the control policy $i_q^t\left(k\right)$ through policy gradient.

$$i_q^t\left(k\right) = i_q^{t-1}\left(k\right) - \lambda_a \nabla_i\left(V_{i^{t-1}}^t\left(\tilde{\omega}\left(k\right)\right)\right)\big|_{i=i_q^{t-1}} \quad (7)$$

Step 3: When $\left| V_{i^t}^t \left(\tilde{\omega} \left(k \right) \right) - V_{i^{t-1}}^t \left(\tilde{\omega} \left(k \right) \right) \right| > \varepsilon$, go back to step 1. Otherwise iteration stops.

Output: Approximate value of optimal control policy $i_q^* \left(k \right)$.

Theorem 1 gives the convergence proof of the policy iteration algorithm.

Theorem 1. *Suppose that $i_q^0 \left(k \right)$ is the admissible control policy. Generate $V_{i^{t-1}}^t \left(\tilde{\omega} \left(k \right) \right)$ and $i_q^t \left(k \right)$ through policy iteration algorithm for $t = 1, 2, \cdots$. Then, $\lim\limits_{t \to \infty} V_{i^{t-1}}^t \left(k \right) = V^* \left(k \right)$ and $\lim\limits_{t \to \infty} i_q^t \left(k \right) = i_q^* \left(k \right)$.*

Proof. Suppose that $V^\infty \left(k \right)$ is the boundary of $V_{i^{t-1}}^t \left(k \right)$. Rewrite (6) and (7) as:

$$V^\infty \left(\tilde{\omega} \left(k \right) \right) = D \left(\tilde{\omega} \left(k \right), i_q^\infty \left(k \right) \right) + V^\infty \left(\tilde{\omega} \left(k + 1 \right) \right) \tag{8}$$

$$i_q^\infty \left(k \right) = i_q^\infty \left(k \right) - \lambda_a \nabla_i \left(V^\infty \left(\tilde{\omega} \left(k \right) \right) \right) |_{i = i_q^\infty} \tag{9}$$

According to (9), $\nabla_i \left(V^\infty \left(\tilde{\omega} \left(k \right) \right) \right) |_{i = i_q^\infty} = 0$.

Therefore, (8)-gradient equation is:

$$0 = \nabla_i D \left(\tilde{\omega} \left(k \right), i_q^\infty \left(k \right) \right) + \nabla_i V^\infty \left(\tilde{\omega} \left(k + 1 \right) \right) |_{i = i_q^\infty} \tag{10}$$

Based on Global Nash Equilibrium, it can be concluded that

$$0 = \left\{ \nabla_i D \left(\tilde{\omega} \left(k \right), i_q^* \left(k \right) \right) + \nabla_i V^* \left(\tilde{\omega} \left(k + 1 \right) \right) \right\} |_{i = i_q^*} \tag{11}$$

Thus,

$$\begin{aligned} \lim_{t \to \infty} i_q^t \left(k \right) &= i_q^* \left(k \right) \\ \lim_{t \to \infty} V_{i^{t-1}}^t \left(\tilde{\omega} \left(k \right) \right) &= V^* \left(\tilde{\omega} \left(k \right) \right) \end{aligned} \tag{12}$$

The proof is completed.

Theorem 2 gives the optimality proof of the policy iteration algorithm.

Theorem 2. *Suppose that $i_q^0 \left(k \right)$ is the admissible control policy. Generate $V_{i^{t-1}}^t \left(\tilde{\omega} \left(k \right) \right)$ and $i_q^t \left(k \right)$ through policy iteration algorithm for $t = 1, 2, \cdots$. We make the learning rate $\lambda_a = \frac{1}{\eta}$. If*

$$H \geq \frac{2 \left(w - \vartheta \right) \eta}{M} + h \tag{13}$$

$V_{i^{t-1}}^t \left(\tilde{\omega} \left(k \right) \right)$ *converges to near-optimal value.*

$$V_{i^{H-1}}^H \left(\tilde{\omega} \left(k \right) \right) - V^* \left(\tilde{\omega} \left(k \right) \right) \leq \vartheta \tag{14}$$

where $\vartheta > 0$. The arbitrary positive constant w satisfies $w \geq V_{i^{h-1}}^h \left(\tilde{\omega} \left(k \right) \right) - V^* \left(\tilde{\omega} \left(k \right) \right)$. And $M = \max \left(\left\| \nabla_i \left(V_{i^{t-1}}^t \left(\tilde{\omega} \left(k \right) \right) \right) \right\|^2 \right)$ for $t = 1, 2, \cdots$.

Proof. According to local Lipschitz gradients [7], $V_{i^t}^t\left(\tilde{\omega}\left(k\right)\right) - V_{i^{t-1}}^t\left(\tilde{\omega}\left(k\right)\right) \le -\frac{1}{2\eta}\left\|\nabla_i\left(V_{i^{t-1}}^t\left(\tilde{\omega}\left(k\right)\right)\right)\right\|$ and $V_{i^t}^{t+1}\left(\tilde{\omega}\left(k\right)\right) \le V_{i^{t-1}}^t\left(\tilde{\omega}\left(k\right)\right)$. Therefore,

$$V_{i^t}^t\left(\tilde{\omega}\left(k\right)\right) \le V_{i^{t-1}}^t\left(\tilde{\omega}\left(k\right)\right) - \frac{1}{2\eta}\left\|\nabla_i\left(V_{i^{t-1}}^t\left(\tilde{\omega}\left(k\right)\right)\right)\right\|^2 \tag{15}$$

where both $i_q^t\left(k\right)$ and $i_q^{t-1}\left(k\right)$ are the admissible control policies.

Subtracting $V^*\left(\tilde{\omega}\left(k\right)\right)$ from both sides of inequality (15) yields

$$\begin{aligned} V_{i^t}^t\left(\tilde{\omega}\left(k\right)\right) - V^*\left(\tilde{\omega}\left(k\right)\right) &\le V_{i^{t-1}}^t\left(\tilde{\omega}\left(k\right)\right) - V^*\left(\tilde{\omega}\left(k\right)\right) \\ &\quad - \frac{1}{2\eta}\left\|\nabla_i\left(V_{i^{t-1}}^t\left(\tilde{\omega}\left(k\right)\right)\right)\right\|^2 \end{aligned} \tag{16}$$

From $V_{i^t}^{t+1}\left(\tilde{\omega}\left(k\right)\right) \le V_{i^{t-1}}^t\left(\tilde{\omega}\left(k\right)\right)$, it can be inferred that

$$\begin{aligned} V_{i^t}^{t+1}\left(\tilde{\omega}\left(k\right)\right) - V^*\left(\tilde{\omega}\left(k\right)\right) &\le V_{i^{t-1}}^t\left(\tilde{\omega}\left(k\right)\right) - V^*\left(\tilde{\omega}\left(k\right)\right) \\ &\quad - \frac{1}{2\eta}\left\|\nabla_i\left(V_{i^{t-1}}^t\left(\tilde{\omega}\left(k\right)\right)\right)\right\|^2 \end{aligned} \tag{17}$$

Therefore, for $t = h, \cdots, H$, we can obtain

$$\begin{aligned} V_{i^h}^{h+1}\left(\tilde{\omega}\left(k\right)\right) - V^*\left(\tilde{\omega}\left(k\right)\right) &\le V_{i^{h-1}}^h\left(\tilde{\omega}\left(k\right)\right) - V^*\left(\tilde{\omega}\left(k\right)\right) \\ &\quad - \frac{1}{2\eta}\left\|\nabla_i\left(V_{i^{h-1}}^h\left(\tilde{\omega}\left(k\right)\right)\right)\right\|^2 \end{aligned} \tag{18}$$

$$\begin{aligned} V_{i^{h+1}}^{h+2}\left(\tilde{\omega}\left(k\right)\right) - V^*\left(\tilde{\omega}\left(k\right)\right) &\le V_{i^h}^{h+1}\left(\tilde{\omega}\left(k\right)\right) - V^*\left(\tilde{\omega}\left(k\right)\right) \\ &\quad - \frac{1}{2\eta}\left\|\nabla_i\left(V_{i^h}^{h+1}\left(\tilde{\omega}\left(k\right)\right)\right)\right\|^2 \end{aligned}$$

$$\vdots$$

$$\begin{aligned} V_{i^H}^{H+1}\left(\tilde{\omega}\left(k\right)\right) - V^*\left(\tilde{\omega}\left(k\right)\right) &\le V_{i^{H-1}}^H\left(\tilde{\omega}\left(k\right)\right) - V^*\left(\tilde{\omega}\left(k\right)\right) \\ &\quad - \frac{1}{2\eta}\left\|\nabla_i\left(V_{i^{H-1}}^H\left(\tilde{\omega}\left(k\right)\right)\right)\right\|^2 \end{aligned}$$

So,

$$\begin{aligned} V_{i^H}^{H+1}\left(\tilde{\omega}\left(k\right)\right) - V^*\left(\tilde{\omega}\left(k\right)\right) &\le V_{i^{h-1}}^h\left(\tilde{\omega}\left(k\right)\right) - V^*\left(\tilde{\omega}\left(k\right)\right) \\ -\frac{1}{2\eta}\left(\left\|\nabla_i\left(V_{i^{h-1}}^h\left(\tilde{\omega}\left(k\right)\right)\right)\right\|^2 \right. &+ \cdots + \left.\left\|\nabla_i\left(V_{i^{H-1}}^H\left(\tilde{\omega}\left(k\right)\right)\right)\right\|^2\right) \end{aligned} \tag{19}$$

According to [16], there must be an iterative index h such that $w \ge V_{i^{h-1}}^h\left(\tilde{\omega}\left(k\right)\right) - V^*\left(\tilde{\omega}\left(k\right)\right)$. Meanwhile, from the continuous differentiable monotone non-increment of $V_{i^{t-1}}^t\left(k\right)$, the derivative of $V_{i^{t-1}}^t\left(k\right)$ is bounded. Therefore, it can be defined $M = \max\left(\left\|\nabla_i\left(V_{i^{t-1}}^t\left(\tilde{\omega}\left(k\right)\right)\right)\right\|^2\right)$. (19) can be rewritten as

$$V_{i^H}^{H+1}\left(\tilde{\omega}\left(k\right)\right) - V^*\left(\tilde{\omega}\left(k\right)\right) \le w - \frac{M}{2\eta}\left(H - h\right) \tag{20}$$

From (14), it can be concluded that

$$w - \frac{M}{2\eta}(H - h) \leq \vartheta \tag{21}$$

From (13), it can be inferred that (21) holds true. The proof is completed.

Theorem 3 gives the stability proof of system (1) under the iterative control policy.

Theorem 3. *Suppose that $i_q^0(k)$ is the admissible control policy. Generate $V_{i^{t-1}}^t(\tilde{\omega}(k))$ and $i_q^t(k)$ through policy iteration algorithm for $t = 1, 2, \cdots$. Iterative control policy $i_q^t(k)$ is admissible.*

Proof. Let $t = 0$. And $i_q^0(k)$ is admissible. Let $t = f - 1$, $f = 2, 3, \cdots$. Assume that $i_q^t(k)$ is admissible, i.e., $i_q^{f-1}(k)$ is admissible. For $i_q^{f-1}(k)$, $V_{i^{f-1}}^f(\tilde{\omega}(k))$ satisfies

$$V_{i^{f-1}}^f(\tilde{\omega}(k)) = D\left(\tilde{\omega}(k), i_q^{f-1}(k)\right) + V_{i^{f-1}}^f(\tilde{\omega}(k+1)) \tag{22}$$

Choose $V_{i^{f-1}}^f(\tilde{\omega}(k))$ as the Lyapunov function. The difference of the Lyapunov function is

$$\begin{aligned}\Delta V_{i^{f-1}}^f(\tilde{\omega}(k)) &= V_{i^{f-1}}^f(\tilde{\omega}(k+1)) - V_{i^{f-1}}^f(\tilde{\omega}(k)) \\ &= -D\left(\tilde{\omega}(k), i_q^{f-1}(k)\right) < 0\end{aligned} \tag{23}$$

Therefore, error is asymptotically stable, i.e., $\tilde{\omega}(k) \to 0$ ($k \to \infty$).

For $t = f$, $i_q^f(k)$ is generated by (7). According to the definition of admissible control [17] and $V_{i^f}^{f+1}(\tilde{\omega}(k)) \leq V_{i^{f-1}}^f(\tilde{\omega}(k)) < \infty$, $i_q^f(k)$ is admissible. The proof is completed.

4   Implementation Based on Actor-Critic Neural Network

In order to implement the policy iteration algorithm, in this section, $V_{i^{t-1}}^t(\tilde{\omega}(k))$ and $i_q^t(k)$ are approximated through the actor NN and critic NN, respectively.

4.1   Critic Neural Network

The performance function $V_{i^{t-1}}^t(\tilde{\omega}(k))$ (6) can be approximated by the critic NN

$$\hat{V}_{i^{t-1}}^t(\tilde{\omega}(k)) = \hat{\kappa}_c^{tT}(k)\psi_c\left(\mathrm{H}_c^T z_c(k)\right) \tag{24}$$

where the weight estimate of the hidden-output layer is represented by $\hat{\kappa}_c^t(k)$ in the critic network. the activation function is represented by $\psi_c\left(\mathrm{H}_c^T z_c(k)\right)$, in which $z_c(k) = \left[\tilde{\omega}^T(k), i_q^{(t-1)T}(k)\right]^T$ and the weight vector of the input-hidden layer is represented by H_c. Select the activation function is $\psi_c(m) = \frac{1-\exp(-m)}{1+\exp(-m)}$. Therefore, $0 < \psi_c(m) < 1$ and $0 < \psi_c^T\left(H_c^T z_c(k)\right)\psi_c\left(H_c^T z_c(k)\right) <$

n_c, in which the node number of the critic NN is represented by n_c and $n_c > 1$. The ideal $V_{it-1}^t (\tilde{\omega}(k))$ is $V_{it-1}^t (\tilde{\omega}(k)) = \kappa_c^{*T}(k)\psi_c (H_c^T z_c(k)) + \varepsilon_c(k)$, where the approximation error is represented by $\varepsilon_c(k)$ for the critic network. Define $\tilde{\kappa}_c^t(k) \triangleq \hat{\kappa}_c^t(k) - \kappa_c^*(k)$.

Based on (6) and the existence of neural network approximation error, define the error function of the critic network as $e_c^t(k) = D(\tilde{\omega}(k), i_q^{t-1}(k)) + \hat{V}_{it-1}^t(\tilde{\omega}(k)) - \hat{V}_{it-1}^t(\tilde{\omega}(k-1))$. The minimum value of the error function can be obtained through $E_c(k) = \frac{1}{2}e_c^{tT}(k)e_c^t(k)$. Correspondingly, the tuning law $\hat{\kappa}_c^t(k)$ for critic NN is as follows:

$$
\hat{\kappa}_c^{t+1}(k) = \hat{\kappa}_c^t(k) - \lambda_c \frac{\partial E_c(k)}{\partial \hat{\kappa}_c^t(k)} \tag{25}
$$
$$
= \hat{\kappa}_c^t(k) - \lambda_c \left[D\left(\tilde{\omega}(k-1), i_q^{t-1}(k-1)\right) \right.
$$
$$
\left. = +\hat{V}_{it-1}^t(\tilde{\omega}(k)) - \hat{V}_{it-1}^t(\tilde{\omega}(k-1)) \right] \psi_c (H_c^T z_c(k))
$$

where $\lambda_c > 0$ stands for the learning rate.

4.2 Actor Neural Network

Design the actor NN to approximate the control policy i_q^t (7).

$$
\hat{i}_q^t(k) = \hat{\kappa}_a^{tT}(k)\psi_a (H_a^T \tilde{\omega}(k)) \tag{26}
$$

where the weight estimate and the activation function are represented by $\hat{\kappa}_a^t(k)$ and $\psi_a (H_a^T \tilde{\omega}(k))$ in the actor network. And the weight vector of the input-hidden layer is represented by H_a. The activation function of actor NN is the same as that of critic NN. The ideal $i_q^t(k) = \kappa_a^{*T}(k)\psi_a (H_a^T \tilde{\omega}(k)) + \varepsilon_a(k)$, where the approximation error is represented by $\varepsilon_a(k)$. Define $\tilde{\kappa}_a^t(k) \triangleq \hat{\kappa}_a^t(k) - \kappa_a^*(k)$.

Considering the policy gradient control, the tuning law $\hat{\kappa}_a^t(k)$ for actor NN is as follows:

$$
\hat{\kappa}_a^{t+1}(k) = \hat{\kappa}_a^t(k) - \lambda_a \nabla_i \left(V^t(\tilde{\omega}(k)) \right) \tag{27}
$$
$$
= \hat{\kappa}_c^t(k) - \lambda_a \psi_a (H_a^T \tilde{\omega}(k)) \hat{\kappa}_c^{tT}(k) \dot{\psi}_c (H_c^T z_c(k)) H_c^T \Upsilon
$$

where $\Upsilon = [0,1]^T$. $\lambda_a > 0$ stands for the learning rate.

5 Fault Compensation Strategy

Firstly, the calculated output $\hat{y}(k)$ of the nominal system of (1) is given.

$$
\hat{y}(k) = \alpha^{k-1}\omega(1) + \sum_{h=1}^{k-1} \chi^{h-1}\beta^{k-i}i_q(h) \tag{28}
$$

where $\beta^1 = \widehat{y}(2)/\widehat{i}_q(1), \cdots, \beta^{k-1} = \left(\widehat{y}(k) - \sum_{h=2}^{k-1} \chi^{h-1}\beta^{k-h}\widehat{i}_q(h)\right)/\widehat{i}_q(1)$

and $\alpha^{k-1} = \left(\breve{y}(k) - \sum_{h=2}^{k-1} \chi^{h-1}\beta^{k-h}\breve{i}_q(h)\right)/\breve{i}_q(1)$, in which χ stands for for-

getting   factor. $\left\{\widehat{i}_q(k), \widehat{y}(k), \widehat{\omega}(1) = 0\right\}$ $(\widehat{i}_q(1)$ $\neq$ $0)$

and $\left\{\breve{i}_q(k), \breve{y}(k), \breve{\omega}(1) \neq 0\right\}$ are reference data sets of the nominal system
of (1).

Define $y_e(k) = y(k) - \hat{y}(k)$ and $y(k) = C\omega(k)$. If $\|y_e(k)\| \leq \upsilon$, the system
runs normally and no fault occurs. Otherwise, the actuator has faults and alarms.

Suppose the fault occurs at time m, then $\alpha^m\omega(1) + \beta^m i_q(1) + \cdots + \chi^{m-1}\beta^1 i_q(m) - y(m+1) = y_e(m+1)$ and $\alpha^m\omega(1) + \beta^m i_q(1) + \cdots + \chi^{m-1}\beta^1\left(i_q(m) + i_q^a(m)\right) - y(m+1) = 0$. For time $m+1$,
$\alpha^{m+1}\omega(1) + \beta^{m+1} i_q(1) + \chi\beta^m i_q(2) + \cdots + \chi^{h-1}\beta^2 i_q(m) + \chi^h\beta^1 i_q(m+1) - y(m+2) = y_e(m+2)$ and $\alpha^{m+1}\omega(1) + \beta^{m+1} i_q(1) + \chi\beta^m i_q(2) + \cdots + \chi^{h-1}\beta^2\left(i_q(m) + i_q^a(m)\right) + \chi^h\beta^1\left(i_q(m+1) + i_q^a(m+1)\right) - y(m+2) = 0$.

Therefore, the fault compensation control $i_q^c(k)$ of $k = m+1, m+2, \cdots$ is
(Fig. 1):

$$i_q^c(k) = -\left[(\beta^1)^T\beta^1\right]^{-1}(\beta^1)^T \frac{1}{\chi^{k-2}}\left[y_e(k) + \chi^{m-1}\beta^{k-m}i_q^a(m)\right. \tag{29}$$
$$\left. + \chi^m\beta^{k-m-1}i_q^a(m+1) + \cdots + \chi^{k-3}\beta^2 i_q^a(k-2)\right]$$

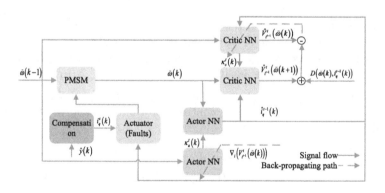

Fig. 1. Overall control strategy diagram

6   Simulation Validation

In simulink, the effectiveness of policy iteration algorithm and fault compensation algorithm for tolerant control of motor with actuator faults is verified. The initial values: $\omega(0) = 4rad/sec$, $i_q(0) = 0A$ and $i_d(0) = 0A$. Motor
parameters: $n = 4$, $B = 1.33 \times 10^{-5}N \cdot s/rad$, $J = 2.4 \times 10^{-6}kg \cdot m^2$,

$\psi = 0.0057Wb$, $T_L = 0N \cdot m$, stator inductance $0.0011mH$ and stator resistance 0.9Ω. $i_q^a(k) = 2, (k > 0.5)$ and $i_q^a(k) = 10*(k - 0.7), (k > 0.7)$ are used to simulate two kinds of actuator faults respectively. $R = 10$ and $Q = 1$ in (2). The structure of actor NN and critic NN are 2-10-1 and 1-10-1 respectively. The initial weights are randomly generated between (0,1). λ_a and λ_c are both 0.1. The maximum number of iterations $t = 50$, the threshold $\varepsilon = 10^{-5}$, and forgetting factor $\chi = 1.0012$.

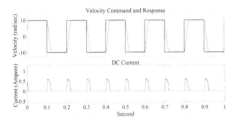

Fig. 2. Policy iteration control based on reinforcement learning

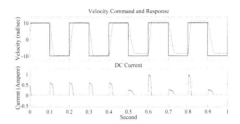

Fig. 3. Policy iteration control without fault compensation

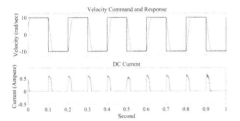

Fig. 4. Tolerant tracking control for $i_q^a(k) = 2$

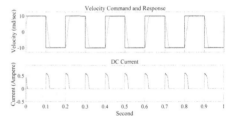

Fig. 5. Tolerant tracking control for $i_q^a(k) = 10*(k - 0.7)$

The simulation results of the velocity and DC current are obtained, as shown in Fig. 2, 3, 4 and Fig. 5. The current loop of the motor still uses a PI controller. When the speed loop actuator has no fault and the system operates normally, the simulation results are shown in Fig. 2. From Fig. 2, it can be seen that the policy iterative algorithm based on reinforcement learning can enable $w(k)$ to track $w_d(k)$. When the speed loop actuator has faults after 0.5 s, $w(k)$ in Fig. 3 deviates from $w_d(k)$ without fault compensation, and the DC current values also change. Figure 4 shows the results of compensation based on the expanded time horizon detection mechanism, which compensates for the policy iteration algorithm after actuator has faults. As shown in Fig. 4, after 0.5 s, $\omega\,(k)$ can still track $\omega_d\,(k)$, and the DC current is basically the same as when there is no fault. When both the initial value of the system and the fault type of the actuator change, as shown in Fig. 5, $\omega\,(k)$ can still track $\omega_d\,(k)$ after 0.7 s.

7   Conclusion

This article focuses on PMSM control with actuator faults and implements tolerant tracking control using methods based on adaptive dynamic programming and fault compensation. In the optimality analysis of the algorithm, a novel convergence speed is introduced by utilizing the properties of the iterative performance function, allowing the function to converge to near-optimal values within a finite number of iterations. To address actuator faults, a detection mechanism with an expanded time horizon is employed to adjust the estimated fault values in the controller, thus enabling tolerant control. The proposed method is particularly beneficial for robotics applications where robust performance and precision under fault conditions are required.

Acknowledgments. This study is funded by National Natural Science Foundation of China (61573113) and Key-Area Research and Development Program of Guangdong Province (2020B0909020001).

Disclosure of Interests. The authors have no competing interests to declare that are relevant to the content of this article.

References

1. Liu, Y., Wang, Z.: Reinforcement learning-based tracking control for a class of discrete-time systems with actuator fault. IEEE Trans. Circuits Syst. II Express Briefs **69**(6), 2827–2831 (2022)
2. Fan, Z.-X., Li, S., Liu, R.: ADP-based optimal control for systems with mismatched disturbances: a PMSM application. IEEE Trans. Circuits Syst. II Express Briefs **70**(6), 2057–2061 (2023)
3. Tan, L.N., Pham, T.C.: Optimal tracking control for PMSM with partially unknown dynamics, saturation voltages, torque, and voltage disturbances. IEEE Trans. Ind. Electron. **69**(4), 3481–3491 (2022)
4. El-Sousy, F.F.M., Amin, M.M., Al-Durra, A.: Adaptive optimal tracking control via actor-critic-identifier based adaptive dynamic programming for permanent-magnet synchronous motor drive system. IEEE Trans. Ind. Appl. **57**(6), 6577–6591 (2021)
5. Luo, B., Liu, D., Wu, H.-N., Wang, D., Lewis, F.L.: Policy gradient adaptive dynamic programming for data-based optimal control. IEEE Trans. Cybern. **47**(10), 3341–3354 (2017)
6. Lin, M., Zhao, B., Liu, D.: Policy gradient adaptive critic designs for model-free optimal tracking control with experience replay. IEEE Trans. Syst. Man Cybern. Syst. **52**(6), 3692–3703 (2022)

7. Lin, M., Zhao, B.: Policy optimization adaptive dynamic programming for optimal control of input-affine discrete-time nonlinear systems. IEEE Trans. Syst. Man Cybern.: Syst. **53**(7), 4339–4350 (2023)
8. Zhang, G., Zhang, H., Huang, X., Wang, J., Yu, H., Graaf, R.: Active fault-tolerant control for electric vehicles with independently driven rear in-wheel motors against certain actuator faults. IEEE Trans. Control Syst. Technol. **24**(5), 1557–1572 (2016)
9. Pang, Z.H., Xia, C.G., Sun, J., Liu, G.P., Han, Q.L.: Active fault-tolerant predictive control of networked systems subject to actuator faults and random communication constraints. Int. J. Control **95**(9), 2357–2363 (2021)
10. Guo, B., Chen, Y.: Robust adaptive fault-tolerant control of four-wheel independently actuated electric vehicles. IEEE Trans. Ind. Inf. **16**(5), 2882–2894 (2020)
11. Liu, L., Wang, Z., Yao, X., Zhang, H.: Echo state networks based data-driven adaptive fault tolerant control with its application to electromechanical system. IEEE/ASME Trans. Mechatron. **23**(3), 1372–1382 (2018)
12. Rizvi, S.A.A., Pertzborn, A.J., Lin, Z.: Reinforcement learning based optimal tracking control under unmeasurable disturbances with application to HVAC systems. IEEE Trans. Neural Netw. Learn. Syst. **33**(12), 17523–7533 (2022)
13. Wang, Y., Wang, Z.: Data-driven model-free adaptive fault-tolerant control for a class of discrete-time systems. IEEE Trans. Circuits Syst. II Express Briefs **69**(1), 154–158 (2022)
14. Han, K., Feng, J., Yao, Y.: An integrated data-driven Markov parameters sequence identification and adaptive dynamic programming method to design fault-tolerant optimal tracking control for completely unknown model systems. J. Franklin Inst. **354**, 5280–5301 (2017)
15. Zhang, S., Zhang, Y.: Introduction to game theory. Chin. Sci. Bull. **48**(9), 841–846 (2003)
16. Li, T., Bai, W., Liu, Q., Long, Y., Chen, C.L.P.: Distributed fault-tolerant containment control protocols for the discrete-time multiagent systems via reinforcement learning method. IEEE Trans. Neural Netw. Learn. Syst. **34**(8), 3979–3991 (2023)
17. Beard, R.W., Saridis, G.N., Wen, J.T.: Galerkin approximations of the generalized Hamilton-Jacobi-Bellman equation. Automatica **33**(12), 2159–2177 (1997)

ROOTED: An Open Source Toolkit for Dialogue Systems in Human Robot Interaction

Antonio Galiza Cerdeira Gonzalez[1]([✉]) [ID], Ikuo Mizuuchi[2] [ID], and Bipin Indurkhya[1] [ID]

[1] Cognitive Science Department, Jagiellonian University, Romana Ingardena 3, Kraków, Poland
{antonio.gonzalez,bipin.indurkhya}@uj.edu.pl
[2] Tokyo University of Agriculture and Technology, BASE, Koganei 2-24-16, Tokyo, Japan
ikuo@mizuuchi.lab.tuat.ac.jp

Abstract. Dialogue Systems are crucial for human-machine interaction, particularly in social robotics where natural communication is essential. However, there is no standardized framework for developing Dialogue Systems, and the integration of Large Language Models (LLMs) faces challenges such as hallucinations, outdated information, and sycophancy, which can compromise trust and effectiveness in high-stakes applications. Also, LLMs often violate Gricean Maxims, affecting user interpretation and system efficacy. To address these issues, we present *ROS2 Opensource Toolkit for Efficient Dialogue* (ROOTED), a framework for developing adaptable dialogue systems for social robots. ROOTED combines rule-based dialogue generation, web search, and LLMs to better adhere to Gricean Maxims by grounding responses. It also includes components for non-verbal communication analysis and generation. The capabilities of ROOTED are demonstrated through its deployment in the Social Plantroid Robot, which uses ROOTED for managing interactions and emotional responses.

Keywords: Dialogue Systems · Human-Robot Interaction · Large Language Models

1 Introduction

Dialogue Systems are responsible for allowing machines to interact with their users through conversation in written or spoken form. Such systems are of particular interest for social robotics, since oral conversations are a natural means of interaction for most humans. Such systems have several components such as automatic speech recognition, natural language understanding, dialogue manager, natural language generation, and speech synthesizer, depending on each application.

H. Li et al. (Eds.): ICSR + InnoBiz 2024, LNAI 15170, pp. 104–118, 2025.
https://doi.org/10.1007/978-981-96-1151-5_11

One problem is that there is no unified framework for how to develop Dialogue Systems. The situation has become even more complicated with the advent of Large Language models, with researchers starting to leverage LLMs into their development [25], for human-like dialogue generation, instruction understanding and broad knowledge domain capabilities.

Introducing such powerful models to dialogue systems, however, also introduces a slew of problems related to LLMs, such as hallucinations [13], lack of current-ness (outdated dataset), and sycophancy (agreeing with humans without regard for truth) [8]. Such shortcomings might be acceptable for some applications, but in high-trust scenarios, e.g. a hospice care robot, such limitations reduce the overall effectiveness of the system by beaching the trust of those who depend on them [4] or, even worse, by providing wrong information that might be harmful [3].

Less critical issues with Dialogue Systems include verbosity, where LLMs often provide excessively long responses. This results in violating several Gricean Maxims: Quantity (overly lengthy answers), Quality (potential inaccuracies), Relation (straying from the intended conversation goal), and Manner (though models generally maintain politeness). Such violations, termed 'flouting', can significantly alter how users interpret the system's responses, leading them to search for deeper meanings or intentions [5]. This can undermine the system's effectiveness. Current research mainly addresses the Maxim of Quality by focusing on reducing hallucinations, with less emphasis on tackling violations of other Gricean Maxims.

Although Dialogue Systems are crucial for social robots, there are currently no open-source, robot-agnostic ROS2-based frameworks for developing dialogue systems for robots. The closest existing system is OAN [6], which was developed for the Nao robot and focuses on general operations than on providing a robust dialogue system.

To address such gaps, we introduce an open-source framework for developing dialogue systems, ROS2 Open-source Toolkit for Efficient Dialogue (ROOTED), which is a versatile tool for social robots. It incorporates both verbal and non-verbal communication elements, such as facial expression analysis and body language generation, and combines rule-based techniques, web search, and large language models to adhere to Gricean Maxims and reduce issues like hallucination. The framework supports both open-domain and task-oriented dialogues and is available at https://gitlab.com/AntonioGCGonzalez/rooted.git.

ROOTED is designed to be a very modular framework, where each component is a python ROS2 package. It also provides several already functional dialogue system components, such as automatic speech recognition, a dialogue state machine, speech synthesis, useful natural language processing functions, a traditional rule-based Python NLTK chatbot, and methods to invoke two different LLMs (Dolly 2 and Llama3). However, the framework goes beyond simple communication by providing a memory module to store conversations and other useful information, a motion module to allow the robot to navigate its environment, a sensing module to allow the robot to better understand its environment, and a flexible vision module that can be used to perform various tasks besides social ones.

The efficacy of the proposed framework is demonstrated through its use in the Social Plantroid Robot (Fig. 1), which helps care for a potted plant by moving it in and out of sunlight and monitoring soil conditions. The robot also

Fig. 1. Social Plantroid Robot

considers human emotional states during conversations and displays appropriate body language and facial expressions. It also performs soil monitoring and robot navigation; all managed by ROOTED.

2   Related Works

2.1   Dialogue Systems and LLMs

Dialogue systems in robotics have evolved from rule-based and probabilistic methods [17] to leverage large language models (LLMs) such as Generative Pre-Trained Transformers (GPT) [19]. LLMs have significantly advanced conversational capabilities, enabling chatbots and dialogue managers to produce human-like responses and exhibit extensive knowledge. This progression has led to new benchmarks for assessing artificial intelligence's human-like intelligence [20].

A new metric is introduced in [26] to evaluate behavior discrepancy for Conversational Recommender Systems that utilize LLMs, as these models tend to give an immediate response instead of investigating the needs of users.

To generate more data for training dialogue state tracking models, [23] used LLMs (GPT4) to simulate multi-turn dialogues between users and agents to train a llama2-based model for tracking the state of conversation. This approach is used in ROOTED, despite using traditional rule-based Natural Language Processing dialogue state tracking.

LLMs are used for automatic API Argument Filling in Task-Oriented Conversational Systems in [15]. Two approaches are investigated; one, for open source models, consisting of supervised fine-tuning (SFT) and rejection sampling (RS), which can be fine-tuned. The other approach is using advanced prompting techniques, which is adapted in ROOTED.

2.2   Grice's Cooperative Principle and LLMs

Large Language Models (LLMs) and other generative models have garnered significant attention from researchers, engineers, and the public. Despite their impressive capabilities, these models often fail to fully adhere to Grice's Cooperative Principle [7], frequently violating one or more of the Gricean Maxims. Most research and guardrails for LLMs focus on mitigating hallucinations (maxim of quality) and preventing toxic or harmful behavior (maxim of politeness) [3]. For instance, [2] tackled hallucination and data staleness by grounding the model with a Knowledge Graph and using the 'According to' prompt.

However, less attention has been given to the issues of quantity and relation. LLMs often produce verbose responses [21], which, though not necessarily harmful, can reduce the communication efficiency. Research in [29] suggests that LLMs have a sense of answer length, though smaller models may need additional fine-tuning. ROOTED addresses this by using prompt engineering to specifically request concise answers.

Miehling *et al.* [14] propose a model to measure the adherence of generative model responses to the Gricean Maxims. Park *et al.* [18] introduce a multilingual suit (MultiPragEval), to test the adherence of models in different languages.

To enhance the ability of LLMs to incorporate Grice's Cooperation Principles—the nuanced meaning behind statements or questions—[29] has shown that when instruction-tuned at the example level, LLMs perform better in resolving implicature. These findings indicate that certain fine-tuning methods can improve an LLM's grasp of pragmatics. However, this research does not specifically target Gricean maxims.

2.3   Plant Caring Robots

The Social Plantroid robot platform is the third iteration in the Plantroid family, following Plantroid Omni [28] and Plantroid Mini [27]. The original Plantroid Omni was designed for moving large plants in greenhouses, while Plantroid Mini operated as a swarm to manage smaller plant pots' light exposure. Unlike its predecessors, which were purely functional, social features were introduced in Social Plantroid to allow it to transform plants into pets.

Among other plant-based social robots, PotPet [12] is similar in its social approach but only communicates non-verbally. Flonaflona [22] responds to hand movements detected by ultrasonic sensors. In [24], an iRobot Create base was combined with a plant with various sensors for artistic installations, making the public rethink the role of decorative plants in human spaces. Unlike these, Social Plantroid can assess user emotions, display facial expressions and speak, offering a more advanced interaction experience.

3   Design Principles

3.1   A Holistic Approach

To develop a framework useful for present and future scientists and engineers, it is necessary to have a highly modular system where the components can be easily replaced to incorporate changes in the technology and different user needs.

Robots do not maintain homeostasis but serve as tools to free up human time for more important tasks and, therefore, must also be designed to not disturb their environment much and attend to human needs.

Finally, there are the needs of the robot itself: it needs to keep its batteries charged and keep its physical integrity, which is also closely intertwined with the environmental needs.

In the following subsections, we propose the design principles for ROOTED grouped in terms of user needs (Subsect. 3.2), environmental factors (Subsect. 3.3) and robot needs (Subsect. 3.4).

3.2 User Needs

ROOTED addresses fundamental user needs in social robotics, ensuring clear communication between humans and robots according to Grice's Cooperative Principle and Gricean Maxims. The core functions of a dialogue system include receiving, understanding, generating, and displaying responses, incorporating both verbal and non-verbal communication elements such as facial expressions and gestures.

Dialogue systems must consider who initiates and controls the conversation flow, varying from human-driven systems like chatbots to mixed-initiative systems like the Social Plantroid robot, which may start a conversation based on plant care needs but otherwise allows human control.

ROOTED integrates automatic speech recognition to convert speech to text, natural language understanding to analyze input, and dialogue management to track and respond appropriately. It also includes human detection through audio and video to manage interactions.

Privacy concerns, such as continuous listening and data storage, are addressed by offering configurable options within ROOTED, balancing the risks and benefits of data collection using ROS2 security enclave and SQLite3 database.

3.3 Environmental Factors

Environmental constraints seem to not matter much for dialogue management systems. However, as the robot might need to move itself in certain states of its dialogue and might have body language, it is necessary to be aware whether the robot can move around freely or if needs obstacle avoidance.

Also, certain settings do not allow for all communication modalities. For example, in a hospital setting, the robot should not have bright blinking lights or make loud sounds; it should be quiet while moving. In a noisy industrial environment, the verbal communication might not be the best medium for quickly conveying messages. ROOTED, then, provides tools for quickly designing voice, text and image based communication systems, while providing vision and sonar-based obstacle avoidance.

3.4 Robot Needs

A robot's needs include charging batteries or being unresponsive during certain tasks. For instance, the Social Plantroid robot prioritizes the plant's needs and will seek human assistance when required, while refusing conversation when moving to avoid obstacles. Also, robots may need to protect themselves from verbal or physical abuse in ways that do not harm humans. ROOTED includes features that allow robots to refuse communication during specific states, addressing these requirements.

4   ROOTED Architecture

To fulfill all general human, environmental and robot needs outlined in Sect. 3, we designed nine distinct modules for ROOTED:

i) MAESTRO; ii) Listening; iii) Vision; iv) Movement; v) Robot Memory; vi) Other Sensors; vii) LLM; viii) Facial Expression; and ix) Voice synthesis.

The overall architecture is shown in Fig. 2.

Each module is described below.

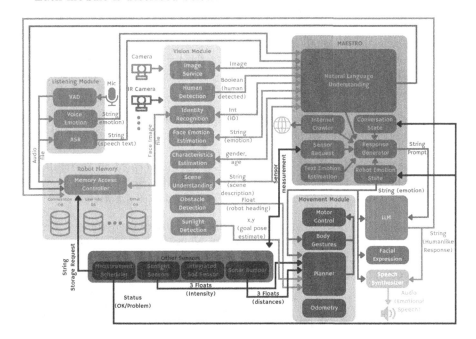

Fig. 2. ROOTED Architecture for the Social Plantroid.

MAESTRO. This is the core of the ROOTED system, managing and integrating its various components. Its primary role is to understand user inputs, consider their emotional state (based on facial expressions, voice tone, and speech content), and generate appropriate high-level responses. These responses are then converted into natural language by a Large Language Model.

The high-level responses of MAESTRO are in the following format, which can be modified by developers as needed:

```
Briefly and politely paraphrase the following text in a <emotion>
tone: <response from NLTK chatbot>
```
MAESTRO allows designers to choose from different models like Ekman's 6 or 7 fundamental emotions [10], Russell's two-dimensional model, Plutchik's wheel of emotion [16]. It tracks the conversation state using a state machine, adjusts the robot's emotional responses accordingly, and issues commands for body language and movement as needed.

To minimize hallucinations and adhere to Gricean Maxims, MAESTRO can seek answers from reliable online sources if the robot lacks information. If an answer cannot be found, the default approach is for the robot to admit lack of knowledge, avoiding potential user trust issues. MAESTRO outputs prompts in a specified format that developers can modify, ensuring that the robot's facial expressions and body language align with the generated emotional tone.

Large Language Module (LLM). This could have been a part of the MAESTRO module. However, as many robots have rather modest computing capabilities, it is expected that more often than not, such models will be run on an external computer and called through an API.

This module is responsible for converting the high-level prompts generated by MAESTRO into a more natural sounding and more diverse response, so the robot can sound more human.

Speech Synthesizer. This module was kept separate for the same reason as above. If more powerful speech synthesis models such as Tortoise-tts-v2 are used, they might not run in modest computing environments.

However, any model can be used; and ROOTED has espeak-ng as its default speech synthesis module, as it is extremely lightweight. Such system, however, requires hard-coded prosody characteristics for the desired emotions.

Listening Module. This is responsible for listening to what users say. Default behavior for ROOTED is to always perform Voice Activity Detection (VAD) using Python vad library and, if human speech is detected, perform Automatic Speech Recognition (ASR) using Google Speech Recognition. The resulting text from ASR is sent to MAESTRO, who will then decide if the robot needs to respond or not.

Current module stores audio from the interactions that are deemed to be a conversation with the robot. But, as this might pose some privacy problems, such behavior can be easily changed.

Vision Module. The is responsible for providing an interface between the cameras of the robot and all the computer vision algorithm and models present in the system. As ROOTED considers that emotion estimation and scene understanding are important to provide a deeper understanding of human communication, such models can be readily adopted in the framework. When keeping a user profile is important, the robot can readily use data from previous interactions. Python Library face-recognition is used for such purpose. Algorithms and models can be added or removed according to each particular system need.

Robot Memory. For the memory of the robot, a simple collection of SQLite3 databases are used, whose access is regulated by a Memory Access Controller node, which receives queries and executes them in a FIFO manner. A more sophisticated system can be used, if it is necessary to have multiple concomitant access to the databases. If heightened security is required, the SQLite Encryption Extension (SEE) can be deployed to protect stored data.

What databases are part of the Robot Memory depends on each application, but ROOTED considers that a history of user conversations and basic user profile are maintained and, thus, those databases are already included. A folder containing the user faces is also kept for the identity recognition: this feature can be removed if deemed not necessary.

Other Sensors. The is responsible for providing a general interface with sensors other than cameras or microphones: sensors like sonars, temperature, moisture, pH and Conductivity sensors. This module is highly customizable as it will vary widely across different applications.

However, ROOTED provides a common service that allows other service to request sensor readings by sending a request with the sensor number. It also provides a Measurement Scheduler to record sensor measurements from time to time. As taking such measurements might require the robot to go to a specific location, it changes the robot state and can send goal poses to the Movement Module.

Movement Module. This is responsible for moving the robot as needed. In the ROOTED framework, it is responsible for both repositioning the robot in its operation environment and for performing the body gestures. This module, then, is responsible for planning and controlling robot movements and obstacle detection and avoidance. As different robots, specially research prototypes, will have different navigation control methods, ROOTED provides only services for sending high-level body gesture commands and sending move goal poses action commands to the robot. It also interfaces directly with the Vision module and the Other Sensors modules to better navigate the environment.

As the current ROOTED implementation focuses on the Dialogue side and just considers that dialogue might drive a robot to move, it was not the focus of development. Currently, it only presents the Social Plantroid end-to-end vision-based neural-network-based navigation system; which requires no mapping, localization or planning from the model. Therefor, these components are not currently available in ROOTED, but one could use the Navigation 2 framework for ROS2, which provides a complete and robust framework for robot navigation together with ROOTED.

Facial Expression. This module is responsible for controlling the facial expressions of the robot. It was created mostly for robots that express their emotions through screens, lights and sounds, as they do not require any parts to move. However, even for robots that have mechanical facial expressions, if it is not possible that changing the expression may cause harm to users or the environment, it is appropriate to keep this module separated from the Movement Module.

As different robot models will have different means of displaying emotions, this module is responsible for receiving high-level emotion commands from MAE-STRO and converting them into lower-level commands, such as changing what images are being displayed on the screen, changing the color and/or brightness of the LEDs of the robot, making a happy/sad noise *etc.*

5   Use Case - Social Plantroid Robot

The Social Plantroid robot extends the social functionality of earlier Plantroid models by turning plant care into a more interactive, pet-like experience. Unlike previous models that only automated plant movement, Social Plantroid maintains human involvement in plant care, aiming to enhance mental well-being of the users by facilitating them to take pride in their plant care activities. The robot monitors soil quality and communicates the needs of the plant, incorporating voice and facial expressions to improve interaction: these features were absent in earlier models.

The idea of developing ROOTED came while working on the notification system for Plantroid, as we were unable to find any existing ROS2 frameworks for quickly developing a Dialogue System for the robot. The architecture implemented for Plantroid is as shown above in Fig. 2.

Not all components are included in the Plantroid version, and some elements may not be relevant for other robots: *e.g.*, the sunlight detection algorithm is not useful for a cashier robot. This section discusses the adaptations needed in the framework (Fig. 2) for the present use case.

5.1   Plantroid's MAESTRO

Plantroid's MAESTRO module is designed to manage simple dialogues focused on two main goals: notifying users of plant care issues and instructing them on how to resolve these problems. It uses a rule-based Python NLTK chatbot to analyze user input and emotional state from voice, facial expressions, and speech content to generate prompts for the Large Language Model (LLM).

The emotional state is determined by a majority rule among the three modalities, with speech content taking precedence in case of discrepancies. MAESTRO employs three strategies for setting the robot's emotional state: S1) mirroring the user's emotion, S2) using positive emotions if the user is negative, or S3) reflecting the plant's condition (happy if all is well, sad or tired if there are issues).

The robot's dialogue system operates on a mixed initiative basis. It does not initiate conversations unless a soil problem is detected, in which case it informs and guides the user based on pre-written instructions. If the robot is busy navigating, it politely defers communication until it can focus on the user. Moreover, as the robot can talk about any topic when there are no problems to be reported, it showcases a mix of both open-domain dialogue (ODD) and task-oriented dialogue (TOD) behaviors.

When idle and addressed by a user, Plantroid engages in conversation, with the NLTK module categorizing the query to determine if it pertains to the plant, general information, or another topic. For soil-related questions, it provides information based on the latest analysis. For general questions, it searches online, defaulting to admitting a lack of knowledge if no information is found. If the query is unrelated to the plant, the LLM handles the response, although the impact of this approach on user trust is still under evaluation.

5.2 Other Sensors Module

Unlike most social robots, Plantroid also functions as an agrobot, using soil and light sensors to monitor the plant's environment and needs. This dual role gives the robot an internal drive and purpose, thereby simulating a living being with biological needs. The Other Sensors Module moves the robot into sunlight when the plant needs light and into the shade when it is too hot or the plant has had enough sun. It measures soil NPK content, pH, and conductivity every six hours, soil moisture every hour and temperature every 5 min. Measurements are stored by the Memory module, which allows to visualize the data over time. Sensors and a moisture plot are visible in Fig. 3.

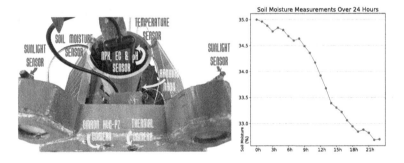

Fig. 3. Left. Social Plantroid's sensors and cameras; Right. Example of synthetic soil moisture percentage measurements along a day.

If measurements fall outside healthy ranges, MAESTRO is alerted, and the robot informs the next human it encounters. All data is stored in the Robot Memory module, aiding in predicting watering and fertilization needs. Also, a Sonar Bumper can be installed to assist with navigation, thereby removing any blind spots in the camera's field of view.

5.3 LLM

The Social Plantroid initially used the Dolly 2 model [9], an open-source GPT-J model fine-tuned for general instruction following and conversation. Due to its large size and GPU requirements, Dolly 2 was run on an external server. It performed well in plant care knowledge, provided concise and varied responses, but occasionally hallucinated despite grounding from internet, sensor data, memory, and scene understanding.

Currently, the robot uses the Llama3 model [1] with 8 billion parameters, offering better performance than Dolly 2. Though Llama3 can in principle be run on the Raspberry Pi 4B, the inference time is too long, so it also operates on a remote server. Switching between LLMs is straightforward, involving a simple API call change, though prompt adjustments by MAESTRO may be needed due to model-specific preferences.

5.4   Vision Module and Emotion Framework

The Vision Module of the Social Plantroid robot relies on an OMRON HVC-P2 B5T-007001-010 camera for human detection, face emotion estimation, and characteristics estimation. This camera detects human bodies, faces, hands, gaze direction, gender, age, and facial emotions, providing scores for five emotions (neutral, happiness, surprise, anger and sadness), which is the emotion framework used for Plantroid. These operations are external to the robot's Raspberry Pi 4B and are requested as needed.

Scene understanding is offloaded to a remote server to conserve local processing power for navigation. Sunlight and shadow detection is handled locally using a Gabor-kernel filter-based algorithm, with a thermal camera assisting in distinguishing hot spots from false positives caused by floor color variations. Both cameras are shown in Fig. 3.

5.5   Listening, Movement, Speech Synthesizer and Robot Memory Modules

The Listening, Speech Synthesizer, and Robot Memory modules of the Social Plantroid robot follow ROOTED standard architecture. Using a common USB microphone, Plantroid must rotate until it visually detects a human due to its inability to locate the interlocutor by sound. As a research platform, it only stores dialogue exchanges for data collection but has the potential to recognize faces and names through communication with the vision and MAESTRO modules, though this feature is currently unused.

The Movement Module is unique, designed to follow sunlight rather than navigate to specific locations, using a VGG-16-based visual navigation system [11]. Plantroid, thus, lacks a Planner component and performs simple body gestures: nodding for agreement, slight rotations for disagreement, and a surprised jolt of its head. More complex gestures could be developed, but further research is needed to ensure they are understood by users, given Plantroid's non-humanoid form. Examples of Social Plantroid's movements can be seen in Fig. 4.

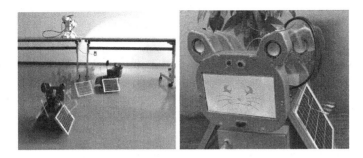

Fig. 4. Left. Social Plantroid avoids obstacle while seeking light. Right. Social Plantroid rotates to find its interlocutor.

5.6 Facial Expressions

The Plantroid's facial expression system uses a screen to display a modular cat-like face, managed by a Python Kivy graphic interface. This allows independent manipulation of the eyes, mouth, and an two emotion markers, chosen to emphasize the cartoonish face's emotional state. There are 13 pre-defined facial expressions, including fear, anger, joy, and others. However, the system can generate hundreds of combinations by varying individual face components, as shown in Fig. 5.

Fig. 5. The many faces of Social Plantroid.

5.7 Demonstration

A brief demonstration of the conversational capabilities provided by ROOTED (using Dolly 2) can be seen in https://mizuuchi.lab.tuat.ac.jp/~antonio/CommVideo.mp4.

One can see that the robot turns to face the interlocutor, and when it says yes it moves its head slightly. It also showcases the mirror emotion conversational strategy and the robot stands up for itself when abusive language is used (an approach that might not be the best, but was adopted in the video to show the emotion engine's capabilities). Also, it features information searching online and a description of the environment where the robot is, as well as readings from its sensors.

6   Conclusions and Future Work

The development of Dialogue Systems in robotics necessitates an adaptable and comprehensive framework to address the multifaceted challenges posed by diverse environments and user needs; and distinct robotic platforms. ROOTED (ROS2 Open-source Toolkit for Efficient Dialogue) represents, thus, a significant step towards creating such a framework, integrating traditional rule-based methods, web search, and Large Language Models to enhance dialogue management while adhering to Gricean Maxims. ROOTED's incorporation of non-verbal communication analysis and generation further enriches interaction quality, as demonstrated in the experiment with the Social Plantroid Robot.

Future work will focus on performing longer validation experiments with human participants to investigate whether they trust a robot that admits not knowing a response more than the robot that hallucinates. Also, it is necessary to investigate which multi-modal emotion estimation approach works better for human-robot interaction, Additionally, it is also necessary to investigate when which one of the proposed robot motion selection strategies work better for a robot that is entrusted with important tasks (such as Plantroid).

Finally, it is necessary to provide better metrics for validating hallucination reduction and higher adherence to the Gricean Maxims, with a model trained for such evaluation, like the analysis performed in [14].

Acknowledgements. AGCG was supported by the Doctoral Program for World-leading Innovative & Smart Education of Tokyo university of Agriculture and Technology. BI was supported by the National Science Center, Poland, under the OPUS call in the Weave programme under the project number K/NCN/000142.

References

1. Abhimanyu, D., et al.: The llama 3 herd of models (2024)
2. Addlesee, A.: Grounding LLMs to in-prompt instructions: reducing hallucinations caused by static pre-training knowledge. In: Proceedings of Safety4ConvAI, pp. 1–7. ELRA and ICCL, Torino, Italia (2024)
3. Ayyamperumal, S.G., Ge, L.: Current state of LLM risks and AI guardrails (2024)
4. Baker, A.L., Phillips, E.K., Ullman, D., Keebler, J.R.: Toward an understanding of trust repair in human-robot interaction: current research and future directions. ACM Trans. Interact. Intell. Syst. (TiiS) **8**(4), 1–30 (2018)
5. Bernsen, N.O., Dybkjær, H., Dybkjær, L.: Cooperativity in human-machine and human-human spoken dialogue. Discourse Process. **21**(2), 213–236 (1996)
6. Bono, A., Brameld, K., D'Alfonso, L., Fedele, G.: Open access NAO (OAN): a ROS2-based software framework for HRI applications with the NAO robot (2024)
7. Brown, K.: Concise Encyclopedia of Pragmatics. Elsevier (2009)
8. Chen, W., et al.: From yes-men to truth-tellers: addressing sycophancy in large language models with pinpoint tuning. In: Forty-First International Conference on Machine Learning (2024)

9. Conover, M., et al.: Free dolly: introducing the world's first truly open instruction-tuned LLM. Databricks Blog (2023). https://www.databricks.com/blog/2023/04/12/dolly-first-open-commercially-viable-instruction-tuned-llm. Accessed 31 May 2023
10. Ekman, P.: Facial expressions of emotion: new findings, new questions (1992)
11. Gonzalez, A.G.C., Venture, G., Mizuuchi, I.: VGG-16 neural network-based visual artificial potential field for autonomous navigation of ground robots. In: International Conference on Intelligent Autonomous Systems, pp. 155–168. Springer (2023)
12. Kawakami, A., et al.: Potpet: pet-like flowerpot robot. In: Proceedings of the Fifth International Conference on Tangible, Embedded, and Embodied Interaction, TEI 2011, pp. 263–264. Association for Computing Machinery, New York (2010). https://doi.org/10.1145/1935701.1935755
13. Li, J., et al.: Banishing LLM hallucinations requires rethinking generalization (2024)
14. Miehling, E., Nagireddy, M., Sattigeri, P., Daly, E.M., Piorkowski, D., Richards, J.T.: Language models in dialogue: conversational maxims for human-AI interactions (2024)
15. Mok, J., et al.: LLM-based frameworks for API argument filling in task-oriented conversational systems (2024)
16. Mondal, A., Gokhale, S.S.: Mining emotions on Plutchik's wheel. In: 2020 Seventh International Conference on Social Networks Analysis, Management and Security (SNAMS), pp. 1–6. IEEE (2020)
17. Ni, J., Young, T., Pandelea, V., Xue, F., Cambria, E.: Recent advances in deep learning based dialogue systems: a systematic survey. Artif. Intell. Rev. **56**(4), 3055–3155 (2023)
18. Park, D., et al.: Multiprageval: multilingual pragmatic evaluation of large language models (2024)
19. Radford, A., et al.: Improving language understanding by generative pre-training. OpenAI (2018)
20. Rein, D., et al.: GPQA: a graduate-level google-proof Q&A benchmark (2023)
21. Saito, K., Wachi, A., Wataoka, K., Akimoto, Y.: Verbosity bias in preference labeling by large language models. arXiv preprint arXiv:2310.10076 (2023)
22. Sawaki, F., Yasu, K., Inami, M.: Flona: development of an interface that implements lifelike behaviors to a plant. In: International Conference on Advances in Computer Entertainment Technology, pp. 557–560. Springer (2012)
23. Sekulić, I., et al.: Reliable LLM-based user simulator for task-oriented dialogue systems (2024)
24. Stocker, J., et al.: Towards adaptive robotic green plants. In: Conference Towards Autonomous Robotic Systems, pp. 422–423. Springer (2011)
25. Vázquez, A., et al.: Dialogue management and language generation for a robust conversational virtual coach: validation and user study. Sensors **23**(3) (2023). https://doi.org/10.3390/s23031423
26. Yang, D., Chen, F., Fang, H.: Behavior alignment: a new perspective of evaluating LLM-based conversational recommendation systems. In: Proceedings of the 47th International ACM SIGIR Conference on Research and Development in Information Retrieval, pp. 2286–2290. Association for Computing Machinery, New York (2024). https://doi.org/10.1145/3626772.3657924
27. Yuasa, M., Mizuuchi, I.: A control method for a swarm of plant pot robots that uses artificial potential fields for effective utilization of sunlight. J. Robot. Mechatron. **26**(4), 505–512 (2014)

28. Yuasa, M., Nishiki, S., Mizuuchi, I.: 1a1-q05 自律移動可能な果樹栽培型 plantroid の開発 (農業用ロボット・メカトロニクス). In: ロボティクス・メカトロニクス講演会講演概要集 2013. pp. _1A1–Q05_1. 一般社団法人 日本機械学会 (2013)

29. Zheng, Z., et al.: Response length perception and sequence scheduling: an LLM-empowered LLM inference pipeline. In: Oh, A., et al. (eds.) Advances in Neural Information Processing Systems, vol. 36, pp. 65517–65530. Curran Associates, Inc. (2023)

Educational-Psychological Dialogue Robot Based on Multi-agent Collaboration

Shiwen Ni and Min Yang[✉]

Shenzhen Institute of Advanced Technology, Chinese Academy of Sciences,
Shenzhen, China
{sw.ni,min.yang}@siat.ac.cn

Abstract. Intelligent dialogue systems are increasingly used in modern education and psychological counseling fields, but most existing systems are limited to a single domain, cannot deal with both educational and psychological issues, and often lack accuracy and professionalism when dealing with complex issues. To address these problems, this paper proposes an intelligent dialog system that combines educational and psychological counseling functions. The system consists of multiple AI agent, including security detection agent, intent identification agent, educational LLM agent, and psychological LLM agent, which work in concert to ensure the provision of accurate educational knowledge Q&A and psychological support services. Specifically, the system recognizes user-input intentions through an intention classification model and invokes a retrieval-enhanced educational grand model and a psychological grand model fine-tuned with psychological data in order to provide professional educational advice and psychological support.

Keywords: Large language model · Multi-agent ·
Educational-Psychological dialogue · Intent identification

1 Introduction

In the field of modern education and psychological counseling, the application of intelligent dialog systems is becoming more and more widespread. Educational intelligent dialog systems can assist students in answering questions, providing learning support and improving learning efficiency. Psychological counseling intelligent dialog systems, on the other hand, can provide users with emotional support and help them relieve psychological pressure [1]. However, most of the existing intelligent dialog systems are limited to a single domain and cannot handle both educational and psychological issues [2–4]. In addition, these systems often lack accuracy and professionalism when dealing with complex issues.

Currently, large-scale pre-trained model [5,6] techniques have made significant progress in semantic understanding and text generation, and are widely used in various natural language processing tasks. These models can effectively understand the context, but still suffer from insufficient answer accuracy and expertise

H. Li et al. (Eds.): ICSR + InnoBiz 2024, LNAI 15170, pp. 119–125, 2025.
https://doi.org/10.1007/978-981-96-1151-5_12

when used alone. To address these problems, retrieval enhancement techniques have been introduced to significantly improve the quality and richness of the model's answers by incorporating external knowledge bases (e.g., Baidu Encyclopedia, Wikipedia). However, these techniques are still insufficiently applied in existing intelligent dialog systems, especially in the combined application in the fields of education and psychological counseling, for which there is no mature solution yet.

In the field of education, students not only need answers to subject knowledge in the learning process, but also may face psychological pressure and emotional distress, in which case a single educational dialog system cannot provide comprehensive help. Similarly, in the field of psychological counseling, users may also need guidance and advice on education while seeking emotional support, and existing psychological dialog systems are not capable of handling such issues. Based on the above background, we propose an intelligent dialog bot that combines educational and psychological counseling functions. It recognizes user-inputted intent through an intent classification model, and invokes an educational grand model based on retrieval enhancement and a psychological grand model fine-tuned with psychological data, respectively, so as to provide professional educational counseling and psychological support. The proposed intelligent dialog bot not only solves the deficiencies in the prior art, but also improves the user experience and provides more comprehensive and accurate services.

2   Methodology

In this paper, we propose an intelligent dialogue system that combines educational and psychological LLMs, and the system consists of multiple AI agents together. As shown in Fig. 1, the user's input is first filtered by a security detection agent, and then the intent of the user input is identified by an intent identification agent, and the different intents are fed to the corresponding LLM agents for processing, respectively, and the system is inter-systemmed through the four different agents in order to provide accurate educational knowledge Q&A and psychological support services.

Security Detection Agent: We use a safety model to determine the safety of input content and filter out unsafe inputs such as insults discrimination, illegal crimes, political sensitivity, violent tendencies, etc. to ensure that the model does not respond to unsafe questions. The safety model is a binary classification model that uses bert-base-chinese [7] as a base model and then fine-tuned using 40k normal questions as positive examples and 40k risky questions as negative examples to ultimately implement a safety classification model. The model uses bert-base-chinese as a base model, which ensures a reliable response time. It also uses 40k positive and negative examples as a dataset to ensure the accuracy of the model. The security model is in the first loop in this system, and all inputs are judged by the security model first, and only those that meet the requirements are allowed to go to the later links.

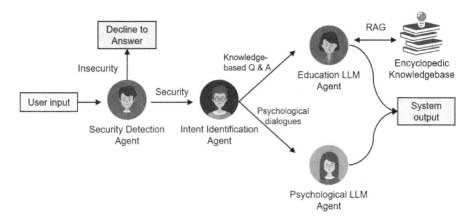

Fig. 1. A figure caption is always placed below the illustration. Please note that short captions are centered, while long ones are justified by the macro package automatically.

Intent Identification Agent: This system designs a BERT-based [7] binary classification model for accurately recognizing the input content of student users and determining whether it should be processed by the psychological or educational LLM. To achieve this goal, a large amount of data including 20,000 educational questions and 700,000 psychological questions were collected as positive and negative examples, respectively. Such a large dataset ensures that the model can cover a wide range of problem types and diverse user needs.

To address the sample imbalance problem, we adopt Focal Loss as the loss function of the classification model, which effectively reduces the impact of simple samples on the total loss by introducing a dynamically adjusted weighting mechanism. This mechanism allows the model to focus on those difficult samples during training, which significantly improves the classification performance in the case of category imbalance. This feature of Focal Loss ensures that the model maintains high accuracy when dealing with the problem of a small number of education classes. In terms of model selection, we choose bert-base-chinese as the base model. Based on the bert-base-chinese model, we added a linear layer to it for further training, and finally constructed an efficient educational-psychological binary classification model.

Educational LLM Agent: We developed a retrieval-enhanced [8] educational large language model. First, the entries in Baidu Encyclopedia are converted into vectors in advance using bge-large-zh [9] as the embedding model, and these vectors are imported into the faiss vector database, for which an efficient HNSW (Hierarchical Navigable Small World) indexing structure is built. This process ensures efficient storage and fast retrieval of data. When a user enters a question, the system uses the embedding model to transform the question into a vector representation, and then searches the educational vector database to quickly find the 100 most relevant data to the user's question. These initially filtered data are able to cover multiple aspects of the user's question, providing a wide range of contextual information. To further improve the accuracy and relevance of the answers, we use bge-reranker-large as a rerank model to reorder these 100 pieces of data at a finer granularity. the rerank model selects the 3 most useful pieces of data by deeply analyzing the content of each piece of data and how well it matches the user's question. These data will be used as the optimal context of the question and added to the prompt (prompt), which greatly improves the quality and accuracy of the answers generated by the large model.

In addition, our educational large language model is based on the fine-tuning of the Qwen1.5-7B model [10] on the COIG-CQIA [11] dataset, which is specifically optimized to fit the needs of the Chinese education domain. In summary, by transforming the massive data of Baidu Encyclopedia into an educational vector database and combining HNSW indexing, embedding model, rerank model, and fine-tuned Qwen1.5-7B LLM, we constructed an efficient and accurate retrieval-enhanced educational large model. This model not only responds quickly to user-input questions, but also provides high-quality, detailed and relevant answers, which greatly improves the user experience and learning effect.

Psychological LLM Agent: In order to build a powerful psychological counseling grand model, we manually combined GPT-4 [12] to generate a large amount of Chinese and English multi-round psychological conversation data. These data cover a wide range of counseling scenarios and issues, enabling the model to provide effective psychological support in multiple contexts. We used these generated data to fine-tune the base model to enhance its performance in psychological counseling.

The base model we chose is Qwen1.5-7B-chat its strong language comprehension and generation capabilities, and it performs particularly well in dialog systems. Through the fine-tuning technique, we further optimize the model's ability to handle counseling conversations while retaining its original advantages. Fine-tuning is able to improve the model's performance in specific domains without significantly increasing the computational overhead, making it more suitable for dealing with counseling-type problems. As a result of this fine-tuning process, the model was significantly improved in terms of its counseling capabilities. Specifically, the model is able to understand the user's psychological needs more accurately, provide more attentive and effective suggestions, and maintain coherence and consistency across multiple rounds of dialog. This enables the model to better support users in practical applications and provide high-quality psychological counseling services.

3   Experiment

We validated the effectiveness of our educational LLM agent using the E-EVAL [13] benchmark. E-EVAL is the first comprehensive assessment benchmark customized for K-12 education in China. E-EVAL comprises 4,351 multiple-choice questions spanning primary, middle, and high school levels, covering a diverse array of subjects. In our comparison, we evaluated the performance of ChatGLM3-6B [14], Qwen1.5-7B [10], GPT-4 [12], and our own Educational

Table 1. Experimental results on E-Eval primary school subjects.

Model	Chinese	Mathematics	English	Science	Ethics
ChatGLM3-6B	56.2	39.2	62.7	71.9	83.9
Qwen1.5-7B	73.9	72.5	80.8	78.0	93.1
GPT-4	70.8	69.6	92.5	85.3	94.2
Educational LLM Agent (our)	75.3	73.2	80.9	80.4	94.9

LLM Agent. Initially, we present the results from experiments on primary subjects in Table 1. The results indicate that our Educational LLM agent performs exceptionally well, surpassing both Qwen1.5-7B and ChatGLM3-6B. Notably, in subjects such as Chinese and Ethics, our agent even outperformed GPT-4.

Table 2. Experimental results on E-Eval middle school subjects.

Model	Chinese	Math	English	Physics	Chemistry	Biology	Politics	History	Geography
ChatGLM3-6B	52.0	37.2	70.2	69.7	67.5	72.1	82.7	81.1	70.1
Qwen1.5-7B	68.2	68.6	89.1	68.4	80.4	80.4	90.2	89.7	90.0
GPT4	54.7	59.8	93.4	76.3	67.5	87.5	83.9	88.9	81.9
Our	70.4	68.9	89.3	69.4	81.2	83.1	92.2	94.5	93.7

The results of the experiment for middle school subjects are shown in Table 2. The experimental results show that our Educational LLM agent outperforms the GPT-4 in the English subject and performs optimally in all other subjects. In language subjects our intelligences achieved an accuracy rate of 70.4%, far exceeding the 54.7% of the GPT-4. Improvements were evident in politics, history, and geography, but less so in math, physics, and chemistry, indicating that the RAG was more effective in improving liberal arts skills.

The results of the experiment for high school subjects are shown in Table 3. The overall performance of LLMs in high school subjects was somewhat lower than in middle school because high school is more difficult. Similarly except for English subject where our educational proxy is below GPT-4, we have the best performance in all subjects. Our method continues to perform very brightly in language and literature, for example, with an accuracy rate of 67.5% in language and a staggering 83.5% in history.

It should be noted that we are a whole multi-agent collaborative system, not a single LLM, so our system can have better security, as well as the ability to call different agents to meet the educational knowledge quiz and professional counseling.

Table 3. Experimental results on E-Eval high school subjects.

Model	Chinese	Mathematics	English	Physics	Chemistry	Biology	Politics	History	Geography
ChatGLM3-6B	40.5	33.8	64.7	52.1	51.1	56.1	70.1	68.5	57.0
Qwen1.5-7B	62.9	43.8	80.0	58.9	71.0	73.0	80.6	79.7	77.6
GPT4	39.3	42.6	88.5	61.5	59.0	63.8	65.5	78.2	78.8
Our	67.5	44.8	81.1	62.2	72.1	77.4	82.3	83.5	80.7

4   Conclusion

In this study, we developed an educational-counseling dialog robot based on multi-agent collaboration, which breaks through the limitations of existing single-domain intelligent dialog systems by combining educational and counseling functions. Our experimental results on the E-EVAL benchmark test show that our educational LLM agent outperforms existing models in several subjects, including Qwen1.5-7B and ChatGLM3-6B, and even exceeds GPT-4 in subjects such as Chinese and ethics. Our system demonstrated a high degree of safety, accuracy, and professionalism, validating the effectiveness of multi-intelligence collaboration in providing comprehensive educational and counseling services.

Acknowledgement. This work was supported by China Postdoctoral Science Foundation (2024M753398), Postdoctoral Fellowship Program of CPSF (GZC20232873), GuangDong Basic and Applied Basic Research Foundation (2023A1515110718 and 2024A1515012003).

References

1. Zhang, C., et al.: CPsycoun: a report-based multi-turn dialogue reconstruction and evaluation framework for Chinese psychological counseling. arXiv preprint arXiv:2405.16433 (2024)
2. Dan, Y., et al.: Educhat: a large-scale language model-based chatbot system for intelligent education. arXiv preprint arXiv:2308.02773 (2023)
3. Dinh, H., Tran, T.K.: Educhat: an AI-based chatbot for university-related information using a hybrid approach. Appl. Sci. **13**(22), 12446 (2023)
4. Oster, N., Henriksen, D., Mishra, P.: Chatgpt for teachers: insights from online discussions. TechTrends, pp. 1–7 (2024)
5. Vaswani, A., et al.: Attention is all you need. In: Advances in Neural Information Processing Systems, vol. 30 (2017)
6. Chu, Z., et al.: History, development, and principles of large language models-an introductory survey. arXiv preprint arXiv:2402.06853 (2024)
7. Devlin, J., Chang, M.W., Lee, K., Toutanova, K.: BERT: pre-training of deep bidirectional transformers for language understanding. arXiv:1810.04805 (2018)
8. Huang, Y., Huang, J.: A survey on retrieval-augmented text generation for large language models. arXiv preprint arXiv:2404.10981 (2024)
9. Xiao, S., Liu, Z., Zhang, P., Muennighof, N.: C-pack: packaged resources to advance general Chinese embedding. arXiv preprint arXiv:2309.07597 (2023)

10. Bai, J., et al.: Qwen technical report. arXiv preprint arXiv:2309.16609 (2023)
11. Bai, Y., et al.: Coig-cqia: quality is all you need for Chinese instruction fine-tuning. arXiv preprint arXiv:2403.18058 (2024)
12. Brown, T., et al.: Language models are few-shot learners. Adv. Neural. Inf. Process. Syst. **33**, 1877–1901 (2020)
13. Hou, J., et al.: E-eval: a comprehensive Chinese k-12 education evaluation benchmark for large language models. arXiv preprint arXiv:2401.15927 (2024)
14. GLM, Team, et al.: ChatGLM: a family of large language models from GLM-130b to GLM-4 all tools. arXiv preprint arXiv:2406.12793 (2024)

Human-Robot Pose Tracking Based on CNN with Color and Geometry Aggregation

Yue Xu[1] , Yinlong Zhang[1,2,3,4,5]([✉]) , Shuai Liu[3,4,5]([✉]) ,
Yuanhao Liu[3,4,5] , Wei Liang[3,4,5] , and Hongsheng He[6]

[1] Shenyang University of Technology, Shenyang 110020, China
xuyue@sia.cn
[2] Guangzhou Institute of Industrial Intelligence, Guangzhou 511458, China
[3] State Key Laboratory of Robotics, Shenyang Institute of Automation, Chinese
Academy of Sciences, Shenyang 110016, China
{zhangyinlong,liushuai,liuyuanhao,weiliang}@sia.cn
[4] Key Laboratory of Networked Control Systems, Chinese Academy of Sciences,
Shenyang 110016, China
[5] University of Chinese Academy of Sciences, Beijing 100049, China
[6] Department of Computer Science, The University of Alabama,
Tuscaloosa,
AL 35487, USA
hongsheng.he@ua.edu

Abstract. Accurately tracking the robotic arm and human joints is crucial to ensure safety during human-robot interaction. However, traditional pose tracking methods often exhibit insufficient performance and
robustness in complex environments. The variations in the robotic arm's
environment and posture make it challenging for traditional methods
to accurately capture the positions and posture of its joints. Specifically, when addressing challenges such as high similarity, occlusion, background complexity, and joint recognition failures, they often struggle
to provide reliable and accurate results. To address these challenges,
this paper proposes a human-robot pose tracking algorithm based on a
new convolutional neural network model. To enhance detection accuracy,
an improved color detection module is introduced to resolve joint mis-
classification. A geometric perception module is designed to accurately
locate joints even under occlusion. Additionally, innovative iEMA and
DBB modules are incorporated. The iEMA module employs edge detection technology to dynamically adjust thresholds for correct matching
by improving the edge matching process. The DBB module refines the
boundary box parameters for precise localization by introducing adaptive
bounding box updates in real-time. This algorithm also integrates human
pose recognition, enabling real-time pose recognition, thereby facilitating
more intelligent and natural human-robot interaction. The algorithm has
been rigorously evaluated on a custom-designed robotic arm platform.
Experimental results validate the algorithm's effectiveness and feasibility.

H. Li et al. (Eds.): ICSR + InnoBiz 2024, LNAI 15170, pp. 126–135, 2025.
https://doi.org/10.1007/978-981-96-1151-5_13

Keywords: Robotic Arm · Social Robots · Color Detection ·
Geometry Perception · Joint Tracking · Human-Robot Interaction

1   Introduction

Against the backdrop of accelerating digital transformation, social robotics is reshaping the manufacturing industry, facilitating a deeper integration of digital technologies and practical operations. Robotic arms, known for their precise motion control and high programmability, find extensive applications in tasks such as assembly, picking, placing, and packaging. Typically, robotic arms execute predefined programs to perform tasks autonomously and can interact accurately with humans, demonstrating precise grasping capabilities when handling physical objects, such as delivering items. In modern industrial environments, especially in scenarios where humans and machines coexist, the precise operation of robotic arms is essential for improving production efficiency and ensuring worker safety [1].

With the widespread application of robotic arms in industrial and service sectors, the safety issues of human-robot interaction have become increasingly prominent [2]. For instance, in industrial settings, inaccurate detection of the arm joint positions of both the robot and the operator may lead to misjudgments and collisions, particularly critical in environments requiring precise and close collaboration such as assembly lines or operating rooms. Ensuring the safe coexistence of robots and humans in complex dynamic environments necessitates precise tracking of the positions and postures of robotic arms and human joints [3]. This capability not only helps prevent potential collisions and accidents but also enhances the efficiency and accuracy of collaborative tasks [4].

To enhance accuracy and address safety concerns in human-robot collaboration, researchers have devoted significant efforts to the detection and localization of joints in both robotic arms and humans [5,6]. Hu et al. [7] proposed a lightweight human joint detection algorithm based on multi-source information fusion, achieving precise human pose detection by integrating data from various sources. Li et al. [8] developed a volleyball action pose recognition method based on joint sequences. Szabó et al. [9] introduced a method for robotic arm detection using coarse-grained and fine-grained visual feature extraction. Mišeikis et al. [10] proposed a two-stage transfer learning method for robotic arm detection and 3D joint position estimation.

Although these methods have achieved impressive performance in detecting human and robotic arm joints, they continue to encounter substantial challenges in addressing critical issues. Specifically, they encounter problems with high joint similarity, leading to misdetection and confusion, which reduces detection accuracy. Additionally, during the rotation or rapid movement of the robotic arm, joint occlusion causes missed detections, impacting reliability. Furthermore, in real-time applications, it is difficult to balance high precision with fast detection, particularly when processing high-resolution images or complex scenes, which affects the system's real-time performance and responsiveness.

To tackle the challenges in joint detection of industrial robotic arms, we design a novel post tracking algorithm based on a new convolutional neural network model, aiming at addressing safety concerns in human-machine collaboration, as shown in Fig. 1. Specifically, by integrating color detection and geometric perception modules, we mitigate issues arising from high similarity between joints, leading to false detections, and occlusions during robotic arm movements, causing missed detections. Additionally, we introduce the Detect_DBB module to optimize feature extraction and enhance joint feature information, thereby improving detection accuracy. By integrating human pose recognition functionalities, we achieve the detection and tracking of human and robotic arm joints during human-machine interaction, thereby enhancing workplace safety and efficiency.

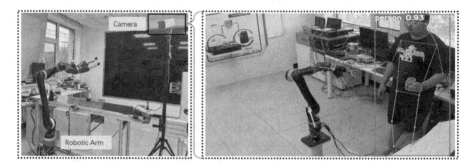

Fig. 1. Illustration on robotic arm and human pose tracking. Different colored bands are affixed to each joint of the robotic arm to ensure and accelerate the pose tracking.

The contributions of this paper can be summarized as follows:

1. We develop an algorithm that tracks the robotic arm pose with the aggregation of color and geometric cues.
2. A color detection module is designed to distinguish color features, addressing false detections and omissions.
3. A geometric perception module is used to analyze the geometric relationships and spatial structures between joints, adding constraints to address missed detections caused by occlusions between joints during robotic arm movements.
4. We design a Detect_DBB module to optimize feature extraction and enhance detection efficiency through multi-level feature fusion.

2 Method

2.1 Network Structure

In the process of industrial robotic arm joint detection, the similarity in size and shape of joints under different postures and occlusion conditions increases the complexity and difficulty of detection. Traditional deep learning models typically rely on fixed-structure convolution operations during feature extraction. Although these operations can effectively capture local information, they have limitations in addressing the issue of joint similarity. To address this problem, this paper proposes a novel robotic arm pose tracking algorithm based on a new convolutional neural network model. This algorithm integrates color detection, geometric perception modules, and the Detect_DBB module to achieve precise detection of robotic arm joints. The algorithm consists of three parts: feature extraction, feature fusion, and prediction output, as shown in Fig. 2.

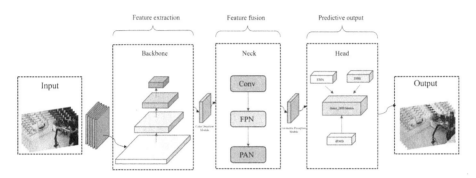

Fig. 2. Human-Robot Pose Tracking Deep-learning Network. The network framework consists of three components: feature extraction, feature fusion, and prediction output. It incorporates color and geometric perception modules, as well as the Detect_DBB module, to enhance feature extraction and acquire key point information.

Firstly, the feature extraction part introduces a color detection module, which utilizes color information to effectively distinguish similar joints, thereby solving the problem of joint similarity and improving the accuracy of initial detection. Secondly, the feature fusion part employs a geometric perception module to add geometric constraints and spatial information to the detection process. This approach addresses the issue of missed detections during the rotation of the robotic arm and enhances the perception of the spatial relationships between joints.

Lastly, to further improve the accuracy and efficiency of joint detection, the prediction output part of our algorithm integrates the Detect_DBB module. This module uses the iEMA [11,12] and DBB [13] modules to fully exploit and utilize the correlation between channels in the feature maps, enhancing the model's ability to perceive multi-scale targets. The network architecture of the Detect_DBB module is shown in Fig. 3. The iEMA module, as shown in Fig. 4, enhancing feature representation during the intermediate stage of feature extraction by using channel attention and spatial attention mechanisms. It dynamically adjusts the weights of the feature maps, enhancing the extraction of key features and reducing irrelevant background information.

Finally, the neck network extracts joint detection results from the fused feature maps, achieving efficient and accurate joint detection. By enhancing the extraction of key features and reducing irrelevant background information, this module significantly improves the detection accuracy and speed, ensuring the safety and efficiency of human-robot collaboration.

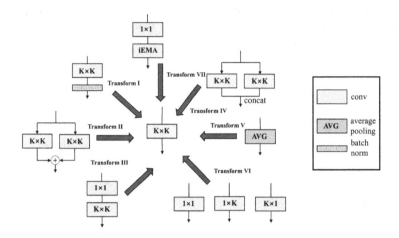

Fig. 3. The structure of the Detect_DBB module. It is a branch structure designed to reduce the computational burden, capable of capturing diverse features in parallel and merging them into a single convolutional layer.

2.2   Loss Function

To effectively train the algorithm, this paper defines a comprehensive loss function. This loss function integrates the contributions of various modules within the network architecture to ensure the model can accurately locate and identify the joints of the robotic arm. The overall loss function L is a weighted sum of several component losses, including joint localization loss, color detection loss, and geometric perception loss.

The loss function is defined as follows:

$$L = \lambda_{jo}L_{jo} + \lambda_{col}L_{col} + \lambda_{geo}L_{geo} \tag{1}$$

λ_{jo}, λ_{col} and λ_{geo} are the weights for joint localization loss, color detection loss and geometric perception loss, respectively. L_{jo} measures the difference between predicted joint coordinates and true joint coordinates. L_{col} assesses the accuracy of the color detection module in recognizing joint colors. L_{geo} captures geometric relationships between joints.

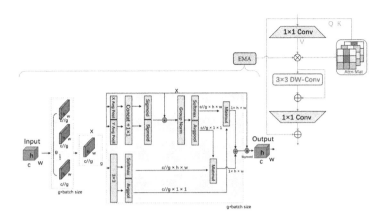

Fig. 4. The structure of the iEMA module. It is based on an inverted residual structure, utilizing channel and spatial attention mechanisms to dynamically adjust weights and enhance feature representation.

L_{jo} measures the difference between predicted joint coordinates and actual joint coordinates. In this study, Mean Squared Error (MSE) [14] is used to compute the difference between joint predictions and ground truth values.

$$L_{\text{jo}} = \frac{1}{N} \sum\nolimits_{i=1}^{N} ||\hat{p}_i - p_i|| \tag{2}$$

where $\hat{p}_i$ represents the predicted position of the i-th joints, p_i represents the true position of the i-th joint, and N is the total number of joints.

L_{col} measures the accuracy of the color detection module in recognizing joint colors. This paper employs cross-entropy [15] loss to evaluate the performance of color classification.

$$L_{\text{col}} = -\frac{1}{M} \sum\nolimits_{j=1}^{M} ||y_i \log(\hat{y}_i) + (1 - y_i) \log(1 - \hat{y}_i)|| \tag{3}$$

where $\hat{y}_i$ represents the predicted probability of the i-th color category, y_i denotes the true label of the i-th color category, and M is the total number of color categories.

L_{geo} captures the geometric relationships between joints to ensure that the model understands the spatial constraints between them. This paper employs a geometric loss function [16] to measure the difference between the predicted distances and the actual distances between joints.

$$L_{geo} = \frac{1}{N} \sum\nolimits_{i=1}^{N} \sum\nolimits_{j=1}^{N} ||d(\hat{p}_i, \hat{p}_j) - d(p_i, p_j)||^2 \tag{4}$$

where $d(\hat{p}_i, \hat{p}_j)$ represents the distance between the predicted joints i and j, and $d(p_i, p_j)$ represents the distance between the true joints i and j.

The effectiveness of this comprehensive loss function has been validated through experiments conducted on multiple benchmark datasets.

3   Experimental Results and Analysis

3.1   Experimental Platform

In this study, we have comprehensively evaluated the proposed method on the developed platform, as shown in Fig. 1. The robotic arm used is the Kinova 6 DOF-KG3, which has 6 degrees of freedom. The images are collected using a Hikvision camera (DS-2CD2626FWD). This camera has a 12VDC power supply and a 4 mm fixed-focus lens. It features a frame rate of 30 fps and a resolution of 1920×1080. To verify the effectiveness of the algorithm in detecting joins of industrial robotic arms, 1,809 images have been collected. Each image is labeled with 6 joints, with the joints of the robotic arm tied with different colored tapes for differentiation. The deep-learning experimental platform is equipped with an Intel Core i7 processor and 16 GB of memory, running the software environment of Ubuntu 20.04 LTS and ROS Noetic, along with tools such as Python 3.7 and CUDA 11.8.

3.2   Results and Analysis

In a simulated work environment, we have created a dataset capturing various poses of a robotic arm and humans within the same scene. This dataset consists of a robotic arm, simulated workers. We have performed real-time scene capture under different conditions to conduct joint detection, which is subsequently highlighted with corresponding color markers to emphasize the position information of each node. The generated joint detection images and results of human-machine interaction are illustrated in Fig. 5. Despite challenges such as joint similarity, occlusion, and background interference in diverse work scenarios, our algorithm accurately detects the varying poses of both the robotic arm and humans.

To evaluate the performance of joint detection for both robotic arms and humans in the same scene, several performance metrics including PCK, mAP, FPS, and Inference Time are employed in this study. Our algorithm is compared with Hourglass Network [17], HRNet [18], DSC-HRNet [19], OpenPose [20], and Simple Baseline [21]. We use PCK, mAP, FPS, and Inference Time to evaluate the pose tracking performance. These metrics are given below:

$$PCK = \frac{1}{N} \sum_{i=1}^{N} [\frac{||P_i - G_i||}{\max(H, W)} \leq \alpha] \tag{5}$$

where N is the total number of joints, P_i and G_i are the predicted and true positions of the joints, respectively. H and W represent the height and width of the target, and α denotes the threshold.

$$mAP = \frac{1}{Q} \sum_{q=1}^{Q} AP(q) \tag{6}$$

where Q is the total number of classes, and $AP(q)$ denotes the average precision of class q.

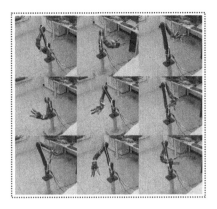 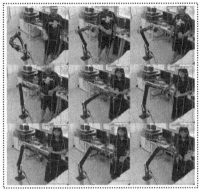

Fig. 5. Schematic of joint detection results. The schematic shows the camera capturing a robotic arm and a person in the environment. Various poses are detected by swinging the robotic arm through different poses to locate joints in different directions.

$$FPS = \frac{1}{T} \tag{7}$$

where T denotes the time required to process one frame of image data.

$$Inference\ Time = \frac{\sum_{i=1}^{N} T_i}{N} \tag{8}$$

where N represents the total number of images, and T_i denotes the time required to process the ith image.

In our experiments, we have rigorously evaluated the proposed algorithm using performance metrics such as PCK, mAP, FPS, and inference time. The results are shown in Table 1. The Hourglass Network [17] captures multi-scale spatial relationships and contextual information through repeated pooling and upsampling to extract features at different scales. Although it has a multi-level structure, it tends to lose information at the detail level. HRNet [18] fuses

Table 1. Comparisons on joint detection performances between ours and state-of-the-art methods

Method	PCK	mAP	FPS	Inference Time
Hourglass Network [17]	0.85	0.75	30	33 ms
HRNet [18]	0.90	0.80	25	40 ms
DSC-HRNet [19]	0.92	0.83	28	30 ms
OpenPose [20]	0.88	0.78	20	50 ms
Simple Baseline [21]	0.83	0.70	35	28 ms
Ours	0.93	0.85	40	25 ms

multi-scale features and uses parallel branches to capture features at different resolutions. While it maintains high-resolution representations, its structure is overly complex. DSC-HRNet [19] achieves a lightweight design through depthwise separable convolutions, reducing computational overhead, but its accuracy and robustness are limited in complex scenarios. OpenPose [20] associates human body parts through Part Affinity Fields (PAFs), enabling multi-person 2D pose estimation, but it performs poorly in handling complex backgrounds. Simple Baseline [21] uses a direct network with a few deconvolution layers to predict heatmaps of joint locations. Although it provides a simple benchmark model, its joint localization accuracy is insufficient, and it lacks the ability to capture detailed variations.

4   Conclusion

In this paper, we have proposed a Human-Robot Pose Tracking model. The algorithm integrates color detection, geometric perception, and the Detect_DBB module for feature extraction, fusion, and prediction output. It accurately detects joint positions of robotic arms and humans working in the same scene under different conditions, addressing challenges such as high similarity between joints and occlusion. Additionally, the Detect_DBB module enhances detection accuracy and speed, providing a more efficient and reliable working environment for personnel and promoting safer human-machine interaction. We have conducted comprehensive evaluations of our algorithm on the platform, demonstrating significant improvements in performance across all metrics.

Acknowledgments. This work was supported by Guangdong Basic and Applied Basic Research Foundation (2023A1515011363), the National Natural Science Foundation of China (62273332), the Youth Innovation Promotion Association of Chinese Academy of Sciences (2022201), and Liaoning Applied Basic Research Foundation (2023JH26/10300028).

Disclosure of Interests. The authors declare that they have no conflict of interest.

References

1. Kang, S., Kim, M., Kim, K.: Safety monitoring for human robot collaborative workspaces. In: 2019 19th International Conference on Control, Automation and Systems (ICCAS), pp. 1192–1194. IEEE (2019)
2. Iqbal, K.F., Kanazawa, A., Ottaviani, S.R., Kinugawa, J., Kosuge, K.: A real-time motion planning scheme for collaborative robots using HRI-based cost function. Int. J. Mechatron. Autom. 8(1), 42–52 (2021)
3. Srinivasan, K., Porkumaran, K., Sainarayanan, G.: A new approach for human activity analysis through identification of body parts using skin colour segmentation. Int. J. Signal Imaging Syst. Eng. 3(2), 93–104 (2010)
4. Saravanakumar, S., Vadivel, A., Ahmed, C.S.: Object tracking and failure recovery in motion video sequences using the properties of HSV colour space. Int. J. Signal Imaging Syst. Eng. 5(1), 29–42 (2012)

5. Kshirsagar, K.P., Doye, D.D.: Comparing key frame selection for one-two hand gesture recognition using different methods. Int. J. Signal Imaging Syst. Eng. **8**(5), 273–285 (2015)
6. Amri, S., Barhoumi, W., Zagrouba, E.: Detection and matching of multiple occluded moving people for human tracking in colour video sequences. Int. J. Signal Imaging Syst. Eng. **4**(3), 153–163 (2011)
7. Hu, Z., Zhang, C., Wang, X., Ge, A.: Light-adaptive human body key point detection algorithm based on multi-source information fusion. Sensors **24**(10), 3021 (2024)
8. Li, X.: Study on volleyball-movement pose recognition based on joint point sequence. Comput. Intell. Neurosci. **2023**(1), 2198495 (2023)
9. Szabó, R., Gontean, A.: Robotic arm detection in the 2D space. In: 2014 IEEE 20th International Symposium for Design and Technology in Electronic Packaging (SIITME), pp. 215–220. IEEE (2014)
10. Mišeikis, J., Brijačak, I., Yahyanejad, S., Glette, K., Elle, O.J., Torresen, J.: Two-stage transfer learning for heterogeneous robot detection and 3D joint position estimation in a 2D camera image using CNN. In: 2019 International Conference on Robotics and Automation (ICRA), pp. 8883–8889. IEEE (2019)
11. Ouyang, D., et al.: Efficient multi-scale attention module with cross-spatial learning. In: ICASSP 2023-2023 IEEE International Conference on Acoustics, Speech and Signal Processing (ICASSP), pp. 1–5. IEEE (2023)
12. Zhang, J., et al.: Rethinking mobile block for efficient attention-based models. In: 2023 IEEE/CVF International Conference on Computer Vision (ICCV), pp. 1389–1400. IEEE Computer Society (2023)
13. Ding, X., Zhang, X., Han, J., Ding, G.: Diverse branch block: building a convolution as an inception-like unit. In: Proceedings of the IEEE/CVF Conference on Computer Vision and Pattern Recognition, pp. 10886–10895 (2021)
14. Mayyas, K., Aboulnasr, T.: Leaky LMS algorithm: MSE analysis for gaussian data. IEEE Trans. Signal Process. **45**(4), 927–934 (1997)
15. Mao, A., Mohri, M., Zhong, Y.: Cross-entropy loss functions: theoretical analysis and applications. In: International Conference on Machine Learning, pp. 23803–23828. PMLR (2023)
16. Kendall, A., Cipolla, R.: Geometric loss functions for camera pose regression with deep learning. In: Proceedings of the IEEE Conference on Computer Vision and Pattern Recognition, pp. 5974–5983 (2017)
17. Newell, A., Yang, K., Deng, J.: Stacked hourglass networks for human pose estimation. In: Computer Vision–ECCV 2016: 14th European Conference, Amsterdam, The Netherlands, 11–14 October 2016, Proceedings, Part VIII 14, pp. 483–499. Springer (2016)
18. Sun, K., Xiao, B., Liu, D., Wang, J.: Deep high-resolution representation learning for human pose estimation. In: Proceedings of the IEEE/CVF Conference on Computer Vision and Pattern Recognition, pp. 5693–5703 (2019)
19. Zhao, Z., Song, A., Zheng, S., Xiong, Q., Guo, J.: DSC-HRNet: a lightweight teaching pose estimation model with depthwise separable convolution and deep high-resolution representation learning in computer-aided education. Int. J. Inf. Technol. **15**(5), 2373–2385 (2023)
20. Cao, Z., Simon, T., Wei, S.-E., Sheikh, Y.: Realtime multi-person 2D pose estimation using part affinity fields. In: Proceedings of the IEEE Conference on Computer Vision and Pattern Recognition, pp. 7291–7299 (2017)
21. Wu, Y., Jiang, L., Yang, Y.: Revisiting embodiedqa: a simple baseline and beyond. IEEE Trans. Image Process. **29**, 3984–3992 (2020)

Cued Speech-Integrated Audio-Visual Variational Autoencoder for Speech Enhancement

Lufei Gao, Yan Rong, and Li Liu[✉]

The Hong Kong University of Science and Technology (Guangzhou), Guangzhou, China
avrillliu@hkust-gz.edu.cn

Abstract. Speech enhancement (SE) is essential for improving the quality and intelligibility of speech signals, particularly in noisy environments. In this paper, we propose an innovative approach to Audio-Visual Speech Enhancement (AVSE) by modifying an audio-visual variational autoencoder (AV-VAE) framework to integrate both lip movements and hand gestures from Cued Speech (CS) as visual cues. This is the first work to incorporate hand gestures, in addition to lip movements, within the AVSE task. By introducing hand cues, our approach aims to address the inherent challenges of lip reading, such as the high ambiguity in interpreting lip movements, which can limit the effectiveness of traditional AVSE methods. Leveraging deep learning and computer vision techniques, our method offers a more comprehensive representation of spoken content. Through empirical evaluation, we demonstrate the effectiveness of our approach in enhancing the clarity and quality of speech signals, even in challenging acoustic conditions. The results indicate that the integration of hand cues significantly improves speech quality, providing a promising solution for AVSE in noisy environments.

Keywords: Audio-Visual Speech Enhancement · Variational Auto-Encoder · Audio-Visual VAE · Cued Speech

1 Introduction

Speech enhancement seeks to enhance the audio quality and clarity of speech in noisy environments. Audio-visual speech enhancement (AVSE) leverages visual cues, like the lip movements of the speaker, to boost the effectiveness of SE [18]. These visual cues offer additional information, such as the place of articulation, which is especially beneficial in situations with low signal-to-noise ratios (SNRs). In particular, in the present of acoustic noise, visual information can aid in distinguishing the target speaker from other potential speakers speaking concurrently. In the past decade, owing to the remarkable advancements in computer vision and deep learning, there has been a significant reexamination of the AVSE issue [1, 4, 18].

© The Author(s), under exclusive license to Springer Nature Singapore Pte Ltd. 2025
H. Li et al. (Eds.): ICSR + InnoBiz 2024, LNAI 15170, pp. 136–145, 2025.
https://doi.org/10.1007/978-981-96-1151-5_14

However, most existing studies focus on English datasets, while the advancement of Chinese lip-reading technology is in its early phases. Chinese poses greater complexity compared to English due to its intricate structure. Unlike English, which primarily comprises letters, Chinese Pinyin encompasses over 400 pronunciation combinations, and the language boasts a repertoire of more than 3500 characters[1]. Additionally, the scarcity of Chinese datasets adds further complexity to the task of lip reading in this language.

Indeed, relying solely on lip movements for speech processing has limitations, especially in languages like Chinese where the ambiguity of lip movements can lead to high error rates in lip reading. Studies have shown that the word error rate for Chinese lip reading can be as high as 60% or more [12], highlighting the challenges associated with interpreting lip movements accurately. Therefore, this further limits the effectiveness of lip-related visualized cues in enhancing speech, particularly in the context of Chinese.

Cued Speech (CS) is a visual coding system designed to assist individuals with hearing impairments in learning spoken language [3]. By mapping phonemes to specific hand shapes and positions, it allows for the systematic encoding of syllables. Since the encoding rules are based on the phonetic system, CS has different adaptations for various languages. Mandarin Chinese CS was first introduced in [13]. In this system, 25 consonants are represented by eight hand shapes, while 16 vowels are indicated by five positions near the face, enabling the cuer[2] to manually spell out *Pinyin*. It has been demonstrated that CS is effective in helping children with hearing impairments develop reading skills, spoken accuracy and overall communication abilities [24]. Naturally, the hand gestures used in CS serve as a complementary cue to lip reading, thereby enhancing speech expression, particularly in scenarios where the speaker's articulation is unclear. Even for individuals with normal hearing, incorporating a small number of CS hand gestures as cues can improve speech comprehension in noisy environments. Intuitively, adding more visual information to noisy speech during speech reconstruction could be beneficial in enhancing speech quality.

In this work, we present a CS-integrated approach to AVSE by implementing an AV-VAE framework. To the best of our knowledge, this is the first work to incorporate visual cues beyond lip movements in the AVSE task. Our method leverages both lip movements and predefined hand gestures from Chinese CS to explore the impact of coded hand cues on improving AVSE performance. This approach aims to mitigate the inherent ambiguity of relying solely on lip reading and to further enhance the effectiveness of SE. By providing a more comprehensive representation of spoken content, our method ultimately improves the overall quality and clarity of the enhanced speech signal. Through empirical evaluation and comparative analysis, we demonstrate the efficacy of our approach, particularly in challenging acoustic conditions.

---

[1] https://zh.wikipedia.org/wiki/%E5%B8%B8%E7%94%A8%E5%AD%97

[2] The people who use cued speech for communication.

2   Related Work

Audio Visual Speech Enhancement. In the area of AVSE, a prevalent strategy involves the development and training of multi-modal deep neural networks (DNNs). These architectures aim to integrate audio and visual features extracted from video and noisy audio data, respectively, with the primary goal of directly estimating the clean speech signal. The effectiveness and generalization performance of this data-driven approach heavily depend on the volume and diversity of the training data, particularly concerning various types of noise.

In contrast to the traditional supervised AVSE framework, a recent alternative approach combines classical model-based techniques, such as maximum a posteriori (MAP) estimation, with the flexibility of DNNs for unsupervised AVSE [19–22]. This method involves an initial pre-training phase where a deep generative model, based on VAEs [8], learns the statistical properties of speech signals in the time-frequency domain using only clean audio-visual data. The trained generative model, which serves as a deep speech prior, is then combined with a parametric noise model. During testing, the parameters of this integrated model, along with the clean speech signal, are estimated using an Expectation-Maximization (EM) algorithm. By modeling noise during the testing phase, unsupervised AVSE can adapt to unexpected noise conditions and potentially offers better generalization compared to supervised methods [22].

However, existing AV-VAE models developed for unsupervised AVSE overlook the sequential nature of speech data. They operate under the assumption of statistical independence between consecutive speech time frames, thus disregarding their inherent correlations. Recent advancements have introduced dynamical variants of VAEs, known as DVAEs [7], which capture the temporal dynamics of speech data. While these models have shown promise in audio-only SE, their integration into AVSE complicates the EM step during testing due to the intricate temporal dependencies of latent variables in the models.

Cued Speech. Cued Speech (CS) was originally introduced in 1967 as a visual system to aid individuals with hearing impairments in learning spoken language. Despite its long history, Mandarin Chinese CS was only developed in 2019 [13], resulting in a relatively limited body of research. Existing studies primarily focus on automatic CS recognition [11,12,15,16,25,26], CS generation [10], and the analysis of hand and lip movement patterns [6,14,17]. This paper pioneers the application of CS in a broader speech research context, aiming to explore new insights and potential improvements in speech processing by integrating CS into conventional speech enhancement methodologies.

3   Method

In this section, we will introduce the AV-VAE framework for speech enhancement, detailing its architecture, latent space modeling, training objectives, and the integration of CS visual features. Additionally, we will explain the speech

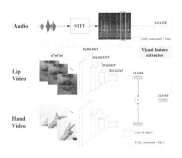 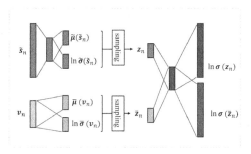

(a) Illustration of audio and visual feature extraction

(b) AV-VAE network pipeline for learning
audio-visual priors for speech enhancement.

Fig. 1. The overall framework of our proposed CS-integrated AV-VAE incorporating
hand gesture videos for visual speech encoding.

enhancement process, which employs a point-estimate EM algorithm to iteratively optimize the latent variables and model parameters.

3.1 Audio-Visual VAE

Audio VAE. The input audio features, represented by the Short-Time Fourier
Transform (STFT) coefficients $\mathbf{s_n} = [s_{fn}]_{f=1}^{F} \in \mathbb{C}^{F}$, is mapped into a latent
representation $\mathbf{z_n} \in \mathbb{R}^{L}(L \ll F)$ that captures the essential characteristics of
the speech signal. The VAE framework is used in the estimation procedure.
Specifically, the model referred to as Audio-VAE (A-VAE) is as following:

$$s_{fn}|\mathbf{z}_n \sim \mathcal{N}_c(0, \sigma_f(\mathbf{z}_n)), \tag{1}$$

$$\mathbf{z}_n \sim \mathcal{N}(\mathbf{0}, \mathbf{I}), \tag{2}$$

where $\mathcal{N}_c(0, \sigma)$ is a univariate complex proper Gaussian distribution and
$\{\sigma_f(\cdot)\}_{f=1}^{F}$ are functions modeled Multi-Layer Perceptrons (MLPs) parameterized by θ. We follow [22] to optimize the Evidence Lower Bound (ELBO), which
defines the approximate posterior distribution $q(\mathbf{z}|\mathbf{s}; \psi)$ as:

$$z_{ln}|\mathbf{s}_n \sim \mathcal{N}(\tilde{\mu}_l(\tilde{\mathbf{s}}_n), \tilde{\sigma}_l(\tilde{\mathbf{s}}_n)), \tag{3}$$

where $\tilde{\mathbf{s}}_n \triangleq (|s_{1n}|^2 \ldots |s_{Fn}|^2)^\top$. The non-linear functions $\tilde{\mu}_l(\cdot)$ and $\tilde{\sigma}_l(\cdot)$ are mod-
eled as MLPs, which is parameterized by ψ.

Visual Feature Extractor. The visual feature extractor is responsible for
processing the visual inputs, which can include lip movements, hand gestures,
or both. This extractor employs a series of 3D convolutional layers, followed
by ReLU activations, to capture temporal and spatial features from the input
video frames. Figure 1a illustrates the structure of the feature extractor. When
both lip and hand features are available, they are concatenated and processed as

$\mathbf{v} = \mathrm{ReLU}(\mathbf{W}_c \cdot \mathrm{concat}(\mathbf{v}_{\mathrm{lip}}, \mathbf{v}_{\mathrm{hand}}) + \mathbf{b}_c)$, where $\mathbf{v}_{\mathrm{lip}}$ and $\mathbf{v}_{\mathrm{hand}}$ are the features extracted from the lip and hand video streams, respectively.

The approximate posterior distribution $q(\bar{\mathbf{z}}|\mathbf{v}; \gamma)$ is defined as:

$$\bar{z}_{ln}|\mathbf{v}_n \sim \mathcal{N}(\bar{\mu}_l(\mathbf{v}_n), \bar{\sigma}_l(\mathbf{v}_n)), \tag{4}$$

where $\bar{\mu}_l(\cdot)$ and $\bar{\sigma}_l(\cdot)$ are parameterized by γ. Specifically, $\bar{\mu}(\mathbf{v}) = \bar{\mathbf{W}}_\mu \mathbf{v} + \bar{\mathbf{b}}$, $\ln \bar{\sigma}^2(\mathbf{v}) = \bar{\mathbf{W}}_\sigma \mathbf{v} + \bar{\mathbf{b}}_\sigma$. The latent variable $\bar{\mathbf{z}}$ is then sampled from the prior distribution using the reparameterization trick.

Latent Space and Decoder. The latent space representation is where the information from both the audio and visual inputs is integrated. The model generates two latent variables: $\mathbf{z}$, sampled from the posterior distribution conditioned on the audio input, and $\bar{\mathbf{z}}$, sampled from the prior distribution conditioned on the visual input. The decoder is structured with linear layers that apply Tanh activations to transform the latent variables back into the audio feature space.

Training Objective. The model parameters $\boldsymbol{\Phi} = \{\theta, \phi, \gamma\}$ are learned by maximizing the ELBO. Similar to [22], the objective function consists of reconstruction loss and the Kullback-Leibler divergence. Using (1), (2), (3) and (4), we obtain the following loss function:

$$\mathcal{L}(\mathbf{s}; \theta, \psi, \gamma) \overset{c}{=} - \alpha \sum_f \sum_n \mathbb{E}_{q(\mathbf{z}_n|\mathbf{s}_n; \psi)}[d_{\mathrm{IS}}(|s_{fn}|^2; \sigma_f(\mathbf{z}_n))]$$
$$- (1-\alpha)(\sum_f \sum_n \mathbb{E}_{q(\bar{\mathbf{z}}_n|\mathbf{v_n}; \gamma)}[d_{\mathrm{IS}}(|s_{fn}|^2; \sigma_f(\bar{\mathbf{z}}_n))])$$
$$+ \frac{\alpha}{2} \sum_l \sum_n [\ln \frac{\bar{\sigma}_l(\tilde{\mathbf{s}}_n)}{\bar{\sigma}_l(\mathbf{v}_n)} - \frac{\ln \tilde{\sigma}_l(\tilde{\mathbf{s}}_n) + (\tilde{\mu}_l(\tilde{\mathbf{s}}_n) - \bar{\mu}_l(\mathbf{v}_n))^2}{\bar{\sigma}_l(\mathbf{v}_n)}], \tag{5}$$

where $\alpha \in [0, 1]$ is a trade-off hyper-parameter and $d_{\mathrm{IS}}(x; y) = x/y - \ln(x/y) - 1$ is the Itakura-Saito divergence [5].

3.2 Speech Enhancement

For the SE task, we employ a variant of the Expectation-Maximization (EM) algorithm, specifically the Point-Estimate EM method [23]. This approach integrates VAE with Non-negative Matrix Factorization (NMF) to iteratively optimize latent variables and model parameters.

Point-Estimate E-Step. Let $\mathbf{x} = \{x_n\}_{n=0}^{N-1}$ denote the STFT frames of the mixture speech, where $x_{fn} = \sqrt{g_n} s_{fn} + b_{fn}$. Here, $\{g_n\}$ denotes the gain parameters to be estimated and $b_{fn} \sim \mathcal{N}_c(0, (\mathbf{W}_b \mathbf{H}_b)_{fn})$ models the unsupervised NMF-based Gaussian noise. The VAE model is then employed to generate the speech variance $\sigma_f(z_n)$. The objective function in this step is composed of a data likelihood term and a regularization term for the latent variables:

$$\mathcal{L}(\mathbf{x}; \theta, \phi) = \sum_n \sum_f \left(\frac{|x_{fn}|^2}{g_n \sigma_f(z_n) + \hat{\sigma}_{fn}} + \ln(g_n \sigma_f(z_n) + \hat{\sigma}_{fn}) \right) + \sum_n \frac{(z_n - \tilde{\mu}(x_n))^2}{\tilde{\sigma}(x_n)} \tag{6}$$

where $\hat{\sigma}_{fn} = (\mathbf{W}_b \mathbf{H}_b)_{fn}$. The latent variables $\mathbf{z}$ are optimized using the Adam optimizer with a learning rate of 0.01.

M-Step. In the M-step, the model parameters $\phi = \{\mathbf{W}_b, \mathbf{H}_b, \mathbf{g}\}$ are updated while keeping the latent variables $\mathbf{z}$ fixed. The power spectrogram of the noise is first computed using the current estimates $\sigma(b_{fn}) = (\hat{\mathbf{W}}_b \hat{\mathbf{H}}_b)_{fn}$. Subsequently, the variance of the mixture signal $\sigma(x_{fn})$ is computed by combining the speech variance and the noise variance, scaled by the gain parameter g_n, i.e. $\sigma(x_{fn}) = g_n \sigma_f(z_n) + \sigma(b_{fn})$. The NMF parameters $\mathbf{W}_b$ and $\mathbf{H}_b$ are updated to minimize the Itakura-Saito divergence between the observed power spectrogram and estimated spectrogram. Finally, the gain vector g_n is also updated to further refine the model's fit to the observed data.

Speech Reconstruction. The set of estimated parameters is represented as $\phi^* = \{\mathbf{W}_b^*, \mathbf{H}_b^*, g_n^*\}$. Hence, the enhanced speech signal is reconstructed by applying a Wiener-like filtering approach to the mixture signal, using the computed speech variance and noise variance:

$$\hat{s}_{fn} = \mathbb{E}_{p(\mathbf{z}_n | \mathbf{x}_n; \phi^*)} \left[\frac{g_n^* \sigma_f^2(\mathbf{z}_n)}{g_n^* \sigma_f^2(\mathbf{z}_n) + (\mathbf{W}_b^* \mathbf{H}_b^*)_{f,n}} \right] x_{fn}. \tag{7}$$

The resulting coefficients are transformed back into the time domain using the inverse STFT, yielding the final enhanced speech signal.

4 Experiment and Analysis

4.1 Experiment Setup

Dataset. We use one cuer's videos from the Mandarin Chinese Cued Speech (MCCS) dataset[3] in this experiment. Each video corresponding to one sentence, of length ranging from four words to 25 words. For each sentence in our dataset, we first extracted the corresponding audio clips. These audio clips serve as the primary modality for our analysis and were prepared in a consistent format suitable for further processing and feature extraction. Using Mediapipe's facemesh[4], we extracted the region of interest (ROI) around the lips for each frame in the video corresponding to the audio clips. These lip ROI images were resized to

---

[3] https://mccs-2023.github.io/.
[4] https://mediapipe.readthedocs.io/en/latest/solutions/face_mesh.html.

$T \times 67 \times 67$. Interpolation was performed to align these visual features with the audio clip, ensuring synchronous multi-modal data. Similarly, hand ROI images were extracted using Mediapipe's hands module[5] by detecting and cropping the region of interest around the hands for each frame. These images were processed and stored for further analysis, ensuring consistent alignment with the corresponding audio and lip ROI data.

To simulate realistic conditions, we added noise to the audio clips using the noises selected randomly from the MS-SNSD dataset[6]. The chosen noise types are Babble_1, Park_1, VaccumCleaner_3, WasherDryer_6 and Washing_1. Each noise type was applied at four different signal-to-noise ratios (SNR): -5 dB, 0 dB, 5 dB, and 10 dB.

The dataset was derived from a single speaker (HS), comprising 1000 sentences. We divided the dataset into training, validation, and test sets in a 14:3:3 ratio.

Metrics. To assess the quality of the enhanced speech signals, we utilize three standard metrics, i.e. the scale-invariant signal-to-distortion ratio (SI-SDR) measured in dB, the short-term objective intelligibility (STOI) measure ranging from 0 to 1, and the perceptual evaluation of speech quality (PESQ) score ranging from -0.5 to 4.5. For all these metrics, higher values indicate better performance.

Model Architecture and Parameter Settings. The architecture of the VAE considered in our experiments follows the models in [2,9], with the dimension of the latent space $L = 32$, batch size $N = 128$, the number of frequency bins $F = 513$. The model was trained using the Adam optimizer with a learning rate of 10^{-4}. Early stopping strategy was employed, i.e. validation loss not improved within 20 epochs. For SE, the number of EM iterations is set to 100 for all the methods. The number of iterations in the E-step is set to 10. The rank of NMF model is set to 8.

4.2 Results and Discussion

The results under the above settings are shown in Table 1, where the dropout probability is 0 and one noise type (Babble_1) is used. With the setting of early stopping strategy, A-VAE was trained for 442 epochs, AV-VAE (lip) for 220 epochs, AV-VAE (hand) for 70 epochs and AV-VAE (lip+hand) for 65 epochs. The results in the table show clear differences between the models in terms of SI-SDR, PESQ, and STOI metrics. The A-VAE model demonstrates good performance across all SNR levels, with noticeable improvement as SNR increases. However, the AV-VAE models, which incorporate visual information, outperform A-VAE across most metrics. Notably, the AV-VAE (hand) model achieves the highest SI-SDR scores across higher SNRs like 5 and 10 dB, suggesting

---

[5] https://mediapipe.readthedocs.io/en/latest/solutions/hands.html.
[6] https://github.com/microsoft/MS-SNSD.

Table 1. Average SI-SDR, PESQ, and STOI for the test audios with early stopping and single noise type Babble_1.

Metric	SI-SDR (db)				PESQ				STOI			
Noise SNR	−5	0	5	10	−5	0	5	10	−5	0	5	10
Input (unprocessed)	−7.22	−2.27	2.77	7.83	1.19	1.16	1.30	**1.65**	0.33	0.44	0.56	**0.67**
A-VAE	−7.04	−0.43	10.14	8.85	1.36	1.13	1.52	1.50	0.27	0.37	0.52	0.53
AV-VAE (lip)	−6.17	**2.80**	11.50	10.63	**1.50**	**1.20**	**1.56**	1.53	0.31	0.45	0.59	0.57
AV-VAE (hand)	−4.95	2.25	**11.63**	**11.20**	1.13	1.18	**1.56**	1.44	0.31	0.44	**0.60**	0.57
AV-VAE (lip+hand)	**−4.11**	1.20	5.93	10.06	1.11	1.17	1.32	1.56	**0.35**	**0.46**	0.58	**0.67**

Table 2. Average SI-SDR, PESQ, and STOI for the test audios with 500 training epochs and five noise types.

Metric	SI-SDR (db)				PESQ				STOI			
Noise SNR	−5	0	5	10	−5	0	5	10	−5	0	5	10
Input (unprocessed)	−10.06	−5.12	−0.11	4.91	1.13	1.19	1.37	1.76	0.40	0.51	0.62	0.72
A-VAE	2.42	6.27	9.51	11.82	1.25	1.37	1.54	1.75	0.47	0.56	0.64	0.71
AV-VAE (lip)	2.09	6.02	9.31	12.19	1.22	1.35	1.54	1.80	0.46	0.55	0.64	0.72
AV-VAE (hand)	**2.56**	**6.34**	**9.58**	12.31	1.23	1.34	1.52	1.75	0.47	0.56	0.64	0.72
AV-VAE (lip+hand)	2.36	6.27	**9.58**	**12.40**	1.23	1.35	1.53	1.78	0.47	0.55	0.64	0.71

that hand gestures contribute significantly to speech enhancement in this noise condition. Additionally, the AV-VAE (lip+hand) model shows competitive performance, with the highest SI-SDR at −5 dB and the best STOI scores at −5 dB, 0 dB and 10 dB, indicating enhanced intelligibility at these SNR levels. Besides, the different training epochs required for each model indicate that the multi-modal AV-VAE models converge faster than the audio-only A-VAE model, likely because the visual inputs provide complementary information that simplifies the learning process. The rapid convergence of the AV-VAE (lip+hand) model suggests that combining lip and hand cues allows the model to extract useful features more efficiently, requiring fewer training epochs to achieve good performance.

Table 2 shows the results with a dropout probability of 0.5 and training for 500 epochs using five different noise types. The AV-VAE (hand) and AV-VAE (lip+hand) models again demonstrate their effectiveness. The AV-VAE (hand) model, in particular, excels in SI-SDR at lower SNRs (−5 dB and 0 dB), indicating its robustness in more challenging noise environments. The AV-VAE (lip+hand) model shows balanced performance across all metrics, with notable improvements in SI-SDR at high SNRs, demonstrating that combining both visual modalities leads to a comprehensive improvement in speech enhancement.

The relatively lower performance of AV-VAE models on PESQ and STOI in Table 2 suggests that while these models are effective at reducing distortion as indicated by SI-SDR, they may struggle with improving perceptual quality and speech intelligibility. This could be due to the trade-off between signal distortion reduction and perceptual quality or the inherent limitations of the VAE architecture for these tasks. To address these issues, future work could focus on enhancing the perceptual focus of the models, improving multi-modal fusion strategies, or using more targeted loss functions that account for human perception and intelligibility.

5   Conclusions

In this work, we proposed an innovative CS-integrated approach to AVSE by extending the AV-VAE framework to incorporate two video streams from cued speech. Our experiments demonstrated that hand cues offer promising additional information in speech enhancement tasks, leading to improved speech quality and intelligibility, particularly in noisy environments. Future work could focus on refining the model to handle more diverse and real-world noisy conditions.

Acknowledgments. This work was supported by the National Natural Science Foundation of China (No. 62101351), Guangzhou Municipal Science and Technology Project: Basic and Applied Basic research projects (No. 2024A04J4232).

References

1. Afouras, T., Chung, J.S., Zisserman, A.: The conversation: deep audio-visual speech enhancement. arXiv preprint arXiv:1804.04121 (2018)
2. Bie, X., Leglaive, S., Alameda-Pineda, X., Girin, L.: Unsupervised speech enhancement using dynamical variational autoencoders. IEEE/ACM Trans. Audio Speech Lang. Process. **30**, 2993–3007 (2022)
3. Cornett, R.O.: Cued speech. Am. Ann. Deaf **112**(1), 3–13 (1967)
4. Ephrat, A., et al.: Looking to listen at the cocktail party: a speaker-independent audio-visual model for speech separation. ACM Trans. Graph. (TOG) **37**(4), 1–11 (2018)
5. Févotte, C., Bertin, N., Durrieu, J.L.: Nonnegative matrix factorization with the Itakura-Saito divergence: with application to music analysis. Neural Comput. **21**(3), 793–830 (2009)
6. Gao, L., Huang, S., Liu, L.: A novel interpretable and generalizable re-synchronization model for cued speech based on a multi-cuer corpus. arXiv preprint arXiv:2306.02596 (2023)
7. Girin, L., Leglaive, S., Bie, X., Diard, J., Hueber, T., Alameda-Pineda, X.: Dynamical variational autoencoders: a comprehensive review. arXiv preprint arXiv:2008.12595 (2020)
8. Kingma, D.P., Welling, M.: Auto-encoding variational bayes. arXiv preprint arXiv:1312.6114 (2013)
9. Leglaive, S., Alameda-Pineda, X., Girin, L., Horaud, R.: A recurrent variational autoencoder for speech enhancement. In: ICASSP 2020-2020 IEEE International Conference on Acoustics, Speech and Signal Processing (ICASSP), pp. 371–375. IEEE (2020)

10. Lei, W., Liu, L., Wang, J.: Bridge to non-barrier communication: Gloss-prompted fine-grained cued speech gesture generation with diffusion model. arXiv preprint arXiv:2404.19277 (2024)
11. Liu, L., Liu, L.: Cross-modal mutual learning for cued speech recognition. In: Proceedings of IEEE-ICASSP, pp. 1–5 (2023)
12. Liu, L., Liu, L., Li, H.: Computation and parameter efficient multi-modal fusion transformer for cued speech recognition. IEEE/ACM Trans. Audio Speech Lang. Process. (2024)
13. Liu, L., Feng, G.: A pilot study on mandarin Chinese cued speech. Am. Ann. Deaf **164**(4), 496–518 (2019)
14. Liu, L., Feng, G., Beautemps, D.: Inner lips feature extraction based on CLNF with hybrid dynamic template for cued speech. EURASIP J. Image Video Process. **2017**, 1–15 (2017)
15. Liu, L., Feng, G., Beautemps, D., Zhang, X.P.: A novel resynchronization procedure for hand-lips fusion applied to continuous French cued speech recognition. In: 2019 27th European Signal Processing Conference (EUSIPCO), pp. 1–5. IEEE (2019)
16. Liu, L., Feng, G., Denis, B., Zhang, X.P.: Re-synchronization using the hand preceding model for multi-modal fusion in automatic continuous cued speech recognition. IEEE Trans. Multimedia **23**, 292–305 (2020)
17. Liu, L., Feng, G., Ren, X., Ma, X.: Objective hand complexity comparison between two mandarin Chinese cued speech systems. In: Proceedings of IEEE-ISCSLP, pp. 215–219 (2022)
18. Michelsanti, D., et al.: An overview of deep-learning-based audio-visual speech enhancement and separation. IEEE/ACM Trans. Audio Speech Lang. Process. **29**, 1368–1396 (2021)
19. Sadeghi, M., Alameda-Pineda, X.: Robust unsupervised audio-visual speech enhancement using a mixture of variational autoencoders. In: ICASSP 2020-2020 IEEE International Conference on Acoustics, Speech and Signal Processing (ICASSP), pp. 7534–7538. IEEE (2020)
20. Sadeghi, M., Alameda-Pineda, X.: Mixture of inference networks for VAE-based audio-visual speech enhancement. IEEE Trans. Signal Process. **69**, 1899–1909 (2021)
21. Sadeghi, M., Alameda-Pineda, X.: Switching variational auto-encoders for noise-agnostic audio-visual speech enhancement. In: ICASSP 2021-2021 IEEE International Conference on Acoustics, Speech and Signal Processing (ICASSP), pp. 6663–6667. IEEE (2021)
22. Sadeghi, M., Leglaive, S., Alameda-Pineda, X., Girin, L., Horaud, R.: Audio-visual speech enhancement using conditional variational auto-encoders. IEEE/ACM Trans. Audio Speech Lang. Process. **28**, 1788–1800 (2020)
23. Sadeghi, M., Serizel, R.: Fast and efficient speech enhancement with variational autoencoders. In: ICASSP 2023-2023 IEEE International Conference on Acoustics, Speech and Signal Processing (ICASSP), pp. 1–5. IEEE (2023)
24. Trezek, B.J.: Cued speech and the development of reading in english: examining the evidence. J. Deaf Stud. Deaf Educ. **22**(4), 349–364 (2017)
25. Wang, J., Tang, Z., Li, X., Yu, M., Fang, Q., Liu, L.: Cross-modal knowledge distillation method for automatic cued speech recognition (2021)
26. Zhang, Y., Liu, L., Liu, L.: Cuing without sharing: a federated cued speech recognition framework via mutual knowledge distillation. arXiv preprint arXiv:2308.03432 (2023)

Semi-supervised Speaker Localization with Gaussian-Like Pseudo-labeling

Xinyuan Qian[1($\boxtimes$)], Chen Lu[1], Yating Zhang[1], Kainan Chen[2], and Haizhou Li[3]

[1] University of Science and Technology Beijing, Beijing, China
qianxy@ustb.edu.cn
[2] Eigenspace GmbH, Munich, Germany
[3] The Chinese University of Hong Kong, Shenzhen, China

Abstract. Speaker localization is important for many human-robot interaction applications. Most existing localization studies train models with fully-annotated data through supervised learning strategies, which doesn't fit the real-world scenarios where labeled data is scarce. To address the challenge of limited labeled data, we propose a semi-supervised deep learning algorithm for Direction of Arrival (DoA) estimation. Specifically, the model is enhanced through a process where it generates pseudo-labels for unlabeled data and incorporates a sophisticated filtering mechanism. This refined approach retrains the model by integrating both the labeled data and the data enriched with these pseudo-labels, thereby optimizing its learning capabilities. Experimental results show that it outperforms both supervised learning algorithms and other semi-supervised learning algorithms.

Keywords: Semi-supervised learning · Pseudo label · Speaker localization · DoA prediction

1 Introduction

Sound Source Localization (SSL) is essential for numerous applications, such as video conferencing, smart homes, and surveillance systems [1–3]. Accurate SSL enhances user experience by enabling more natural and intuitive interactions with technology, which is the critical task to be addressed in this paper.

Traditional methods of SSL often rely on beamforming techniques, where signals from multiple microphone arrays are weighted, summed and subjected to power spectral analysis or cross-correlation analysis [4,5]. Specifically, the directional beamformed signals are then processed to determine the azimuth of the sound source through calculations of temporal and spatial delays. However, these methods exhibit limited generality, requiring tailored algorithms for different environments, and often demonstrate poor resistance to interference.

With the advancement in computational capabilities and the rapid development of neural network technology, deep learning-based SSL methods have emerged [6–9], which exhibit advantages such as autonomous learning, high precision and robustness compared to traditional methods. However, these approaches also have significant limitations. For example, they require large amounts of high-quality annotated data for training, which is often difficult to obtain in traditional application scenarios. This reliance on extensive labeled datasets makes these methods impractical for many real-world environments where labeled data is scarce.

Given these challenges, semi-supervised learning, which requires minimal labeled data, stands out as an advantageous choice. Thus, in this paper, our goal is to develop a robust SSL method that overcomes the limitations of existing approaches by using semi-supervised learning algorithms combined with neural networks. Our approach is inspired by prior work that has demonstrated the efficacy of high-confidence pseudo labels in semi-supervised learning scenarios, where they have been shown to effectively bridge the gap between labeled and unlabeled data. For instance, studies have illustrated that the use of confident pseudo labels can lead to significant improvements in model generalization and accuracy [10,11]. By employing a model to generate pseudo labels for unlabeled data and utilizing a filtering mechanism, we can retrain the model using both labeled and pseudo-labeled data. Our approach improves training performance and localization accuracy, particularly in scenarios with fewer human annotations.

2   Proposed Method

2.1   Problem Formulation

In this paper, we tackle the SSL problem where our goal is to train a network to estimate the DoA of sound sources in a semi-supervised manner. We begin by defining the necessary notation and mathematical formulations. Unless otherwise specified, matrices are in bold uppercase letters, e.g., X, Y, vectors are in bold lowercase letters, e.g., x, y and scalars by lowercase letters, e.g., x, y. Let (X_{tr}, Θ_{tr}) denote training data and labels, X_{un} denotes unlabeled data, (X_{te}, Θ_{te}) denote test data and labels, Θ_{pred} denote the prediction results of our model, and (X_{ps}, Θ_{ps}) denotes pseudo labeled data and pseudo labels. In our task, x represents the input audio feature vector and i denotes the sample index. Our goal is to estimate the DoA of sound sources, denoted as θ, where $\theta \in [0°, 360°)$.

We formulate the SSL problem as a regression task with DoA a discrete value among 360 classes. For the i-th set of input features x_i, our model $f(\cdot; \Omega)$, parameterized by Ω, predicts a probability distribution $\hat{p}_i(\theta)$ for the i-th sample:

$$\hat{p}_i(\theta) = f(x_i; \Omega) \tag{1}$$

Then, the most likely sound source direction is computed as:

$$\hat{\theta}_i = \arg\max_\theta \hat{p}_i(\theta) \tag{2}$$

where $\hat{\theta}_i$ is the DoA estimate whose posterior probability achieves the highest predicted value:

$$p_{max,i} = \max \, \hat{\boldsymbol{p}}_i(\theta) \tag{3}$$

Instead of using a one-hot encoding, we adopt a Gaussian-like vector representation, to model the posterior probability of the speaker's presence. For the i-th sample:

$$\boldsymbol{g}(\theta, \theta_i) = \exp\left(-\frac{(\theta - \theta_i)^2}{2\sigma^2}\right) \tag{4}$$

where $\theta \in [0°, 360°)$ is the DoA index and $\boldsymbol{g}(\theta, \theta_i)$ is centered on the ground truth predicted angle θ_i with a standard deviation σ. This smooths the output to reflect the spatial continuity of DoA and is subsequently used to optimize the model parameters.

To be mentioned, unlabeled data refer to the data containing only multidimensional audio features while labeled data refer to the data containing both the audio features and DoA labels of sound sources. The challenge of the task lies in how to achieve model training and more accurate predictions using extremely limited labeled data and a large amount of unlabeled data.

2.2 Audio Features

Among different acoustic features, Generalized Cross Correlation-Phase Transform (GCC-PHAT) is the most widely used for the estimation of time delays [12]. The peak value is obtained by calculating the mutual correlation function between two microphone signals, which corresponds to the time delay between the signals. The location and direction of the sound can be estimated by comparing the peaks. Given two microphone signals $\boldsymbol{s_1}$ and $\boldsymbol{s_2}$, GCC-PHAT is derived with the following formula:

$$C_{s1,s2}(\tau) = \frac{1}{B} \sum_{b=0}^{B-1} \frac{\hat{\mathbf{R}}_{s1,s2}(\tau, f_b) \hat{\mathbf{R}}^*_{s1,s2}(\tau, f_b)}{\left|\hat{\mathbf{R}}_{s1,s2}(\tau, f_b)\right| \left|\hat{\mathbf{R}}_{s1,s2}(\tau, f_b)\right|} \tag{5}$$

where the summation is taken over B frequency bins, $*$ denotes the complex conjugate, and $\hat{R}_{s1,s2}(\tau, f_b)$ represents the cross-power spectral density between the signals $\boldsymbol{s_1}$ and $\boldsymbol{s_2}$ at frequency f_b. The denominator $\left|\hat{\mathbf{R}}_{s1,s2}(\tau, f_b)\right| \left|\hat{\mathbf{R}}_{s1,s2}(\tau, f_b)\right|$ normalizes the cross-power spectral density, emphasizing the phase information over the amplitude.

2.3 Neural Network Architecture

Multilayer Perceptron (MLP) is able to handle complex non-linear relationships with good generalization ability by nonlinear mapping of input data through activation functions [13, 14]. It is also capable of receiving multiple feature inputs to handle high-dimensional data.

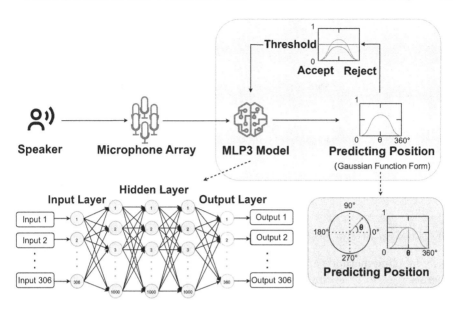

Fig. 1. The structure of our proposed method and the inter-level details.

We propose an MLP model for SSL. Specifically, the model takes an audio feature vector $\boldsymbol{x}$ (consists of concatenated GCC-PHAT of all possible microphone pairs) as the input and produces the predicted probabilities $\hat{\boldsymbol{p}}(\theta)$ for each of the 360° which represent the probabilities of the sound source being at an angle θ_i, through multiple non-linear transformations (Fig. 1).

Specifically, the MLP model consists of an input layer, three hidden layers, and an output layer. For the lth hidden layer ($l = 1, 2, 3$), the forward propagation can be represented as:

$$z^{(l)} = \boldsymbol{W}^{(l)}\boldsymbol{a}^{(l-1)} + \boldsymbol{b}^{(l)} \tag{6}$$

$$\boldsymbol{a}^{(l)} = f(\boldsymbol{z}^{(l)}) = \text{ReLU}(\text{BN}(\boldsymbol{z}^{(l)})) \tag{7}$$

where $\boldsymbol{W}^{(l)}$ and $\boldsymbol{b}^{(l)}$ denote the weight matrix and bias vector of the lth layer, respectively. BN($\cdot$) represents the batch normalization function, and ReLU($\cdot$) is the rectified linear unit activation function.

Each hidden layer contains 1000 neurons, fully connected to all neurons in the previous layer. We use the ReLU activation function between hidden layers to introduce a nonlinear transformation, enhancing the network's ability to fit nonlinear data [15]. To avoid overfitting, we apply batch normalization (BN) and dropout in the hidden layers. BN normalizes the input to each layer, accelerating convergence and improving generalization, while randomly drops hidden neuron activations during training, serving as a regularizer. Finally, at the output layer, we apply the Sigmoid function to normalize the weighted sum:

$$\hat{\boldsymbol{p}}_i(\theta) = \text{Sigmoid}(\boldsymbol{a}^{(3)}) \tag{8}$$

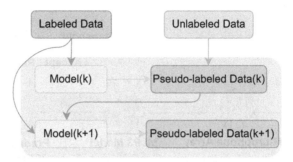

Fig. 2. The pseudo labeling and iterative model update process.

2.4   Design of the Semi-supervised Algorithm

Proxy labeling methods are a class of Semi-Supervised Learning algorithms that generate pseudo labels on unlabeled data to train the original model [11,16,17]. Our proposed method is illustrated in Fig. 2 and described as follows:

An initial Model(k) is trained based on labeled data, as depicted by the arrow from labeled data to the Model(k) in Fig. 2 (variable k represents the iteration round in the model training process). Subsequently, unlabeled data is fed into the initial model to generate pseudo-labeled data. Not all predictions are used as pseudo-labels. We propose a novel scheme for evaluating the prediction's confidence, involving fitting a Gaussian function to the Mean Squared Error (MSE) between predictions and their targets, to select high-confidence ones as pseudo-labels. Finally, the model is retrained using both labeled and pseudo-labeled data to generate an updated Model($k + 1$). This process is iterated.

The process of obtaining high-confidence model predictions is described as follows. We generate the Gaussian-like pseudo-label as:

$$g(\theta, \hat{\theta}_i) = \exp\left(-\frac{(\theta - \hat{\theta}_i)^2}{2\sigma^2}\right) \qquad (9)$$

where $\hat{\theta}_i$ represents the pseudo DoA label, which corresponds to the angle at which the model predicts the highest probability among 360 possible directions; we set $\sigma = 10$.

To be noted, only predictions whose posterior probability $p_{max,i} > \alpha$ and error below a threshold ϵ are eventually used to form the set of high-confidence pseudo-labels $\boldsymbol{\Theta}_{ps}$:

$$\begin{cases} \boldsymbol{\Theta}_{ps,i} = \{\theta \mid p_{max,i} > \alpha \text{ and } |\hat{\boldsymbol{p}}_i(\theta), g(\theta, \hat{\theta}_i)| < \epsilon\} \\ \boldsymbol{X}_{ps,i} = \{\boldsymbol{X}_{un,i} \mid \exists \boldsymbol{\Theta}_{ps,i}\} \end{cases} \qquad (10)$$

Finally, these high-confidence pseudo labels are merged into our training set, augmenting the labeled data:

$$\begin{cases} \boldsymbol{X}_{tr} = \boldsymbol{X}_{tr} \cup \boldsymbol{X}_{ps} \\ \boldsymbol{\Theta}_{tr} = \boldsymbol{\Theta}_{tr} \cup \boldsymbol{\Theta}_{ps} \end{cases} \tag{11}$$

Finally, we use MSE to optimize the model parameters. Specifically, the MSE is computed between the model prediction with the real posterior probability (Eq. 4) or the generated Gaussian-like pseudo labels (Eq. 9).

Algorithm 1: Pseudo-Label Generation and Model Training

Input : Training data and labels $(\boldsymbol{X}_{tr}, \boldsymbol{\Theta}_{tr})$, unlabeled data $\boldsymbol{X}_{un}$, pseudo-labeling threshold (α, ϵ)
Output: Pseudo labels $\boldsymbol{\Theta}_{ps}$
Initialize model parameters Ω;

Semi-Supervised learning pipeline:
for *each data point* $\boldsymbol{x}_i$ *in* $\boldsymbol{X}_{un}$ **do**

> **Forward pass:**
> $\hat{\boldsymbol{p}}_i(\theta) \leftarrow f(\boldsymbol{x}_i; \Omega)$;
> **Highest predicted value**
> $\hat{\theta}_i = \arg\max_\theta \hat{\boldsymbol{p}}_i(\theta)$;
> $p_{max,i} = \max \hat{\boldsymbol{p}}_i(\theta)$;
> **Gaussian function error calculation:**
> $g(\theta, \hat{\theta}_i) \leftarrow \exp\left(\frac{-(\theta-\hat{\theta}_i)^2}{2\sigma^2}\right)$;
> error $\leftarrow |\hat{\boldsymbol{p}}_i(\theta), g(\theta, \hat{\theta}_i)|$;
> **High-confidence pseudo label selection:**
> **if** $p_{max,i} > \alpha$ *and* error $< \epsilon$ **then**
>> $\boldsymbol{\Theta}_{ps,i} \leftarrow \hat{\theta}_i$;
>> $\boldsymbol{X}_{ps,i} \leftarrow \{\boldsymbol{X}_{un,i} \mid \exists \boldsymbol{\Theta}_{ps}\}$;
>> $(\boldsymbol{X}_{tr}, \boldsymbol{\Theta}_{tr}) \leftarrow \{(\boldsymbol{X}_{tr}, \boldsymbol{\Theta}_{tr}) \cup (\boldsymbol{X}_{ps,i}, \boldsymbol{\Theta}_{ps,i})\}$

Model training and Supervised learning pipeline:
for *each data point* $(\boldsymbol{x}_i, \theta_i)$ *in* $(\boldsymbol{X}_{tr}, \boldsymbol{\Theta}_{tr})$ **do**

> Shuffle training data;
> **for** *each mini-batch* **do**
>> **Forward pass:**
>> $\hat{\boldsymbol{p}}_i(\theta) \leftarrow f(\boldsymbol{x}_i; \Omega)$;
>> **Backward pass:**
>> compute MSE error
>> Update model parameters Ω

Through the formulations and principles described above, the proposed multilayer perceptron model can learn feature representations from the input audio features to predict the source DoA angle, while employing reasonable regularization strategies to mitigate overfitting.

Table 1. Hyperparameter settings

Hyperparameters	Value
Learning rate	0.001
Batch size	256
Epoch	10
Drop	0.2
Number of layers	3
Number of hidden units	1000
Optimization algorithm	Adam
Pseudo-label classification threshold	0.5, 0.09
Accuracy calculation threshold	5

3 Experiments

3.1 Dataset and Performance Metrics

We use the publicly available Sound Source Localization for Robots (SSLR) dataset for experiments. It enables us to explore and validate our approach effectively, leveraging both labeled and pseudo-labeled data to enhance model performance in scenarios with limited annotated data. We utilized the loudspeaker and human talker sections of the dataset, excluding the noise section, which was sufficient to train and test our model.

We use Mean Absolute Error (MAE) and Accuracy (ACC) as the evaluation metric. The MAE is defined as the average absolute error between the predicted value and the true label,

$$\text{MAE} = \frac{1}{N} \sum_{n=1}^{N} \left| \theta_i - \hat{\theta}_i \right| \tag{12}$$

where $i = 1, ..., N$ denotes the number of samples, θ_i denotes the true DoA label and $\hat{\theta}_i$ denotes the prediction. The accuracy is calculated as:

$$\text{ACC} = \frac{\sum_i \delta(\left| \theta_i - \hat{\theta}_i \right| \leq \beta)}{\text{Number of Samples}} \tag{13}$$

where δ is the indicator function whose value sets to 1 if the content in parentheses is correct and 0 otherwise; β is the threshold.

3.2 Parameter Settings

The hyperparameter settings are listed in Table 1. We use the Adam optimizer [18] and all models are trained for 10 epochs. Specifically, the SSLR dataset is recorded in a physical setup with one or two concurrent speakers and with

Table 2. A summary of MAE ($°$) and ACC (%) of speaker and human speaker DoA estimation on the SSLR test set with different learning methods (S indicates the number of speakers; the number of audio frames for each subset is given in bracket).

Split Ratio	Method	Loudspeaker				Human				Overall	
		S = 1(178K)		S = 2(29K)		S = 1(788K)		S = 2(141K)			
		MAE	ACC	MAE	ACC	MAE	ACC	MAE	ACC	MAE	ACC
25%	Supervised Learning	4.74	94.0	10.12	64.9	5.34	93.0	7.65	71.3	5.49	89.9
	Meta Pseudo Labels	4.51	94.3	9.58	66.8	3.78	95.6	4.32	77.7	5.21	90.4
	Our Method	**4.52**	**94.2**	**9.32**	**67.3**	**4.54**	**95.6**	**4.42**	**76.7**	**5.19**	**90.4**
30%	Supervised Learning	4.85	93.0	9.81	65.3	4.90	91.9	4.34	75.5	5.54	89.1
	Meta Pseudo Labels	4.46	94.5	9.35	67.4	5.90	93.1	6.23	67.0	5.15	90.7
	Our Method	**4.40**	**94.2**	**8.74**	**69.8**	**2.35**	**96.7**	**4.74**	**78.7**	**4.99**	**90.8**
35%	Supervised Learning	4.23	94.0	8.76	68.0	3.61	96.4	5.03	78.7	4.86	90.4
	Meta Pseudo Labels	4.23	94.6	8.80	68.6	5.65	95.1	4.49	74.1	4.87	91.0
	Our Method	**4.21**	**94.5**	**8.92**	**68.2**	**4.83**	**94.5**	**5.53**	**74.8**	**4.87**	**90.8**
40%	Supervised Learning	4.53	94.0	8.99	67.6	5.02	95.6	6.00	74.5	5.15	90.3
	Meta Pseudo Labels	4.22	94.6	8.80	68.9	4.34	94.8	6.77	69.9	4.86	91.0
	Our method	**4.22**	**94.3**	**8.16**	**70.5**	**4.68**	**94.7**	**4.23**	**77.3**	**4.77**	**91.0**

adequate target 3D annotations. It consists of 4-channel audio recordings at 48 kHz sampling rate, which is organized into three subsets, namely training, testing-Human, and testing-Loudspeaker. We randomly select two microphones from four, resulting in 6 pairs. Thus, the input data to our neural network are of dimension $(6, 51)$, representing the GCC-PHAT coefficients from the 6 pairs, with each pair contributing 51 coefficients ($\tau \in [-25, 25]$ samples). In this process of pseudo labeling, the threshold α for the predicted probability is set to 0.5, and the threshold ϵ for the mean squared error (MSE) is set to 0.09. The ACC threshold β is set to $5°$.

3.3   Results

We evaluated our proposed semi-supervised learning method against the supervised learning method (only using data with annotations) and another semi-supervised learning approach i.e., meta pseudo labels [19]. All methods are tested under identical conditions using the aforementioned MLP3 model architecture.

The results are listed in Table 2 where split ratio represents the proportion of labeled data in the training set. For instance, a Split Ratio of 25% indicates that 25% of the data is used as labeled data while the remaining 75% is used as unlabeled data, under the condition that the total amount of data remains constant.

Our experiments demonstrate that our proposed method consistently outperforms methods with supervised learning and meta pseudo labels in terms of both MAE and ACC across all data split ratios (25% to 40% labeled data). In particular, even in the least favorable scenario with a 25% split ratio, our method achieves an average MAE of 5.19° and an accuracy of 90.4%.

In contrast, the supervised learning method, which relies solely on labeled data without leveraging the additional information from unlabeled data, performs less effectively. When the proportion of labeled data is low, the MAE and ACC of supervised learning show a significant disparity compared to the two semi-supervised learning methods. For example, with a Split Ratio of 30%, the ACC of supervised learning is nearly 2% lower than that of the other methods.

Compared to the meta pseudo labels method, our method not only outperforms it in the majority of cases but also demonstrates greater stability. The instability of the meta pseudo labels method may be attributed to the teacher model updating its parameters based on the student model, which may contain insuitable parameters [16]. For example, with split ratios of 30%, 35%, and 40%, and testing on Human ($S = 2$), the ACC of the meta pseudo labels method (67.0%, 74.1%, and 69.9%) is significantly lower than that of the other two methods.

4 Conclusions

In this paper, we proposed a novel deep-learning-based semi-supervised SSL algorithm. Our method addresses the critical challenge of limited availability of labeled data in practical applications of speaker localization. Our comprehensive evaluation results demonstrate that our approach significantly outperforms the traditional supervised learning method and other competitive semi-supervised learning methods. In conclusion, our work contributes significantly to the challenge of data scarcity, paving the way for a more robust and practical implementation of DoA estimation systems in various real-world applications.

For future work, we plan to extend this application to more complex acoustic environments with multiple moving speakers and varying noise conditions.

Acknowledgements. This work is supported by National Natural Science Foundation of China under Grant No. 62306029 and Beijing Natural Science Foundation under Grant L233032.

References

1. Qian, X., Brutti, A., Lanz, O., Omologo, M., Cavallaro, A.: Audio-visual tracking of concurrent speakers. IEEE Trans. Multimedia (2021)
2. Qian, X., Liu, Q., Wang, J., Li, H.: Three-dimensional speaker localization: audio-refined visual scaling factor estimation. IEEE Signal Process. Lett. **28**, 1405–1409 (2021)
3. Qian, X., Pan, Z., Zhang, Q., Chen, K., Lin, S.: GLMB 3D speaker tracking with video-assisted multi-channel audio optimization functions. In: Proceedings of IEEE International Conference on Audio, Speech and Signal Processing, pp. 8100–8104. IEEE (2024)

4. Chen, J., Yao, K., Hudson, R.: Source localization and beamforming. IEEE Signal Process. Mag. **19**(2), 30–39 (2002). https://doi.org/10.1109/79.985676
5. Chen, J.C., Yao, K., Hudson, R.E.: Acoustic source localization and beamforming: theory and practice. EURASIP J. Adv. Signal Process. **2003**, 1–12 (2003)
6. He, W., Motlicek, P., Odobez, J.M.: Deep neural networks for multiple speaker detection and localization. In: Proceedings of International Conference on Robotics and Automation, pp. 74–79 (2018)
7. Wang, J., Qian, X., Pan, Z., Zhang, M., Li, H.: GCC-PHAT with speech-oriented attention for robotic sound source localization. In: Proceedings of International Conference on Robotics and Automation, pp. 74–79 (2021)
8. Qian, X., Madhavi, M., Pan, Z., Wang, J., Li, H.: Multi-target DOA estimation with an audio-visual fusion mechanism. In: Proceedings of IEEE International Conference on Audio, Speech and Signal Processing, pp. 2814–2818 (2021)
9. Qian, X., Yue, X., Wang, J., Zhuang, H., Li, H.: Analytic class incremental learning for sound source localization with privacy protection. arXiv preprint arXiv:2409.07224 (2024)
10. Cascante-Bonilla, P., Tan, F., Qi, Y., Ordonez, V.: Curriculum labeling: revisiting pseudo-labeling for semi-supervised learning. In: Proceedings of the AAAI Conference on Artificial Intelligence, pp. 4358–4366 (2018)
11. Lee, D.H.: Pseudo-label: the simple and efficient semi-supervised learning method for deep neural networks. In: Workshop on Challenges in Representation Learning, ICML, pp. 896–906 (2013)
12. Knapp, C., Carter, G.: The generalized correlation method for estimation of time delay. IEEE/ACM Trans. Audio Speech Lang. Process. **24**(4), 320–327 (1976)
13. Werbos, P.: Beyond regression: new tools for prediction and analysis in the behavioral sciences. Ph.D. thesis, Committee on Applied Mathematics, Harvard University, Cambridge, MA (1974)
14. Rumelhart, D.E., McClelland, J.L., Group, P.R., et al.: Parallel Distributed Processing, Volume 1: Explorations in the Microstructure of Cognition: Foundations. The MIT Press (1986)
15. Agarap, A.F.: Deep learning using rectified linear units (relu). arXiv preprint arXiv:1803.08375 (2018)
16. Ouali, Y., Hudelot, C., Tami, M.: An overview of deep semi-supervised learning. arXiv preprint arXiv:2006.05278 (2020)
17. Arazo, E., Ortego, D., Albert, P., O'Connor, N.E., McGuinness, K.: Pseudo-labeling and confirmation bias in deep semi-supervised learning. In: Proceedings of International Joint Conference on Neural Networks, pp. 1–8. IEEE (2020)
18. Kingma, D.P., Ba, J.: Adam: a method for stochastic optimization. arXiv preprint arXiv:1412.6980 (2014)
19. Pham, H., Dai, Z., Xie, Q., Le, Q.V.: Meta pseudo labels. In: Proceedings of International Conference on Computer Vision and Pattern Recognition, pp. 11557–11568 (2021)

MCCS: The First Open Multi-Cuer Mandarin Chinese Cued Speech Dataset and Benchmark

Li Liu[1(✉)], Lufei Gao[1], Wentao Lei[1], Yuzhi He[2], Yuxing He[2], Che Feng[1], Yue Chen[1,3], and Zheyu Li[1,4]

[1] The Hong Kong University of Science and Technology, Guangzhou, China
`avrillliu@hkust-gz.edu.cn`
[2] The Experimental High School Attached to Beijing Normal University, Beijing, China
[3] University of Edinburgh, Edinburgh, UK
[4] University of Nottingham Ningbo China, Ningbo, China

Abstract. Cued Speech (CS) is an innovative communication system that enhances lip reading by incorporating hand gestures. This method significantly improves comprehension for individuals with hearing impairments. The development of automatic CS recognition and generation facilitates more effective communication between deaf individuals and the hearing community. The CS dataset is essential for establishing an AI-based automatic recognition and generation model for CS. Previous CS datasets were mainly in English and French, and the data volume was small with a single cuer (*i.e.*, people who perform CS), which hinders research progress in this field. Therefore, we have constructed, for the first time, a **Mandarin Chinese CS Dataset (MCCSD)** containing 4000 CS videos from four native Chinese CS cuers. Importantly, we propose a novel GAN-based CS Video Gesture Generation baseline for the first time. To further validate the effectiveness of this dataset, we build a benchmark for both automatic CS video recognition and generation. Experimental results demonstrate that MCCS serves as a valuable benchmark for CS recognition and generation, presenting new challenges and insights for future research. The complete dataset, benchmark, and source codes, will be made publicly available.

Keywords: Mandarin Chinese Cued Speech · Dataset and Benchmark · Automatic CS Recognition · Automatic CS Video Generation

1 Introduction

To assist the hearing impaired in better understanding speech, Cued Speech (CS) was developed by Dr. Cornett [7] as a visual communication system. CS employs

---

L. Liu, L. Gao and W. Lei—Equal contribution.

© The Author(s), under exclusive license to Springer Nature Singapore Pte Ltd. 2025
H. Li et al. (Eds.): ICSR + InnoBiz 2024, LNAI 15170, pp. 156–166, 2025.
https://doi.org/10.1007/978-981-96-1151-5_16

a set of hand shapes and positions, known as cues, to represent phonemes such as consonants and vowels. The details of Mandarin Chinese CS (MCCS) [14,18] is illustrated in Fig. 1, showing five hand positions for Chinese vowels and eight hand shapes for consonants. In CS, hand gestures supplement lip-reading by providing visual cues for phonetic elements that may not be clearly distinguished from lip movements alone. This combination helps eliminate ambiguities often encountered in lip-reading. By offering a clear visual representation of speech, CS serves as an effective alternative to audio input for hearing-impaired individuals. This system enhances their ability to comprehend and differentiate spoken language, which in turn promotes the development of their verbal skills, improves reading proficiency, and strengthens overall communication capabilities.

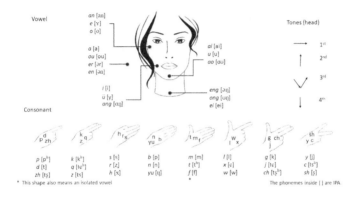

Fig. 1. Table of the combinations between hand shapes and hand positions in MCCS, shown separately for vowels and consonants. Image from [14].

As shown in Fig. 2, automatic CS recognition aims to convert CS videos into text, categorizing it as a video recognition task designed to help hearing individuals better understand the content expressed by those with hearing impairments. On the other hand, automatic CS generation aims to convert text or audio signals into corresponding CS gesture videos, making it a video generation task primarily intended to help hearing-impaired individuals visually comprehend the content expressed by hearing individuals without barriers.

Previously, there were only two public CS datasets. One is in French[1] [15,20] and the other is in British English[2] [19]. On the one hand, these existing datasets are very small (i.e., French dataset contains 476 CS videos, and the British English dataset contains 97 CS videos) and consist of data from a single cuer[3]. On the other hand, there are currently no Chinese CS datasets available.

---

[1] https://zenodo.org/record/5554849#.ZBBCvOxBx8Y.
[2] https://zenodo.org/record/3464212#.ZBBAJuxBx8Y.
[3] People who perform CS are called cuer.

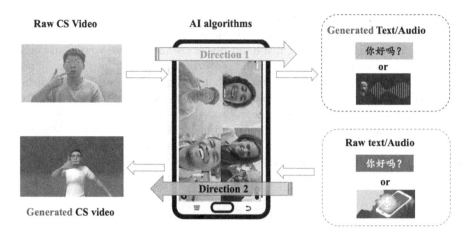

Fig. 2. The bidirectional framework for CS and text/audio conversion. Direction 1: CS to text/audio recognition, enabling normal-hearing individuals to understand CS users. Direction 2: Text/audio to CS gesture generation, helping hearing-impaired individuals visually interpret speech from normal-hearing people.

To address the lack of Mandarin Chinese CS data and enlarge the amount of data and cuers, in this work, we establish the first open dataset for Mandarin Chinese CS called MCCS, which is larger in scale and in cuer amount. Table 1 is a summary of these open CS datasets. Moreover, to validate the effectiveness of our dataset, we established a CS benchmark containing CS recognition and generation for the first time. Importantly, for automatic CS generation, we proposed a GAN-based baseline model for the task of CS gesture video generation.

Table 1. Details of the three public CS datasets with different languages (*i.e.*, French, British English and our MCCSD).

Dataset	French	British	MCCSD
#Cuer	1	1	4
#CS Video	476	97	4000
#Character	12872	2741	131581
#Word	1190	485	42248

2   Related Work

French CS Database. The data collection took place in a specially designed sound-proof chamber at France's GIPSA-lab. Two female CS speakers with normal hearing, identified as LM and SC, participated in the recording process. The setup captured color video footage of the speakers' upper body regions, utilizing a frame rate of 50 fps and producing RGB images with resolution of 720×576. It's worth noting that the LM corpus was recorded without the use of any artificial markers. For her contribution, LM articulated and coded a set of 238 French sentences in CS, which were adapted from a corpus previously described in [1,17]. To enhance the dataset's robustness, each sentence was repeated, resulting in a total of 476 recorded sentences.

British English CS Dataset. The first British English CS dataset was created at Deaf Choices UK (formerly Cued Speech UK)[4]. This dataset is unique as it's the first to focus on continuous recognition in British English CS and was recorded without any special markers. A skilled CS user with normal hearing was chosen to speak and code 97 British English sentences at the same time. The recordings show the upper body of the CS user in color video, taken at 25 frames per second, with each image being 720×1280 resolution.

3   MCCS Dataset

Reading Material. The text acquisition process comprises three key stages: raw text collection, data cleaning, and data filtering. During the raw text collection phase, we first select content from reliable, widely circulated sources with significant impact. These texts are not only closely related to daily life but also span multiple domains, ensuring the quality and diversity of our dataset. Following these principles, we carefully choose materials from diverse sources such as social media, news reports, novels, and poetry. This diverse selection strategy aims to build a comprehensive and representative text database. Finally, the dataset contains 23 primary scenario categories, such as communication, transportation, and shopping, further subdivided into 72 specific subcategories including meetings, dating, and introductions. In particular, when designing the text, we have included as many of the commonly used syllables as possible. There are a total of 413 Chinese pinyin syllables, and our corpus includes 399 of them. The distribution of the syllables is shown in Fig. 3, which follows a long-tailed distribution. The text on the chart lists all the syllables in order of frequency. The distribution of sentence length is shown in Fig. 4.

CS Video Recording. All CS videos are recorded by a mobile phone with 30 fps and 1280×720 format. All the participants have received at least one month of systematic training and can complete the MCCS recording smoothly and accurately. Four cuers (two female and two male) utter 4000 sentences using CS (see Fig. 5). Since these four cuers are all normal hearing, they were required to produce audio sound to facilitate our experiment for rhythmic information extraction. The background of the recording was kept white, with no shadows allowed. Before annotation, each video was cross-checked by four cuers to ensure there were no errors.

---

[4] https://www.deafchoicesuk.com/.

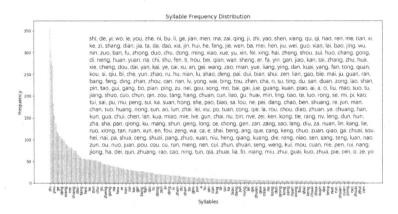

Fig. 3. The syllable distribution and all syllables presented in the text corpus. The horizontal axis lists every fifth syllable.

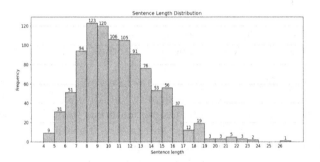

Fig. 4. The sentence length (*i.e.*, the number of words in the sentence) distribution in the text corpus.

Data Annotations. As our CS data contained audio and images sampled from videos, we annotated the audio and CS video, respectively. It should be noted that since the lips feature is assumed to be synchronous with the audio signal [2], we regard the temporal segments on the audio signals as the temporal segments for lip reading. The *Praat* tool [23] is used for audio annotation. *ELAN* [9] is used for temporal annotation of hand movements in CS video, which is to label the hand position and hand shape sequences. We manually annotate all temporal boundaries of lip and hand movements for all phonemes in our MCCSD by checking the semantic meaning of lip shapes, hand shapes and hand positions in the CS videos.

The ground truth CS gesture landmarks are obtained using 3D pose estimation from the CS video. *OpenPose*'s pose detection [5] was used to obtain the lip and hand gesture landmarks (containing 70 for the face including 20 for the lip and 42 for the hand). We only select a subset of landmarks as ground truth to reduce the complexity of the task while ensuring a good visualization effect.

(a) Cuer HS expresses syllable "yan" (b) Cuer LF expresses syllable "wei" (c) Cuer WT expresses syllable "a" (d) Cuer XP expresses syllable "lai"

Fig. 5. The four MCCS cuers in MCCSD (two females and two males). They are all native Chinese, and the data annotations are completed by them.

Open Sourcing of Dataset. All cuers agree to make this MCCSD public and they sign a consent for the privacy and research morality issue. In summary, our dataset comprises raw Mandarin Chinese Cued Speech videos featuring four skilled cuers, accompanied by audio recordings and a text file containing 1000 sentences. We also provide corresponding annotations at both the audio and video levels. We currently make it public (https://mccs2023.github.io/) to available exclusively to academic and research organizations.

Table 2. Performance comparisons (CER) on British English, French CS datasets and our MCCS.

Dataset	French	British	MCCSD	
#Speaker	single	single	single	multiple
CNN + LSTM [22]	33.4	43.6	55.4	61.4
JLF + COS + CTC [25]	25.8	35.1	33.5	68.2
CMML [12]	24.9	33.6	9.7	24.5
EcoCued [13]	24.8	33.0	9.0	22.2

4 Benchmarks

4.1 Benchmark for Automatic CS Recognition

In this section, we conducted a series of experiments to evaluate the effectiveness of our dataset using previous models [12,13,16]. Specifically, we performed the CS-to-phoneme recognition experiment, which aims to recognize the multi-modal CS gestures and convert them into text (phoneme). This experiment is to validate the quality of our dataset by establishing baseline results. The rationale behind this choice is that there is a wealth of prior research on CS-to-text recognition in French and English CS, allowing us to leverage existing algorithms and assess their performance on MCCSD. The results are presented in Table 2.

The training and test sentences were divided randomly in a 4:1 ratio. The character error rate (CER) was employed as the evaluation metric for the CS phoneme recognition performance of all methods. Here, we consider the 35 phonemes in French, the 36 phonemes in British English, and the 39 phonemes in Chinese. Due to the absence of word-level annotations for French and British English CS datasets, we do not include the Word Error Rate (WER).

As shown in Table 2, our previous Economical Cued Speech Fusion Transformer (EcoCued) [13] outperformed other baselines (Cross-Modal Mutual Learning (CMML) [12], CNN + LSTM [22] and JLF + COS + CTC [25]), both across different CS datasets and different cuer settings based on MCCSD.

Additionally, we observed that the multi-cuer task proved to be more challenging than the single-cuer case, primarily due to cuer adaption issue. In general, there are discrepancies between the characteristics of the cuers in the training set and those in the testing or real-world scenarios. These discrepancies can include differences in speaking style, hand movement rhythm and other individual variations. Therefore, the issue of multiple cuer adaptations is when the testing set comprises cuers who were not included in the training set, resulting in unsatisfactory performance during testing. This finding suggests a valuable direction for future research in CS recognition.

4.2   Benchmark for Automatic CS Generation

To the best of our knowledge, currently, there are no deep learning-based methods for CS gesture video generation. Therefore, we propose a baseline model based on GANs for the first time. It primarily includes a module for extracting text features and a GAN-based generation method. The details are as follows.

Note that, in this work, we do not employ a diffusion model because it typically requires a robust encoder [21,26], often utilizing text encoders like Contrastive Language-Image Pretraining (CLIP) [24]. However, the gesture-text CS dataset is insufficient for training a strong CLIP model. Additionally, using the pre-trained CLIP model can result in domain gaps (*i.e.*, the image-text mapping for CS is image-phoneme, which differs from CLIP's image-text mapping). In contrast, GAN-based methods can generate realistic gestures without needing a large amount of data, making them more suitable for CS gesture generation.

Text Feature Extraction. Text features are extracted by first decomposing text into phonemes, aligning with the video frame rate. These are converted into 300-dimensional word vectors using a Chinese word embedding layer trained on the *Chinese Wikipedia* corpus, derived from *FastText*. These word vectors are then encoded into 64-dimensional text feature vectors using a temporal convolutional network, which outperforms RNNs for our task.

Loss Function for Text Encoder. During the training process of the encoder and gesture generator, our objective is to minimize the discrepancy between the ground truth CS gestures from the training data and their corresponding generated gestures $\hat{M}$. To achieve this, we employ the Huber loss function [10]. The gesture loss L_G^{Huber} is defined as follows:

$$L_G^{\text{Huber}} = \frac{1}{N} \sum_{i=1}^{N} \mathrm{H}\left(M_i, \hat{M}_i\right), \tag{1}$$

Here, H denotes the Huber loss function, and N represents the total number of frames in a video sequence. We define M_i as the directional vectors representing human poses in the i-th frame, while $\hat{M}$ signifies the corresponding generated semantic gesture. To ensure consistency, all directional vectors are normalized to unit length. The L_G^{Huber} can be characterized as a smoothly differentiable fusion of $L1$ and $L2$ losses, often referred to as the smooth $L1$ loss. This formulation offers a balance between the robustness of $L1$ and the stability of $L2$, making it particularly suitable for our gesture generation task.

GAN-Based Semantic CS Video Gesture Generator. Since our text features and speech features are aligned with the frame number of our gesture sequence, we directly concatenate the text features and speech features to obtain our final input features $f = (f^{text}, f^{audio})$. Here $f \in R^{128 \times N}$. The semantic gesture generator $G(\cdot)$ uses the final input features f as input and generates the semantic gestures $\hat{M}$. We represent a gesture sequence using a coordinate vector of keypoints. Here $\hat{M} \in R^{K \times N}$, where K is the number of key landmarks of gestures and N is the number of frames. Each gesture contains 137 key landmarks (*i.e.*, 70 for the face, 42 for the hand, and 25 for the pose). To ensure consistency in time length N, we align the input time length with the output gesture, enabling our proposed framework to process information frame by frame for gesture generation.

Loss Function for Semantic Gesture Generator and Discriminator. To enhance the realism of generated gestures, we implement an adversarial training strategy, drawing inspiration from [8]. This approach utilizes a generator-discriminator architecture. Our gesture generator's model architecture is based on a multi-layered bidirectional GRU [6], an adaptation influenced by the NS-GAN [8]. The loss function is:

$$L_G^{\text{GAN}} = -\mathbb{E}[\log(D(\hat{M}))], \tag{2}$$

where the discriminator D functions as a binary classifier, tasked with differentiating between GT and generated gestures. Specifically, we employ a Bi-GRU architecture, which produces a binary output for each frame, followed by an FC layer for final classification. The generator processes fused feature vectors $f_i = (f_i^{text}, f_i^{audio})$, combining text and audio encodings for each frame i. It sequentially produces the next pose $\hat{M}i + 1$ based on each input fi.

The loss function L_D to train the discriminator is defined as follows:

$$L_D = -\mathbb{E}[\log(D(M))] - \mathbb{E}[\log(1 - D(\hat{M}))]. \tag{3}$$

By alternately optimizing the generator and the discriminator, the generator will fool the discriminator by improving its performance, ending up with a better generator.

Total Loss is $\mathcal{L} = \lambda_1 L_G^{Huber} + \lambda_2 L_G^{GAN} + \lambda_3 L_D$, where λ_j $(j = 1, 2, 3)$ are the balancing weights for each loss.

Results on MCCS Dataset. Table 3 summarizes the performance of various methods on the MCCS Dataset. Our proposed method demonstrates the lowest values for the Percentage of Correct Keypoint (PCK) [27], Mean Absolute Joint Errors (MAJE) [28], Mean Acceleration Difference (MAD) [28], and Fréchet Gesture Distance (FGD) [28]. Notably, the FGD values of our method are significantly lower than those of other methods, indicating that the gestures synthesized by our methods possess higher perceptual quality.

Table 3. Experiment results on MCCS Dataset compared with SOTA methods. ↑ means the higher the better, ↓ means the lower the better.

Methods	PCK (%)↑	FGD↓	MAJE (mm)↓	MAD (mm/s^2)↓
GES [11]	31.5	36.7	60.87	2.87
GTC [28]	33.2	34.1	58.46	2.65
S2AG [4]	37.8	31.9	53.75	1.92
RG [3]	43.2	29.5	49.53	0.97
Ours	**45.7**	**28.3**	**37.21**	**0.67**

5 Conclusion and Insights

This work presents the first Mandarin Chinese Cued Speech (MCCS) dataset that includes four cuers and introduces, for the first time, a baseline model for GAN-based CS gesture video generation. These contributions are expected to advance the fields of CS recognition and generation. This task raises higher demands for the understanding of fine-grained gestures and the precise generation of fine-grained multi-modal gestures. Combining the advantages of large multi-modal models with prompt learning to achieve better results is one of the potential future research directions in this field. Additionally, due to privacy concerns, the dataset currently includes CS data from individuals with normal hearing. In the future, it will be essential to explore how to construct a dataset, including CS data recorded by hearing-impaired individuals, while protecting privacy, and to establish a more comprehensive benchmark for this dataset. Besides, speaker adaption for CS recognition and the multi-modal conditional diffusion model for CS video generation are worth exploring.

Acknowledgments. This work was supported by the National Natural Science Foundation of China (No. 62101351), Guangzhou Municipal Science and Technology Project: Basic and Applied Basic research projects (No. 2024A04J4232).

References

1. Aboutabit, N.: Reconnaissance de la Langue Française Parlée Complété (LPC): décodage phonétique des gestes main-lèvres. Ph.D. thesis, Institut National Polytechnique de Grenoble-INPG (2007)

2. Angela, T., Mark, G., Abdel, N.D.: The effect of onset asynchrony in audio-visual speech and the uncanny valley in virtual characters. Int. J. Mech. Rob. Syst. **2**(2), 97–110 (2015)
3. Ao, T., Gao, Q., Lou, Y., Chen, B., Liu, L.: Rhythmic gesticulator. ACM Trans. Graph. **41**(6), 1–19 (2022). https://doi.org/10.1145/3550454.3555435
4. Bhattacharya, U., Childs, E., Rewkowski, N., Manocha, D.: Speech2affectivegestures: synthesizing co-speech gestures with generative adversarial affective expression learning. In: ACM MM (2021)
5. Cao, Z., Gines, H., Tomas, S., Shih-En, W., Yaser, S.: Openpose: realtime multiperson 2d pose estimation using part affinity fields. TPAMI **43**(1), 172–186 (2021). https://doi.org/10.1109/TPAMI.2019.2929257
6. Cho, K., van Merrienboer, B., Gulcehre, C., Bougares, F., Schwenk, H., Bengio, Y.: Learning phrase representations using rnn encoder-decoder for statistical machine translation. In: EMNLP (2014)
7. Cornett, R.O.: Cued speech. Am. Ann. Deaf **112**(1), 3–13 (1967)
8. Goodfellow, I., et al.: In: NeurIPS (2014)
9. Hennie, B., Albert, R., Xd, N.: Annotating multi-media/multi-modal resources with elan. In: LREC (2004)
10. Huber, J.: Robust estimation of a location parameter. Ann. Math. Stat. **35**(1), 73–101 (1964). https://doi.org/10.1214/aoms/1177703732
11. Kucherenko, T., et al.: Gesticulator: a framework for semantically-aware speech-driven gesture generation. In: ICMI (2020). https://doi.org/10.1145/3382507.3418815
12. Liu, L., Liu, L.: Cross-modal mutual learning for cued speech recognition. In: Proceedings of IEEE-ICASSP, pp. 1–5 (2023)
13. Liu, L., Liu, L., Li, H.: Computation and parameter efficient multi-modal fusion transformer for cued speech recognition. IEEE/ACM Trans. Audio Speech Lang. Process. (2024)
14. Liu, L., Feng, G.: A pilot study on mandarin Chinese cued speech. Am. Ann. Deaf **164**(4), 496–518 (2019)
15. Liu, L., Feng, G., Beautemps, D.: Automatic temporal segmentation of hand movements for hand positions recognition in French cued speech. In: Proceedings of IEEE-ICASSP, pp. 3061–3065 (2018)
16. Liu, L., Feng, G., Beautemps, D., Zhang, X.P.: A novel resynchronization procedure for hand-lips fusion applied to continuous French cued speech recognition. In: Proceedings of IEEE-EUSIPCO, pp. 1–5 (2019)
17. Liu, L., Feng, G., Denis, B., Zhang, X.P.: Re-synchronization using the hand preceding model for multi-modal fusion in automatic continuous cued speech recognition. IEEE Trans. Multimedia **23**, 292–305 (2020)
18. Liu, L., Feng, G., Ren, X., Ma, X.: Objective hand complexity comparison between two mandarin Chinese cued speech systems. In: Proceedings of IEEE-ISCSLP, pp. 215–219 (2022)
19. Liu, L., Li, J., Feng, G., Zhang, X.P.S.: Automatic detection of the temporal segmentation of hand movements in British English cued speech. In: Proceedings of Interspeech, pp. 2285–2289 (2019)
20. Liu, L., Thomas, H., Feng, G., Denis, B.: Visual recognition of continuous cued speech using a tandem cnn-hmm approach. In: INTERSPEECH, pp. 2643–2647 (2018)
21. Minguk, K., Jun-Yan, Z., Richard, Z., Jaesik, P., Eli, S., Sylvain, P., Taesung, P.: Scaling up gans for text-to-image synthesis. In: CVPR (2023)

22. Papadimitriou, K., Potamianos, G.: A fully convolutional sequence learning approach for cued speech recognition from videos. In: Proceedings of IEEE-EUSIPCO, pp. 326–330 (2021)
23. Paul, B., Vincent, V.H.: Speak and unspeak with praat. Glot. Int. **5**, 341–347 (2001)
24. Radford, A., et al.: Learning transferable visual models from natural language supervision. In: Proceedings of ICML, pp. 8748–8763 (2021)
25. Wang, J., Tang, Z., Li, X., Yu, M., Fang, Q., Liu, L.: Cross-modal knowledge distillation method for automatic cued speech recognition. In: Proceedings of Interspeech, pp. 2986–2990 (2021)
26. Yang, L., et al.: Diffusion models: a comprehensive survey of methods and applications. arXiv:2209.00796 (2023)
27. Yi, Y., Deva, R.: Articulated human detection with flexible mixtures of parts. TPAMI **35**(12), 2878–2890 (2013). https://doi.org/10.1109/TPAMI.2012.261
28. Youngwoo, Y., et al.: Speech gesture generation from the trimodal context of text, audio, and speaker identity. ACM Trans. Graph. **39**(6), 1–16 (2020). https://doi.org/10.1145/3414685.3417838

A Review of Human Mesh Reconstruction: Beyond 2D Video Object Segmentation

Peng Wu[1], Zhicheng Wang[1], Feiyu Pan[1], Fangkai Li[1], Hao Hu[1],
Xiankai Lu[1](✉), and Yiyou Guo[2]

[1] School of Software, Shandong University, Jinan 250000, Shandong, China
`carrierlxk@126.com`
[2] School of Mathematics and Computer Science, Fujian Provincial Key Laboratory of Data-Intensive Computing, Fujian University Laboratory of Intelligent Computing and Information Processing, Quanzhou Normal University, Quanzhou, China

Abstract. Video object segmentation aims to extract 2D object masks by segmenting video frames into multiple objects, which is crucial in various practical applications such as medical imaging, *etc.*. However, traditional video object segmentation methods produce 2D masks, which are not suitable for 3D scenarios where depth information is essential, such as in robotic grasping, virtual reality, and autonomous driving, *etc.*. In this paper, we present a comprehensive review of 3D human mesh reconstruction (HMR) as an extension beyond 2D video object segmentation. We begin by reviewing the mainstream video object segmentation methods, then transition from 2D video object segmentation to 3D HMR. We further categorize recent HMR methods based on key characteristics that define this research field, including the type of model input and the use of statistical models. Finally, we provide detailed information on HMR datasets and evaluation metrics.

Keywords: Video Object Segmentation · Human Mesh Reconstruction · Deep Learning

1 Introduction

Video object segmentation, which leverages temporal information to segment target objects, is a fundamental task in computer vision and has been applied in various fields such as medical image segmentation. However, many scenarios, such as robotic grasping, autonomous driving, and virtual reality, require 3D models rather than 2D masks. To support the advancement of techniques suitable for 3D application scenarios, we present a systematic review of recent developments in 3D human mesh reconstruction.

In the presented paper, we firstly review the mainstream video object segmentation paradigms, including zero-shot video object segmentation (Fig. 2 (a)), One-shot video object segmentation (Fig. 2 (b)), language-guided video object

© The Author(s), under exclusive license to Springer Nature Singapore Pte Ltd. 2025
H. Li et al. (Eds.): ICSR + InnoBiz 2024, LNAI 15170, pp. 167–176, 2025.
https://doi.org/10.1007/978-981-96-1151-5_17

segmentation (Fig. 2 (c)) and interaction video object segmentation (Fig. 2 (d)). Compared with traditional video object segmentation methods which predict 2D masks, human mesh reconstruction (HMR) aims to predict 3D human body meshes (Fig. 2 (e)) that are more practical in 3D scenarios. Specifically, we categorize the recent contributions of HMR into three classes based on the model input, *i.e.*, pose-based methods, imgae-based methods and video-based methods.

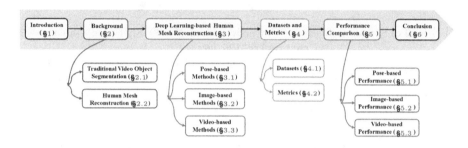

Fig. 1. Overview of this survey.

Figure 1 shows the structure of this survey. Section 2 gives the study history of traditional video object segmentation (Sect. 2.1) and research background of HMR (Sect. 2.2). We review representative papers on HMR in Sect. 3, including pose-based methods (Sect. 3.1), image-based methods(Sect. 3.2) and video-based methods (Sect. 3.3). Section 4 introduces details of HMR datasets (Sect. 4.1) and metrics (Sect. 4.2) while Sect. 5 conducts performance evaluation and analysis. Finally, we make concluding remarks in Sect. 6.

2   Background

In this section, we begin by reviewing the key paradigms of traditional video object segmentation, including Zero-shot Video Object Segmentation (ZVOS), One-shot Video Object Segmentation (OVOS), Language-guided Video Object Segmentation (LVOS), and Interactive Video Object Segmentation (IVOS). Following this, we provide an overview of the background of human mesh reconstruction (HMR).

2.1   Traditional Video Object Segmentation

Video Object Segmentation Formulation (2D). Video object segmentation (VOS) focuses on separating the foreground objects from the background throughout a video sequence. In the simplest scenario, the object category is not specified, making $\mathcal{Y}$ binary. Deep learning-based VOS methods typically aim to learn an *ideal* video-to-segment mapping function, $f : \mathcal{X} \mapsto \mathcal{Y}$, where $\mathcal{X}$ and $\mathcal{Y}$ represent the input and output spaces, respectively (Fig. 3).

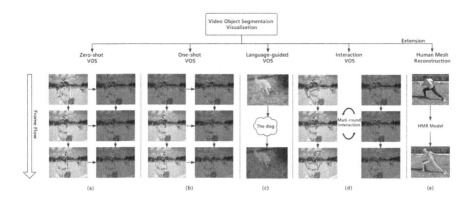

Fig. 2. Overview of the mainstream video object methods and human mesh reconstruction. (a) zero-shot video object segmentation (ZVOS), (b) one-shot object segmentation (OVOS), (c) langugae-guided video object segmentation (LVOS), (d) interaction video object segmentation (IVOS), (e) human mesh reconstruction.

Taxonomy for 2D Video Object Segmentation. VOS methods can be further categorized into four types: zero-shot, one-shot, language-guided, and interactive, according to how and how many interventions are involved during inference.

- **Zero-shot Video Object Segmentation (ZVOS).** ZVOS (also named *Unsupervised video object segmentation*, also known as *automatic video object segmentation*, performs VOS without any human intervention, including manual initialization (Fig. 2 (a)). While ZVOS is effective for video analysis, it is less suitable for video editing tasks that require flexible segmentation of arbitrary objects or their parts. A common application of ZVOS is in autonomous driving.

- **One-shot Video Object Segmentation (OVOS).** One-shot video object segmentation (OVOS) is performed with minimal human guidance, typically relying on the first frame to identify the target objects (Fig. 2 (b)). The most common form of human intervention is a first-frame object mask, in which case OVOS is also referred to as *pixel-wise tracking* or *mask propagation*. Other forms of human input include bounding boxes and scribbles [21]. OVOS enhances the flexibility of Zero-shot Video Object Segmentation (ZVOS) by allowing users to define target objects, though it requires additional human intervention. OVOS is commonly used in user-friendly applications, such as video content creation on mobile devices. A key challenge in OVOS is maximizing the effectiveness of target information provided through minimal human input.

- **Language-guided Video Object Segmentation (LVOS).** As a sub-branch of OVOS, language-guided video object segmentation involves linguistic descriptions as a form of intervention for defining the target objects, enabling more efficient human-computer interaction (Fig. 2 (c)).

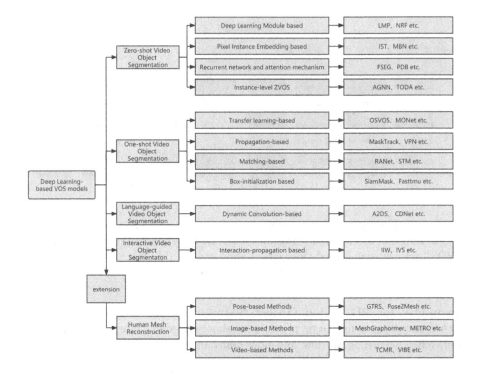

Fig. 3. Method Classification. This survey covers deep learning methods for 2D video object segmentation and human mesh reconstruction. The 2D video segmentation includes zero-shot, one-shot, language-guided and interactive methods. Human mesh reconstruction methods as an extension of the traditional video segmentation methods can be regarded as 3D video segmentation methods.

- **Interactive Video Object Segmentation (IVOS).** Compared to ZVOS and OVOS, IVOS incorporates human guidance throughout the analysis process (Fig. 2 (d)), which leads to high-quality segments. For IVOS, The input space $\mathcal{X}$ for IVOS is $\mathcal{V} \times \mathcal{S}$, where $\mathcal{S}$ typically refers to human scribbling. IVOS is suitable for computer-generated imagery and video post-production, where tedious human supervision is possible.

2.2   Human Mesh Reconstruction

Human Mesh Reconstruction which can be regarded as expansion of 2D VOS focus on reconstructing 3D human mesh from single image or video. Compared to traditional VOS methods, HMR focus on predicting 3D human models instead of 2D masks. There exist numerous deep learning-based methods for human mesh reconstruction which are categorized into three classes based on the input type: (1) **pose-based** methods [2,22,26,31] takes 2D poses as input; (2) **image-**

based methods [3,4,8,9,13–15,17,18,20,27,28,30] takes image as input directly; (3) **video-based** methods [1,5,6,10,12,16,25] takes video frames as input.

3   Deep Learning-Based Human Mesh Reconstruction

In this section, we review the representative HMR methods of the three categories: **pose-based** methods [2,22,26,31], **image-based** methods [3,4,8,9,13–15,17,18,20,27,28,30] and **video-based** methods [1,5,6,10,12,16,25].

3.1   Pose-Based Methods

Pose-based methods typically follow this pipeline: (1) an off-the-shelf detector is used to obtain the 2D pose or key points, and (2) the 2D pose is then fed into the proposed models to reconstruct the mesh and pose. For instance, GTRS [31] extracts the 2D pose using the DARK method [29], which is then input into their model, which combines Transformer [23] and graph convolutional neural networks (GCNN) [11].

3.2   Image-Based Methods

In this category, the original image or a single video frame is directly input into the model. The model first extracts features from the input, which are then used to regress the SMPL parameters or reconstruct the mesh and pose. Some approaches incorporate auxiliary models, such as a template mesh from SMPL, to provide depth information. Examples include I2L-MeshNet [20], GraphCMR [14], and METRO [17]. Additionally, MeshGraphormer [18] combines Transformer and Graph Convolutional Networks (GCN) to reconstruct the human mesh based on human structure.

3.3   Video-Based Methods

Compared to the previous two categories, video-based methods take cross-frame information into account. For instance, in [5,6], consistency among video frames is utilized to enhance performance. In summary, leading approaches often incorporate Transformers and Graph Convolutional Networks (GCNs) because of their ability to capture both global and local information within video frames.

4   Datasets and Metrics

Deep learning-based models have achieved great success due to the development of datasets to some extent. In this paper, we introduce the most representative three HMR datasets, including **Human3.6M** [7], **3DPW** [24] and **MPI-INF 3DHP** [19]

Table 1. Quantitative Hmr Results on Human3.6M [7] and 3dPW [24] in terms of MPJPE, PA-MPJPE and MPVE.

Class	Method	Protocol1			Protocol2			Protocol3			Protocol4		
		MJ↓	PMJ↓	MV↓	MJ↓	PMJ↓	MV↓	MJ↓	PMJ↓	MV↓	MJ↓	PMJ↓	MV↓
Pose based	GTRS [31]	**64.3**	**45.4**	–	**97.4**	**62.4**	**117.2**	**88.5**	58.5	106.7	–	–	–
	Skeleton2Mesh [26]	87.1	55.4	–	–	–	–	–	–	–	–	–	–
	Pose2Mesh [2]	64.9	47	–	100.5	63	117.5	88.9	**58.3**	**106.3**	89.2	**58.9**	–
	DSD-SATN [22]	–	–	–	–	–	–	–	–	–	–	69.5	–
Image based	PyMAF [30]	57.7	40.5	–	–	–	–	92.8	58.9	110.1	–	–	–
	MeshGraphormer [18]	51.2	**34.5**	–	–	–	–	**74.7**	**45.6**	**87.7**	–	–	–
	METRO [17]	54	36.7	–	–	–	–	–	–	–	–	–	–
	DSR [4]	–	–	–	–	–	–	91.7	54.1	105.8	–	–	–
	THUNDR [28]	**48**	34.9	–	–	–	–	74.8	51.5	88	–	–	–
	HUND [27]	–	–	–	–	–	–	87.7	56.5	–	–	–	–
	ProHMR [15]	–	41.2	–	–	–	–	–	–	–	–	–	–
	I2LMeshNet [20]	–	–	–	–	–	–	93.2	57.7	110.1	**93.2**	58.6	–
	EFT [8]	–	–	–	–	–	–	–	–	–	–	**55.7**	–
	SPIN [13]	–	41.1	–	**313.8**	**156**	**344.3**	96.9	59.2	116.4	96.9	59.2	–
	Sim2Real [3]	–	–	–	–	–	–	–	–	–	–	74.7	–
	GraphCMR [14]	–	50.1	–	332.5	177.4	380.8	–	70.2	–	–	70.2	–
	HMR [9]	88	56.8	–	377.3	165.7	481	–	81.3	–	130	76.7	–
Video based	TCMR [1]	62.3	41.1	–	–	–	–	95	**55.8**	**111.5**	–	–	–
	UAHMR [16]	**58.4**	**38.4**	–	–	–	–	–	–	–	–	–	–
	BOA [6]	–	–	–	–	–	–	–	–	–	77.2	49.5	–
	DyBOA [5]	–	–	–	–	–	–	–	–	–	**65.5**	**40.4**	–
	VIBE [12]	65.6	41.4	–	–	–	–	**93.5**	56.5	113.4	–	–	–
	HMMR [10]	–	–	–	–	–	–	–	–	–	116.5	73.6	–

[1] **Protocol1**-Train and test on human3.6M,

[2] **Protocol2**-Train on human3.6M and test on 3dPW,

[3] **Protocol3**-Train on multi-datasets and test on 3dPW,

[4] **Protocol4**-Train on human3.6M and 3dPW and test on 3dPW.

[5] *MJ* represents *MPJPE*.

[6] *PMJ* represents *PA-MPJPE*.

[7] *MV* represents *MPVE*.

4.1 Datasets

- **Human3.6M** [7] is a widely used large-scale indoor dataset for 3D Human Pose Estimation (HPE) and mesh reconstruction, consisting of 3.6 million video frames captured from 11 professional actors performing 17 different actions.
- **3DPW** [24] is an in-the-wild dataset comprising 60 video sequences (51K video frames) captured in outdoor environments.
- **MPI-INF-3DHP** [19] consists of over 1.3 million frames of outdoor video footage of 11 humans, captured simultaneously by 14 cameras.

4.2   Evaluation Metrics

There are three common used metrics in human mesh reconstruction.

- **MPJPE** is used to evaluate the accuracy of estimated 3D human poses. It measures the mean Euclidean distance between the estimated joints and the ground truth joints.
- **PA-MPJPE** is computed after performing Procrustes Analysis, which rigidly aligns the estimated 3D pose with the ground truth 3D pose. PA-MPJPE measures the errors in the reconstructed structure while excluding the effects of translations and rotations.
- **MPVE** is used to evaluate the estimated 3D mesh vertices. It computes the mean Euclidean distance between the estimated mesh vertices and the ground truth mesh vertices.

5   Performance Comparison

We evaluate some representative methods on Human3.6M and 3dPW and the results are shown in Table 1. Notably, four protocols are utilized totally.

5.1   Pose-Based Performance

From the results in Table 1, we can observe that GTRS [31] achieves better performance than other pose-based methods across most protocols which demonstrates that it is significant to combine graph neural networks and transformer.

5.2   Image-Based Performance

We further discover that MeshGraphormer [18] and THUNDR [28] achieve better performance than other image-based methods. We analyse that these two methods are benefit from the transformer architecture.

5.3   Video-Based Performance

Finally, as for the video-based methods, the results of TCMR [1] and UAHMR [16] set the best performance in this category. Video-based methods have the advantage of exploiting depth information which can help predicting more accurate results.

6   Conclusion

In this paper, we provide a systematic review of 3D human mesh reconstruction (HMR) beyond 2D video object segmentation. Firstly, we review the mainstream video object segmentation methods. Afterward, we transition from 2D video object segmentation to 3D HMR. We further categorize recent HMR methods along main characteristics that underline this research field, including the types of model input and the employment of statistical model. Finally, we provide the details of HMR datasets and evaluation metrics.

Acknowledgments. This work was supported in part by the National Natural Science Foundation of China (No. 62106128, 62101309), the Natural Science Foundation of Shandong Province (No. ZR2021QF001, ZR2021QF109), Shandong Province Science and Technology Small and Medium-sized Enterprise Innovation Capacity Enhancement Project (2023TSGC0115), Shandong Province Higher Education Institutions Youth Entrepreneurship and Technology Support Program (2023KJ027).

Disclosure of Interests. The authors of this paper have no competing interests.

References

1. Choi, H., Moon, G., Chang, J.Y., Lee, K.M.: Beyond static features for temporally consistent 3d human pose and shape from a video. In: Proceedings of the IEEE/CVF Conference on Computer Vision and Pattern Recognition, pp. 1964–1973 (2021)
2. Choi, H., Moon, G., Lee, K.M.: Pose2Mesh: graph convolutional network for 3D human pose and mesh recovery from a 2D human pose. In: Vedaldi, A., Bischof, H., Brox, T., Frahm, J.-M. (eds.) ECCV 2020. LNCS, vol. 12352, pp. 769–787. Springer, Cham (2020). https://doi.org/10.1007/978-3-030-58571-6_45
3. Doersch, C., Zisserman, A.: Sim2real transfer learning for 3d human pose estimation: motion to the rescue. Adv. Neural Inf. Process. Syst. **32** (2019)
4. Dwivedi, S.K., Athanasiou, N., Kocabas, M., Black, M.J.: Learning to regress bodies from images using differentiable semantic rendering. In: Proceedings of the IEEE/CVF International Conference on Computer Vision, pp. 11250–11259 (2021)
5. Guan, S., Xu, J., He, M.Z., Wang, Y., Ni, B., Yang, X.: Out-of-domain human mesh reconstruction via dynamic bilevel online adaptation. IEEE Trans. Pattern Anal. Mach. Intell. **45**(4), 5070–5086 (2022)
6. Guan, S., Xu, J., Wang, Y., Ni, B., Yang, X.: Bilevel online adaptation for out-of-domain human mesh reconstruction. In: Proceedings of the IEEE/CVF Conference on Computer Vision and Pattern Recognition, pp. 10472–10481 (2021)
7. Ionescu, C., Papava, D., Olaru, V., Sminchisescu, C.: Human3. 6m: large scale datasets and predictive methods for 3d human sensing in natural environments. IEEE Trans. Pattern Anal. Mach. Intell. **36**(7), 1325–1339 (2013)
8. Joo, H., Neverova, N., Vedaldi, A.: Exemplar fine-tuning for 3d human model fitting towards in-the-wild 3d human pose estimation. In: 2021 International Conference on 3D Vision (3DV), pp. 42–52. IEEE (2021)
9. Kanazawa, A., Black, M.J., Jacobs, D.W., Malik, J.: End-to-end recovery of human shape and pose. In: Proceedings of the IEEE Conference on Computer Vision and Pattern Recognition, pp. 7122–7131 (2018)
10. Kanazawa, A., Zhang, J.Y., Felsen, P., Malik, J.: Learning 3d human dynamics from video. In: Proceedings of the IEEE/CVF Conference on Computer Vision and Pattern Recognition, pp. 5614–5623 (2019)
11. Kipf, T.N., Welling, M.: Semi-supervised classification with graph convolutional networks. arXiv preprint arXiv:1609.02907 (2016)
12. Kocabas, M., Athanasiou, N., Black, M.J.: Vibe: video inference for human body pose and shape estimation. In: Proceedings of the IEEE/CVF Conference on Computer Vision and Pattern Recognition, pp. 5253–5263 (2020)
13. Kolotouros, N., Pavlakos, G., Black, M.J., Daniilidis, K.: Learning to reconstruct 3d human pose and shape via model-fitting in the loop. In: Proceedings of the IEEE/CVF International Conference on Computer Vision, pp. 2252–2261 (2019)

14. Kolotouros, N., Pavlakos, G., Daniilidis, K.: Convolutional mesh regression for single-image human shape reconstruction. In: Proceedings of the IEEE/CVF Conference on Computer Vision and Pattern Recognition, pp. 4501–4510 (2019)
15. Kolotouros, N., Pavlakos, G., Jayaraman, D., Daniilidis, K.: Probabilistic modeling for human mesh recovery. In: Proceedings of the IEEE/CVF International Conference on Computer Vision, pp. 11605–11614 (2021)
16. Lee, G.H., Lee, S.W.: Uncertainty-aware human mesh recovery from video by learning part-based 3d dynamics. In: Proceedings of the IEEE/CVF International Conference on Computer Vision, pp. 12375–12384 (2021)
17. Lin, K., Wang, L., Liu, Z.: End-to-end human pose and mesh reconstruction with transformers. In: Proceedings of the IEEE/CVF Conference on Computer Vision and Pattern Recognition, pp. 1954–1963 (2021)
18. Lin, K., Wang, L., Liu, Z.: Mesh graphormer. In: Proceedings of the IEEE/CVF International Conference on Computer Vision, pp. 12939–12948 (2021)
19. Mehta, D., et al.: Monocular 3d human pose estimation in the wild using improved cnn supervision. In: 2017 International Conference on 3D Vision (3DV), pp. 506–516. IEEE (2017)
20. Moon, G., Lee, K.M.: I2L-MeshNet: image-to-lixel prediction network for accurate 3D human pose and mesh estimation from a single RGB image. In: Vedaldi, A., Bischof, H., Brox, T., Frahm, J.-M. (eds.) ECCV 2020. LNCS, vol. 12352, pp. 752–768. Springer, Cham (2020). https://doi.org/10.1007/978-3-030-58571-6_44
21. Nagaraja, N.S., Schmidt, F.R., Brox, T.: Video segmentation with just a few strokes. In: Proceedings of the IEEE International Conference on Computer Vision, pp. 3235–3243 (2015)
22. Sun, Y., Ye, Y., Liu, W., Gao, W., Fu, Y., Mei, T.: Human mesh recovery from monocular images via a skeleton-disentangled representation. In: Proceedings of the IEEE/CVF International Conference on Computer Vision, pp. 5349–5358 (2019)
23. Vaswani, A., et al.: Attention is all you need. Adv. Neural Inf. Process. Syst. **30** (2017)
24. Von Marcard, T., Henschel, R., Black, M.J., Rosenhahn, B., Pons-Moll, G.: Recovering accurate 3d human pose in the wild using imus and a moving camera. In: Proceedings of the European Conference on Computer Vision (ECCV), pp. 601–617 (2018)
25. Wu, P., Lu, X., Shen, J., Yin, Y.: Clip fusion with bi-level optimization for human mesh reconstruction from monocular videos. In: Proceedings of the 31st ACM International Conference on Multimedia, pp. 105–115 (2023)
26. Yu, Z., et al.: Skeleton2mesh: kinematics prior injected unsupervised human mesh recovery. In: Proceedings of the IEEE/CVF International Conference on Computer Vision, pp. 8619–8629 (2021)
27. Zanfir, A., Bazavan, E.G., Zanfir, M., Freeman, W.T., Sukthankar, R., Sminchisescu, C.: Neural descent for visual 3d human pose and shape. In: Proceedings of the IEEE/CVF Conference on Computer Vision and Pattern Recognition, pp. 14484–14493 (2021)
28. Zanfir, M., Zanfir, A., Bazavan, E.G., Freeman, W.T., Sukthankar, R., Sminchisescu, C.: Thundr: transformer-based 3d human reconstruction with markers. In: Proceedings of the IEEE/CVF International Conference on Computer Vision, pp. 12971–12980 (2021)
29. Zhang, F., Zhu, X., Dai, H., Ye, M., Zhu, C.: Distribution-aware coordinate representation for human pose estimation. In: Proceedings of the IEEE/CVF Conference on Computer Vision and Pattern Recognition, pp. 7093–7102 (2020)

30. Zhang, H., et al.: Pymaf: 3d human pose and shape regression with pyramidal mesh alignment feedback loop. In: Proceedings of the IEEE/CVF International Conference on Computer Vision, pp. 11446–11456 (2021)
31. Zheng, C., Mendieta, M., Wang, P., Lu, A., Chen, C.: A lightweight graph transformer network for human mesh reconstruction from 2d human pose. In: Proceedings of the 30th ACM International Conference on Multimedia, pp. 5496–5507 (2022)

A Transformer-Based Depression Detection Network Leveraging Speech Emotional Expression Cues

Changqing Xu[1,2], Xinyi Wu[1,2], Nan Li[1], Xin Wang[3], Xu Feng[4], Rongfeng Su[1], Nan Yan[1(✉)], and Lan Wang[1(✉)]

[1] Guangdong-Hong Kong-Macao Joint Laboratory of Human-Machine Intelligence-Synergy Systems, Shenzhen Institute of Advanced Technology, Chinese Academy of Sciences, Shenzhen, China
{cq.xu,xy.wu2,n.li2,rf.su,nan.yan,lan.wang}@siat.ac.cn
[2] University of Chinese Academy of Sciences, Beijing, China
[3] Peking University Shenzhen Institute, Shenzhen, China
xin.wang@imsl.org.cn
[4] Good Mood Health Industry Group Co., Ltd., London, UK
xufeng@haoxinqing.cn

Abstract. In recent years, significant progress has been made in automated depression detection methods using speech and text data combined with deep learning. However, few studies have explored the connection between depression and speech emotions. To address this issue, this paper proposes a novel Transformer-based network leveraging Speech Emotion Information (SEI) for depression detection. The proposed network consists of a primary network used for depression classification and an auxiliary network is employed for speech emotion classification. In the primary network, the pre-trained Hubert and RoBERTa are used to obtain the short-term acoustic and textual features, respectively. And then the long-term audio and text features are aggregated from the shot-term features by using Transformer-based approaches with average pooling. The SEI extracted from the auxiliary network serves as supplementary auxiliary features aimed at augmenting the precision of depression recognition. Based on the proposed method, our best experimental results achieved an accuracy of 76.10% at the subject level. The experimental results demonstrate that incorporating speech emotions in depression detection improves diagnostic accuracy, offering a new perspective for research in this area.

Keywords: Depression Detection · Speech Emotion · Self-Supervised Learning · Transformer

1 Introduction

Depression is a prevalent mental health issue characterized primarily by low mood, slowed thinking processes, and decreased volitional activity [4]. This condition not only profoundly impacts the individuals affected but also imposes

H. Li et al. (Eds.): ICSR + InnoBiz 2024, LNAI 15170, pp. 177–186, 2025.
https://doi.org/10.1007/978-981-96-1151-5_18

significant burdens on the economy and society at large [13]. Therefore, timely and accurate diagnosis of depression is crucial. Currently, questionnaire surveys such as the PHQ-9 [7] and HAMD [5] are commonly used methods for diagnosing depression. However, these methods rely on subjective judgments, which may affect diagnostic accuracy. In light of this, automated methods for depression detection are gaining attention for potentially providing more objective and accurate diagnostic results.

In recent years, significant progress has been made in using deep learning for automated depression detection. Speech and text have become a hot spot for researchers to use for depression research due to their non-invasive and easily accessible properties. Ma et al. [11] proposed the DepAudioNet for classifying the speech of patients with depression. DepAudioNet combines Convolutional Neural Networks (CNN) and Long Short-Term Memory (LSTM) to encode features related to depression in the sound channel, providing a more comprehensive audio representation. Lu et al. [10] proposed a new model that combines the Transformer Encoder and CNN to address the issue of capturing the long-term dependencies in depressive audio due to the vanishing gradient problem. Zhao et al. [20] proposed a deep learning method that combines unsupervised learning, knowledge transfer, and hierarchical attention for classifying the severity of depression based on speech. In [15], after modeling the speech and text modalities separately using GCNN, LSTM, and CNN, LSTM, and then fusing the features, a better depression detection effect than using only single-modal data was achieved. In [1], the interaction of audio and text features was simulated in a Long Short-Term Memory (LSTM) neural network model to detect depression. In [16], the research results proved the effectiveness of word-level multimodal fusion for depression detection, which is superior to early feature-level and late fusion techniques. In addition, a large number of studies have shown that depression detection using speech and text is feasible.

However, there has been limited research connecting depression with emotion in speech, despite depression being a part of emotional experience. Additionally, studies have shown that speech contains rich paralinguistic information such as tone and pitch [8], which can distinguish between depressed and non-depressed populations [4]. Our previous research has also shown that the overall emotional tone of speech in depressed people is more negative than in healthy people [18].

Based on this, this paper integrates speech emotion information (SEI) into a depression detection network to improve the accuracy of depression recognition. Specifically, we propose a multitask depression detection network where the primary network is used for depression classification and the auxiliary network is employed for speech emotion classification. The primary network enhances its performance by integrating speech emotion information extracted from the auxiliary network. Additionally, due to factors like privacy concerns, data available for depression research is limited, which may hinder models from fully learning the complex features of depression. Therefore, this paper introduces pretrained models to alleviate issues caused by data scarcity. Based on the proposed approach, our best experimental results achieve an accuracy of 76.10% at the subject-level, validating the effectiveness of our method.

The remainder of this paper is organized as follows: Sect. 2 describes the methodology, Sect. 3 details the experimental setup and results, and Sect. 4 presents conclusions and future work.

2 Method

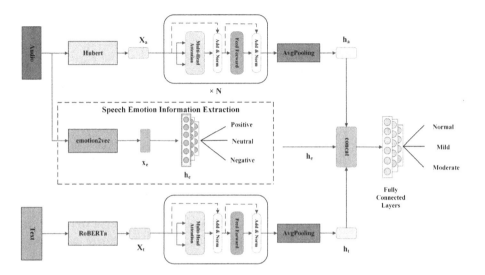

Fig. 1. Proposed Transformer-based Depression Detection Network Leveraging Speech Emotional Expression Cues

2.1 Feature Extraction

Self-Supervised Learning (SSL) is an efficient pre-training strategy that utilizes large amounts of unlabeled training data to train foundational models, thereby providing effective feature representations for subsequent task-specific learning. This approach not only reduces reliance on costly annotated data but also enhances the adaptability and generalization capability of models for new tasks. Therefore, this study utilizes Hubert [6] and RoBERTa [9] to extract features from speech and text, respectively.

For the speech modality, we employ the 24-layer Transformer model (chinese-hubert-large) pretrained on WenetSpeech's 10,000-hour Chinese data[1]. We extract features from the output of the 12th layer, yielding audio features of

---

[1] https://huggingface.co/TencentGameMate/chinese-hubert-large.

dimension 1024. For the text modality, we utilize the RoBERTa-large model pretrained on various text corpora[2] to extract text features, also of dimension 1024.

In addition, emotion2ve [12]has achieved state-of-the-art performance on various paralinguistic tasks. It leverages emotional speech data with utterance-level and frame-level losses, employing additional chunk token embeddings to capture utterance-wise information. In this study, we utilize emotion2vec[3] for extracting emotional features from speech, capturing emotion-related information. The feature extraction involves utterance-level averaging of embeddings, where a simple average of frame-level representations yields a utterance-level embedding of dimension 768.

2.2   Proposed Depression Detection Network

The Transformer [17] model, with its unique self-attention mechanism, has revolutionized the fields of speech and text processing. It is ability to capture long-range dependencies and process information in parallel makes it highly effective in tasks such as speech recognition, synthesis, and transformation. Similarly, in text processing tasks like classification, sentiment analysis, machine translation, and summarization, the Transformer model excels in understanding complex textual structures and semantics, yielding high-quality outputs.

Given these advantages of the Transformer model, this paper proposes a depression classification network based on Transformer. As illustrated in Fig. 1, this network integrates audio, text, and speech emotion information to construct a multimodal classification framework, comprising the following key modules:

Audio Processing Module: In this module, raw audio is initially processed through the Hubert model to extract features X_a. These features are then passed through N Transformer blocks to capture complex dependencies in the audio data. Post-Transformer processing, features undergo average pooling (AvgPooling) to compress them further, resulting in the final audio feature representation h_a.

Text Processing Module: Similar to audio processing, raw text content is processed through the RoBERTa model to obtain features X_t. These features are also fed through N Transformer blocks to obtain more advanced feature representations. After Transformer blocks and average pooling, the final text feature representation h_t is derived.

Speech Emotion Information Extraction Module: Raw audio undergoes emotion2vec model processing to extract segment-level feature vectors x_e. To extract speech emotion embeddings, a Multi-Layer Perceptron (MLP) is utilized

---

[2] https://huggingface.co/FacebookAI/roberta-large.
[3] https://huggingface.co/emotion2vec/emotion2vec_base.

for speech emotion classification on x_e. Specifically, we extract the embedding from the first layer of the MLP as the representation of speech emotion information(512 dimensions), denoted as embedding representation:

$$h_e = W x_e \qquad (1)$$

where W represents the weights of the first fully connected layer.

Furthermore, we also explored using the direct output of the MLP for voice emotion classification (where 0 represents Negative, 1 represents Neutral, and 2 represents Positive) as the Speech Emotion Information (SEI). We denote this method of extracting SEI information as single-number.

Feature-Level Fusion Strategy and Classification: Finally, the audio feature h_a, text feature h_t, and speech emotion embedding h_e are concatenated (concat) and processed through a fully connected layer to output classification results for the three categories: Normal, Mild, and Moderate.

3 Experiments

3.1 Dataset

The data used in this study consists of recordings of consultations between depression patients and experienced psychologists via online conference calls. Topics covered include emotional issues, work-related stress, interpersonal relationships, sleep, and exercise. All recordings are saved in .wav/8kHz.

The dataset comprises 22.9 h of recordings, involving 272 individuals aged between 12 and 45. Among them, there are 100 healthy individuals (53 males and 47 females), 100 with mild depression (49 males and 51 females), and 72 with moderate depression (36 males and 36 females). All individuals diagnosed with depression in the dataset have been professionally diagnosed by psychiatrists. For the assessment of healthy individuals, the Self-Rating Depression Scale (SDS) [22] and the Self-Rating Anxiety Scale (SAS) [21] were used. The SAS and SDS are commonly used psychological assessment tools, employed to evaluate anxiety and depression levels, respectively. Generally, a SAS score below 50 indicates a normal level of anxiety, and an SDS score below 50 indicates a normal level of depression in the Chinese population. In this study, the SAS and SDS scores for the healthy individuals in the dataset were all below 45.

We employed the pyannote-audio tool [3] for speaker diarization to segment audio clips between psychologists and patients. The WeNet toolkit [19] was used for Automatic Speech Recognition (ASR) to obtain corresponding text transcriptions. Subsequently, Praat [2] was utilized for manual correction of audio segment boundaries and text content to ensure accuracy. Overlapping segments with multiple speakers were manually removed, resulting in a total of 9,332 segments. These segments are categorized into 2700 healthy control segments, 3924 mild depression segments, and 2708 moderate depression segments, with an average length of 8.78 s per segment.

To integrate emotional content into the automated depression detection network, we defined the acoustic emotions into five categories: anger, dispirited, neutral, surprise, and joy. Emotional labeling was conducted using a single-blind method to ensure each annotator was unaware of the audio's source. In summary, each audio segment was labeled by five individuals, and the label with the highest consensus was assigned as the emotional label for that segment.

3.2 Experiments Setup

We employed a five-fold cross-validation method to evaluate the model performance, taking special care to address data overlap issues. Specifically, the dataset was randomly divided into five subsets, each approximately 20% of the total data volume. We then conducted five rounds of training and testing, where in each round, one subset was chosen as the test set, and the remaining four subsets were used for training. Throughout this process, we ensured there was no overlap between the training and test sets, ensuring that the same data did not appear simultaneously in both sets.

All deep learning methods were executed using the PyTorch [14] framework on an NVIDIA RTX 4090 GPU. We employed the Adam optimizer with an initial learning rate of 0.00001 and a batch size of 64. The number N of Transformer block is set to 12. The entire network was jointly trained for two tasks—depression classification and speech emotion classification. Both tasks utilized cross-entropy loss:

$$\mathcal{L}_{\text{Total}} = \mathcal{L}_{\text{Depression}} + \mathcal{L}_{\text{SpeechEmotion}} \tag{2}$$

where $\mathcal{L}_{\text{Depression}}$ represents the loss for the depression classification task, and $\mathcal{L}_{\text{SpeechEmotion}}$ represents the loss for the speech emotion classification task.

3.3 Baseline

For the audio baseline, speech data is processed through the HuBERT model to extract features. These features undergo processing by N layers of Transformer Encoder and are then fed into a Multi-Layer Perceptron (MLP) for classifying depression severity (Normal/Mild/Moderate). For the audio-text baseline, speech data is also processed through the HuBERT model to extract features. Simultaneously, text data is processed through the RoBERTa model to extract its own set of features. These two sets of features from speech and text are concatenated after undergoing processing by N layers of Transformer Encoder each. The concatenated features are then input into an MLP for classifying depression severity (Normal/Mild/Moderate).

3.4 Result

The evaluation metrics used for assessing the model performance in our experiment include Accuracy, Precision, Recall, and F1 score. Since our task involves a three-class classification (Normal, Mild depression, Moderate depression), we employ macro-averaging for these metrics. Macro-averaging entails calculating these metrics separately for each class and then averaging them to obtain the final evaluation result. This approach ensures that each class is equally weighted in the evaluation process, thereby avoiding disproportionate influence on the overall assessment due to class imbalance. Additionally, for the purpose of depression detection to determine an individual's depressive state, we aggregate segment-level prediction results to the subject-level through majority voting.

The performance of baseline is presented in Table 1. From the table, it can be observed that the multimodal baseline system slightly outperforms the corresponding system trained solely on acoustic features, achieving a subject-level accuracy of 73.53%.

Table 1. Classification results from baseline models in segment-level and subjecti-level.

Inputs	Segment-level				Subject-level			
	Accuracy	F1	Precision	Recall	Accuracy	F1	Precision	Recall
A	59.74	61.26	59.81	62.79	72.06	72.79	72.59	72.98
A+T	62.67	63.12	62.68	63.57	73.53	74.25	73.79	74.47

We explored the performance of integrating SEI with various depression assessment systems. The SEI extraction module was defined as a three-class classification task (negative/neutral/positive), where emotions such as anger and dispirited were categorized as negative, while surprise and joy were categorized as positive. The results are shown in Table 2. From the results in Table 2, several observations can be made: The depression assessment system with added SEI exhibits higher accuracy compared to the corresponding baseline system without SEI integration. Introducing an additional "single-number" SEI representation improves the performance of the respective baseline model. The depression assessment system using an "embedding" representation method outperforms the system using "single-number" representation method. In summary, integrating SEI and utilizing different representation methods enhances the accuracy of depression assessment systems.

In addition, to investigate whether fine-grained emotion granularity affects the performance of the network, we replaced the previous three-class task (negative/neutral/positive) in the Speech Emotion Information Extraction section with a five-class task (anger/dispirited/neutral/surprise/joy). Experimental results are shown in Table 3. The results demonstrate that a more detailed classification of speech emotions can improve the accuracy of depression detection.

Table 2. The performance of the depression assessment systems with or without the SEI information in segment-level and subjecti-level.

Inputs	SEI Info	Segment-level				Subject-level			
		Accuracy	F1	Precision	Recall	Accuracy	F1	Precision	Recall
A	×	59.74	61.26	59.81	62.79	72.06	72.79	72.59	72.98
	single-number	61.53	62.63	61.99	63.28	72.43	73.22	72.74	73.70
	embedding	63.22	64.23	63.14	65.36	73.16	72.91	72.61	73.20
A+T	×	62.67	63.12	62.68	63.57	73.53	74.25	73.79	74.47
	single-number	63.32	64.02	63.25	64.80	74.63	74.13	73.85	74.41
	embedding	62.74	63.56	62.70	64.45	75.74	75.82	75.33	76.31

Table 3. Classification results with different speech emotion fine-grained in subjecti-level.

Inputs	SEI Info	SEI-3-fine-grained				SEI-5-fine-grained			
		Accuracy	F1	Precision	Recall	Accuracy	F1	Precision	Recall
A	embedding	73.16	72.91	72.61	73.20	74.63	74.49	74.07	74.93
A+T	embedding	75.74	75.82	75.33	76.31	76.10	76.36	75.82	76.91

4   Discussion and Conclusion

Thie paper proposed Transformer-based Depression Detection Network has demonstrated its effectiveness in accurately classifying depression severity by integrating speech emotional expression cues with audio and text features. The study utilized pre-trained models HuBERT and RoBERTa for feature extraction, enhancing the model's adaptability and generalization capability. The incorporation of SEI through the emotion2vec model has shown to significantly improve the accuracy of depression recognition.

The study underscores the critical role of speech emotion information in depression detection. By using SEI as the output for a three-class classification task (Negative/Neutral/Positive), we observed that integrating SEI into the depression assessment system led to higher accuracy compared to the baseline system without SEI. Furthermore, both the "single-number" SEI representation and the "embedding" representation enhanced the performance of their respective baseline models, with the "embedding" representation proving more effective.

We also explored the impact of emotion granularity on the network's performance. By replacing the three-class task in the speech emotion extraction module with a five-class task, experimental results indicated that more detailed speech emotion classification could enhance the accuracy of depression detection. This suggests that finer classification of emotions may help capture more subtle associations with depression.

Experimental results validate the advantages of our approach, with higher accuracy and F1 scores compared to baseline models. The findings underscore the potential of leveraging speech emotional cues in automated depression diagnosis, offering a promising direction for future research and clinical applications in mental health assessment.

In future work, we will further explore integrating other types of data, such as physiological signals and facial expressions, with speech and text data, which may provide a more comprehensive perspective on depression detection.

Acknowledgments. This work is supported by National Natural Science Foundation of China (U23B2018, NSFC 62271477), Shenzhen Science and Technology Program (JCYJ20220818101411025, JCYJ20220818102800001, JCYJ20220818101217037), and Shenzhen Peacock Team Project (KQTD20200820113106007).

References

1. Al Hanai, T., Ghassemi, M.M., Glass, J.R.: Detecting depression with audio/text sequence modeling of interviews. In: Interspeech, pp. 1716–1720 (2018)
2. Boersma, P., Van Heuven, V.: Speak and unspeak with praat. Glot Int. **5**(9/10), 341–347 (2001)
3. Bredin, H., et al.: Pyannote. audio: neural building blocks for speaker diarization. In: ICASSP 2020-2020 IEEE International Conference on Acoustics, Speech and Signal Processing (ICASSP), pp. 7124–7128. IEEE (2020)
4. Cummins, N., Scherer, S., Krajewski, J., Schnieder, S., Epps, J., Quatieri, T.F.: A review of depression and suicide risk assessment using speech analysis. Speech Commun. **71**, 10–49 (2015)
5. Hamilton, M.: A rating scale for depression. J. Neurol. Neurosurg. Psychiatry **23**(1), 56 (1960)
6. Hsu, W.N., Bolte, B., Tsai, Y.H.H., Lakhotia, K., Salakhutdinov, R., Mohamed, A.: Hubert: Self-supervised speech representation learning by masked prediction of hidden units. IEEE/ACM Trans. Audio Speech Lang. Process. **29**, 3451–3460 (2021)
7. Kroenke, K., Spitzer, R.L., Williams, J.B.: The phq-9: validity of a brief depression severity measure. J. Gen. Intern. Med. **16**(9), 606–613 (2001)
8. Lausen, A., Hammerschmidt, K.: Emotion recognition and confidence ratings predicted by vocal stimulus type and prosodic parameters. Human. Soc. Sci. Commun. **7**(1), 1–17 (2020)
9. Liu, Y., et al.: Roberta: a robustly optimized bert pretraining approach. arXiv preprint arXiv:1907.11692 (2019)
10. Lu, J., Liu, B., Lian, Z., Cai, C., Tao, J., Zhao, Z.: Prediction of depression severity based on transformer encoder and cnn model. In: 2022 13th International Symposium on Chinese Spoken Language Processing (ISCSLP), pp. 339–343. IEEE (2022)
11. Ma, X., Yang, H., Chen, Q., Huang, D., Wang, Y.: Depaudionet: an efficient deep model for audio based depression classification. In: Proceedings of the 6th International Workshop on Audio/Visual Emotion Challenge, pp. 35–42 (2016)
12. Ma, Z., et al.: emotion2vec: self-supervised pre-training for speech emotion representation. arXiv preprint arXiv:2312.15185 (2023)
13. Organization, W.H.: World mental health report: Transforming mental health for all. World Health Organization (2022)

14. Paszke, A., et al.: Pytorch: an imperative style, high-performance deep learning library. Adv. Neural Inf. Process. Syst. **32** (2019)
15. Rodrigues Makiuchi, M., Warnita, T., Uto, K., Shinoda, K.: Multimodal fusion of bert-cnn and gated cnn representations for depression detection. In: Proceedings of the 9th International on Audio/Visual Emotion Challenge and Workshop, pp. 55–63 (2019)
16. Rohanian, M., Hough, J., Purver, M., et al.: Detecting depression with word-level multimodal fusion. In: Interspeech, pp. 1443–1447 (2019)
17. Vaswani, A., et al.: Attention is all you need. Adv. Neural Inf. Process. Syst. **30** (2017)
18. Wu, X., Xu, C., Li, N., Su, R., Lan, W., Nan, Y.: Depression enhances internal inconsistency between spoken and semantic. In: Interspeech (2024)
19. Yao, Z., et al.: Wenet: production oriented streaming and non-streaming end-to-end speech recognition toolkit. arXiv preprint arXiv:2102.01547 (2021)
20. Zhao, Z., et al.: Automatic assessment of depression from speech via a hierarchical attention transfer network and attention autoencoders. IEEE J. Sel. Topics Signal Process. **14**(2), 423–434 (2019)
21. Zung, W.W.: A rating instrument for anxiety disorders. Psychosomatics: J. Consult. Liaison Psychiatry (1971)
22. Zung, W.W.: A self-rating depression scale. Arch. Gen. Psychiatry **12**(1), 63–70 (1965)

Am I a Social Buddy? A Literature Review on Socially Appealing Design and Implementation Methods for Social Robots

Andreea Ioana Niculescu$^{(\boxtimes)}$, Kheng Hui Yeo, and Jochen Ehnes

Institute for Infocomm Research, A*STAR Research Entities, Singapore, Singapore
{andreea-n,yeokh,jwehnes}@i2r.a-star.edu.sg

Abstract. This paper reviews socially appealing design and implementation methods for social robots published between 2020 and 2024, focusing on three critical traits: human-like communication, emotional intelligence, and personality. Analyzing 29 recent empirical studies, we highlight key trends in human-robot interaction (HRI). Recent advancements in natural language processing (NLP) and multimodal interaction, such as Large Language Models (LLMs) and context-aware frameworks, have significantly improved robots' ability to handle complex conversations and interact effectively in multi-party settings. Generative Adversarial Networks (GANs) have enhanced robots' expressiveness by generating non-verbal cues like co-speech gestures. Advances in emotion recognition, including multimodal data fusion and physiological sensors, have led to more responsive and emotionally intelligent robots with pleasant personalities. These developments indicate a shift towards robots that not only offer functional assistance but also emotional support, enhancing overall user satisfaction and engagement.

Keywords: human-robot. interaction · socially appealing design · social robotics · literature review · social intelligence · human-like communication; · empathy and emotion · personality

1 Introduction

Human-Robot Interaction (HRI) focuses on designing and evaluating robotic systems tailored for human interaction, integrating fields such as AI, robotics, and social sciences. Social robots, which mimic human behavior through verbal and non-verbal communication, emotional expression, and social relationship-building, require sophisticated skills. As robots transition from science fiction to practical applications in caregiving, education, entertainment, and domestic environments, their ability to engage through verbal and bodily expressions and adhere to contextual behavioral norms becomes crucial [3]. Additionally, robots may interact and learn from each other when necessary [6]. Research highlights that the following core characteristics enhance a social robot's social appeal:

© The Author(s), under exclusive license to Springer Nature Singapore Pte Ltd. 2025
H. Li et al. (Eds.): ICSR + InnoBiz 2024, LNAI 15170, pp. 187–196, 2025.
https://doi.org/10.1007/978-981-96-1151-5_19

- Human-like communication: this encompasses both verbal and non-verbal cues, such as eye contact and facial expression recognition [4].
- Emotional intelligence: the capacity to express empathy and offer emotional support [16].
- Personality: consistent traits that foster more natural interactions [15].
- Adaptive behavior: the ability to interpret and respond appropriately to human actions [9].
- Social learning capabilities: the potential to enhance social skills through interactions [6].
- Appropriate physical appearance: a design that supports social interaction without causing discomfort [7].

In this review, we have chosen to concentrate on the first three characteristics—human-like communication, emotional intelligence, and personality—as they represent the most salient social skills for fostering natural, meaningful, and emotionally resonant interactions between humans and social robots. By focusing on these areas, we aim to explore the current state-of-the-art technologies and reveal recent innovative approaches in social robotics.

2   Methods

For our paper review, we selected empirical studies published between 2020 and 2024 focusing on socially appealing design methodologies and implementation practices for social robots. The bibliography was compiled through research on Google Scholar, IEEE, and BASE databases. We also reviewed the reference lists of included articles and key papers to find additional relevant studies.

Our selection criteria were as follows: only papers available in English, published in peer-reviewed journals or conference proceedings, and focusing on social robots were included. Specifically, we included empirical studies presenting new data or those addressing design methodologies and implementation practices. Review articles, meta-analyses, and studies that focused exclusively on user perceptions of robots or specific robot features were excluded.

3   Results

3.1   Human-Like Communication

Human-like interaction through verbal and non-verbal cues is crucial for engaging effectively with social robots because it fosters a sense of familiarity and comfort. Advancements in sensors, actuators, and processing capabilities now allow robots to converse with humans in a more human-like manner, with seamless use of eye contact and facial expressions. We found that the research on human-like communication in social robots can be organized into three primary categories:**verbal**, **non-verbal** and **multimodal**.

Social robots that communicated with predefined repetitive texts tended to come across as artificial. To enhance natural and engaging **verbal** communication, the study in [24] proposes using advanced natural language generation models. They developed and evaluated two mechanisms: a paraphrasing module that rephrases the robot's utterances while preserving their original meaning and a topic-based speech generation module that customizes content according to the robot's conversation partner. While the models show significant potential, challenges such as computational cost, interaction latency, reliance on proprietary models, and absence of subjective evaluations need to be addressed.

For scenarios where multiple people may interact with a single robot in a public space, the lack of multi-party capabilities becomes a significant limitation. To address this issue, the study in [2] proposes a system leveraging Large Language Models (LLMs) to manage conversations involving multiple people, allowing the robot to determine when to speak, generate clarification requests when users pause, and respond to both in-domain and out-of-domain queries effectively. They describe an architecture that detects the addressee of user utterances, handles incomplete sentences with incremental clarification requests, and utilizes LLMs for general chit-chat and knowledge-based responses. Challenges such as ensuring appropriate responses and preventing harmful outputs are addressed by incorporating safeguards and grounding information in prompts.

Besides verbal exchanges, effective communication also relies on **nonverbal** cues like gestures and eye contact. Integrating such **multimodal** behaviors into social robots has been a key focus of research for many years. In recent times, data-driven, end-to-end learning methods have become the primary approach in this field, providing greater scalability and adaptability for replicating human-like nonverbal communication in robots. Two papers introduce a context-aware Generative Adversarial Network (GAN) framework for generating nonverbal behaviors, specifically co-speech gestures, in dyadic interactions [20,21]. Using GANs and a novel Context Encoder, the new approach integrates the target person's audio with their partner's nonverbal signals to generate appropriate co-speech gestures, such as head tilting and hand movements, which convey emotions, intentions, and verbal content. Tested on the JESTKOD and LISI-HHI datasets, it showed improved gesture generation, especially in agreement scenarios. The gestures were successfully transferred to the Pepper robot, highlighting the approach's potential for practical human-robot interaction scenarios.

Non-verbal cues, such as gaze and breathing cues, also appear to be crucial factors in enhancing interactions with collaborative robots (cobots), significantly improving user engagement and perception. In [23], researchers sought to evaluate these cues by modifying a cobot's appearance and behavior using principles from character animation. Gaze cues were implemented through programmed eye movement patterns and real-time gaze adjustments using servo motors by directing the robot's gripper toward points of interest (i.e. collaborator's face or task locations) to simulate attention and communication. Breathing was simulated through rhythmic physical movements of the robot's chest, synchronized with interaction cues to enhance naturalness and engagement. Results demonstrated that gaze cues significantly enhanced the robot's perceived likeability, intelligence, and social presence, while adding breathing motions made it appear more lifelike further improving the overall users' perceptions.

Additionally, it was shown that robot gaze behavior should mimic human-like gaze movements. In [25], a Furhat robot with a biomimetic neck and a 3D face model tested three gaze patterns with users (n = 21): Neutral Gaze (constant eye contact), Experimental Gaze (dynamic adjustments), and Random Gaze (unpredictable shifts). Results revealed that the Experimental Gaze, which mimicked human-like turn-taking and gaze aversions, received higher ratings in anthropomorphism, animacy, likeability, and intelligence compared to neutral and random gaze patterns. Random Gaze was rated lower, highlighting the need for well-designed gaze behavior for positive user experiences.

3.2 Emotional Intelligence

For social robots to effectively assist people, they must demonstrate emotional intelligence capabilities by recognizing and responding appropriately to emotional cues. By understanding and expressing emotions through facial expressions, vocal intonation, and body language, robots can foster meaningful interactions and adapt to cultural differences.

Emotions in social robotics research have been considered from three main points of view: formalizing robots' emotional states using **frameworks**, enabling robots to **express emotion**, and developing algorithms for robots to **understand human emotions** [27].

We found three papers on emotion recognition **frameworks** for human-robot interaction, each with different approaches and goals. In [12], the authors develop a flexible system for robots using video, audio, and text, with an adaptive fusion method (EmbraceNet+) to handle inconsistent data quality and missing information. The system performed competitively in classifying emotions like happiness or sadness across various modality combinations (e.g., text and audio, face and text).

Hong et al. [13] presented a multimodal HRI architecture that combines body language and vocal intonation for emotion detection. Using a two-layer emotional model (deliberative and reactive) to guide their robot's responses, they were able to demonstrate that robots with emotional expressiveness can improve user experience in a diet/fitness counseling scenario compared to neutral robots.

Also, the study by [11] developed a framework for emotion detection in social robots, incorporating a semantic repository to store and manage emotion data. The framework processes various types of multimedia content and employs NLP transformers for classification, intending to integrate this system into practical applications like museum tour-guide robots.

Research focusing on **emotion expression** looked at empathy expression through verbal and non-verbal cues. For verbal cues, the study by [28] used GPT-3.5 on the text of the conversation to predict the appropriate emotion for a specific social interaction in real-time. In experiments, participants favored the robot interactions where the predicted emotions matched its verbal responses, perceiving the robot as more human-like when it was emotionally accurate.

For nonverbal cues, we found four papers focusing on vocal features and body movements for emotional expression. One study [14] investigated empathetic cues through prosody, including melody and speech rhythm. The study found that effective empathy modeling requires synthesizing both primary and nuanced secondary emotions, such as anxiety or confidence. Using a New Zealand English speech corpus, the study applied the Fujisaki model to adjust pitch and rhythm and machine learning to convert neutral text into expressive speech. The models were tested in two rounds: a pilot and a user study (n = 120, n = 59).

Another study [26] focused on enhancing social robots' empathetic abilities through four types of non-verbal cues: speech, action (gesture), facial expression, and emotion. Researchers developed a conversational system using an LLM to generate responses that include these cues. The LLM enables the robots to modulate their speech tone and pace, use appropriate gestures like nodding, display suitable facial expressions, and convey fitting emotions.

Also, Tuyen et al. [22] focused on non-verbal cues, trying to enable social robots to learn bodily expressions of emotion through human interaction. The proposed model allows robots to learn and imitate human gestures, enhancing their social capabilities. It encodes human actions using a pose estimation module and processes them through a Self-Organizing Map (SOM) for clustering. This approach allows the robot to perform motions of its own based on frequent and similar gestures. Experiments show robots using this reflection of human emotional gestures to produce more meaningful and long-lasting interactions.

Ali et al. [1] investigate how robots can effectively convey emotions through full-body gestures. Using Russell's circumplex model, they define 28 closely related emotions in 8 primary groups. Key features such as speed, frequency, and joint angles of the robot's movements are manipulated to express specific emotions. The gestures were tested with 33 participants, who recognized the robot's emotions with an average accuracy of 79.69% across 28 trials.

In the area of **understanding human emotion**, we found two papers using physiological sensors to capture user's emotional states in response to a stimulus. Fiorini and colleagues [29] sought to verify that social robots could use electrocardial, electrodermal, and brain activity signals to infer emotions induced by social interaction. The sensor data was analyzed with three time-window frames and classified using both supervised and unsupervised methods. With 15 participants and over 100 instances, the study achieved 77% accuracy on the best unsupervised method and 85% on the best supervised method.

Shao et al. [30] investigated how choreographed body movements of the robot Pepper, combined with musical stimuli from a validated dataset, can evoke specific emotions in users. Emotional responses from subjects in various age groups were measured via electroencephalography (EEG). These data were classified using multilayer perceptron neural networks (NNs) and SVMs. Results showed that self-reported emotions matched the intended effects, with NNs achieving higher classification rates.

3.3 Personality

Personality's impact on interactions has been thoroughly examined in human contexts. In human-robot interaction (HRI), personality has been identified as essential for improving these interactions, but research in this area is still fragmented and underdeveloped. As such, the papers reviewed could not be grouped in any particular categories, each deploying a mixture of different techniques.

Zabala et al. [33] present a system that enables a humanoid robot to adapt its body language according to the sentiment of its speech, aiming to convey emotion and personality to generate trust. The system combines talking beat gestures with emotional cues like eye lighting, body posture, voice intonation, and volume, allowing the robot to exhibit a range of personalities from discreet to histrionic. The authors used VADER sentiment analysis to translate text polarity into corresponding robot emotions, modulating gestures, eye lighting, and voice intonation for natural expressions. A GAN model generates talking beat gestures, adjusting their speed and intensity to match emotions. Positive emotions produce lively gestures, while negative emotions result in subdued movements.

Andriella et al. [34] describe a robotic system designed to display context-dependent personality traits in an experiment involving assistive memory games. They used observations from human-human interactions, including verbal cues (speech rate and pitch) and non-verbal cues (gestures), to create a robot with both pre-programmed and real-time adaptive behaviors. A statistical algorithm selected appropriate actions and social cues based on the robot's personality and the interaction context, e.g. the game being played. User studies confirmed that participants could statistically distinguish between the robot's different personalities, demonstrating a successful approach to modeling personality traits.

Otterdijk et al. [35] combined literature reviews, expert feedback, and practical implementation to design the robot's personality. Non-verbal cues and movement analysis differentiated introverted from extroverted behaviors. The Pepper robot was programmed with these cues using Choregraphe software and showcased in videos evaluated by movement analysis experts. Their feedback led to refined design guidelines, emphasizing the need for consistent and congruent cues to effectively represent personality.

Noguchi et al. [36] investigated personality design for non-anthropomorphic voice-assisted robots by creating three personas: Butler, Buddy, and Sidekick. These personas differed in proactivity and emotional impact, using both humanoid cues (speech and intonation) and indirect cues (colors and movements). Employing the Big Five personality theory and a Wizard of Oz study, the research developed verbal cues reflecting traits like Extraversion, Conscientiousness, and Neuroticism. Indirect cues were refined through user feedback and Mechanical Turk studies, resulting in distinct motion patterns and color schemes. Participants successfully identified the intended traits and preferred robots that mirrored their own traits, demonstrating the effectiveness of abstract cues in personality modeling.

The team of Nardelli [19] designed a personality generator that varies three of the Big Five traits to modulate robot's behavior during collaborative tower-building game. Using the Pepper robot, they demonstrated that a small group of users (n = 11) could clearly identify differences in Agreeability and Extraversion. However, distinguishing between Conscientiousness and Unscrupulous behavior was less certain. This approach contrasts with Luo et al. [17], who created ten short videos of a "barebones" robot displaying various archetypes in conversation and then asked users (n = 18) to evaluate the personalities shown in the videos via a questionnaire. Their goal was to assess how well each of the five OCEAN model traits could be rated and which traits were most worth the design effort along with the broader question of whether human emotion models are valid for robots. While most traits were rated no better than random guesses, Conscientiousness and Extraversion showed the clearest, consistent differences in user ratings. Repeating such studies across different cultures and larger groups, potentially focusing on a single trait like Extraversion [32] or non-humanoid form factors [5], could provide further insights into which facets most effectively create distinct personalities. Alternative frameworks, such as the Cognitive-Affective Processing System [18], which was used in [10] to develop a situation-dependent personality model, or the Eysenck Personality Questionnaire [8], as applied by [31], might also offer new perspectives.

4   Discussion

Our review of design and implementation techniques for social robots, with a focus on human-like communication, emotional intelligence, and personality, uncovered several key trends that highlight the increasing sophistication in designing robots capable of engaging users more naturally and meaningfully.

Recent advancements in natural language processing (NLP) and multimodal interaction have been transformative. LLMs and context-aware frameworks have improved robots' ability to handle complex conversational scenarios and interact effectively in multi-party settings, reducing the artificiality of predefined, repetitive text. Natural language generation (NLG) techniques like paraphrasing and topic-based speech generation contribute to more fluid interactions, despite ongoing challenges like computational cost and interaction latency. Beyond verbal communication, integrating non-verbal cues such as gaze, facial expressions, and body language—enhanced by GANs—creates more immersive and lifelike interactions. These developments in co-speech gestures, eye contact, and even subtle human-like behaviors like breathing play a crucial role in improving user perceptions of robots, making them seem more intelligent and engaging.

Another notable trend is the development of emotionally intelligent robots, increasingly equipped with multimodal emotion recognition systems that can understand and express emotions by processing real-world data from video, audio, and text sources. These advancements allow robots to classify and respond to emotions more accurately. Emotion expression is also evolving, with robots now able to convey empathy through verbal cues (tone, pitch) and non-verbal gestures, which enhance emotional alignment and improve user satisfaction. The use of physiological sensors to assess user's emotional states reflects a shift towards emotionally responsive robots, capable of adapting to users' needs in real-time.

Although still fragmented, research in personality design for social robots, highlights the increasing focus on adapting robots' body language, voice, and gestures to match user emotions and personalities. Robots are now designed to adjust their behavior in real-time based on the interaction context, integrating verbal and non-verbal cues to create more dynamic and recognizable personalities. This extends to non-humanoid robots, which use abstract cues such as color schemes and motion patterns to convey distinct personas aligned with user preferences. The use of personality models like the Big Five (OCEAN) allows robots to exhibit traits such as extraversion and agreeableness, although some traits remain less perceptible to users. Overall, while personality design is advancing with a focus on emotion recognition and context-aware adaptation, the field is still developing and needs more standardized methods and broader research to create engaging and relatable robot personalities.

5   Conclusion

We reviewed 29 recent empirical studies focused on socially appealing design methodologies and implementation practices for social robots. Our analysis shows that the field of social robotics is rapidly advancing, driven by innovations in human-like communication, emotional engagement, and personality design. Progress in NLP models, multimodal interaction techniques, and emotion recognition systems has significantly enhanced robots' ability to interact naturally and empathetically with humans.

Future research should expand to account for cultural differences, tailoring robots' emotional and personality responses to diverse user backgrounds while also improving personality design to increase relatability. By refining communication algorithms and boosting emotional intelligence, researchers can advance the field of HRI, creating robots that not only excel in functionality but also form meaningful connections with users through social engagement.

References

1. Ali, S., et al.: Human robot interaction: identifying resembling emotions using dynamic body gestures of robot. In: Proceedings of the 3rd International Conference on Artificial Intelligence (ICAI), pp. 39–44. Islamabad, Pakistan (2023)
2. Angus, A., et al.: A multi-party conversational social robot using LLMs. In: IEEE International Conference on Human-Robot Interaction (HRI 2024), pp.1273–1275. ACM, New York (2024)
3. Bartneck, C., Nomura, T., Kanda, T., Suzuki, T., Kennsuke, K.: A cross-cultural study on attitudes towards robots. In: Proceedings of HCI International, Las Vegas, NV, USA, 22–27 July (2005)
4. Breazeal, C.: Toward sociable robots. Robot. Auton. Syst. **42**(3–4), 167–175 (2003)

5. Chowdhury, A., Ahtinen, A., Wu, C. H., Väänänen, K., Taidi, D., Pieters, R.: Exploring the personality design space of robots: personalities and design implications for non-anthropomorphic wellness robots. In: 32nd IEEE International Conference on Robot and Human Interactive Communication (RO-MAN), pp. 2344–2351, Busan, Republic of Korea (2023)
6. Dautenhahn, K.: Socially intelligent robots: dimensions of human-robot interaction. Philos. Trans. Roy. Soc. B: Biol. Sci. **362**(1480), 679–704 (2007)
7. DiSalvo, C.F., Gemperle, F., Forlizzi, J., Kiesler, S.: All robots are not created equal: the design and perception of humanoid robot heads. In: Proceedings of the 4th Conference on Designing Interactive Systems: Processes, Practices, Methods, and Techniques, pp. 321–326, London, UK (2002)
8. Eysenck, H.J., Eysenck, S.B.G.: Manual of the Eysenck Personality Questionnaire. Hodder and Stoughton, London (1975)
9. Fong, T., Nourbakhsh, I., Dautenhahn, K.: A survey of socially interactive robots. Robot. Auton. Syst. **42**(3–4), 143–166 (2003)
10. Gargano, A., Cominelli, L., Vannucci, C., Cecchetti, L., Scilingo, E.P.: Preliminary personality model for social robots based on the Cognitive-Affective Processing System theory. In: IEEE International Conference on Metrology for Extended Reality, Artificial Intelligence and Neural Engineering (MetroXRAINE), pp. 223–228, Rome, Italy (2022)
11. Graterol, W., Diaz-Amado, J., Cardinale, Y., Dongo, I., Lopes-Silva, E., Santos-Libarino, C.: Emotion detection for social robots based on NLP transformers and an emotion ontology. Sensors **21**(4), 1322 (2021)
12. Heredia, J.P., et al.: Adaptive multimodal emotion detection architecture for social robots. IEEE Access **10**, 20727–20744 (2022)
13. Hong, A., et al.: A multimodal emotional human-robot interaction architecture for social robots engaged in bidirectional communication. IEEE Trans. Cybern. **51**(12), 5954–5968 (2021)
14. James, J., Balamurali, B.T., Watson, C.I., MacDonald, B.: Empathetic speech synthesis and testing for healthcare robots. Int. J. Soc. Robot. **13**, 2119–2137 (2021)
15. Lee, K.M., Peng, W., Jin, S.A., Yan, C.: Can robots manifest personality? An empirical test of personality recognition, social responses, and social presence in human-robot interaction. J. Commun. **56**(4), 754–772 (2006)
16. Leite, I., Martinho, C., Paiva, A.: Social robots for long-term interaction: a survey. Int. J. Soc. Robot. **5**(2), 291–308 (2013)
17. Luo, L., Ogawa, K., Ishiguro, H.: Identifying personality dimensions for engineering robot personalities in significant quantities with small user groups. Robotics **11**(28) (2022)
18. Mischel, W., Shoda, Y.: A cognitive-affective system theory of personality: reconceptualizing situations, dispositions, dynamics, and invariance in personality structure. Psychol. Rev. **102**(2), 246–268 (1995)
19. Nardelli, A., Recchiuto, C., Sgorbissa, A.: A psychological framework for robotic personality. In: Proceedings of I-RIM Conference, pp. 48–50, Rome, Italy (2023)
20. Tuyen, N.T.V., Elibol, A., Chong, N.Y.: A GAN-based approach to communicative gesture generation for social robots. In: IEEE International Conference on Advanced Robotics and Its Social Impacts (ARSO), pp. 58–64 (2021)
21. Tuyen, N.T.V., Celiktutan, O.: It takes two, not one: context-aware nonverbal behaviour generation in dyadic interactions. Adv. Robot. **37**(24), 1552–1565 (2023)

22. Tuyen, N.T.V., Elibol, A., Chong, N.Y.: Learning bodily expression of emotion for social robots through human interaction. IEEE Trans. Cogn. Dev. Syst. **13**(1), 16–30 (2020)
23. Terzioğlu, Y., Mutlu, B., Şahin, E.: Designing social cues for collaborative robots: the role of gaze and breathing in human-robot collaboration. In: 15th ACM/IEEE International Conference on Human-Robot Interaction, pp. 343–357, Cambridge, UK (2020)
24. Sevilla-Salcedo, J., et al.: Using large language models to shape social robots' speech. Int. J. Interact. Multimed. Artif. Intell. **8**(6) (2023)
25. Somashekarappa, V., Howes, Ch., Sayeed, A.: Good looking: how gaze patterns affect users' perceptions of an interactive social robot. In: IEEE International Conference on Advanced Robotics and Its Social Impacts (ARSO), pp. 128–133. Hong Kong (2024)
26. Lee, Y.K., Jung, Y., Kang, G., Hahn, S.: Developing social robots with empathetic non-verbal cues using large language models. In: 32nd IEEE International Conference on Robot Human Interactive Communication (RO-MAN), Busan, Republic of Korea (2023)
27. Spezialetti, M., Placidi, G., Rossi, S.: Emotion recognition for human-robot interaction: recent advances and future perspectives. Front. Robot. AI **7** (2020)
28. Chinmaya, M., Verdonschot, R., Hagoort, P., Skantzel, G.: Real-time emotion generation in human-robot dialogue using large language models. Front. Robot. AI **10** (2023)
29. Fiorini, L., Mancioppi, G., Semeraro, F., Fujita, H., Cavallo, F.: Unsupervised emotional state classification through physiological parameters for social robotics applications. Knowl.-Based Syst. **190**, 105–217 (2020)
30. Shao, M., Snyder, M., Nejat, G., Benhabib, B.: User affect elicitation with a socially emotional robot. Robotics **9**, 44 (2020)
31. Sorrentino, A., Khalid, O., Coviello, L., Cavallo, F., Fiorini, L.: Modeling human-like robot personalities as a key to foster socially aware navigation. In: Proceedings of the 30th IEEE International Conference on Robot & Human Interactive Communication (RO-MAN), pp. 95–101, Vancouver, BC, Canada (2021)
32. Speranza, S., Recchiuto, C.T., Bruno, B., Sgorbissa, A.: A model for the representation of the extraversion-introversion personality traits in the Communication Style of a Social Robot. In: 29th IEEE International Conference on Robot and Human Interactive Communication (RO-MAN), pp. 75–81 Naples, Italy (2020)
33. Zabala, U., Rodriguez, I., Martínez-Otzeta, J.M., Lazkano, E.: Expressing robot personality through talking body language. Appl. Sci. **11**(10) (2021)
34. Andriella, A., et al.: Do I have a personality? Endowing care robots with context-dependent personality traits. Int. J. Soc. Robot. **13**(8), 2081–2102 (2021)
35. Otterdijk, M.V., Song, H., Tsiakas, K., Zeijl, I., Barakova, E: Nonverbal cues expressing robot personality –a movement analysts perspective. In: 31st IEEE International Conference on Robot and Human Interactive Communication (RO-MAN), pp. 1181–1186. Italy, Napoli (2022)
36. Noguchi, Y., Kamide, H., Fumihide, T.: Personality traits for a social mediator robot encouraging elderly self-disclosure on loss experiences. ACM Trans. Hum. Robot Interact. **9**(3), 1–24 (2020)

Optimization-Based Trajectory Planning for Autonomous Ground Vehicles

Haoran Xu and Qinyuan Ren(✉)

College of Control Science and Engineering, Zhejiang University, Hangzhou 310027, People's Republic of China
renqinyuan@zju.edu.cn

Abstract. In social environments, complex interactive scenes and various tasks bring great challenges to the motion planning of autonomous ground vehicles. Application scenarios typically require vehicles to plan a smooth trajectory in real time that takes the shortest amount of time and conforms to all constraints. The construction of an optimal control problem in the state space is a common approach in this field, however, this inevitably entails a compromise between the optimality of the trajectories and the computational efficiency. The proposed method formulates a trajectory optimization problem based on differential flatness theory, which realizes efficient obstacle avoidance while satisfying the nonholonomic constraints of the ground vehicles. The representation of trajectories is simplified and a trajectory planning problem is constructed in the differential flatness space of vehicles. Furthermore, safe driving corridors are utilized to achieve smooth obstacle avoidance. The output trajectories are tracked by a model predictive controller for deployment on autonomous ground vehicles. Experiments in both simulation and real-world are conducted to demonstrate the feasibility of the algorithms in complex scenarios.

Keywords: Motion Planning · Autonomous Vehicles · Obstacle Avoidance

1 Introduction

The development of motion planning problems for mobile robots has yielded more fruitful results. However, due to the complexity of cluttered environments and the fact that most ground vehicles have nonholonomic constraints, trajectory optimization for autonomous vehicles is extremely challenging. Obstacle avoidance in cluttered environments requires accurate modeling of the robot as well as precise trajectory discretization, and nonholonomic constraints bring nonlinearity and nonconvexity to the optimization problem, making it quite difficult to solve.

Optimization-based planning algorithms plan the trajectory of a mobile robot by minimizing a cost function affected by the robot's state variables. The

CHOMP algorithm [14] optimizes the trajectory for the cost function using gradient descent to obtain smooth, collision-free trajectories. However, the algorithm suffers from the problem of easily falling into the local minima. The Time Elastic Band algorithm [8] describes the path planning problem as a multi-objective optimization problem and is accelerated using the g2o [5] solver. However, the computational complexity of the TEB algorithm is still large and the control is unstable. [12] assumed that obstacles are convex and proposed an optimization-based obstacle avoidance (OBCA) algorithm, where they introduced signed distance to represent the distance between the robot and the obstacle and transformed the safety constraints into a continuously differentiable form. [10,13] employ a differential flatness model for quadrotors and parameterize the trajectory using a polynomial, which reduces the difficulty of solving the optimization problem and allows efficient planning with limited computational resources.

Differential flatness systems can transform all state and control variables into functions of the flatness output and its finite derivatives. An important feature of differential flatness systems is that we only need to perform algebraic operations without integration to represent all variables. By introducing differential flatness theory to the motion planning problem of unmanned vehicles, we can avoid dealing with nonholonomic constraints, and perform dimensionality reduction to reduce the nonconvexity and nonlinearity of the optimization problem so that the iteration process could converge faster.

The aim of this paper is to design a trajectory optimization method suitable for nonholonomic ground vehicles in dynamic and complex scenarios, to generate a smooth, low-energy, physically feasible trajectory. Autonomous ground vehicles can reach the end state as soon as possible in complex environments with safety in mind. Starting from the differential flatness theory, we first establish a differential flatness model of the ground vehicle, use the flatness output and its derivatives to represent the state variables of the vehicle, and parameterize the trajectory with polynomial curves; then, the trajectory optimization problem and its constraints are represented using the flatness output, and the penalty function method is used to transform the constrained optimization problem into an unconstrained optimization problem; finally, the optimal trajectory is solved by the quasi-Newton method and the planned trajectory is tracked using a model predictive control algorithm. Experiments in both simulation and real-world are conducted to demonstrate the feasibility of the algorithms in complex scenarios.

2   Differential Flatness Model

This paper focuses on the analysis of differential drive models commonly used in autonomous ground vehicles. The differential drive model is illustrated with state $\boldsymbol{x} = [x, y, \theta, v, \omega]$ consisting of the position $\boldsymbol{p} = [x, y]$ and heading angle θ in the global coordinate system, the linear velocity v and the angular velocity ω in the body frame. The model can be expressed as

$$\dot{x} = v \cos\theta, \ \dot{y} = v \sin\theta, \ \dot{\theta} = \omega, \ \dot{v} = a, \ \dot{\omega} = \beta, \tag{1}$$

where a is linear acceleration and β is angular acceleration.

[1] proves that wheeled robots are differential flatness systems and the position of the drive center $s = [s_x, s_y]^T = [x, y]^T$ can be used as a flatness output of the system. For the differential drive model of the ground vehicle, its state variables and control variables can be transformed into functions of the flatness output and its finite order derivatives:

$$\theta = \arctan 2(\eta \dot{s}_y, \eta \dot{s}_x), \ v = \eta \|\dot{s}\|_2, \ a = \eta \frac{\ddot{s}^T \dot{s}}{\|\dot{s}\|_2}, \ \omega = \frac{\ddot{s}^T B \dot{s}}{\|\dot{s}\|_2^2}, \tag{2}$$

where $\eta = \pm 1$ means the vehicle moves forward or backward, $B = \begin{bmatrix} 0 & -1 \\ 1 & 0 \end{bmatrix}$.

3 Trajectory Optimization Problem

In this section, a spatio-temporal trajectory planning problem in differential flatness space is introduced and we design a numerical iterative algorithm to solve the optimization problem. In trajectory optimization problems for mobile robots, the most common optimization objective is the comfort of the trajectory, defined as the derivative of acceleration with respect to time. Usually, we optimize the trajectory by minimizing the integral of the square of jerk in the spatial domain.

We represent the trajectory as a polynomial curve of n segments in two dimensions, and the ith segment of the trajectory can be represented as: $s_i(t) = c_i^T h(t)$, where $c_i \in \mathbb{R}^{(r+1) \times q}, h(t) = [1, t, t^2, \cdots, t^r]^T, i \in \{1, 2, \cdots, n\}, t \in [0, T_i]$, $r = 5$ is the order of the polynomial, $q = 2$ is the dimension of the trajectory, T_i is the duration time of the i-th segment. The total time required for the entire trajectory is $T_s = \sum_{i=1}^n T_i$. We set each segment of the trajectory to be uniformly distributed in duration time and optimize the trajectory by adjusting the points connected to adjacent trajectories so that $T_i = \frac{T_s}{n}$.

The planned trajectory aims to achieve smooth obstacle avoidance while maintaining perfect dynamic performance. After parameterizing the vehicle's trajectory in the flatness output space, we can define the following trajectory optimization problem:

$$\min_{c, T_s} \mathcal{J}(c, T_s) = \int_0^{T_s} V(t)^T W V(t) dt + w_T T_s, \tag{3a}$$

$$s.t. V(t) = s^{(\rho)}(t), \forall t \in [0, T_s], \tag{3b}$$

$$s^{[\rho-1]}(0) = s_0^{[\rho-1]}, s^{[\rho-1]}(T_s) = s_f^{[\rho-1]}, \tag{3c}$$

$$s_i^{[\tilde{\rho}]}(T_i) = s_{i+1}^{[\tilde{\rho}]}(0), 1 \leq i < n, \tag{3d}$$

$$\mathcal{G}_d(s(t), ..., s^\rho(t), t) \preceq 0, \forall d \in \mathcal{D}, \forall t \in [0, T_s], \tag{3e}$$

$$T_s > 0, T_i = \frac{T_s}{n}. \tag{3f}$$

where $c = [c_1, c_2, \cdots, c_n] \in \mathbb{R}^{(n \times (r+1)) \times q}, W \in \mathbb{R}^{q \times q}$ is the weight parameter matrix of the quadratic term, $w_T \in \mathbb{R}^+$ is the weight of the trajectory's duration time. $s^{(\rho)}(t)$ denotes the ρ-th derivative of the trajectory. The typical choice for adjusting overall trajectory smoothness is to set $\rho = 3$, which minimizes the sum of squared jerk of the entire trajectory. We define $s^{[\rho-1]} = [s, s^{(1)}, \cdots, s^{(\rho-1)}]$ as a representation of vehicle's state, $s_0^{[\rho-1]}$ and $s_f^{[\rho-1]}$ are start states and end states of the vehicle. (3d) is the continuity constraint between adjacent trajectory segments, and $\tilde{\rho}$ represents that the trajectory is continuous at $\tilde{\rho}$-th order; (3e) represents inequality constraints consisting of dynamics constraints, safety constraints, etc., $\mathcal{D} = \{v, a, \omega, C\}$.

According to the previous work [2,10], when $\tilde{\rho} = 4$, the trajectory's parameter c can be uniquely determined from the $n - 1$ constraint points and the total time T_s, so (3c) and (3d) can be written as $M(T_s)c = b$, where $M(T_s) \in \mathbb{R}^{(n \times (r+1)) \times (n \times (r+1))}$ is a non-singular matrix containing $n \times (r+1)$ linear equality constraints' parameters, $b \in \mathbb{R}^{(n \times (r+1)) \times q}$ is the matrix associated with continuity of the trajectory. Assuming that $p = [p_s, p_1, \cdots, p_{n-1}, p_g] \in \mathbb{R}^{q \times (n+1)}$ represents all waypoints on the trajectory, p_s is the start position and p_g is the goal position, $p_1, \cdots, p_{n-1}$ are constraint points, we can design $M(T_s)$ and b as:

$$
M = \begin{bmatrix}
F_0 & 0 & 0 & \cdots & 0 \\
E_1 & F_1 & 0 & \cdots & 0 \\
0 & E_2 & F_2 & \cdots & 0 \\
\vdots & \vdots & \vdots & \ddots & \vdots \\
0 & 0 & 0 & \cdots & F_{n-1} \\
0 & 0 & 0 & \cdots & E_n
\end{bmatrix}, b = \begin{bmatrix}
D_0 \\
D_1 \\
0_{\tilde{\rho} \times q} \\
\vdots \\
D_{n-1} \\
0_{\tilde{\rho} \times q} \\
D_n
\end{bmatrix} \tag{4}
$$

where $D_0 = (s_0^{[\rho-1]})^T, D_n = (s_f^{[\rho-1]})^T, D_i = p_i^T$, as for $E_i, F_i \in \mathbb{R}^{(r+1) \times (r+1)}$, they satisfy the following equation:

$$
E_i = \left[h(T_i), h(T_i), ..., h^{(\tilde{\rho})}(T_i) \right]^T, F_i = \left[0, -h(0), ..., -h^{(\tilde{\rho})}(0) \right]^T, \tag{5}
$$

so that c can be uniquely determined by p and T_s:

$$
c = M(T_s)^{-1}b(p). \tag{6}
$$

The equation constraints disappear after the variable substitution, we can handle the inequality constraints through penalty functions, transforming the constrained optimization problem into an unconstrained optimization problem:

$$
\min_{p, T_s} \mathcal{W}(p, T_s) = \mathcal{J}(c(p, T_s), T_s) + \mathcal{K}_{\Sigma}(c(p, T_s), T_s), \tag{7}
$$

where $\mathcal{K}_{\Sigma} = \sum_{i \in \mathcal{D}} L_1(\mathcal{K}_i)$ is the sum of penalty functions for inequality constraints, $L_1(\cdot)$ is a first-order relaxation function.

We often require ground vehicles to operate within a certain speed range due to safety, physical limitations, and environmental uncertainty. We define v_m as the max linear velocity, the linear velocity penalty function for the differential vehicle can be written in the following form:

$$
\mathcal{K}_v(\dot{s}) = \dot{s}^T \dot{s} - v_m^2. \tag{8}
$$

To prevent the drive wheels from slipping, the acceleration of the ground vehicle needs to be limited. We can write the linear acceleration penalty function as:

$$\mathcal{K}_a(\dot{s}, \ddot{s}) = \frac{(\ddot{s}^T \dot{s})^2}{\dot{s}^T \dot{s}} - a_m^2, \tag{9}$$

where a_m is the max linear acceleration. In the normal direction, the acceleration of the unmanned vehicle is $a_n = \omega v$, so a limit on angular velocity is needed and we can write the penalty function as:

$$\mathcal{K}_\omega(\dot{s}, \ddot{s}) = \left(\frac{\ddot{s}^T B \dot{s}}{\|\dot{s}\|_2^2} \right)^2 - \omega_m^2 \tag{10}$$

Analogous to UAVs, in the 2D plane, we can generate a series of 2D convex polygons to form a safe driving corridor, which constrains the vehicle to be within the concatenation set formed by convex polygons to achieve safe obstacle avoidance, as shown in Fig. 1.

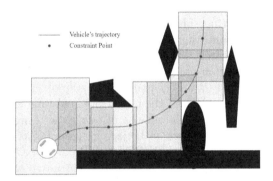

Fig. 1. The trajectory planning in safe corridors.

The set of points within a convex polygon can be expressed as $\mathcal{F} = \{s \in \mathbb{R}^q | A_k s \le b_k\}$, so for every hyperplane of the k-th convex polygon, the obstacle avoidance penalty function is:

$$\mathcal{K}_{C,e}(s) = A_{k,e} s - b_{k,e}, e \in \{1, \cdots, m\}, \tag{11}$$

where m is the number of hyperplanes.

Following the previous work [6], we choose rectangles as the polygons that combine to form safe corridors, the construction of the safe corridors is shown in Fig. 2. Consequently, we have:

$$A_k = \begin{bmatrix} -1 & 0 \\ 1 & 0 \\ 0 & -1 \\ 0 & 1 \end{bmatrix}, b_k = \begin{bmatrix} -x_{min} \\ x_{max} \\ -y_{min} \\ y_{max} \end{bmatrix}. \tag{12}$$

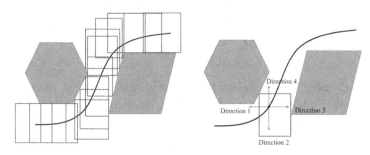

(a) Rectangles in the safe corridor.   (b) Expansion of the rectangle.

Fig. 2. The construction of safe corridors.

4   Experiments

We conduct experiments in both simulation and real-world to verify the feasibility of the proposed algorithm. The trajectory planning module needs a sequence of collision-free points connecting the start point and the end point. We choose the JPS (Jump Point Search, [3]) algorithm as a collision-free path searcher to provide an initial solution for trajectory optimization. As for mapping and localization, we first construct an occupancy grid map of the environment using the Cartographer algorithm [4] and then use it for real-time localization during trajectory planning. Due to the dominance of quadratic terms in the objective function, the optimization problem in trajectory planning is solved by the L-BFGS method [7]. We employ an MPC(Model Predictive Control) controller [11] that minimizes position and velocity errors to track planned trajectories, the nonlinear optimization problem in MPC controller is solved by IPOPT [9].

First, we conduct experiments in simulation to test the performance of the proposed method, as shown in Fig. 3. The size of the map is 10 m × 10 m, the configuration of the robot is $v_m = 0.5\,\text{m/s}, a_m = 2.0\,\text{m/s}^2, \omega_m = 2.0\,\text{rad/s}, r = 0.1\,\text{m}$, where r is the radius of the robot.

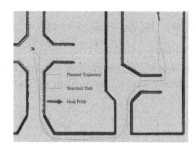

Fig. 3. The experiment in simulation.

The quantitative information of the planned trajectory in simulation is shown in Table 1, where $t_{compute}$ is the time consumption of solving the optimization problem, $J = \frac{1}{T_s} \int_0^{T_s} \sqrt{(s^{(3)})^T s^{(3)}} dt$ means average jerk. It can be seen that the linear velocity, angular velocity and linear acceleration obtained from the trajectory optimization are all within the preset limits, and the average jerk is relatively low, which achieves the minimum energy control. Furthermore, the optimization problem is solved rapidly, which allows it to meet the real-time requirement.

Table 1. Experiment data in simulation.

Parameter	Value
$t_{compute}$	45.0 ms
T_s	52.39 s
J	$0.063 \, \text{m/s}^3$
v_m	0.5 m/s
w_m	0.45 rad/s
a_m	$0.155 \, \text{m/s}^2$

In order to demonstrate the superiority of the proposed algorithm in terms of solution speed and trajectory quality, we carried out comparison experiments in the simulation. The selected baseline was the TEB algorithm [8], which was analyzed in terms of trajectory smoothness, trajectory time, and computation time respectively. We selected three different scenarios for our experiments: 13 m × 5 m, 12 m × 7 m, 20 m × 15 m, as shown in Fig. 4.

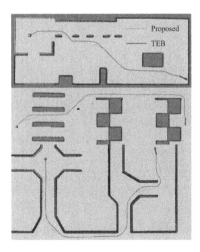

Fig. 4. The comparison between the proposed method and TEB method.

Table 2. The comparative analysis of the performance of trajectory planning.

Map	$t_{compute}(ms)$		$T_s(s)$		$v_m(m/s)$		$\omega_m(rad/s)$	
	TEB	Ours	TEB	Ours	TEB	Ours	TEB	Ours
13 m × 5 m	1048.0	**16.0**	**30.2**	32.7	0.5	0.5	1.948	**0.247**
12 m × 7 m	1809.0	**42.0**	**48.4**	51.8	0.5	0.5	2.0	**0.450**
20 m × 15 m	8551.0	**69.0**	**40.3**	44.5	0.5	0.5	2.0	**0.568**

From Fig. 4 and Table 2, TEB slightly outperforms the proposed method in terms of the duration of the trajectory. However, our method's trajectory result is smoother and TEB's trajectory almost reaches the limit of the given constraints such as linear velocity and angular velocity, which is easy to have large errors in the trajectory tracking. In addition, there is a big gap between TEB and our algorithm in terms of solving time, especially in long-distance trajectory optimization. TEB is seriously time-consuming so it can not meet the real-time requirements of motion planning. While the computation time of our algorithm can still be controlled within 70 ms in long-distance cases, efficient optimization is still possible on an onboard computer.

We deploy the entire motion planning framework on a differential wheeled robot and conduct real-world experiments to verify the feasibility of our planner on a real physical platform. The experimental scene is a 6 m × 5 m cluttered environment, as shown in Fig. 6, the robot needs to pass through the obstacles to reach the specified position. All modules are implemented in C++ and run on an onboard computer configured with an Intel i7-8565U CPU, 16G RAM, and Ubuntu 18.04 operation system.

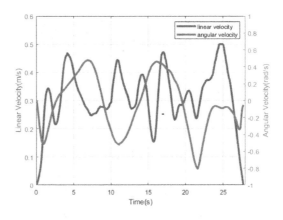

Fig. 5. The velocity profile of the planned trajectory.

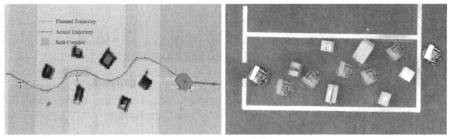

(a) The trajectory in Rviz.   (b) The trajectory in real world.

Fig. 6. The trajectory of the vehicle in the real-world experiment.

As shown in Fig. 5, the planned velocity profile is very smooth, and the maximum linear and angular velocities do not exceed the set thresholds, which facilitates the controller to track the trajectory accurately. In Fig. 6, the robot smoothly avoids obstacles to reach the specified position, and the whole trajectory is constrained into the safe corridor, which meets the safe obstacle avoidance constraints. Figure 7 demonstrates the tracking effect of the MPC controller on the planned trajectory, the controller is able to track the whole trajectory completely with a maximum positional tracking error of 0.1 m.

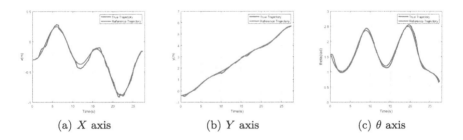

(a) X axis   (b) Y axis   (c) θ axis

Fig. 7. The reference trajectory and the real trajectory of the vehicle.

5 Conclusions

In this paper, a hierarchical motion planning system is established utilizing differential flat theory and applied to differential wheeled mobile robots. The feasibility of the system in complex scenarios is verified through experiments. The motion planning system designed in this paper has good performance and can efficiently plan high-quality motion trajectories using limited computation resources. In the future, we will work on dynamic obstacle avoidance in unknown environments.

References

1. Fliess, M., Lévine, J., Martin, P., Rouchon, P.: Flatness and defect of non-linear systems: introductory theory and examples. Int. J. Control **61**(6), 1327–1361 (1995)
2. Han, Z., et al.: An efficient spatial-temporal trajectory planner for autonomous vehicles in unstructured environments. IEEE Trans. Intell. Transp. Syst. (2023)
3. Harabor, D., Grastien, A.: Online graph pruning for pathfinding on grid maps. In: Proceedings of the AAAI Conference on Artificial Intelligence, vol. 25, pp. 1114–1119 (2011)
4. Hess, W., Kohler, D., Rapp, H., Andor, D.: Real-time loop closure in 2D lidar slam. In: 2016 IEEE International Conference on Robotics and Automation (ICRA), pp. 1271–1278. IEEE (2016)
5. Kümmerle, R., Grisetti, G., Strasdat, H., Konolige, K., Burgard, W.: G 2 O: a general framework for graph optimization. In: 2011 IEEE International Conference on Robotics and Automation, pp. 3607–3613. IEEE (2011)
6. Li, B., et al.: Optimization-based trajectory planning for autonomous parking with irregularly placed obstacles: a lightweight iterative framework. IEEE Trans. Intell. Transp. Syst. **23**(8), 11970–11981 (2021)
7. Liu, D.C., Nocedal, J.: On the limited memory BFGS method for large scale optimization. Math. Program. **45**(1), 503–528 (1989)
8. Rösmann, C., Feiten, W., Wösch, T., Hoffmann, F., Bertram, T.: Efficient trajectory optimization using a sparse model. In: 2013 European Conference on Mobile Robots, pp. 138–143. IEEE (2013)
9. Wächter, A., Biegler, L.T.: On the implementation of an interior-point filter line-search algorithm for large-scale nonlinear programming. Math. Program. **106**, 25–57 (2006)
10. Wang, Z., Zhou, X., Xu, C., Gao, F.: Geometrically constrained trajectory optimization for multicopters. IEEE Trans. Rob. **38**(5), 3259–3278 (2022)
11. Zavala, V.M., Biegler, L.T.: The advanced-step NMPC controller: optimality, stability and robustness. Automatica **45**(1), 86–93 (2009)
12. Zhang, X., Liniger, A., Borrelli, F.: Optimization-based collision avoidance. IEEE Trans. Control Syst. Technol. **29**(3), 972–983 (2020)
13. Zhou, X., Wang, Z., Ye, H., Xu, C., Gao, F.: Ego-planner: an ESDF-free gradient-based local planner for quadrotors. IEEE Robot. Autom. Lett. **6**(2), 478–485 (2020)
14. Zucker, M., et al.: Chomp: covariant Hamiltonian optimization for motion planning. Int. J. Robot. Res. **32**(9–10), 1164–1193 (2013)

Alzheimer's Disease Detection Based on Large Language Model Prompt Engineering

Tian Zheng[1,2], Xurong Xie[1(✉)], Xiaolan Peng[1], Hui Chen[1], and Feng Tian[1]

[1] Institute of Software, Chinese Academy of Sciences, Beijing 100190, China
{xurong,xiaolan,chenhui,tianfeng}@iscas.ac.cn
[2] University of Chinese Academy of Sciences, Beijing 100049, China
zhengtian24@mails.ucas.ac.cn

Abstract. In light of the growing proportion of older individuals in our society, the timely diagnosis of Alzheimer's disease has become a crucial aspect of healthcare. In this paper, we propose a non-invasive and cost-effective detection method based on speech technology. The method employs a pre-trained language model in conjunction with techniques such as prompt fine-tuning and conditional learning, thereby enhancing the accuracy and efficiency of the detection process. To address the issue of limited computational resources, this study employs the efficient LORA fine-tuning method to construct the classification model. Following multiple rounds of training and rigorous 10-fold cross-validation, the prompt fine-tuning strategy based on the LLAMA2 model demonstrated an accuracy of 81.31%, representing a 4.46% improvement over the control group employing the BERT model. This study offers a novel technical approach for the early diagnosis of Alzheimer's disease and provides valuable insights into model optimization and resource utilization under similar conditions. It is anticipated that this method will prove beneficial in clinical practice and applied research, facilitating more accurate and efficient screening and diagnosis of Alzheimer's disease.

Keywords: Prompt learning · Large language model · Alzheimer's disease

1 Introduction

In recent years, the ageing of the world's population has become one of the new features of demographic change. With advances in medical care, the average life expectancy of human beings has lengthened, country-specific differences in population health have become more pronounced, and the prevalence of chronic diseases has risen globally. China is a large country with a large population and a seriously aging population. As the severity of aging increases, a variety of geriatric diseases follow, including Alzheimer's disease (AD), Parkinson's disease type of neurodegenerative diseases, and some statistics [7] show that there are

H. Li et al. (Eds.): ICSR + InnoBiz 2024, LNAI 15170, pp. 207–216, 2025.
https://doi.org/10.1007/978-981-96-1151-5_21

about 15 million dementia patients and more than 3 million Parkinson's patients among the elderly aged sixty years and above in China.Considering the global imbalance of healthcare resources, it is more difficult to diagnose AD by clinical visits, extensive neuropsychological testing or invasive means, but digital health tools can ideally address such issues. Completing a digital assessment at home via a smartphone or tablet would greatly increase the accessibility of Alzheimer's screening.

The current speech-language data used for AD research suffers from high difficulty in data collection, limited number of samples, insufficient data diversity, and data quality problems. And the big language model can effectively deal with the above challenges. The large amount of pre-training data can compensate for the sparsity of data; the robust deep feature extraction of the large model can solve the problem of large individual differences in data [13]; and compared with ordinary neural network models, the large language model can extract multi-level linguistic features that can help to comprehensively assess the patient's linguistic ability and capture potential AD symptoms.

In summary, this paper proposes the use of a large language model (LLAMA2) combined with a prompt engineering approach for AD detection method. The specific research methods are 1) using Prompt Learning combined with LORA to fine-tune the model; 2) using Prompt Tuning method to fine-tune the promptd utterances; and 3) using Conditional Learning to fine-tune the model. Experiments were conducted on the ADReSS2020 dataset, in which the method using Prompt Learning combined with LORA fine-tuning model achieved a classification accuracy of 81.31%, which is higher than the BERT-based Prompt Learning method (76.85%).

2   Related Work

The extant literature on the detection of AD using speech-language data can be classified into three principal categories. The first category comprises studies that employ machine learning classification using manually extracted features. The second category encompasses studies that utilize automatic extraction of embedded features and classification using deep neural networks, among other techniques. The third category includes studies that employ fine-tuning and classification using pre-trained large language models.

Manually extracted features can be classified into two main categories: language-related features and acoustic-related features. Linguistic features encompass syntax, semantics, fluency/pause, word frequency, discourse continuity, and readability. Acoustic features, while not exhaustive, include spectral, rhythmic, jittery, and tonal qualities, as well as paralinguistic features such as rate of speech, phoneme accuracy, and so forth. In a previous study, the authors [10]achieved a classification accuracy of 73.9% using a simple Bayesian classifier after extracting the features contained in the eGeMAPS feature set. The eGeMAPS feature set [4] is based on the OpenSMILE tool and the associated feature design and consists of 88 acoustic features, the values of which can be computed by analyzing the recording clips. These features encompass a range of characteristics, including frequency-dependent attributes such as pitch, jitter, and resonance peaks, as well as energy-dependent functions like shimmer, loudness, and the harmonic noise ratio. Additionally, they include spectral parameters like the alpha ratio and the Hammarberg ratio, harmonics, and ratios related to six temporal features.

Furthermore, neural extraction is a prevalent methodology for implicit embedding characterization. The Distillable BERT model, as described in the literature [8], is a lightweight version based on the Bidirectional Encoder Representations from Transformers (BERT) [3] model. The complexity of the BERT model is reduced through the process of model distillation, thereby enhancing the inference speed and resource efficiency of the model. The data set is then fed into the back-end classifier, which achieves an 88% classification accuracy. In the literature [2], a Google VGGish model, pre-trained through Google's AudioSet, is employed to transform audio input features into linguistically and semantically meaningful high-level 128-dimensional embeddings [11]. Wav2Vec 2.0, as detailed in literature [5,12], is a self-supervised learning framework for speech recognition. It learns high-quality speech representations directly from raw audio waveforms through self-supervised learning, offering the advantages of lower data requirements and multilingual support.

The advent of large language models that have been pre-trained on vast quantities of data has given rise to novel approaches for the detection of AD. Pre-trained language models can be classified into two main categories: masked language models and autoregressive generative language models. The most prevalent masked language model is BERT and its numerous variants, including RoBERTa and Sentence BERT. Supervised model fine-tuning can be performed directly using labeled text, or the classification task can be converted into a prediction token using methods such as prompt. Study [1] demonstrated the feasibility of this detection method by using spontaneous speech for the first time to classify text embeddings extracted from a large amount of pre-trained semantic knowledge on GPT-3. Nevertheless, the considerable number of parameters inherent to these large language models presents a challenge. For instance, GPT-3 has 175 billion parameters.

3 Data Set and Experimental Methods

In order to solve the problem of high computational cost, this experiment adopts two solutions: 1) using a smaller scale model LLAMA2-7b; and 2) reducing the scale of the parameters to be computed by using a fine-tuning method such as LORA during the fine-tuning.

3.1 Dataset

The dataset is the ADReSS (Alzheimer's Dementia Recognition through Spontaneous Speech) Challenge 2020 dataset. The dataset comprises transcribed text in

CHAT (Codes for the Human Analysis of Transcripts) format. In particular, the dataset comprises 108 data sets, each of which contains a description of an image (Cookietheft) provided by the subject and the corresponding label (Health/AD). The data are distributed in a quantitative manner, with the healthy and AD groups each comprising 54 of the data set. Additionally, the language utilized in the data set is English. In order to effectively utilize this data for the training of large-scale language models such as LLAMA2, a series of preprocessing steps are required. Initially, the text data must be cleaned and normalized in order to ensure data quality and consistency. Subsequently, text processing operations, such as word splitting and the removal of labeled words, are necessary in order to provide a clean and uniform input for the model.

3.2   BERT-Based Prompt Learning

The present study employs BERT-based experiments as a baseline for comparison. The methodology employed involved fixing the prompt template and adjusting the model parameters during the training phase. The pre-training models selected are BERT and RoBERTa. Robustly Optimized BERT Approach (RoBERTa) [9] is an improvement to BERT proposed by the Facebook AI Research team. Task reconstruction is achieved by reconstructing AD and non-AD classification tasks as labeled words in filled prompted phrases. The implementation is divided into the following steps:

(1) Prompt phrase design: manually design the prompt phrases and select appropriate labeling words. "Diagnosis is <MASK>." is the main template used in this paper, in which "dementia" and "healthy" are used as label words for AD and non-AD respectively.
(2) Combination of text and prompt phrases: The speech transcription text is combined with prompt phrases and input into PLM for prediction. The logits of the corresponding tagged words are generated from the prediction results, and the probability distribution of the tagged words is calculated by Softmax layer and optimized based on the binary cross-entropy loss.

3.3   LLAMA2-Based Prompt Learning

The experiments employed the Prompt Engineering with Frozen Transformers (PeFT) methodology and quantization techniques. The pre-training models were selected from the "Large Language Model Meta AI version 2," which was released by Meta. The LLAMA2 model is based on the decoder-only architecture of Transformer, which is a neural network structure designed for text generation tasks. The model's architectural configuration is illustrated in Fig. 1.

The LLAMA2 model's decoder-only architecture and autoregressive generation mechanism facilitate effective performance in complex text generation tasks. The model is capable of discerning the subtleties in the input data and generating text of a high quality that is consistent with the context. Furthermore, as the model is designed with a focus on the decoding aspect, it is capable of demonstrating enhanced flexibility and efficiency in text generation, thereby providing users with expedient and precise responses.

The reconstruction of the text categorization task is achieved through the generation of responses based on prompts, which is facilitated by the utilization of LLAMA2. The implementation is divided into the following steps:

(1) Prompt phrase design: The prompt template is manually designed, and suitable labeling words are selected. The main template used in this experiment is "Input: input Instruction: instruction Response:". The response template utilized in this experiment is as follows:
(2) The combination of text and prompt phrases: The text data should then be combined with the prompt phrases and input into the model for prediction.
(3) Model quantization: The model weights are loaded into memory in the form of 8-bit integers using the quantization technique provided by the BitsAndBytes library, thereby improving the running efficiency of the model.
(4) LoRA Adaptation: The model is fine-tuned by introducing low-rank matrices in the key parts of the model.

Low-Rank Adaptation of Large Language Models (LoRA) is an approach to reduce the computational resource requirements for fine-tuning large language models (LLMs). The core idea of LoRA is to insert a pair of special low-rank projection matrices in each layer of the pre-trained model, thus restricting the update space of model parameters to these low-rank matrices. Specifically, LoRA introduces two small projection matrices, $\mathbf{A}$ and $\mathbf{B}$. Matrix $\mathbf{A}$ is of the form $\mathbf{A} \in \mathbb{R}^{r \times m}$, where m and n are the dimensions of the input and output layers, respectively. Matrix $\mathbf{B}$ is of the form $\mathbf{B} \in \mathbb{R}^{n \times r}$. The rank value r is much smaller than m and n. The projection matrices $\mathbf{A}$ and $\mathbf{B}$ represent the dimensions of the input and output layers, respectively.

The prompt-based fine-tuning method can effectively solve the problem of inconsistency between the loss function of the pre-trained model and the downstream task goal without changing the main structure of the pre-trained model. The overall schematic diagram is shown in Fig. 1.

3.4 LLAMA2-Based Prompt Tuning

The fundamental premise of Prompt-Tuning is that by fixing the parameters of the pre-trained model and adjusting only the parameters of the prompt statement component, the model is compelled to generate outputs that are more aligned with the task requirements specified by the prompt statements.

Specifically, Prompt-Tuning comprises the following steps: firstly, an initial prompt statement is designed, based on the task requirements for cognitive impairment detection; secondly, an initial prompt statement template is created. To illustrate, the prompt utterance "Is there a speech disorder in this text?" can be designed to guide the model in recognizing the speech abnormality in the dialogue.

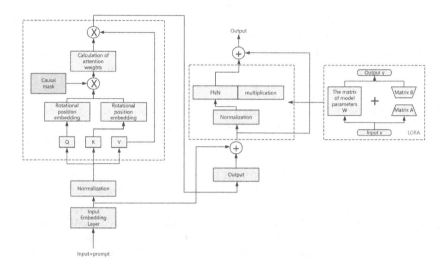

Fig. 1. Schematic diagram of the fine-tuning method based on the LLAMA2 model using prompt in combination with LORA.

Once the model has been loaded, the next stage is to fine-tune the prompt parameters. During the training process, the parameters in the prompt statements are adjusted by the back-propagation algorithm, and the performance of the model on the validation set is optimized by means of cross-entropy. In contrast to traditional hard prompts, which are typically fixed text fragments, soft prompts are learnable vectors. These vectors are incorporated into the input embedding of the model and optimized during training through techniques such as gradient descent. In general, soft prompts can be adapted to different task requirements in a flexible manner, thereby enhancing the model's generalization ability and ultimately leading to improved results.

3.5   LLAMA2-Based Conditional Learning

In previous experiments, labels were predicted based on input text. The text is about the image description in the dataset. The experimental method of conditional learning is to use an autoregressive model to compute the probability of a text given a label and then compute the probability of the same text under two different labels. The text with the higher probability is the predicted text. During training, the label is linked to the text and given to the autoregressive model to predict the next token.

The reconstruction of the text categorization task is reconstructed by computing the generation loss and probability. This is done by using a template with the label and text, with the label before or after the text. The text constitutes a description of the image. The label may be either "The following passage has a speech disorder" or "There is no speech disorder in the following passage."

4   Experiments

The experimental environment consists of the following configurations: the GPU model used is NVIDIA A40, with a total of five GPUs; the Python version is 3.7.0; the CUDA version is 11.6.0; and the server operating system is Linux.

4.1   BERT-Based Prompt Learning

The fine-tuning process was implemented using the OpenPrompt framework, which is based on Pytorch for prompt fine-tuning. The BERT and RoBERTa models (bertbase-uncased and roberta-base) were selected for use, with their standard splitters employed in each case. The maximum length of the input text is set to 512. The hyperparameters are optimized on the cross-validation (CV) set through a greedy search. The hyperparameters that were prompted for fine-tuning included the learning rate, batch size, and AdamW optimizer. A weight decay of 0.01 should be applied to the LayerNorm module. Ten rounds of prompt fine-tuning are to be performed, with the 10-fold CV average accuracy serving as the scheduling criterion. The outputs of the final three epochs of fine-tuning are employed in a majority voting scheme to mitigate the risk of overfitting and to attenuate performance fluctuations.

The prompted fine-tuning performance is as follows: The performance of the prompted fine-tuning of the PLM on the training data with 10-fold cross-validation is illustrated in Table 1. The accuracy of each fold in the 10-fold cross-validation is shown in the Fig. 2.

Table 1. Experimental results.

Model	Approach	Accuracy	Precision	Recall	F1-score	Acc Std Dev	F1 Std Dev
BERT	Prompt Learning	0.7685	0.8372	0.6667	0.7423	0.0816	0.1214
LLAMA2	Prompt Learning(1)	**0.8131**	0.8269	0.7963	**0.8113**	0.1844	0.1380
LLAMA2	Prompt Learning(2)	0.7938	0.7049	0.9556	0.8113	0.1890	0.1492
LLAMA2	Conditional Learning	0.5741	0.5769	0.5556	0.5660	0.1112	0.2271

4.2   LLAMA2-Based Prompt Learning

The fine-tuning process was implemented using the PeFT framework. The LLAMA2-7b model was selected for use, and its standard splitter was employed. The maximum length of the input text is set to 512. The hyperparameters are optimized on the training set through cross-validation. The fine-tuned hyperparameters include the learning rate, microbatch size, gradient accumulation step, and AdamW optimizer. The model was subjected to multiple rounds of fine-tuning, with the 10-fold cross-validation average accuracy serving as the evaluation criterion.

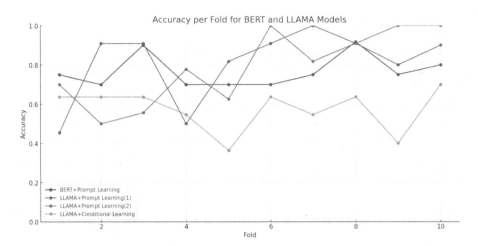

Fig. 2. 10-fold cross-validation accuracy results.

1) Utilize the prompt "Is there a speech disorder to the above text?" and categorize the response as "No speech disorder/Presence of speech disorder."
2) Employ the prompt "Is there a dementia to the above text?" and categorize the response as "Healthy/Dementia."

The final 10-fold cross-validation performance obtained using the optimal model saved during training is presented in Table 1.

4.3 LLAMA2-Based Prompt Tuning

The configuration of the tokenizer, the preprocessing of data, the fine-tuning of hyperparameters, and the evaluation of results are essentially the same as in the Prompt Learning section.

Due to the flexibility of the generative model, the effect of only training hints is very unsatisfactory. After many rounds of fine-tuning, the loss of cross-entropy is always greater than 1, and the results of many experiments do not exceed 50% classification accuracy. Further experimental tuning is needed.

4.4 LLAMA2-Based Conditional Learning

The configuration of the tokenizer, the preprocessing of data, the fine-tuning of hyperparameters, and the evaluation of results are essentially the same as in the Prompt Learning section. The same LORA fine-tuning method was used.

During the experiment, several rounds of fine-tuning verification are attempted, which may be limited by the computational resources, the results of several rounds are not very good, and the performance is shown in Table 1.

5   Discussion

In terms of average accuracy, the LLAMA2-based model (81.31%) slightly outperformed the BERT-based method (76.85%), suggesting that the LLAMA2 model performed better on the cognitive impairment classification task.

Although both methods used prompt fine-tuning, they differed in terms of model architecture, optimization techniques, and performance. The LLAMA2 model performed slightly better in the experiments, possibly because the input text was long descriptions, and the autoregressive nature of the generative model allowed for a more comprehensive understanding of the text. The seq2seq model was able to deal with longer contextual information, whereas the BERT model only needed to predict the words, and the generative model was can generate complete sequences. In addition, generative models are more flexible in adapting to new tasks and data distributions, especially when dealing with rare or new categories. In contrast, masking models require more fine-tuning to adapt to specific classification tasks.

The lower classification accuracy of the LLAMA2 model using the conditional learning approach may be due to label space constraints, the computation of generative probabilities, and the lack of label diversity in small datasets affecting the model's performance. The poor performance of cue fine-tuning in the AD classification task may be due to the complexity of the task making simple cue fine-tuning insufficient to capture and utilize complex patterns and features.

It is important to note that these advantages do not mean that the generative model outperforms the masked model in all scenarios. Masked models also perform well in many NLP tasks, especially in tasks that require contextual understanding and accurate prediction. Model selection should be based on specific task requirements, data characteristics, and performance goals.

6   Conclusion

The objective of this paper is to examine the efficacy of a large-scale language model based on prompt engineering techniques for the efficient detection of cognitive impairment. The experiment initially selects prompt learning based on the BERT model as a performance baseline. Moreover, Prompt Learning and Prompt Tuning methods are innovatively explored in conjunction with the LLAMA2-7B model, with the objective of enhancing the model's capacity to identify cognitively impaired texts through the application of Prompt Engineering techniques. Additionally, experiments were conducted on conditional learning. To address the high computational demands of the large model, we employ a semi-precision quantization model and LoRA fine-tuning method, which effectively reduce the model's resource consumption. The experimental results demonstrate that the Prompt Learning method based on LLAMA2-7B attains an accuracy of 81.31%, which is superior to the 76.85% achieved by the control group. Nevertheless, there is considerable scope for improvement in the areas of Conditional Learning and Prompt Tuning, due to the limitations of their fine-tuning range and dataset size. To address this challenge, future work will focus on optimizing the Prompt Tuning and Conditional Learning strategies. Additionally, experiments will be extended to the Chinese dataset, with the aim of further improving the detection performance and practicality of the model, and providing strong technical support for the early diagnosis of cognitive impairment.

Acknowledgments. The research work of this thesis was funded by the National Science and Technology Major Project on New Generation Artificial Intelligence (No. 2022ZD0118002) and the Basic Research Program of Institute of Software, Chinese Academy of Sciences (No. ISCAS-JCMS-202306).

References

1. Agbavor, F., Liang, H.: Predicting dementia from spontaneous speech using large language models. PLOS Dig. Health **1**(12), e0000168 (2022)
2. Cai, H., et al.: Exploring multimodal approaches for Alzheimer's disease detection using patient speech transcript and audio data. arXiv preprint arXiv:2307.02514 (2023)
3. Devlin, J., Chang, M.W., Lee, K., Toutanova, K.: Bert: pre-training of deep bidirectional transformers for language understanding. arXiv preprint arXiv:1810.04805 (2018)
4. Eyben, F., et al.: The Geneva minimalistic acoustic parameter set (GeMAPS) for voice research and affective computing. IEEE Trans. Affect. Comput. **7**(2), 190–202 (2015)
5. Gauder, M.L., Pepino, L.D., Ferrer, L., Riera, P.: Alzheimer disease recognition using speech-based embeddings from pre-trained models (2021)
6. Hu, E.J., et al.: Lora: low-rank adaptation of large language models. arXiv preprint arXiv:2106.09685 (2021)
7. Jia, L., et al.: Prevalence, risk factors, and management of dementia and mild cognitive impairment in adults aged 60 years or older in china: a cross-sectional study. Lancet Public Health **5**(12), e661–e671 (2020)
8. Liu, N., Luo, K., Yuan, Z., Chen, Y.: A transfer learning method for detecting Alzheimer's disease based on speech and natural language processing. Front. Public Health **10**, 772592 (2022)
9. Liu, Y., et al.: RoBERTa: a robustly optimized BERT pretraining approach. arXiv preprint arXiv:1907.11692 (2019)
10. Luz, S., Haider, F., Fromm, D., Lazarou, I., Kompatsiaris, I., MacWhinney, B.: Multilingual Alzheimer's dementia recognition through spontaneous speech: a signal processing grand challenge. In: ICASSP 2023-2023 IEEE International Conference on Acoustics, Speech and Signal Processing (ICASSP), pp. 1–2. IEEE (2023)
11. Mittal, A., Sahoo, S., Datar, A., Kadiwala, J., Shalu, H., Mathew, J.: Multi modal detection of Alzheimer's disease from speech and text. arXiv preprint arXiv:2012.00096 (2020)
12. Pan, Y., et al.: Using the outputs of different automatic speech recognition paradigms for acoustic-and BERT-based Alzheimer's dementia detection through spontaneous speech. In: Interspeech, pp. 3810–3814 (2021)
13. Utama, P.A.: Robustness of pre-trained language models for natural language understanding (2024)

Mapless Navigation in Factory Environments with Safe RL Approach

Junyi Hou🔟 and Qinyuan Ren$^{(\boxtimes)}$🔟

College of Control Science and Engineering, Zhejiang University, Hangzhou 310027, People's Republic of China
`renqinyuan@zju.edu.cn`

Abstract. Navigation of Automated Guided Vehicles (AGVs) in factory environments is a vital application scenario of autonomous systems. However, due to the complexity and variability of these environments, designing collision-free navigation strategies is highly challenging. To address this, this paper introduces a framework that leverages Deep Reinforcement Learning (DRL) for AGV navigation within factory environments. We prioritize safety throughout both the training phase and the execution of navigation strategies. Specifically, we employ a Signed Distance Function (SDF) to accurately represent the spatial relationship between the AGVs and obstacles, and integrating these constraints within the Markov Decision Process (MDP). The proposed method is evaluated in GAZEBO simulating environments, where AGVs navigate safely to reach designated storage racks. The experimental outcomes reveal that the proposed method is able to successfully learn obstacles avoiding navigation, exhibiting strong generalization capabilities across various environment settings.

Keywords: Mapless navigation · Factory environments · Safe reinforcement learning

1 Introduction

Autonomous robot navigation, i.e., moving a robot from one point to another without colliding with any obstacle, has been studied by the robotics community for decades [9]. In the field of modern industrial automation, the complexity and dynamism of factory environments pose higher demands on the navigation systems of Automated Guided Vehicles. Traditional navigation schemes rely on pre-planned routes and precise trajectory tracking, which perform well in static or minimally changing environments [12]. However, the limitations of traditional methods become increasingly apparent when faced with unpredictable obstacles, frequent layout changes, and diverse task requirements common in factory settings. Moreover, traditional methods often require re-planning and system tuning when faced with new or unknown environments, which is not only time-consuming and labor-intensive but also fails to meet the modern industry's demands for flexibility and adaptability.

H. Li et al. (Eds.): ICSR + InnoBiz 2024, LNAI 15170, pp. 217–226, 2025.
https://doi.org/10.1007/978-981-96-1151-5_22

In contrast, as a data-driven learning method, reinforcement learning adjusts strategies through trial and error to maximize cumulative rewards. It shows significant advantages in dealing with complex, dynamic, and partially observable environments, particularly because it does not require the specific construction of a map of the environment [1]. More importantly, navigation scheme base on reinforcement learning exhibit strong generalization capabilities, capable of adapting to different obstacle layouts and environmental changes, thus achieving effective navigation without the need for re-planning. Therefore, this study aims to explore a RL-based AGV navigation scheme, with the expectation of achieving a more safe, flexible, reliable, and cost-effective navigation strategy in factory environments.

Safety reinforcement learning not only focuses on the effectiveness of strategies but also places greater emphasis on safety during the execution of strategies. By introducing safety constraints into the reinforcement learning framework, AGVs avoid collisions and other potential hazards during navigation, thereby achieving more secure and reliable automated operations. This safety-oriented learning mechanism will provide a more solid guarantee for AGV navigation in complex factory environments.

For navigation in factory environments, we set the constraints as the distance between the AGV and obstacles. Moreover, Signed Distance Function is used to precisely depict the spatial relationship between the AGVs and obstacles. Furthermore, we introduce a Safe Critic to assess the safety of state-action pairs. Finally, we construct a Constrained Markov Decision Process, incorporating constraints into the update of the action network by using the Lagrange multiplier. The experimental results demonstrate the safety and effectiveness of our proposed navigation framework.

2   Related Works

Mapless navigation with reinforcement learning presents several challenges, including (1) the uncertainty of partially observable states and sensor data, (2) safety concerns, (3) learning from limited trial-and-error data, and (4) generalization to diverse and novel environments [9]. To address the issue of RL algorithms getting trapped in local minima due to partial observable states in mapless navigation, [3] utilizes artificially designed rules to identify points of interest (POI) from LIDAR data and then navigates towards selected POI, overcomes the issue of becoming stuck in local optima. In [11], the Asynchronous Advantage Actor-Critic (A3C) framework enhances mapless navigation by incorporating a curiosity module. This module supplements the reward system with a curiosity score, encouraging the robot to explore unfamiliar areas and thus overcoming data limitations. [6] trains strategies by alternating between different environments, improving generalization to diverse and novel settings. In the majority of previous studies, safety, particularly obstacle avoidance, is typically managed through reward engineering. However, in scenarios with multiple objectives, crafting a well-suited and high generalized reward function for efficient and safe navigation poses a significant challenge.

Safe reinforcement learning addresses the aforementioned challenges by explicitly incorporating constraints and employing methodologies based on Lyapunov or Lagrangian approaches [2]. The Lyapunov-based methodology maintains the robot within a safe regions by constraining the policy network. [5] introduces Generalized Control Barrier Functions (GCBF) to limit policy gradient updates, ensuring that the robot's states remain within safety boundaries by considering safety in several next steps. However, there are limitations to manually designed control barrier functions. In [7], Support Vector Machine (SVM)-based technique is suggested for synthesizing barrier functions from dataset that encompasses both safe and unsafe samples, leading to a more accurate estimation of safety boundaries. Lagrangian-based methods integrate constraints into the policy network's update process, optimizing the policy and the associated Lagrange multipliers iteratively to improve safety. While traditional methods typically use a Safe Critic to assess safety, [10] introduces the Conditional Value at Risk (CVaR) to consider the costs in the tail distribution of unsafe scenarios, which is particularly effective for training reinforcement learning strategies with high safety demands. Given that Lyapunov-based approaches, while challenging to implement, do not offer a better performance as noted in [2], this paper adopts a Lagrangian-based method, aims to improve both the convergence rate and the safety of reinforcement learning algorithms during navigation in factory environments.

3   Preliminaries

3.1   Constrained Markov Decision Process

We assume an environment modeled by a Constrained Markov Decision Process, which is formally defined as a 7-tuple $(S, A, \rho, r, c, C_{max}, \gamma)$. In this CMDP, S and A denote the state and action space respectively, which are both multidimensional, continuous and bounded. A probabilistic transition function $\rho : S \times A \times S \rightarrow \mathbb{R}$ indicates the transition probabilities to the next state given a current state and action. A reward function $r : S \times A \rightarrow [r_{min}, r_{max}]$ represents the instant step reward after taking action $a \in A$ in state $s \in S$. A cost function $c : S \times A \rightarrow [c_{min}, c_{max}]$ evaluates how well the constraints are satisfied in a step. The parameter C_{max} is a predefined threshold for safety, and the parameter γ is a discount factor for reward.

The goal of the agent is to learn a policy that maximizes the expected return for each episode when costs remain below the given threshold:

$$
\begin{aligned}
\max_{\pi} \quad & f(\pi) = \mathbb{E}_{(s_t, a_t) \sim \rho_\pi} \left[\sum_{t=0}^{\infty} \gamma^t r(s_t, a_t) \right] \\
\text{s.t.} \quad & g(\pi) = \mathbb{E}_{(s_t, a_t) \sim \rho_\pi} \left[\sum_{t=0}^{\infty} \gamma^t c(s_t, a_t) \right] - C_{max} \leq 0.
\end{aligned}
\tag{1}
$$

3.2 Lagrangian Methods

Lagrangian methods are a powerful optimization approach, particularly useful for solving problems that involve constraints. These methods involve the introduction of auxiliary variables, known as Lagrange multipliers, which help in finding the local maxima or minima of a function subject to equality constraints. In the context of Constrained Markov Decision Processes, Lagrangian methods are employed to handle the constraints inherently present in the decision-making process.

The Lagrangian $\mathcal{L}$ for a CMDP can be formulated as follows:

$$\max_{\pi} \min_{\lambda \geq 0} \mathcal{L}(\pi, \lambda) \doteq f(\pi) - \lambda g(\pi), \tag{2}$$

where $f(\pi)$ is the objective function, $g(\pi)$ represents the constraints, and λ is the vector of Lagrange multipliers. The goal is to minimize $\mathcal{L}$ with respect to π and λ, which effectively seeks to optimize the objective function while satisfying the constraints.

3.3 Sign Distance Function

The Sign Distance Function is a mathematical concept that describes the signed distance from a point to the nearest point on a boundary. It is defined as the shortest distance from a point to the surface, with the sign indicating the direction relative to the surface normal.

In factory environments, AGVs require precise navigation and obstacle avoidance. Many previous works treated robots as point masses or circles, but in factory environments, the shape of AGVs is more akin to a rectangle, such simplification which may lead to collisions or space wasted. Employing the SDF allows for a more accurate representation of an AGV's shape, enabling more precise distance calculations to ensure safety.

To account for both the shapes of obstacles and vehicles, we calculate the positions of the laser radar points projected by the LiDAR in the vehicle's coordinate system as $\mathbf{p}$. Subsequently, we determine the SDF from these points on the obstacles to the vehicle body, using the minimum value as a measure of safety. The SDF of rectangular can be calculated as follows:

$$\mathbf{d} = \begin{bmatrix} d_x \\ d_y \end{bmatrix} = \mathbf{p} - \mathbf{b} = \begin{bmatrix} p_x - b_x \\ p_y - b_y \end{bmatrix}, \tag{3}$$

$$\text{SDF}_{\text{rectangular}}(\mathbf{p}) = \left\| \begin{bmatrix} \max(d_x, 0) \\ \max(d_y, 0) \end{bmatrix} \right\| + \min(\max(d_x, d_y), 0), \tag{4}$$

where $\mathbf{b}$ is the coordinates of the vertices of the rectangle. The point closest to the rectangular vehicle body is selected as d_{min} to measure the safety:

$$d_{min} = min(\text{SDF}_{\text{rectangular}}(\mathbf{p}_i)), \quad i \in \text{obstacle range}. \tag{5}$$

To further illustrate the concept, Fig. 1 provides a visual representation of the SDF. During operation, we iterate through not-full-value LiDAR data point, searching for the point with the smallest SDF to calculate d_{min}.

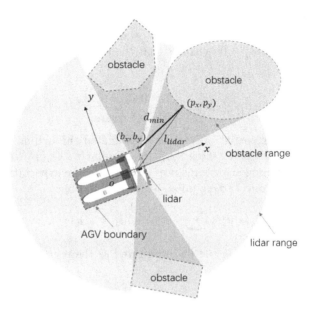

Fig. 1. SDF Illustration. The point closest to the rectangular vehicle body is selected as d_{min}.

4 Methods

4.1 Reward and Cost Settings

The sparse reward problem is a core challenge faced by Deep Reinforcement Learning in task-solving, and sparse rewards are common in practical applications, including factory navigation [4]. Here, the robot is rewarded based on its distance to the target $r_{dis} = k_1/l_{goal}(t)$, as well as the change in distance from the previous to the current step $r_{\triangle dis} = k_2(l_{goal}(t) - l_{goal}(t-1))$. This ensures that the robot is incentivized to move towards the target, even if it has not yet arrived. Furthermore, a modest negative reward $-r_{col}$ is imposed when the robot comes close to obstacles, instead of a huge penalty, to prevent the value network from struggling with learning state value discontinuities [2]. At each time step, a small negative reward $-r_{step}$ is imposed based on the steps taken in this episode, which encourages the robot to reach the target promptly. The overall reward is as follows:

$$r(s,a) = \begin{cases} r_{\text{success}}, & \text{if AGV reaches the goal safely} \\ -r_{\text{col}}, & \text{if } d_{min} < d_{safe} \\ r_{dis} + r_{\triangle dis} - r_{step}, & \text{otherwise.} \end{cases} \quad (6)$$

As for the safety cost, if a collision occurs, the cost function $c(s,a) = 1$. If it travels safely, $c(s,a) = 0$, ensures that the discount-weighted value is always between 0 and 1:

$$c(s,a) = \begin{cases} 1, & \text{if } d_{min} < d_{safe} \\ 0, & \text{otherwise.} \end{cases} \quad (7)$$

Typically, the expected safety cost is estimated through an evaluative function, known as the safety critic [2,8,10]. Similar to Q_a in some value-based reinforcement learning algorithms, we define Q_c as the expectation of long-term cumulative costs from starting point (s, a), denoted by:

$$Q_c(s,a) = \sum_t \gamma^t c(s_t, a_t) | s_0 = s, a_0 = a, \pi, \quad (8)$$

the value of $Q_c \in (0,1)$ can be interpreted as the probability of collision.

4.2   SAC-Lagrangian

In reinforcement learning, the Soft Actor-Critic (SAC) algorithm is known for optimizing policies using maximum entropy. But with tasks requiring strict safety constraints, standard SAC may not guarantee policy safety.

By introducing the Lagrangian multiplier λ, we incorporate the constraint into the policy optimization process. This approach facilitates an iterative process in which the actor, critic, safety critic, and Lagrangian multiplier are updated alternately, using data from dataset $\mathcal{D}$ to refine their parameters and performance. The update rules are as follows:

Actor: The policy network is tasked with learning the mapping from states to actions, aiming to maximize the cumulative reward while considering the imposed constraints. Besides the Lagrangian multiplier λ, here we multiply the safety critic value $Q_c(s,a)$ with the critic value $Q_a(s,a)$. This can be understood as the state safety acting as a proportional multiplier, affecting the robot's ability to obtain the reward given by the critic:

$$Q_{\text{composite}}(s,a) = (1 - Q_c(s,a))Q_a(s,a) - \lambda Q_c(s,a), \quad (9)$$

ω is also added in loss function to penalize large steering angles. Finally, the actor loss can be formulated as follows, where β_{ent} is the entropy coefficient and β_ω is the steering penalization coefficient:

$$J_\pi(\theta) = \mathbb{E}_{(s,a)\sim\mathcal{D}} \left[\beta_{\text{ent}} \log \pi_\theta(a|s) - Q_{\text{composite}}(s,a) + \beta_\omega \omega^2 \right]. \quad (10)$$

Critic: Similar to standard SAC, the critic network is updated by loss function:

$$J_a(\phi) = \mathbb{E}_{(s,a)\sim\mathcal{D}} \left[Q_a(s,a) - \left(r(s,a) + \gamma \mathbb{E}_{a'\sim\pi_\theta, s'\sim\rho_\pi} \left[Q_a(s',a') \right] \right) \right]. \quad (11)$$

Safety Critic: The safe critic network serves as a critical component in assessing the risk of state-action pairs. $Q_a(s,a) \in (0,1)$ indicates the collision probability of a trajectory start from (s,a). The safe critic network is updated based on Bellman equation, γ_c is the discount factor, and the loss function is characterized by:

$$J_c(\psi) = \mathbb{E}_{(s,a)\sim\mathcal{D}} \left[Q_c(s,a) - \left(c(s,a) + \gamma_c \mathbb{E}_{a'\sim\pi_\theta, s'\sim\rho_\pi} \left[Q_c(s',a') \right] \right) \right]. \quad (12)$$

Lagrangian Multiplier: The multiplier λ is used as a tool for balancing the trade-off between the objective function and the constraints. Here C_{max} is the limit of $Q_c(s,a)$, when $Q_c(s,a) > C_{max}$, the Lagrangian multiplier is increased to pay more attention to constrains. The update rule for the Lagrange multiplier can be described in (13),

$$\lambda = max \left(\mathbb{E}_{(s,a)\sim\mathcal{D}} \left[\lambda + \gamma_\lambda \left(Q_c(s,a) - C_{max} \right) \right], \lambda_{min} \right). \quad (13)$$

5 Experiments

We evaluated the performance of the algorithm in the GAZEBO virtual environment. Walls and cubes are used to simply model the shelves and obstacles in a factory environment, simulating the scenario where an AGV navigates around obstacles to goal shelves. To enhance generalizability, domain randomization was employed during training, with the green target point appearing randomly between the shelves and two obstacles randomly placed on the map. The observation is a tuple composed of the sensory input from LiDAR scans and the relative goal position in the robot frame, and the action is (v, ω).

The study utilizes a differentially driven AGV for experimentation, which is divided into two sections. The first section analyzes the navigation performance of the vehicle under different layouts of obstacle and target points. The second section compares our algorithm with the standard SAC, verifying the effectiveness of the additional collision network and Lagrange multiplier. The control frequency is $10\,\mathrm{Hz}$. The simulation experiment is run on the GPU of GeForce RTX 2070 SUPER.

Different Obstacles Layout: To verify the generalizability of the policies in this paper across different environments, we conducted experiments under various obstacle layouts. The robots starts from a random position and is required to navigate around obstacles to reach a randomly selected target location. The experimental results are shown in the Fig. 2.

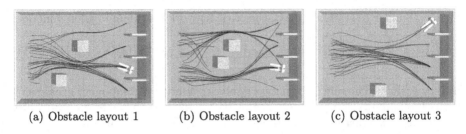

(a) Obstacle layout 1   (b) Obstacle layout 2   (c) Obstacle layout 3

Fig. 2. Trajectories of the robot navigating 50 times in four different obstacle layouts.

From the trajectories in Fig. 2, it can be seen that under different obstacle layouts, the robot can successfully choose a suitable and relatively short path to the target point, with a very high success rate. The few instances of failure happened when the car started near an obstacle and was facing it, thus a large steering angle is required to maneuver around it.

Comparison: In the second part of the experiment, the standard SAC algorithm is selected to compare with the algorithm proposed in this paper. The following Fig. 4 depicts the variations observed throughout the training process.

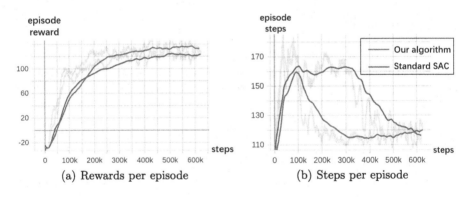

(a) Rewards per episode   (b) Steps per episode

Fig. 3. Comparison between our algorithm and standard SAC.

From 3(a), our algorithm converged more quickly to a higher reward per episode, which means a shorter path and higher navigation efficiency according to the design of the reward as previously described. In terms of training convergence time, when the reward gets 100, our algorithm only needs to train for 200k steps, while the standard SAC algorithm requires 250k steps. This is also evident from Fig. 3(b), the steps per episode of our algorithm decrease more rapidly, indicating that the proposed strategy can find feasible solutions more quickly. This may be due to the safe critic's ability to share the burden of learning feedback from environment, assisting in the identification of unsafe states.

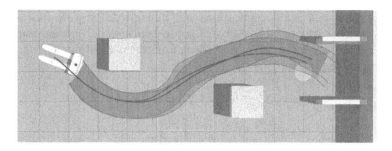

Fig. 4. Spatial occupancy of AGV trajectory. The red one is drawn by standard SAC policy, the blue one is drawn by our policy. (Color figure online)

As can be seen from Fig. 4, the blue trajectory demonstrates a smoother path that maintains a safer distance from obstacles, characterized by its ability to make turns earlier when encountering obstacles ahead. Additionally, Table 1 reveals that the policy trained by our proposed algorithm achieves a higher success rate. Although the robot moves at a lower average speed, it achieves shorter trajectories and maintains a safer distance from obstacles, highlighting a more cautions approach in navigation that prioritizes safety.

Table 1. Comparison of navigation performance.

Algorithm	Success Rate	Minimal Distance to Obstacle (m)	Trajectory Length (m)	Average Speed (m/s)
Ours	90.8%	0.4189	8.6344	0.6891
Standard SAC	75.3%	0.4001	8.8805	0.7005

6 Conclusions and Limitations

This paper introduces a reinforcement learning framework focused on safety for AGVs navigating in factory environments. Specifically, the framework integrates safety constraints into the learning process through the use of the Lagrangian multiplier, and refines obstacle avoidance process by considering the shapes of both the robots and obstacles. The GAZEBO experimental outcomes show that the algorithm introduced in this study successfully trains navigation strategies that are more efficient and safer compared to those developed by the standard SAC algorithm.

Despite the promising results, the study acknowledges certain limitations. One of the main limitations is that our approach encourages safety during training but cannot guarantee it. Furthermore, while the algorithm shows strong generalization capabilities, its adaptability to unforeseen or rapidly changing environments in real-world applications may be limited. Future work could concentrate on investigating policy-switching mechanisms under hazardous conditions, or refining the information processing from the perception module, thereby further enhancing safety.

References

1. Arce, D., Solano, J., Beltrán, C.: A comparison study between traditional and deep-reinforcement-learning-based algorithms for indoor autonomous navigation in dynamic scenarios. Sensors **23**(24), 9672 (2023)
2. Bührer, N., Zhang, Z., Liniger, A., Yu, F., Van Gool, L.: A multiplicative value function for safe and efficient reinforcement learning. In: 2023 IEEE/RSJ International Conference on Intelligent Robots and Systems (IROS), pp. 5582–5589. IEEE (2023)
3. Cimurs, R., Suh, I.H., Lee, J.H.: Goal-driven autonomous exploration through deep reinforcement learning. IEEE Robot. Autom. Lett. **7**(2), 730–737 (2021)
4. Li, S., Wang, X., Zhang, W., Zhang, X.: A model-based approach to solve the sparse reward problem. In: 2021 4th International Conference on Pattern Recognition and Artificial Intelligence (PRAI), pp. 476–480. IEEE (2021)
5. Ma, H., et al.: Model-based constrained reinforcement learning using generalized control barrier function. In: 2021 IEEE/RSJ International Conference on Intelligent Robots and Systems (IROS), pp. 4552–4559. IEEE (2021)
6. Miranda, V.R., Neto, A.A., Freitas, G.M., Mozelli, L.A.: Generalization in deep reinforcement learning for robotic navigation by reward shaping. IEEE Trans. Ind. Electron. (2023)
7. Srinivasan, M., Dabholkar, A., Coogan, S., Vela, P.A.: Synthesis of control barrier functions using a supervised machine learning approach. In: 2020 IEEE/RSJ International Conference on Intelligent Robots and Systems (IROS), pp. 7139–7145. IEEE (2020)
8. Stooke, A., Achiam, J., Abbeel, P.: Responsive safety in reinforcement learning by PID Lagrangian methods. In: International Conference on Machine Learning, pp. 9133–9143. PMLR (2020)
9. Xu, Z., Liu, B., Xiao, X., Nair, A., Stone, P.: Benchmarking reinforcement learning techniques for autonomous navigation. In: 2023 IEEE International Conference on Robotics and Automation (ICRA), pp. 9224–9230. IEEE (2023)
10. Yang, Q., Simão, T.D., Tindemans, S.H., Spaan, M.T.: WCSAC: worst-case soft actor critic for safety-constrained reinforcement learning. In: Proceedings of the AAAI Conference on Artificial Intelligence, vol. 35, pp. 10639–10646 (2021)
11. Zhelo, O., Zhang, J., Tai, L., Liu, M., Burgard, W.: Curiosity-driven exploration for mapless navigation with deep reinforcement learning. arXiv preprint arXiv:1804.00456 (2018)
12. Zhu, K., Zhang, T.: Deep reinforcement learning based mobile robot navigation: a review. Tsinghua Sci. Technol. **26**(5), 674–691 (2021)

Video Question Answering Based on Audio-Visual Hyper Graphs

Shuai Zhang$^{(\boxtimes)}$

Beijing University of Posts and Telecommunications, Beijing, China
`zshuai@bupt.edu.cn`

Abstract. In this paper, we address the Visual-Audio Question Answering (VQA) task, which involves answering questions about objects, sounds, and their relationships in videos. Effective VQA requires capturing the presence and evolving relationships of subjects and objects over time, utilizing both video and audio modalities. We propose a novel framework, Audio-Visual Hyper-Graph VQA (AVHG-VQA), that constructs situation audio-visual hyper-graphs (AVHG) for answering video-related questions. AVHG offers a structured representation by detailing sub-graphs for individual frames and connecting them with hyper-edges, encapsulating relevant information compactly. Our framework trains a hyper-graph decoder to infer associations between people and objects from video snippets, using cross-attention between predicted AVHG and question embeddings to determine answers. The training process involves two stages: extracting relationships from video frames using a pre-trained scene graph model as labels and optimizing the model with cross-entropy and Hungarian matching loss functions.

We extensively evaluate our framework on the challenging MUSIC-AVQA dataset, which focuses on video-audio modality information.

Keywords: Question answering · Audio-Visual modalities · Hyper graph

1 Introduction

Visual Question Answering (VQA) poses significant challenges in practical scenarios due to the integration of scene perception, language understanding, and reasoning. It benefits from knowledge representation through graph structures such as scene graphs, spatial-temporal graphs, and knowledge graphs, which primarily focus on visual attributes.

Our work addresses audio-visual VQA, aiming to answer questions about visual objects, sounds, and their associations, which requires effective multimodal understanding and reasoning for complex audio-visual scenes. We propose incorporating audio information into structured scene representations by generating situation hyper-graphs from both video and audio modalities. Our method captures actor-object relationships frame-by-frame without relying on

H. Li et al. (Eds.): ICSR + InnoBiz 2024, LNAI 15170, pp. 227–232, 2025.
https://doi.org/10.1007/978-981-96-1151-5_23

explicit object detection, simplifying spatial-temporal graph learning into a set prediction task.

We evaluate our method extensively on the MUSIC-AVQA benchmark, which includes visual, audio, and audio-visual questions based on the MUSIC dataset. Our results indicate that our situation hyper-graph encoding significantly enhances VQA performance by facilitating accurate answers through spatio-temporal graph analysis. Our contributions are as follows:

- We innovatively introduced audio-visual situation hyper-graphs for the VQA task.
- Experimental results demonstrate that our method is effective.

2   Related Work

2.1   Answering Question Through Different Modalities

Originally derived from text-based questioning and answering (QA) [1], intelligent QA tasks are progressively combining an increasing amount of text, image, video, and audio multimodal data. This has led to the creation of Visual QA [2], Video QA [3], Audio QA [4], and the recently developed Audio-Visual QA (AVQA) [5–7] tasks. The AVQA job in this study is the most difficult of them because it calls for synthesizing audiovisual data in order to provide answers to the questions.

2.2   Graph-Based VQA

Another branch of this work is graph-based VQA techniques [8]. Some of these techniques apply to object features taken from a trained detector [9], while others operate on frame-level [10], clip-level features [11]or transformer-based backbones [12].

3   Method

The VQA task involves three key steps: 1) perceiving the video scene through visual and audio information; 2) understanding the question's language; and 3) reasoning based on the previous representations. We propose an implicit structure that integrates audio and visual information for learning video scene representations. The model is trained to predict this underlying structure, which encompasses entities and their relationships. Given that the MUSIC-AVQA dataset lacks scene graph labels, we utilize a two-stage training process: first, generating scene graph labels with a scene graph generation model, and second, using these labels to train the VQA model. Our architecture is shown in Fig. 1.

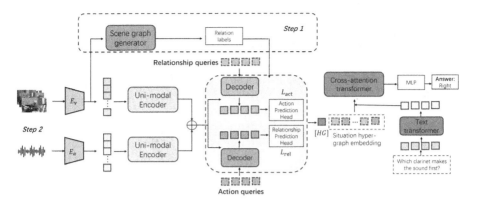

Fig. 1. The proposed AVHG-VQA model is trained in two steps. First, video embeddings are processed by a pre-trained scene graph generation model to obtain subject-object categories and relationship labels for each frame. Second, unimodal encoders extract video, audio, and text features, which are summed to form a fused video feature. This feature is then input to two relational decoders to derive situation hyper-graph embeddings, optimized with a binary loss function. Finally, cross-attention between text features and hyper-graph embeddings is used for classification to obtain the final answer.

3.1 Input Processing

We encode the video, audio, and question inputs through the unimodal encoder as described below:

Unimodal Encoder. To incorporate global context, we employ a uni-modal encoder for visual, audio and text features, constructed with stacked transformer encoder layers featuring multi-head self-attention and feed-forward networks.

The extracted video and audio features, denoted as X_v and X_a, are concatenated to form fused features X_m. These features are then fed into the decoders of action and relationship to generate the situation hyper-graph, which captures entities and their relationships. A class token that is initialized at random $[HG]$ is appended, and the hyper-graph embeddings are processed by a multi-layer cross-attention transformer encoder to refine interactions between the question and the video's structured semantic knowledge. Finally, the output features are passed to an answer classifier to produce the final response.

3.2 Relation Labels Generation

We first feed the video embeddings into a pre-trained scene generation model to obtain the triplet relationships for each frame, which are then used as labels for training in Step 2.

3.3   Hyper Graph Generation

To characterize the activities and relationships between items in the provided video, we portray it as a "situation graph". For each time step $t \in \{1, 2, \ldots, T\}$, given an input video, we wish to learn a situation graph that captures the entities and their relationships present in that frame. The set of situation graphs thus represents the hyper-graph for a single video.

Let X_m represent the encoded video features. A prediction of relationship p characterizes interactions between different entities in the form of actor-relation-object triplets. Our approach aims to predict two sets for each video frame: the relationship predicates R and the predicted actions A. Specifically, at each time step t, The set of relationship predicates what we forecast $R_t = \{p_1, p_2, \ldots, p_M\}$, where p_i denotes the predicate between two entities in i-th, and $M = |R_t|$ is the size of the set. Similarly, we determine the set of actions A_t, which contains N actions at time t. In our system, M and N are both hyperparameters. We then use the decoded queries for relationships and actions to create situation hyper-graph embeddings for every time step. t.

3.4   Learning Objective

The AVHG-VQA model is optimized with the goal of:

$$L = \lambda_1 L_{\text{act}} + \lambda_2 L_{\text{rel}} + L_{\text{vqa}} \tag{1}$$

where L_{act} and L_{rel} are the losses for predicting the action and relationship sets, λ_1 and λ_2 are hyperparameter, and L_{vqa} is a cross-entropy loss which is used to predict the answer to a question.

Action and Relationship Prediction Loss: The model infers fixed sizes of action and relationship sets for each video frame.

Let A represent the ground-truth actions and $\hat{A} = \{\hat{a}_i\}_{i=1}^{|N| \times T}$ denote the predicted actions, where N is a hyperparameter. If $\hat{A}$ contains more actions than A, the latter is padded with a special class ϕ. Using the Hungarian algorithm, we calculate a bipartite matching between the ground truth labels and the predicted actions:

$$\hat{\sigma_a} = \sum_t^T \text{argmin}_{\sigma_t \in \zeta_{|N|}} \sum_i^{|N|} \mathcal{L}_{\text{match}} \left(a_{t_i}, \hat{a}_{\sigma_t(i)}\right) \tag{2}$$

The loss is:

$$L_{\text{act}}(a, \hat{a}) = \sum_{i=1}^{|N| \times T} -\log \hat{p}_{\hat{\sigma}(i)}(c_i) \tag{3}$$

$\hat{p}(c_t^{(i)})$ is the action prediction's class probability at $\sigma_t^{(i)}$, $L_{match}(a_t^{(i)}, \hat{a}_{\sigma_t^{(i)}})$ would be $-1_{\{c_{t(i)} \neq \phi\}} \hat{p}_{\sigma_t(i)} \left(c_{t(i)}\right)$. Similarly for relationships. The inferred graph is then used with the question and answer choices in a cross-attentional transformer module. With the labels get in step one, the network is trained end-to-end.

4 Experiment

4.1 Dataset

The MUSIC-AVQA dataset [7], which consists of over 45K QA pairings spread over 9,288 movies, is used for the experiments. Nine different types of QA pairings pertaining to different modalities are included in the collection; a large percentage of the questions are audio-visual and encompass existential, counting, geographical, comparison, and temporal elements.

4.2 Evaluation Metric

We evaluate the model's performance for each type of question, and the metric we use is the average answer prediction accuracy, or Avg. It can be calculated by taking the total number of questions of each specific type, dividing the number of accurate occurrences by that number, and then averaging.

4.3 Implementation Details

Each video is divided into $T = 16$ segments, producing T audio segments and T video frames. Audio features are extracted using the pretrained VGGish network, while video frames are processed with a pretrained convolutional network. Our model employs $M = 6$ relation queries and $N = 4$ action queries per situation. During training, the initial learning rate is set to 1.80×10^{-4} and using the Adam optimizer. The batch size is 64, and training lasts for 20 epochs.

4.4 Performance Comparison

We compare our model with others and report performance across different question types. Our method outperforms the previous STG model [7] in both audio and visual question answering, as shown in Table 1, with average accuracy improvements of 0.59% and 0.93%, respectively, resulting in a total average improvement of 0.97%. These enhancements demonstrate that our proposed method offers superior scene modeling capabilities.

Table 1. We compare our method with existing approaches on the MUSIC-AVQA dataset. The abbreviations 'CNT', 'Comp', 'LOC', 'Exist', and 'Temp' correspond to the question types 'Counting', 'Comparative', 'Location', 'Existential', and 'Temporal', respectively.

Method	Audio question			Visual Question			Audio-Visual Question						All
	CNT	Comp	Avg.	CNT	LOC	Avg.	Exist	LOC	CNT	Comp	Temp	Avg.	Avg.
AVSD [13]	72.47	62.46	68.78	66.00	74.53	70.31	80.77	64.03	57.93	62.85	61.07	65.44	67.32
Pano-AVQA [6]	75.71	65.99	72.13	70.51	75.76	73.16	82.09	65.38	61.30	63.67	62.04	66.97	69.53
STG [7]	77.78	67.17	73.87	73.52	75.27	74.40	82.49	64.24	69.88	64.67	65.82	69.53	71.59
AVHG	77.63	67.89	74.46	74.89	75.77	75.33	83.03	66.11	71.47	64.35	65.67	70.12	72.56

5 Conclusion

For the challenging video question answering task, we propose an audiovisual situation hyper-graph method that implicitly captures object relationships in the video. This approach, which enables the model to first learn high-level semantic information, effectively enhances its capabilities.

References

1. Mishra, A., Jain, S.K.: A survey on question answering systems with classification. J. King Saud Univ. Comput. Inf. Sci. **28**(3), 345–361 (2016)
2. Zhou, S., Guo, D., Li, J., et al.: Exploring sparse spatial relation in graph inference for text-based VQA. IEEE Trans. Image Process. (2023)
3. Shen, X., Li, D., Zhou, J., et al.: Fine-grained audible video description. In: Proceedings of the IEEE/CVF Conference on Computer Vision and Pattern Recognition, pp. 10585–10596 (2023)
4. Li, G., Xu, Y., Hu, D.: Multi-scale attention for audio question answering. arXiv preprint arXiv:2305.17993 (2023)
5. Lao, M., Pu, N., Liu, Y., et al.: Coca: collaborative causal regularization for audiovisual question answering. In: Proceedings of the AAAI Conference on Artificial Intelligence, vol. 37. no. 11, pp. 12995–13003 (2023)
6. Yun, H., Yu, Y., Yang, W., et al.: Pano-AVQA: grounded audio-visual question answering on 360deg videos. In: Proceedings of the IEEE/CVF International Conference on Computer Vision, pp. 2031–2041 (2021)
7. Li, G., Wei, Y., Tian, Y., et al.: Learning to answer questions in dynamic audiovisual scenarios. In: Proceedings of the IEEE/CVF Conference on Computer Vision and Pattern Recognition, pp. 19108–19118 (2022)
8. Kant, Y., et al.: Spatially aware multimodal transformers for TextVQA. In: Vedaldi, A., Bischof, H., Brox, T., Frahm, J.-M. (eds.) ECCV 2020. LNCS, vol. 12354, pp. 715–732. Springer, Cham (2020). https://doi.org/10.1007/978-3-030-58545-7_41
9. Seo, P.H., Nagrani, A., Schmid, C.: Look before you speak: visually contextualized utterances. In: Proceedings of the IEEE/CVF Conference on Computer Vision and Pattern Recognition, pp. 16877–16887 (2021)
10. Lei, J., Li, L., Zhou, L., et al.: Less is more: clipbert for video-and-language learning via sparse sampling. In: Proceedings of the IEEE/CVF Conference on Computer Vision and Pattern Recognition, pp. 7331–7341 (2021)
11. Yang, A., Miech, A., Sivic, J., et al.: Just ask: learning to answer questions from millions of narrated videos. In: Proceedings of the IEEE/CVF International Conference on Computer Vision, pp. 1686–1697 (2021)
12. Qian, T., Chen, J., Chen, S., et al.: Scene graph refinement network for visual question answering. IEEE Trans. Multimed. **25**, 3950–3961 (2022)
13. Schwartz, I., Schwing, A.G., Hazan, T.: A simple baseline for audio-visual scene-aware dialog. In: Proceedings of the IEEE/CVF Conference on Computer Vision and Pattern Recognition, pp. 12548–12558 (2019)

Synergized Twin Layer for Federated Action Recognition

Yanshu He$^{(\boxtimes)}$ [ID]

Beijing University of Posts and Telecommunications, Beijing, China
hys@bupt.edu.cn

Abstract. In recent years, Federated Learning (FL) has gained significant traction as an effective solution for various computer vision applications, particularly due to its strengths in preserving data privacy and minimizing communication overhead. However, its application to advanced tasks like video-based action recognition introduces unique complications. Additionally, the client drift caused by data heterogeneity remains a significant challenge. To address this challenge, we introduce a novel framework, Synergized Twin Layer for Federated Action Recognition (STL-FAR), which leverages both local and global layers to harmonize client-specific patterns with a global model representation. Specifically, the STL-FAR framework is composed of two main components in Synergized Twin Layer (STL): a local classifier that adapts to local client data, enhancing the robustness and accuracy of action recognition on individual clients, and a global classifier that unifies the local models into a consolidated global model through federated averaging, thereby reducing inter-client discrepancies and improving overall model generalization. Moreover, we incorporate a Cloud-to-Client Knowledge Distillation (CCKD) mechanism within the framework, where the server supervises the client, ensuring consistent and robust performance across clients. We demonstrate the efficacy of STL-FAR through extensive experiments on two benchmark action recognition datasets. Our findings indicate that STL-FAR outperforms existing federated learning methods. This work advances federated action recognition and provides a promising solution to the issue of data heterogeneity in federated learning scenarios.

Keywords: Federated learning · Action recognition · Knowledge distillation

1 Introduction

Action Recognition (AR) has attracted increasing attention due to its promising applications in many fields, including smart home environments, human-robot interaction, security monitoring, and video understanding. With the popularity of surveillance cameras and smartphones, collecting video data has become easier, and this rich data has improved the performance of video-based action recognition methods. Recent advancements in deep neural networks have shown significant progress in action recognition. Though successful, traditional AR models heavily rely on large-scale, centrally collected action videos, which raise substantial concerns regarding user privacy, data storage requirements, and communication costs. To address these issues, Federated Learning (FL) has emerged as a pioneering approach that enables decentralized training of action recognition models. This paradigm not only enhances privacy protection but also reduces communication overhead.

Despite the advancements, Federated Action Recognition (FAR) introduces several unique challenges. One critical challenge is the heterogeneity of client data, which leads to client drift. This issue arises from non-independent and identically distributed (non-IID) data among clients, which could be due to differences in device location or environmental factors. Compared with conventional FAR tasks, the main contributions of STL-FAR are summarized as follows:

- We propose a framework that applies federated learning to action recognition, addressing privacy and security issues when training action recognition models using video datasets.
- The proposed STL-FAR method utilizes the Synergized Twin Layer (STL) structure, which builds its own unique output layer for private and public data to alleviate the aggregation imbalance caused by data heterogeneity.
- Supervision from the server to the client through Cloud-to-Client Knowledge Distillation (CCKD) helps distill global information into local models, thus solving the problem of client drift.
- Experimental comparisons on two public datasets demonstrate that STL-FAR outperforms existing federated learning methods.

By combining STL and CCKD, STL-FAR produces impressive performance and offers useful solutions for federated learning in action recognition.

2   Related Work

Action Recognition. Modeling video information, optical flow information, or skeletal information is the main emphasis of the deep learning techniques now in use for action recognition. The video-based methods include 2D-CNN, 3D-CNN, and Transformer structure methods. 2D-CNN methods involve analyzing the image content within the video and extracting information from the temporal relationships between frames [1,2]. 3D-CNN methods analyze video segment features by directly incorporating both temporal and spatial information [3].

Federated Learning. Federated Learning (FL) is first proposed by McMahan et al. [4], presenting a mechanism for aggregating local models based on their respective weights. In order to limit local model updates and maintain them closer to the global model, FedProx [5] adds a proximal term. MOON [6] refines local training by using model representation similarity.

Action Recognition with Federated Learning. Researchers have delved into various FL frameworks for numerous computer vision challenges. Within the

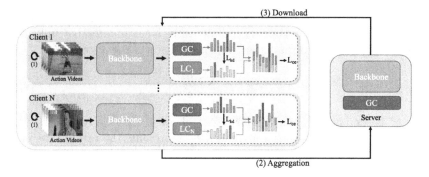

Fig. 1. Overview of the proposed Synergized Twin Layer for Federated Action Recognition (STL-FAR). The local clients utilize our STL mechanism by Global Classifier (GC) and Local Classifier (LC) for better modeling , and are optimized with the CCKD loss through the knowledge distillation from sever to client. One client-server training round include: (1) local models are trained by clients; (2) parameters are uploaded and aggregated by the server; (3) clients then download the combined models.

action recognition domain, self-supervised learning frameworks for video comprehension within the framework of federated learning were proposed by Rehman et al. [7] and Dave et al. [8]; FSAR [9] proposed a federated skeleton-based action recognition method; Yang et al. [10] proposed a cross-modal federated human activity recognition framework. Unlike them, our method focuses on addressing client drift issues in video-based FAR tasks.

3 Method

3.1 Vanilla FAR

Overview. First, we established the Federated Learning (FL) paradigms [4], following the Vanilla Federated Action Recognition (Vanilla FAR) benchmark. Assume that there are N clients and a central server. Every client has a local model and a private dataset v_i ($i \in N$). Initially, we optimize the local models on the clients utilizing their individual private datasets, then transferring the model parameters to the central server for aggregation. The revised server model is transmitted to each client for the subsequent training round.

Client and Server Updates. In the k-th local iteration, the backbone $\Phi(\phi_i^k)$ of the i-th client encodes the input x_i as the local feature h_i.

$$h_i = \Phi(\phi_i^k; x_i) \tag{1}$$

where ϕ_i^k is the parameter of backbone, and x_i is the transformed frame image of v_i. The update rule for every client can be expressed as:

$$\phi_i^{k+1} \leftarrow \phi_i^k - \eta \nabla \phi_i^k \tag{2}$$

where η represents the learning rate, and ∇ represents the gradient update. After each client participating in training completes the local update, they upload their respective parameters to the server, which then starts the aggregation:

$$\phi_g^{r+1} \leftarrow \sum_{i=1}^{N} \frac{n_i}{n} \phi_i^r \qquad (3)$$

where ϕ_i^r is the backbone parameter of i-th client in the r-th round, ϕ_g^{r+1} is the global parameter for the next round, and $\frac{n_i}{n}$ represents the ratio of the current client's data volume to the entire data volume. Then the clients download the global parameters from the server and start the next round: $\phi_i^{r+1} \leftarrow \phi_g^{r+1}$.

3.2   STL-FAR

Synergized Twin Layer Structure. The overall architecture of our proposed method is illustrated in Fig. 1. Previous research [9] has found that the shallower layers of a network learn more generalized features from local data, acting similarly to a global encoder; the deeper layers' parameters are more representative of the characteristics of the local data and learn more about the distribution of heterogeneous data. Therefore, we designed an STL structure that learns shared parameters from the server while retaining unique parameters that differ due to local data, to prevent the client from being affected by other clients with different data distributions. Specifically, the local update strategy for the classifier is as follows:

$$\psi_i^{k+1} \leftarrow \psi_i^k - \eta \nabla \psi_i^k \qquad (4)$$

where ψ_i^k is the parameter of i-th client classifier in the k-th local iteration, whether it is global ψ_i^g or local ψ_i^l. Notably, for ψ_i^g, we aggregate parameters, while for ψ_i^l, we cache private parameters on each client and keeping them unchanged until the next training round. The aggregation formula is:

$$\psi_i^{r+1,g} \leftarrow \sum_{i=1}^{N} \frac{n_i}{n} \psi_i^{r,g} \qquad (5)$$

Cloud-to-Client Knowledge Knowledge Distillation. Due to their limited exposure to private datasets, local classifiers may overly rely on this localized information, leading to overfitting. Therefore, through Cloud-to-Client Knowledge Distillation (CCKD), we can not only mitigate overfitting but also gain additional insights into the relationships between different categories. Therefore, the cloud-to-client knowledge distillation loss is defined as follows:

$$\mathcal{L}_{KD} = KL(\Psi_i^g(\psi_i^g, h_i), \Psi_i^l(\psi_i^l, h_i)) \qquad (6)$$

where the i-th global or local classifier is $\Psi_i(\psi_i)$, and the Kullback Leibler divergence is denoted by $KL(\cdot)$. The following is the formulation for the classification loss:

$$\mathcal{L}_{CE} = CE(\Psi_i^g(\psi_i^g, h_i) + \Psi_i^l(\psi_i^l, h_i), y) \qquad (7)$$

where $CE(\cdot)$ represents cross entropy and y is the truth-label.

3.3   Optimization Strategy

The unique i-th client is trained end-to-end using the sum of the losses in every client-server communication round.

$$\mathcal{L}_{TOTAL} = \alpha\mathcal{L}_{CE} + \beta\mathcal{L}_{KD} \tag{8}$$

where the values used to balance the loss are β and α.

4   Experiments

4.1   Datasets and Federated Scenarios

We test our approach on two popular action recognition datasets. UCF-101 [12] has 13,320 films from 101 classes, whereas HMDB-51 [11] has 6,766 videos from 51 action classes. We report classification accuracy on the mean of three test splits for both datasets. We divide them into shards to obtain a private dataset, and other federated scenario settings are also the same as FedAVG [4].

4.2   Implementation Details

We employ the pytorch framework, and all networks are trained on 1 GPU with 24G memory, using the pretrained I3D model [3] as the backbone. We follow the standard data augmentation that all input images are resized to 224×224. We initialize the learning rate to 0.01. It has decay rate 1×10^{-4}, and momentum 0.9 to update parameters. The maximum rounds are 300. The loss weights α, β are set as 1.

Table 1. Test accuracy comparison on HMDB-51 [11] dataset and UCF-101 [6] dataset

Methods	Datasets	
	HMDB-51 [11]	UCF-101 [12]
FedAVG [4]	0.6765	0.9218
FedProx [5]	0.6839	0.9255
MOON [6]	0.6270	0.8014
STL-FAR(ours)	**0.7052**	**0.9337**

4.3 Results

In Table 1, we utilize several aggregation strategies for comparison: FedAVG [4], FedProx [5] and MOON [6]. Result show that FedProx is beneficial for improving the performance of Vanilla FAR, while others are limited. This is because other algorithms do not take into account the handling of heterogeneous video data, whereas FedProx has corrected for data heterogeneity. Conversely, our STL-FAR, constructed by STL and CCKD, surpasses existing FL approaches in the identical situations by reevaluating the update strategy. On two datasets, the test accuracy has improved, demonstrating the efficacy of FAR within the framework of federated learning paradigms.

5 Conclusion

This paper presents a novel paradigm, STL-FAR, and leads the way in adding FL into the action recognition problem. We show that the primary issue impeding training stability is client drift. In order to achieve this, we independently learn the global and local feature distributions using a Synergized Twin Layer structure. Additionally, a mechanism called Cloud-to-Client Knowledge Distillation is being developed to bridge the gap that exists between the central server and the local clients. Our suggested benchmark and technique provide workable answers for FL in action recognition, which enhances privacy protection. One limitation is that there is still room of improvement in selecting the classifier, which could adaptively be either global or local.

References

1. Simonyan, K., Zisserman, A.: Two-stream convolutional networks for action recognition in videos. In: Advances in Neural Information Processing Systems, vol. 27 (2014)
2. Wang, L., Xiong, Y., Wang, Z., et al.: Temporal segment networks for action recognition in videos. IEEE Trans. Pattern Anal. Mach. Intell. **41**(11), 2740–2755 (2018)
3. Carreira, J., Zisserman, A.: Quo vadis, action recognition? a new model and the kinetics dataset. In: Proceedings of the IEEE Conference on Computer Vision and Pattern Recognition, pp. 6299–6308 (2017)
4. McMahan, B., Moore, E., Ramage, D., et al.: Communication-efficient learning of deep networks from decentralized data. In: Artificial Intelligence and Statistics. PMLR, pp. 1273–1282 (2017)
5. Li, T., Sahu, A.K., Zaheer, M., et al.: Federated optimization in heterogeneous networks. Proc. Mach. Learn. Syst. **2**, 429–450 (2020)
6. Li, Q., He, B., Song, D.: Model-contrastive federated learning. In: Proceedings of the IEEE/CVF Conference on Computer Vision and Pattern Recognition, pp. 10713–10722 (2021)
7. Rehman, Y.A.U., Gao, Y., Shen, J., et al.: Federated self-supervised learning for video understanding. In: European Conference on Computer Vision, pp. 506–522. Springer, Cham (2022)

8. Dave, I.R., Chen, C., Shah, M.: Spact: self-supervised privacy preservation for action recognition. In: Proceedings of the IEEE/CVF Conference on Computer Vision and Pattern Recognition, pp. 20164–20173 (2022)

9. Guo, J., Liu, H., Sun, S., et al.: FSAR: federated skeleton-based action recognition with adaptive topology structure and knowledge distillation. In: Proceedings of the IEEE/CVF International Conference on Computer Vision, pp. 10400–10410 (2023)

10. Yang, X., Xiong, B., Huang, Y., et al.: Cross-modal federated human activity recognition. IEEE Trans. Pattern Anal. Mach. Intell. **46**(8) (2024)

11. Kuehne, H., Jhuang, H., Stiefelhagen, R., Serre, T.: Hmdb: a large video database for human motion recognition. In: High Performance Computing in Science and Engineering, vol. 12, pp. 571–582. Springer (2013)

12. Soomro, K., Zamir, A.R., Shah, M.: Ucf101: a dataset of 101 human actions classes from videos in the wild. arXiv preprint arXiv:1212.0402 (2012)

Controllable Talking Head Synthesis by Equivariant Data Augmentation for Spatial Coordinates

Wan Ding[1], Dong-Yan Huang[2,3(✉)], Zehong Zheng[2], Tianyu Wang[3],
Linhuang Yan[2], Xianjie Yang[2], and Penghui Li[2]

[1] Xinyang AI Technology Co. Ltd., Hangzhou, China
[2] UBTech Robotics Corp, Shenzhen, China
dongyan.huang@ubtrobot.com
[3] Tsinghua Shenzhen International Graduate School, Shenzhen, China

Abstract. Traditional talking head synthesis algorithms decompose the lips and head pose information from the facial landmark points based on the spatial point registration. In this paper, we show that the hypothesis of the traditional point registration methods is too strong to result in unnatural talking head. Instead of registration, we propose a latent lip-head pose coding method. The proposed method performs self-supervised learning and equivariant data augmentation to the facial landmark points. The experimental results show that the proposed latent lip-head pose coding method outperforms the traditional registration-based methods and can generate natural looking talking head with accurate mouth shapes.

Keywords: Self-supervised learning · Equivariant data augmentation · Controllable talking head synthesis · Multimodal human-computer interaction · Virtual assistant

1 Introduction

The audio-visual talking head video contains rich information such as the lip motions, the head pose and the facial identity. Controllable talking head synthesis (CTHS) targets to take several inputs, for example, the audio and the images, that each input defines part of the values of the information, to drive the talking head synthesis. Controllable talking head synthesis is one of the key technologies for the multimodal human-computer interaction and it can find many applications such as the virtual assistant, content creation and avatar etc. One of the research problems for CTHS is how to quantify the control information. Model-based [1–10] and end2end [11–16] are two main kinds of the control information modeling methods. The model-based approaches define the control information space as the existing models such as the facial landmark points and the 3D movie maker coefficients. The end2end approaches define the control

H. Li et al. (Eds.): ICSR + InnoBiz 2024, LNAI 15170, pp. 240–249, 2025.
https://doi.org/10.1007/978-981-96-1151-5_25

information as latent code and train the audio-visual encoder and decoder in an end2end manner.

Facial landmark points are very popular control information definitions for the model based CTHS [1,2,5,6,8–10]. Traditional facial landmark based approaches explicitly decompose the head pose and lip motions, which are originally entangled in the facial landmarks data, by point registration (to a fixed reference face) methods. The decomposition results are then used to train audio-to-lip and head pose estimation models. The registration-based decomposition methods depend heavily on the stable points hypothesis, i.e., the eye corner and nose keypoints are stable unless the head pose changes. However the stable point hypothesis is too strong to that the lip-head pose decomposition errors result in unnatural talking head synthesis. For lip-head pose decomposition, the accurate modeling may not be easy to do due to the complex human facial motions. On the other hand, it is possible to "bypass" the explicit decomposition problem for the model based CTHS. In this paper, the "latent-coding + self-supervised learning" framework is applied to the spatial coordinate domain, i.e., the facial landmark points. This framework has been widely used for the end2end CTHS, which takes the sensor data (audio and images) as inputs and outputs of the system. One reason of using latent coding for model-based CTHS is that it does not require for the explicit lip-head pose decomposition. Another reason is that there is not any strong presumption about the I/O data distribution for the "latent coding+self-supervised learning" framework. If it works in the audio and image domain, it should work as well in the spatial coordinates domain, i.e., the facial landmark points. The third reason is that it is very intuitive to formulate the lip-head motion coding as a self-supervised learning problem in the spatial coordinate domain, by taking the audio and mouth-region-masked facial landmarks as input and the full facial landmarks as output.

One of the difficulties of self-supervised learning for latent coding is to collect enough data. To solve this problem, the data augmentation methods have been proved to be effective by the end2end CTHS approaches [11–13]. Most end2end CTHS approaches applied to pixel intensity or spatial frequency data augmentation methods can generate the invariant data pairs. For example, removing the high spatial frequency information from the input images by presuming the low frequency information is enough for head pose estimation. However, there is no pixel in the facial landmark points, i.e., the spatial coordinates domain, so the pixel augmentation methods are not applicable. On the other hand, the rotation for spatial coordinates can be modeled as matrix multiplication (e.g., affine transformation). The rotation defines a kind of equivariant data augmentation, since the input landmarks for head pose control rotates, the output landmarks should also rotate the same degrees.

Our contributions can be summarized as follows: the experiments on the Databaker dataset show that the stable point hypothesis for model based CTHS is too strong to result in talking head synthesis errors. We propose a "latent coding + self-supervised learning" framework to the spatial coordinate domain to overcome the limitations of the registration-based lip-head pose coding methods.

We design an equivariant data augmentation method to be successfully used to the spatial coordinates self-supervised learning to generate super-realistic talking head video frames. The paper is organized as follows: Sect. 2 describes the related work; Sect. 3 introduces the details of the proposed approach; Sect. 4 represents the experiments and Sect. 5 gives the conclusions and future work (Fig. 1).

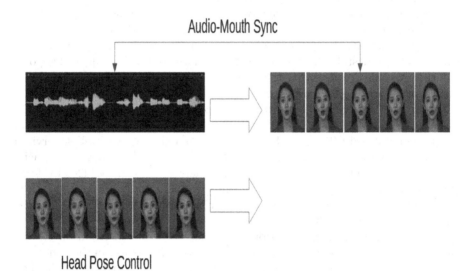

Fig. 1. Illustration of the controllable talking head synthesis Problem.

2   Related Work

One of the state-of-the-art methods for training end2end CTHS models is the self-supervised learning. Instead of manually collecting and annotating data for supervised learning the end2end CTHS, self-supervised learning takes the distorted data as inputs and the origin data as outputs. Distortion functions were designed to keep the desired control original information, while distorting the irrelevant information. For example, Burkov et al. improved their previous version of Head Reenact algorithm, which is to convert facial landmarks to facial images, by end2end modeling the control information as latent code, for capturing richer information [11]. They exploited bottleneck design and the data augmentation functions such as lossy compression and color contrast change to the head pose control videos. Zhou et al. extended the image end2end latent code based head reenact algorithm to audio-visual domain, they also used invariant functions for image data augmentations for self-supervised learning (SSL) [12]. Liang et al. assumed the independence between lips move, head pose, and facial expression. The image masking processes (for example mask the mouth region of the input for head pose control) were designed for latent coding [13]. Hong et al. also applied image self-supervised learning for talking head synthesis [7]. Instead of predict talking head results from audio-visual inputs, they conducted SSL to estimate the depth information from 2D images from same person but with different head poses.

For model based CTHS, most approaches design explicitly decomposition functions for the control information. Fu et al. applied the pretrained models to decompose the information (head pose, facial expression, etc.) from the extracted facial boundary images, and applied the pix2pixHD algorithm to learn the mappings from boundary image to face image [17]. They also collected a high-resolution Multi-View Face (MVF-HQ) database for experiments. Lu et al. proposed unsupervised audio representation learning, and a linear approximation algorithm to solve the source-target speaker gap problem for audio driven talking head synthesis [2]. Then they trained model to predict the registered lip landmark points from the audio representation. Yao et al. proposed registration + interpolation-based data augmentation methods to generate new facial landmarks points for self-supervised learning [6]. Instead of using GAN, they conducted NeRF to model the landmarks-to-image mapping. Zhang et al. defined the parameters of the Computer Graphic Models (e.g., 3DMM) as the control information space [3]. They also decomposed head pose and mouth information based on the registration.

The main difference between the proposed approach and the traditional approaches is that we apply the "latent coding+self-supervised learning" framework to the model-based CTHS. In consequence, the equivariant data augmentation method is designed for the spatial coordinates domain.

3   The Approach

3.1   System Overview

The proposed CTHS approach is composed of three sub-modules:

- Feature extraction: the audio features are defined as 13 dimension MFCC, the visual head pose features are defined as the 48 of facial landmark points (in total 68, the 20 lip keypoints are masked)[1].
- Audio-visual facial landmarks prediction: given audio (controls the lip motions) and landmarks (control the head pose), predict the correspond facial landmark sequence. The problem was defined as a self-supervised learning regression problem. The data pairs are collected from the audiovisual talking head video for training;
- Facial landmarks to talking head video, which applies the vid2vid synthesis algorithm (Fig. 2).

---

[1] The cascade of regressors based algorithm [18] is applied for the 68 Facial landmarks points detection.

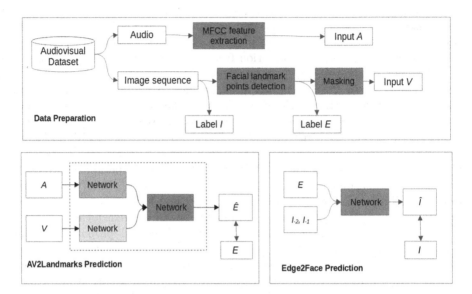

Fig. 2. Overview of the proposed talking head synthesis algorithm. The architectures of the three networks for AV2Landmarks prediction are presented in Fig. 3.

3.2   AudioVisual Landmarks Prediction

Network Design. The main architectures of the audio encoder, the visual encoder and the decoder are 1D-CNN, Fully connected network and unidirectional LSTM in respect. The details of the network architectures are presented in Fig. 3. The input of the audio encoder is four consecutive MFCC frames (e.g., 1–4, 5–8, to align with visual frames). For CNNs the second parameters denote the channel dimensions.

Data Augmentation. The data augmentation function is defined as rotation, as if the input headpose rotates a certain degree, the output facial landmarks should also rotate the same degree. The input head pose and the output facial landmarks were both defined on spatial coordinates domain, and the rotation for spatial coordinates domain can be defined as the matrix multiplication:

$$T_{\theta,t} = \begin{bmatrix} \cos(\theta) & -\sin(\theta) & t_x \\ \sin(\theta) & \cos(\theta) & t_y \\ 0 & 0 & 1 \end{bmatrix}$$

where $T_{\theta,t}$ is the transform matrix, θ is the rotation degree along z dimension (yaw). Since the extracted facial landmarks are two dimensional and the yaw rotation defines in the three-dimension space, we empirically define the range of θ as $[-10, 10]$ (Degree) for approximation. t_x and t_y are the shift along the spatial x and y dimension, during training the t_x and t_y were randomly sampled from $[-10, 10]$.

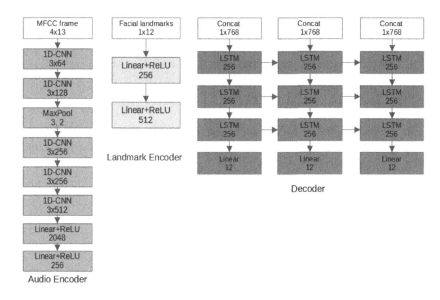

Fig. 3. The audio-visual encoder and decoder architectures.

Table 1. Comparison of the talking head synthesis results. The experiments conducted four algorithms to generate talking head videos from the same audio. The video frames correspond to the same audio phonemes, were then sampled for comparison.

Frame ID:	25	50	75	100	125	150	175	200
Phoneme:	ch ao2	s e4	h **uang2**	c **ai3 sp**	r en2	**fu2**	j **ian4**	sh iii3
Registration								
SSL1								
SSL2								
GT								

于是从唐朝起，黄色就成了代表皇家的色彩，其他人不得在服饰和建筑上使用。   v2, sh iii4, c ong2, t ang2, ch ao2, q i3 ,

So since the Tang Dynasty, yellow has become the color representing the royal   h uang2, s e4, j iou4, ch eng2, l e5, d ai4, b iao3, h uang2, j ia1, d e5, s e4, c ai3 ,

family, and others are not allowed to use it in clothing and architecture.   q i2, t a1, r en2, b u4, d e2, z ai4, f u2, sh iii4, h e2, j ian4, zh u4, sh ang5, sh iii3. iong4 .

Training Algorithm. The training loss for facial landmarks prediction was defined as mean squared error, as follows:

$$Loss = \sum ||T_{\theta,t}\hat{v} - T_{\theta,t}v||_2 \tag{1}$$

$$T_{\theta,t}\hat{v} = G(F(a), H(T_{\theta,t}v)) \tag{2}$$

where $T_{\theta,t}$ is the rotation matrix, v is the ground truth, $\hat{v}$ is the network outputs, G is the LSTM decoder, F is the audio encoder and H is the visual encoder.

3.3 Edge2Face Prediction

The predicted sequence of facial landmark points were first converted from the spatial coordinates domain to the image domain, by point interpolation and drawing, then the vid2vid algorithm [19] was applied to map the drawed edge images (sequence) to the face images (sequence).

4 Experiments

4.1 Dataset

The proposed algorithm was tested on the Databaker Audiovisual TTS Dataset[2]. The content of the dataset is a video that an actress speaking mandarin in broadcasting style. The length of the video is ten minutes. The original video(image) is 1920×1080 resolution, 50 fps, the original audio is 48000 Hz sampling rate, 16 bit-rate. For experiments the video was down-sampled to 25 fps, then the region containing head and shoulder was cropped and rescale to 256×256 resolution; the audio was down-sampled to 16000 Hz; the first 9.5 min data was for training and the last 0.5 min was for testing.

4.2 Hyper Parameters

For Audio2Landmark, the learning rate was set to $1e^{-3}$, the regression loss was Mean Squared Error, the batch size was 16 (number of sequences) $\times$ 16 (length of sequence), The gradient descent algorithm was Adam method and the training stop criterion was Stoped after 1000 epochs. For Landmark2Video, the training follows the vid2vid algorithm [19].

4.3 Results and Discussion

As shown in Table 1, four algorithms were tested for comparison. Registration denotes the traditional lips-headpose decomposition based methods; SSL1 and SSL2 are the proposed latent code based methods with equivariant data augmentation; GT denotes the ground truth. The inputs were the same audio and the audio information is presented at the bottom of Table 1. The bottom left is the audio texts (Chinese) and the English translation, the bottom right is the phonemes. From Table 1 we can see that: for the Registration method, the mouth and the head pose were obviously not aligned in Frame 175. The results supported the argument that the Stable Point Hypothesis mentioned in Sect. 1 is

---

[2] Provided by Databaker Technology Co., Ltd.

too strong in practice and may cause the registration error that affects the synthesis results. For the SSL methods, the mouth and the head pose were aligned much better, but the mouth shapes of SSL1, which directly predicts the 68 facial landmarks by regression, is not very accurate. The explanation was the relations between the audio features and the mouth shape may not be determinate, so the regression may predict the mean and it is not on the manifold. So SSL2 conducted PCA to model the regression and noises, and the predictions are closer to the ground truth than SSL1 results (e.g., the Frame 50 and Frame 175). The experimental results also showed that some of the detailed mouth information was lost after PCA, for example the Frame 150 (the fu2 of SSL2 and the fu2 of GT).

We also conducted the MOS tests to the algorithms for experiments[3]. Table 2 presents the results. For SSL1, since the audio2landmark network and the landmark2face network were trained separately, the outliers of the landmark point predications may cause the blur and inaccurate mouth shapes, thus the clarity and accuracy scores are relatively low. SSL2 algorithm exploited PCA to regularize the regression targets, and achieved higher clarity and accuracy scores. However as indicated in Table 1. The PCA also removed some of the detailed lips move information, and thus the Naturalness score was relatively low.

Table 2. The MOS results of talking head synthesis.

Algorithm	Clarity	Naturalness	Accuracy	Mean
SSL1	3.95	4.21	3.67	3.94
SSL2	4.28	4.1	4.04	4.14

5   Conclusions and Future Work

In this paper, we proposed a facial landmark point-based controllable talking head synthesis algorithm. Instead of the decomposition of point registration-based lip-head pose information, the proposed algorithm conducted latent coding, self-supervised learning and equivariant data augmentation to the spatial coordinate domain. The experimental results showed that the proposed latent coding method achieves more accurate lip-head pose alignment results and the proposed algorithm can generate natural and accurate talking head results. The future work will conduct mainly in three folds: Firstly, we will develop algorithms to overcome the limitations of the Regression+PCA based landmark prediction method. Secondly, we will extend the controllable information of the algorithm,

---

[3] Three MOS scores are defined: video clarity, video naturalness and video accuracy (how the lips move synchronize to the audio). The score range is from 1 (lowest) to 5 (highest). We randomly selected 20 videos from the testing data and invited 40 people for the MOS tests.

such as face identity and facial expressions. Thirdly, we will study the combinations of data augmentation methods for self-supervised learning for different modalities.

References

1. Chen, L., Maddox, R.K., Duan, Z., Xu, C.: Hierarchical cross-modal talking face generation with dynamic pixel-wise loss. In: Proceedings of the IEEE Conference on Computer Vision and Pattern Recognition (CVPR 2019) (2019)
2. Lu, Y., Chai, J., Cao, X.: Live speech portraits: real-time photorealistic talking-head animation. ACM Trans. Graph. 40(6) (2021)
3. Zhang, Z., Li, L., Ding, Y., Fan, C.: Flow-guided one-shot talking face generation with a high-resolution audio-visual dataset. In: Proceedings of the IEEE/CVF Conference on Computer Vision and Pattern Recognition, pp. 3661–3670 (2021)
4. Zhang, S., Yuan, J., Liao, M., Zhang, L.: Text2Video: text-driven talking-head video synthesis with personalized phoneme - pose dictionary. In: Proceedings of the IEEE International Conference on Acoustics, Speech and Signal Processing (ICASSP), pp. 2659–2663 (2022)
5. Wang, X., Xie, Q., Zhu, J., Xie, L., Scharenborg, O.: AnyoneNet: synchronized speech and talking head generation for arbitrary person (2021)
6. Yao, S., Zhong, R.Z., Yan, Y., Zhai, G., Yang, X.: DFA-NeRF: personalized talking head generation via disentangled face attributes neural rendering (2022)
7. Hong, F.-T., Zhang, L., Shen, L., Xu, D.: Depth-aware generative adversarial network for talking head video generation (2022)
8. Li, L., et al.: Write-a-speaker: text-based emotional and rhythmic talking-head generation. In: Proceedings of the AAAI Conference on Artificial Intelligence, vol. 35, no. 3, pp. 1911–1920 (2021)
9. Meshry, M., Suri, S., Davis, L.S., Shrivastava, A.: Learned spatial representations for few-shot talking-head synthesis. In: Proceedings of the IEEE/CVF International Conference on Computer Vision (ICCV), pp. 13809–13818 (2021)
10. Fried, O., Tewari, A., Zollhfer, M., Finkelstein, A., Agrawala, M.: Text-based editing of talking-head video. ACM Trans. Graph. (TOG) (2019)
11. Burkov, E., Pasechnik, I., Grigorev, A., Lempitsky, V.: Neural head reenactment with latent pose descriptors. In: Proceedings of IEEE/CVF Conference on Computer Vision and Pattern Recognition (CVPR) (2020)
12. Zhou, H., Sun, Y., Wu, W., Loy, C.C., Wang, X., Liu, Z.: Pose-controllable talking face generation by implicitly modularized audio-visual representation. In: Proceedings of the IEEE Conference on Computer Vision and Pattern Recognition (CVPR) (2021)
13. Liang, B., et al.: Expressive talking head generation with granular audio-visual control. In: Proceedings of the IEEE/CVF Conference on Computer Vision and Pattern Recognition, pp. 3387–3396 (2022)
14. Tandon, P., et al.: Txt2Vid: ultra-low bitrate compression of talking-head videos via text (2021)
15. Wang, J., Zhao, Y., Liu, L., Xu, T., Li, Q., Li, S.: Emotional talking head generation based on memory-sharing and attention-augmented networks. In: Proceedings of INTERSPEECH, pp. 2–6 (2023)
16. Wang, J., et al.: Memory-augmented contrastive learning for talking head generation. In: Proceedings of the IEEE International Conference on Acoustics Speech and Signal Processing (ICASSP), pp. 1–5 (2023)

17. Chaoyou, F., Yibo, H., Xiang, W., Wang, G., Zhang, Q., He, R.: High-fidelity face manipulation with extreme poses and expressions. IEEE Trans. Inf. Forensics Secur. **16**, 2218–2231 (2021)
18. Kazemi, V., Sullivan, J.: One millisecond face alignment with an ensemble of regression trees. In: Proceedings of the IEEE Conference on Computer Vision and Pattern Recognition, pp. 1867–1874 (2014)
19. Wang, T.-C., et al.: Video-to-video synthesis. In: Conference on Neural Information Processing Systems (NeurIPS) (2018)

Multi-source-Domain Adaptation for TMS-EEG Based Depression Detection

Jingdong Zhou[1,2]([envelope]), Nan Li[1], Chongyuan Lian[3], Yudong Yang[1], Lan Wang[1,2], Yi Guo[3,4], Nan Yan[1,2], and Rongfeng Su[1,2]

[1] Guangdong-Hong Kong-Macao Joint Laboratory of Human-Machine Intelligence-Synergy Systems, Shenzhen Institute of Advanced Technology, Chinese Academy of Sciences, Shenzhen, Guangdong, China
[2] University of Chinese Academy of Sciences, Beijing, China
{jd.zhou,lan.wang,nan.yan}@siat.ac.cn
[3] Institute of Neurological and Psychiatric Disorders, Shenzhen Bay Laboratory, Shenzhen, Guangdong, China
[4] Department of Neurology, Shenzhen People's Hospital, Shenzhen, Guangdong, China

Abstract. The development of Brain-Computer-Interface (BCI) technology requires accurate decoding of brain activities measured by EEG. However, due to the non-stationary characteristics of EEG signals and intra- and inter-individual variability, it is not easy to construct a reliable and universal evaluation model for different subjects. In practical applications, most of the target domains are invisible, yet the current transfer learning models based on EEG signals mostly are target-domains-visable. To address this problem, this paper proposes a deep migration learning framework that reduces individual differences through intra-subject alignment and inter-subject alignment, extracts stable features after superposition averaging using a multi-scale spatio-temporal graph neural network, and employs a multi-source domain distribution normalization method, which enables the model to be effectively generalized to the target domain. The adaptive subject normalization layer introduced in the model gradually realizes the alignment of different source domain distributions during the training process, and executes the Test-Time-Adaptation (TTA) strategy in the testing phase to achieve dynamic adaptation to the target domain data.

The experimental results show that the model outperforms traditional deep learning models on TMS-EEG data, while the ablation experiments verify the effectiveness of the subject-level normalization module in improving the model generalization ability.

Keywords: TMS-EEG · Transfer Learning · Domain Adaptation · Normalization · Inter-Subject Alignment · Test-Time Adaptation

© The Author(s), under exclusive license to Springer Nature Singapore Pte Ltd. 2025
H. Li et al. (Eds.): ICSR + InnoBiz 2024, LNAI 15170, pp. 250–261, 2025.
https://doi.org/10.1007/978-981-96-1151-5_26

1   Introduction

In EEG experiments, subjects are required to follow specific experimental paradigm to accomplish a given task, and these experimental paradigms are usually scenario-driven data paradigms. The cortical responses to different stimuli are recorded as different potential patterns in the EEG [1]. TMS-EEG (Transcranial Magnetic Stimulation Electroencephalography) has been developed as a technique that combines TMS and EEG to study brain function and neural mechanisms more accurately [2] recent years. TMS-EEG stimulates the cerebral cortex by TMS and records EEG signals at the same time in order to probe the brain's response to a specific stimulus, a method that is of great significance in the study of neuroscience and in clinical applications, such as in research on how depression affecting functional pattern in response to stimuli [3].

Individual-specific models achieved good results in EEG data processing and analysis [4], but disadvantage of requiring complex training for specific individuals remains. It has been shown that within-subject models usually achieve better performance on data from the same individuals. However, a cross-modal classification study of visually stimulated EEG signals from subjects viewing **ImageNet** [5] showed that unvalidated block design can lead to erroneous EEG experimental results, emphasizing the importance of experimental paradigm design on results [6].

Thus, many researchers have started to employ transfer learning into deep learning models to mine potential signaling patterns in EEG data [7, 8]. In the field of EEG, the exploration of transfer learning mainly focuses on domain-adversarial learning and multi-model learning [9], where point-to-point is performed by setting the target and source domains in advance [10]. However, the target domain is usually unknown in practical applications, which requires the establishment of a dynamic knowledge migration framework that enables the model to adapt quickly and maintain good performance in the face of unknown individuals or environments, thus overcoming the problem of insufficient generalization ability.

In this paper, we propose a deep transfer learning model for Depression detection based on EEG signals. The model reduces individual difference in the embedding space by intra-subject adaptation and inter-subject adaptation, then it extracts stable features after superposition averaging using a multi-scale graph neural network based on a weighted attention mechanism for a depression classification task. In addition, the multi-source domain normalization method adopted by the model allows the model learned on the source domain to be effectively generalized to the target domain.

2   Related Work

2.1   Graph Network Based on EEG Data

Graph neural networks (GNNs) have demonstrated excellent performance in EEG data analysis. While traditional methods usually ignore the graph structural information in EEG signals, GNNs are able to effectively model the functional connectivity of brain regions, thus enhancing feature extraction. Studies have shown that graph convolutional networks (GCNs) [11] significantly improve the accuracy of EEG classification and prediction. For example, in the emotion recognition task, Li et al. [12] used a multi-domain fusion GCN architecture, which was able to effectively capture the complex temporal and spatial patterns of the EEG signals and identify the brain region activity patterns related to the cognitive task in the frequency domain analysis.

Graph Attention Network (GATs) [13] capture nonlinear relationships and temporal dependencies amongst brain regions to aggregate features. For example, a study on self-attention pooling based on graph construction demonstrated excellent performance in a depression classification task [14] by capturing complex brain region dependencies through attention modeling, they also taking into account dynamically interrelationships between different graphs. They only modeled the scalp EEG channels and did not consider the non-stationary properties of EEG signals. However Dynamic Graph Convolutional Networks (DGCNs) can effectively model the time-varying dependency, [15] proposed a multilayer dynamic network by taking both local and global graph connections into consideration, the accuracy of predicting epileptic seizures was enhanced.

2.2   Normalization Methods

Batch Normalization (BN) [16] accelerates training and mitigates the problem of vanishing or exploding gradients by reducing Internal Covariate Shift (ICS). However, BN is sensitive to batch size and has limited effect in small batches of training or sequence data. To address these issues, Layer Normalization (LN) [17] and Group Normalization (GN) [18] have been introduced in the field of computer vision. LN performs normalization within each sample, which is suitable for variable-length sequential data, whereas GN performs normalization on feature channels, which enhances the robustness to small batch training. In addition, Instance Normalization (IN) [19] is another alternative method widely used in image generation and style migration tasks by normalizing each channel independently for each sample.

3   Preliminaries

In this section, we introduce the definitions and notations related to multi-source domain transfer learning in our work and the transfer learning model based on EEG signals. Given $D_{s_i} = \{X_i^n, y_i^n\}_{n=1}^{N_i}$, $i \in \{1, ..., K\}$ denoted the i th of K source domain which each domain included N_i EEG trials. $X_i^n \in \mathbb{R}^{C \times T}$, where C represented EEG channels and T for the time samples in the recording, unlabeled target domain (UT) and labeled target domain (LT) $D_{tl} = \{X_{tl}^n, y_{tl}^n\}_{n=1}^{N_l}$, $D_{tu} = \{X_{tu}^n\}_{n=N_l+1}^{N_l+N_u}$. The objective of this work is to enable the model learned from the source domains to generalize to the target domain through a multi-source domain normalization method, which can be written as:

$$f(\theta; p(s)) \rightarrow f(\delta; p(s, t)) \tag{1}$$

$p(s)$, $p(t)$ represented the distribution of source domain and target domain respectively. This goal is particularly important given the significant individual discrepancy and variability in EEG signals.

3.1 EEG Based Multi-source Style Transfer Mapping

Li *et al.* [20] proposed a multi-source domain transfer learning algorithm based on EEG signals. By using a small amount of unlabeled data from the target domain, affine transform was performed to align with the prototype cluster centers in the source domains. Define the target domain sample points as o and the source domain sample points as sp. The optimization problem of the multi-source domain style transfer algorithm can be expressed as:

$$\min_{A \in R^{m \times m}, b \in R^m} \sum_{i=1}^{n} f_i \|Ao_i + b - d_i\|_2^2 + \beta \|A - I\|_F^2 + \gamma \|b\|_2^2 \tag{2}$$

where $o_i \in \mathbb{R}^m$ represented samples in source domain, and $d_i \in \mathbb{R}^m$ denoted destination point, $\| \cdot \|_F^2$ is the Frobenius norm of matrix and $\|\cdot\|_2$ is the L_2-norm of vector. Second item in Eq. (2) encourages transformation coefficient to adhere identity matrix I and the third item restricts the scale of bias, β and γ are hyperparameters determined through cross-validation. Equation (2) is a convex quadratic programming problem, which has a closed-form solution:

$$A = QP^{-1}, b = \frac{1}{\hat{f}}\left(\hat{d} - A\hat{o}\right) \tag{3}$$

$$Q = \sum_{i=1}^{n} f_i d_i o_i^T - \frac{1}{\hat{f}}\hat{d}\hat{o}^T + \beta I \tag{4}$$

$$P = \sum_{i=1}^{n} f_i o_i o_i^T - \frac{1}{\hat{f}}\hat{o}\hat{o}^T + \beta I \tag{5}$$

$$\hat{o} = \sum_{i=1}^{n} f_i o_i, \hat{d} = \sum_{i=1}^{n} f_i d_i \tag{6}$$

$$\hat{f} = \sum_{i=1}^{n} f_i + \gamma. \tag{7}$$

3.2 Domain-Specific Batch Normalization

DSBN is implemented through two different normalization branches: one is the source domain normalization layer, and the other is the target domain normalization branch. The training of the model using DSBN consists of two stages.

First, we train the pseudo-label generator F_T^1 for the target domain. In the second training stage, we use data and their labels from both domains to train the final model under a supervised learning framework. The loss function is given by the sum of the losses from the two domains:

$$\mathcal{L} = \mathcal{L}_{\text{cls}}(\mathcal{X}_S) + \mathcal{L}_{\text{cls}}^{\text{pseudo}}(\mathcal{X}_T) \tag{8}$$

$$\mathcal{L}_{\text{cls}}(\mathcal{X}_S) = \sum_{(x,y)\in\mathcal{X}_s} \ell(F_S^2(x), y), \tag{9}$$

$$\mathcal{L}_{\text{cls}}^{\text{pseudo}}(\mathcal{X}_T) = \sum_{x\in\mathcal{X}_T} \ell(F_T^2(x), y'). \tag{10}$$

$\ell(\cdot, \cdot)$ in Eq. (9), (10) is discriminative loss function and y' is target domain pseudo-label assigned by:

$$y' = \underset{c\in C}{\text{argmax}} \left\{ (1-\lambda)F_T^1(x)[c] + \lambda F_T^2(x)[c] \right\} \tag{11}$$

where $F_T^i(x)[c]$ is prediction score of the class c given by F_T^1 and λ is a weight factor that changes gradually from 0 to 1 during training. The potentially noisy pseudo-labels were suppress by [21] increasing as a sigmoid like function.

4   Method

The proposed model mainly consists of three parts: a multi-scale spatiotemporal graph network, a dynamic attention module, and an adaptive subject normalization layer. More importantly, our proposed adaptive subject normalization layer is a plug-and-play module, and experiments have demonstrated that it achieves better performance on downstream tasks across various EEG-specific networks. The overall model structure is shown as followed (Fig. 1).

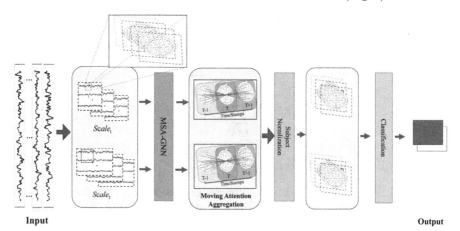

Fig. 1. Illustration of the proposed model.

4.1 Multi-scale Spatiotemporal Graph Neural Network

As mentioned in the Introduction, the ERP signals in EEG are highly sensitive to the time window, and the induced time signal period varies among different individuals, often within tens of milliseconds. However, in the long term, the induced EEG signals are also influenced by the experimental paradigm. The experimental data in this paper use the rTMS (Repetitive Transcranial Magnetic Stimulation) paradigm (details are provided in the Experimental section), meaning that the signals repeatedly appear within an error time range in individual time windows. We use a multi-scale spatiotemporal dynamic graph neural network to capture the time range in which these sensitive signals appear.

For a preprocessed input EEG signal $X \in \mathbb{R}^{C \times T}$, we segment it into multiple patches $X_i \in \mathbb{R}^{C \times P_s}, (i = 1, ..., [\frac{T}{P_s}])$ to facilitate the capture of information both intra and inter time information, where P_s represents the patch size of each graph. Then, we feed each patch into the encoder to obtain feature-level vectors $e(X_i)$ and perform positional encoding for each EEG channel:

$$f_p(t)^{(m)} := \begin{cases} sin(\omega_k \cdot t) & \text{if} m = 2k, \\ cos(\omega_k \cdot t) & \text{if} m = 2k + 1. \end{cases} \tag{12}$$

$$\boldsymbol{\nu}_c = e(X_i) + f_p(t) \tag{13}$$

where m is the feature dimension of encoded time series, and s is the amount of different scale graph. We use an attention layer to measure the connectivity between each spatiotemporal node as adjacency matrix:

$$e_{wx,yz} = \frac{(\boldsymbol{\nu}_{wy} W_A)(\boldsymbol{\nu}_{xz} W_A)^T}{\sqrt{m}} \tag{14}$$

Hence, the spatiotemporal graph at each scale can be represented as $\mathcal{G}_s = (\nu, E)$ where $\boldsymbol{\nu} = \{\nu_c\}_{c=1}^C$, $E = \{\{e_{wx,yz}\}_{y,z=1}^{[\frac{T}{P_s}]}\}_{w,x=1}^C$.

Moving Attention Aggregation. To obtain both intra and inter patch information, we adapt Moving Attention Aggregation to aggregate the spatiotemporal node-level information of the EEG network. The aggregated features from different scales are concatenated and fed into the next unit.

First, we aggregate the features of neighboring nodes for each spatiotemporal node based on the previously computed node-level attention scores e:

$$h'_w = \sigma \left(\sum_{w \in C} \sum_{y \in [\frac{T}{P_s}]} e_{wy} \mathbf{W} h_y \right) \tag{15}$$

Then, we use a window of fixed length M that moves along the patch dimension with a stride of st. Within each window, we perform weighted averaging of the patch-level features to obtain new features $\frac{1}{N} \sum_N W_s H_{P_s}$ of N length, noting that $N = \frac{M-K}{st} + 1$.

Compared to directly multiplying the adjacency matrix and feature matrix to obtain first-order and second-order walk matrices, this method has stronger expressive capability and can capture the dependencies between complex structural nodes in the spatiotemporal graph.

Finally, we concatenate the node representations obtained from all scales into a projection head, and output them to the next module:

$$H_G = MLP([\frac{1}{N} \sum_N W_s H_{P_1}, ..., \frac{1}{N} \sum_N W_s H_{P_s}]) \tag{16}$$

4.2   Normalization on Subject-Level

Considering a representation H_G learned from a multi-scale network, we first use a domain encoder to encode domain information for each sample. Domain encoder can use either semi-supervised or unsupervised methods to encode the domain labels for each sample.

During the training phase, we update the statistical information of each source domain using exponential moving averages and update the affine transformation parameters for each source domain through backpropagation.

To address the issue of using the same statistical information of the data distribution in both training and testing phases in BN, we implemented a Test-Time Adaptation (TTA) strategy during testing. This involves calculating the Wasserstein distance between each sample and the different source domains in the feature space and using the nearest statistical information in the feature space to align the target domain with the source domains. The specific algorithms for training and testing are shown in Algorithm 1 and Algorithm 2 respectively:

Algorithm 1 Subject Normalization for Domain Adaptation (Training process)

1: **Training Input:** Multi-source domains $D_{s_i} = \{X_i^n, y_i^n\}_{n=1}^{N_i}$, domain labels $i \in \{1, ..., K\}$; Hyperparameters $K, e, \epsilon, bs > 0$
2: **Training Output:** Normalized features of source domains X_s
3: Initialize training domain set $T \leftarrow None$;
4: Initialize affine parameters γ, β **When** $affine$ is True;
5: Initialize statistics storage $S = \{m, \nu\} \leftarrow 0$;
6: **repeat**
7:     Find each unique domain D_u in B_i
8:     **for** $x \in D_u$ **to** bs **do**
9:         **if** $u \notin T$ **then**
10:             $T \leftarrow T + u$
11:         **end if**
12:         $x_m \leftarrow Mean(x)$, $x_\nu \leftarrow Var(x)$
13:         $m_u \leftarrow e \times x_m + (1 - e) \times m_u$
14:         $\nu_u \leftarrow e \times x_\nu + (1 - e) \times \nu_u$
15:     **end for**
16:     $\bar{x} \leftarrow (x - m_u)/\sqrt{\nu_u + \epsilon}$
17:     **if** $affine$ **then**
18:         $X_s \leftarrow \gamma_u \cdot \bar{X} + \beta_u$
19:     **end if**
20: **until** $i = [\frac{D}{bs}] + 1$
21: **Return** X_s

[!t] **Algorithm 2** Subject Normalization for Domain Adaptation (Test-Time-Adaptation)

1: **Require:** Training domain set T; Training statistics storage $\{S_m, S_\nu\}_{i=1}^{N_T}$; Training affine parameters γ, β **When** $affine$ is True
2: **Testing Input:** Labeled target domains $D_{tl} = \{X_{tl}^n, y_{tl}^n\}_{n=1}^{N_l}$; Unlabeled target domains $D_{tu} = \{X_{tu}^n\}_{n=N_l+1}^{N_l+N_u}$; Target domain labels $i \in \{1, ..., K\}$; Hyperparameters $K, e, \epsilon, bs > 0$
3: **Testing Output:** Normalized features of source domains X_t
4: Initialize testing domain set $\Gamma \leftarrow None$;
5: Initialize statistics storage $\{\Omega_m, \Omega_\nu\}_{i=1}^{N_T} \leftarrow 0$;
6: **repeat**
7:     Find each unique domain D_u in B_i
8:     **for** $x \in D_u$ **to** bs **do**
9:         **if** $u \in T$ **then**
10:             $\{x_m, x_\nu\} \leftarrow \{S_m^u, S_\nu^u\}$
11:         **end if**
12:         **if** $u \notin \Gamma$ **then**
13:             $\Gamma \leftarrow \Gamma + u$
14:             $\{x_m, x_\nu\} \leftarrow \{Mean(x), Var(x)\}$
15:         **else**
16:             $\Omega_m^u \leftarrow e \times x_m + (1 - e) \times \Omega_m^u$
17:             $\Omega_\nu^u \leftarrow e \times x_\nu + (1 - e) \times \Omega_\nu^u$

18:     **end if**
19:     **end for**
20:     $\{X_m, X_\nu\} \leftarrow \{\Omega_m, \Omega_\nu\}$
21:     $\bar{X} \leftarrow (X - X_m)/\sqrt{X_\nu + \epsilon}$
22:     **if** $affine$ **then**
23:         $t^* \leftarrow \arg\min_{t_i \in T} \left(\|\mu_u - \mu_{t_i}\|^2 + \text{Tr}(\Sigma_u + \Sigma_{t_i} - 2 \cdot (\Sigma_u^{1/2} \Sigma_{t_i} \Sigma_u^{1/2})^{1/2}) \right)$
24:         $X_t \leftarrow \gamma_{t^*} \cdot \bar{X} + \beta_{t^*}$
25:     **end if**
26: **until** $i = [\frac{D}{bs}] + 1$ or model convergence
27: **Return** X_t

5 Experimental Set Up

5.1 Data Collection and Preprocess

In this study, TMS-EEG data were collected from 60 participants, comprising 30 normal healthy controls (Ages: 45.1 ± 12.6) and 30 subjects diagnosed with Major Depressive Disorder (Ages: 42.6 ± 13.4).

Preprocessing. All experimental data compared have been processed with a bandpass filter of 2–42 Hz [22,23]. The TMS-EEG data was selected from 0.5 s before the TMS stimulation and 1.5 s after the TMS stimulation [24], further we downsampled to 500 Hz. Due to the constraints of the ERP experimental paradigm, we used raw data with non-overlapping sample points as input (Fig. 2).

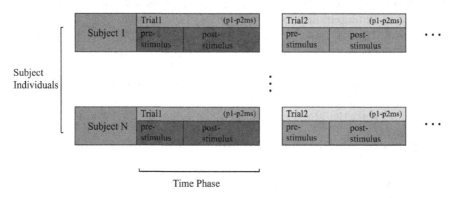

Fig. 2. Overall TMS-EEG dataset architecture of 60 TMS stimulated subjects.

5.2 Validation Setting

To validate the performance of our proposed EEG-based transfer learning model, we adopted a subject-independent approach, meaning that subjects present in the training set will not appear in the test set. In other words, our model will be applied to the test dataset without any calibration steps solely relying on our normalization transfer method. We randomly split the dataset into a training set (70%) and a validation/test set (30%).

6   Results

We utilized the PyTorch framework and conducted the training on NVIDIA GPUs (RTX 3090) with 24 GB of memory. The training process involved the following key components. For the optimizer, we used the RAdam optimizer with a momentum of 0.9. The learning rate for all models was uniformly set to 0.00001. The optimizer's weight decay was managed using a cosine annealing warm restarts scheduler with a period of 5 epochs, scheduling between 0.0005. The batch size for training 128, and the number of epochs for one training phase is 300 (Table 1).

Table 1. Comparisons with Classification Results of the Model on TMS-EEG Dataset

Methods	Accuracy	Precision	F1-Score
MS-AGNN w/SN	**0.73530**	**0.81254**	**0.78634**
MS-AGNN w/IN	0.65815	0.67024	0.65163
MS-AGNN w/BN	0.67014	0.67153	0.66891
MS-AGNN w/GN	0.63139	0.63189	0.63094
EEGNet w/SN	0.62280	0.70530	0.62404
EEGNet w/IN	0.55257	0.47880	0.59533

7   Conclusion

In this study, we propose a novel transfer learning model for ERP task detection based on EEG. This model addresses the adverse factors hindering model generalization due to variations in EEG data by employing adaptive subject normalization, thereby enhancing the network's generalization capability across different scenarios and subjects. The model includes a spatiotemporal dynamic attention graph network for extracting domain-invariant features from EEG signals, coupled with a subject-level normalization domain adaptation module.

The proposed model has been validated on TMS-EEG dataset and demonstrates superior performance compared to other models. Additionally, we conducted ablation experiments by replacing the subject-level normalization module with traditional BN, LN, and GN. The results indicate that our proposed model effectively aligns different domain distributions in multi-subject transfer learning tasks, reduces dependence on domain information, and achieves improved performance in EEG-based tasks.

Acknowledgments. This work is supported by National Natural Science Foundation of China (U23B2018), National Natural Science Foundation of China (NSFC62271477), Shenzhen Science and Technology Program (JCYJ20220818101411025), Shenzhen Science and Technology Program (JCYJ20220818102800001), Shenzhen Science and Technology Program (JCYJ20220818101217037), Shenzhen Peacock Team Project (KQTD 20200820113106007).

References

1. Delorme, A., Makeig, S.: EEGLAB: an open source toolbox for analysis of single-trial EEG dynamics including independent component analysis. J. Neurosci. Methods **134**(1), 9–21 (2004)
2. Hopman, H.J., et al.: Personalized prediction of transcranial magnetic stimulation clinical response in patients with treatment-refractory depression using neuroimaging biomarkers and machine learning. J. Affect. Disord. **290**, 261–271 (2021)
3. Leuchter, A.F., Wilson, A.C., Vince-Cruz, N., Corlier, J.: Novel method for identification of individualized resonant frequencies for treatment of Major Depressive Disorder (MDD) using repetitive Transcranial Magnetic Stimulation (rTMS): a proof-of-concept study. Brain Stimul. **14**(5), 1373–1383 (2021)
4. Dadebayev, D., Goh, W.W., Tan, E.X.: EEG-based emotion recognition: review of commercial EEG devices and machine learning techniques. J. King Saud Univ.-Comput. Inf. Sci. **34**(7), 4385–4401 (2022)
5. Deng, J., Dong, W., Socher, R., Li, L.J., Li, K., Fei-Fei, L.: ImageNet: a large-scale hierarchical image database. In: 2009 IEEE Conference on Computer Vision and Pattern Recognition, pp. 248–255. IEEE (2009)
6. Li, R., et al.: The perils and pitfalls of block design for EEG classification experiments. IEEE Trans. Pattern Anal. Mach. Intell. **43**(1), 316–333 (2021). https://doi.org/10.1109/TPAMI.2020.2973153
7. Lawhern, V.J., Solon, A.J., Waytowich, N.R., Gordon, S.M., Hung, C.P., Lance, B.J.: EEGNet: a compact convolutional neural network for EEG-based brain-computer interfaces. J. Neural Eng. **15**(5), 056013 (2018). https://doi.org/10.1088/1741-2552/aace8c
8. Xie, J., et al.: A transformer-based approach combining deep learning network and spatial-temporal information for raw EEG classification. IEEE Trans. Neural Syst. Rehabil. Eng. **30**, 2126–2136 (2022). https://doi.org/10.1109/TNSRE.2022.3194600
9. Li, Y., Zheng, W., Zong, Y., Cui, Z., Zhang, T., Zhou, X.: A bi-hemisphere domain adversarial neural network model for EEG emotion recognition. IEEE Trans. Affect. Comput. **12**(2), 494–504 (2018)
10. Miao, Z., Zhang, X., Menon, C., Zheng, Y., Zhao, M., Ming, D.: Priming cross-session motor imagery classification with a universal deep domain adaptation framework (2023). https://doi.org/10.48550/arXiv.2202.09559
11. Kipf, T.N., Welling, M.: Semi-supervised classification with graph convolutional networks. arXiv preprint arXiv:1609.02907 (2016)
12. Li, R., Wang, Y., Lu, B.L.: A multi-domain adaptive graph convolutional network for EEG-based emotion recognition. In: Proceedings of the 29th ACM International Conference on Multimedia, MM '21, pp. 5565–5573. Association for Computing Machinery, New York (2021). https://doi.org/10.1145/3474085.3475697
13. Veličković, P., Cucurull, G., Casanova, A., Romero, A., Liò, P., Bengio, Y.: Graph attention networks (2018). https://doi.org/10.48550/arXiv.1710.10903

14. Chen, T., Guo, Y., Hao, S., Hong, R.: Exploring self-attention graph pooling with EEG-based topological structure and soft label for depression detection. IEEE Trans. Affect. Comput. **13**(4), 2106–2118 (2022)
15. Tao, T.L., Guo, L.H., He, Q., Zhang, H., Xu, L.: Seizure detection by brain-connectivity analysis using dynamic graph isomorphism network. In: 2022 44th Annual International Conference of the IEEE Engineering in Medicine & Biology Society (EMBC), pp. 2302–2305. IEEE (2022)
16. Ioffe, S., Szegedy, C.: Batch normalization: accelerating deep network training by reducing internal covariate shift. In: International Conference on Machine Learning, pp. 448–456. PMLR (2015)
17. Ba, J.L., Kiros, J.R., Hinton, G.E.: Layer normalization. arXiv preprint arXiv:1607.06450 (2016)
18. Wu, Y., He, K.: Group normalization. In: Proceedings of the European Conference on Computer Vision (ECCV), pp. 3–19 (2018)
19. Ulyanov, D., Vedaldi, A., Lempitsky, V.: Improved texture networks: maximizing quality and diversity in feed-forward stylization and texture synthesis. In: Proceedings of the IEEE Conference on Computer Vision and Pattern Recognition, pp. 6924–6932 (2017)
20. Li, J., Qiu, S., Shen, Y.Y., Liu, C.L., He, H.: Multisource transfer learning for cross-subject EEG emotion recognition. IEEE Trans. Cybern. **50**(7), 3281–3293 (2020). https://doi.org/10.1109/TCYB.2019.2904052
21. Ganin, Y., et al.: Domain-adversarial training of neural networks. J. Mach. Learn. Res. **17**(59), 1–35 (2016)
22. Chen, P., Gao, Z., Yin, M., Wu, J., Ma, K., Grebogi, C.: Multiattention adaptation network for motor imagery recognition. IEEE Trans. Syst. Man Cybern. Syst. **52**(8), 5127–5139 (2022). https://doi.org/10.1109/TSMC.2021.3114145
23. Schirrmeister, R.T., et al.: Deep learning with convolutional neural networks for EEG decoding and visualization. Hum. Brain Mapp. **38**(11), 5391–5420 (2017). https://doi.org/10.1002/hbm.23730
24. Hopman, H.J., et al.: Personalized prediction of transcranial magnetic stimulation clinical response in patients with treatment-refractory depression using neuroimaging biomarkers and machine learning. J. Affect. Disord. **290**, 261–271 (2021). https://doi.org/10.1016/j.jad.2021.04.081

Structured Dialogue System for Mental Health: An LLM Chatbot Leveraging the PM⁺ Guidelines

Yixiang Chen[1,2,3], Xinyu Zhang[1,4], Jinran Wang[1,5], Xurong Xie[3], Nan Yan[1], Hui Chen[3], and Lan Wang[1(✉)]

[1] Guangdong-Hong Kong-Macao Joint Laboratory of Human-Machine Intelligence-Synergy Systems, Shenzhen Institute of Advanced Technology, Chinese Academy of Sciences, Shenzhen, China
{yx.chen7,xy.zhang14,jr.wang2,nan.yan,lan.wang}@siat.ac.cn
[2] University of Chinese Academy of Sciences, Beijing, China
[3] Institute of Software, Chinese Academy of Sciences, Beijing, China
{xurong,chenhui}@iscas.ac.cn
[4] East China Normal University, Shanghai, China
[5] Wuhan Research Institute of Posts and Telecommunications, Wuhan, China

Abstract. The Structured Dialogue System, referred to as SuDoSys, is an innovative Large Language Model (LLM)-based chatbot designed to provide psychological counseling. SuDoSys leverages the World Health Organization (WHO)'s Problem Management Plus (PM+) guidelines to deliver stage-aware multi-turn dialogues. Existing methods for employing an LLM in multi-turn psychological counseling typically involve direct fine-tuning using generated dialogues, often neglecting the dynamic stage shifts of counseling sessions. Unlike previous approaches, SuDoSys considers the different stages of counseling and stores essential information throughout the counseling process, ensuring coherent and directed conversations. The system employs an LLM, a stage-aware instruction generator, a response unpacker, a topic database, and a stage controller to maintain dialogue flow. In addition, we propose a novel technique that simulates counseling clients to interact with the evaluated system and evaluate its performance automatically. When assessed using both objective and subjective evaluations, SuDoSys demonstrates its effectiveness in generating logically coherent responses. The system's code and program scripts for evaluation are open-sourced (https://github.com/EthanLifeGreat/SuDoSys).

Keywords: Large language model · Psychological counseling · Multi-turn dialogue system

1 Introduction

In today's fast-paced world, mental health has risen to the forefront of global health priorities, recognized as a critical component of overall well-being [1].

© The Author(s), under exclusive license to Springer Nature Singapore Pte Ltd. 2025
H. Li et al. (Eds.): ICSR + InnoBiz 2024, LNAI 15170, pp. 262–271, 2025.
https://doi.org/10.1007/978-981-96-1151-5_27

Structured Dialogue System for Mental Health   263

However, access to professional mental health services like psychological counseling remains a challenge, particularly in regions lacking specialists. Advancements of Natural Language Processing (NLP) and Large Language Models (LLMs) [2] offer a promising avenue to bridge this gap. LLMs like ChatGPT[1], LLaMA [3, 4], ChatGLM [5] and Qwen [6], characterized by their vast capacity to understand instructions and generate human-like responses, have the potential to serve as empathetic listeners and psychological consultants, providing immediate assistance to help-seeking individuals.

However, LLMs must be adapted for psychological counseling, as they are primarily pre-trained for general purposes. Previous studies have utilized (real or synthetic) counseling dialogues to fine-tune pre-trained LLMs for multi-turn dialogue systems. For example, ExTES-LLaMA [7], MEChat [8], SoulChat [9], and CPsyCounX [10] are LLMs fine-tuned on generated multi-turn dialogues. PsyChat [11] is a dialogue system fine-tuned on dialogues with counselor's strategy and user's behavior labeled by human. However, these fine-tuning approaches often do not consider the different stages of counseling, resulting in dialogues that lack direction and coherence.

To address these limitations, we propose **St**ructured **D**ialogue **Sys**tem (SuDoSys), an LLM-based multi-turn dialogue system designed for stage-aware counseling. To enhance the system's intelligence in counseling, we leverage the World Health Organization (WHO)'s guidelines for structured psychological interventions—Problem Management Plus (PM+) [12]. By adhering to the PM+'s seven-step framework for problem management (see Chapter 7 of PM+), we have meticulously crafted a series of prompts that guide SuDoSys through the entire problem management process while providing emotional support.

In this paper, we introduce SuDoSys and propose a novel automatic evaluation method utilizing counseling dialogues collected from actual PM+ interventions. We then conduct both objective and subjective evaluations of SuDoSys. The experimental results demonstrate that our approach excels in generating coherent dialogues compared to existing fine-tuning methods. Notably, all the experiments conducted in this work are in Chinese.

2   SuDoSys and Automatic Evaluation

2.1   Stage-Unaware Prompting: A Baseline Method

An intuitive approach to priming pre-trained Large Language Models (LLMs) for the role of psychological counselors involves explicitly assigning the counselor role and responsibilities to the model prior to the commencement of the counseling session.

However, such a stage-unaware approach overlooks the distinct stages inherent to the counseling process. Besides, LLMs are prone to exhibit suboptimal performance (such as forgetting information) as the context length increases, which can lead to a lack of coherence in the dialogue. Consequently, the stage-unaware method is employed as a baseline in this study.

---

[1] https://chatgpt.com/.

2.2 SuDoSys: A Stage-Aware Multi-turn Dialogue System

In each stage of a psychological counseling, a counselor engages the client by inviting them to express their thoughts and responds with a strategic approach. Simultaneously, the counselor assesses whether to advance to the next stage, based on the sufficiency of the information gathered from the client and the client's readiness for the subsequent stage of discussion. Inspired by these practices, we propose a dialogue system that not only responds to the user's input appropriately, but also accounts for the progression of the conversation through different stages.

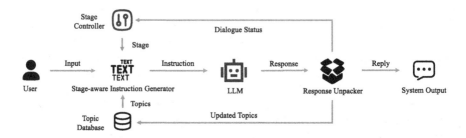

Fig. 1. The overview structure of SuDoSys. It consists of 5 parts: a stage controller, a stage-aware instruction generator, a topic database, a pre-trained LLM, and a response unpacker.

As illustrated in Fig. 1 SuDoSys comprises five modules: a stage controller, a stage-aware instruction generator, a topic database, a pre-trained LLM, and a response unpacker. In each turn (denoted as t) of the conversation, the instruction receives the current stage number S, the turn's user input utterance u_t, the conversation topics stored in all previous stages $\{\mathbb{T}_s\}_{s=1}^{S}$ and forms instruction I, where $\mathbb{T}_s = \{T_s^k\}_{k=1}^{K_s}$, and each T_s^k is a topic that can be discussed around, and K_s is the number of topics in stage s, as defined in topic database D. As instructed by I, the LLM then 1) extract updated conversation topics $\mathbb{T}'_S$, 2) determine the dialogue status $c \in \{-1, 0, 1\}$, where $c = -1$ indicates going to the previous stage, $c = 0$ indicates staying at current stage and $c = 1$ indicates moving to the next stage, and 3) yield a reply r_t towards the user. As soon as the topics $\mathbb{T}'_S$ and status c are produced, they are sent to the topic database and the stage controller respectively for instruction generation of the next turn.

Stage-Aware Instruction Generator. The stage-aware instruction generator is the core of SuDoSys as it sends information-retriving commands to the LLM. In stage S, an instruction I is made up of 4 parts:

– **Stage-dependent Base Instruction B_S.** This is a hand-crafted directive that specifies the role and responsibilities of the LLM within the current stage of interaction. The instruction is derived from the PM+ guidelines and serves to remind the LLM of its focus during the conversation, the timing for stage shifts, and the manner in which it should respond with both empathy and professionalism. It is selected from base instruction library $\mathbb{B}$ by the generator according to S: $B_S = \mathbb{B}[S]$.

- **Stage-dependent Topics** $\{\mathbb{T}_s\}_{s=1}^S$. For each stage s, the stage dependent topics $\mathbb{T}_s$ represents a series of key-value pairs that define the topics to be discussed. Each key corresponds to a specific issue to be addressed, while the value provides a description of the issue. These descriptions may be revised (expanded or pruned) after each turn's discussion, with revisions applicable only to the current stage. Descriptions for topics in previous stages remain unchanged and serve as references. Similar to the base instruction, the issues for each stage are predefined based on the guidelines, and all descriptions are initialized as empty at the beginning of the dialogue. It should be distinguished with the *slot pairs* proposed in Dialogue State Tracking [13,14]—slot values are typically constrained to a predefined set of options, whereas topic values are unrestricted descriptive sentences.

- **User Input of the Turn** u_t. The input utterance is crucial for the LLM to comprehend the user's sentiments and gather relevant information for revising the topics above.

- **Response Template** R_S^T. This is typically represented as a Python dictionary that specifies the structure of the desired output in stage S, which includes the updated topics $\mathbb{T}_S'$, the dialogue status $c \in \{-1, 0, 1\}$ and the user-oriented reply r_t.

With base instruction library $\mathbb{B}$ and Response Template R_S^T stored inside, the stage-aware instruction generator G_I reorganizes the values and operates as follows:

$$I = G_I(S, \{\mathbb{T}_s\}_{s=1}^S, u_t) = [\mathbb{B}[S]; \{\mathbb{T}_s\}_{s=1}^S; u_t; R_S^T],$$

where I denotes the generated instruction; S represents the current stage; $\{\mathbb{T}_s\}_{s=1}^S$ is the set of topics for stages starting from one up to the current number S; u_t is user's input utterance; and the square brackets $[\cdot; \cdot]$ means direct text concatenation. Examples of the instructions are available in our open-source project.

LLM and Response Unpacker. The decoder-only LLM is the core of the system functioning because it is responsible for comprehending user's input, extracting new topics $\mathbb{T}_S'$, and generating output r_t and dialogue status c. The text-formatted output of the LLM, denoted as o, is expected to contain and only contain the values above. However, due to the lack of Human Preference Alignment Training [15,16], the LLMs sometimes fail to generate responses that are pure JSON and contain exactly the dictionary keys as required. For instance, the LLM might generate incompatible quotation marks or provide additional explanations of the JSON, making the output unable to be parsed. In such cases, the response unpacker is responsible for fixing the format errors and removing the redundant messages, and parse the revised output to the values of $\mathbb{T}_S'$, r_t

and c. As for more complex situations where the unpacker cannot handle, the LLM is required to regenerate the response. The LLM and the response unpacker together, denoted as F_{LLM}, function as follows:

$$\mathbb{T}'_S, r_t, c = F_{LLM}(I),$$

where $\mathbb{T}'_S$ is the updated topics for stage S; r_t is the reply towards user; c dialogue status; and I is the instruction input to the LLM. It is worth noting that, theoretically, the LLM in the SuDoSys can be any pre-trained LLM, and the processing speed of function F_{LLM} is positively correlated with the degree of the LLM's alignments with human preferences.

Stage Controller. The stage controller changes the stage number s according to the c dialogue status:

$$s := s + c,$$

where $c \in \{-1, 0, 1\}$ is the dialogue status.

Topic Database. The topic database stores the aforementioned topics for each chatting stages, denoted as $\{\mathbb{T}_s\}_{s=1}^N$ where N is the total number of stages in the dialogue. During each stage S, the database updates only the topics of the stage:

$$\mathbb{T}_S := \mathbb{T}'_S,$$

but it sends to the instruction generator all topics of previous stages (including the current one): $\{\mathbb{T}_s\}_{s=1}^S$.

2.3 Automatic Evaluation Method for Stage-Aware Multi-turn Dialogue Systems

To automatically evaluate the AI-generated responses, many researches [17,18] employ GPT-4 to assess the quality of such responses. In the context of psychological counseling, existing methods [8,9,11,19] for evaluating multi-turn dialogue systems often focus on comparing single-round outputs between/among different models given the same dialogue history. However, these approaches cannot be directly applied to evaluate a stage-aware dialogue system. This is because a randomly selected dialogue history may diverge significantly from a structured dialogue, thereby rendering the comparison between models less meaningful.

To address such issues, we propose an automatic evaluation method for assessing the quality of multi-turn responses. As illustrated in Fig. 2, we first employ GPT-4 to extract client portraits from dialogues transcribed from raw PM+ intervention recordings. Subsequently, we prompt the GLM-4 [5] model to act as these clients and engage in conversations with the evaluated systems to generate dialogues that will undergo further assessments. Details of the components in the figure are as follows:

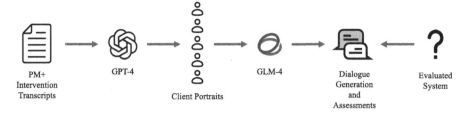

Fig. 2. The overview structure of our proposed evaluation method. We make use of GPT-4 to extract portraits of actual PM+ clients. The GLM-4 model then plays the role of these clients and make conversations with dialogue systems to generate dialogues for evaluation.

- **PM+ Intervention Transcripts**. These are 148 dialogues transcribed from recordings of psychological counseling sessions in Chinese, in which counselors apply the PM+ intervention guidelines. Each session has a duration of approximately 90 min. Each dialogue comprises approximately 20,000 Chinese characters and encompasses over 100 turns of utterances.
- **Client Portraits**. Profiles of clients participating PM+ interventions encompass various aspects including age, gender, occupation, hobbies, health conditions, sources of distress, current mood, and psychiatric symptoms. The number of the portraits is equal to the transcripts.
- **Dialogue Generation**. The dialogues are the result of turn-by-turn interactions between the evaluated systems and the 148 clients simulated by the GLM-4 model. We limit the number of turns to 20 as most models typically complete the conversation within this number of turns.
- **Dialogue Assessments**. In this part, we utilize GPT-4 to automatically evaluate the overall quality of the AI psychological counselor's utterances generated during the dialogues. Specifically, by prompting GPT-4 to provide ratings, we assess four key aspects of the AI's responses: logical coherence, professionalism, empathy, and authenticity.

Due to page limitations, we provide the prompts for portrait extraction, the scripts for dialogue generation, and the detailed evaluation metrics in our open-source project.

3   Experiments

3.1   Experimental Setup

We compare SuDoSys with the fine-tuning model CPsyCounX [10], which has backbone model with 7B parameters. To ensure a fair comparison, we utilize Qwen2-7B-Instruct [6] as the base LLM for SuDoSys. Additionally, we employ the stage-unaware prompt stated in Sect. 2 to instruct Qwen2-7B-Instruct, serving as a baseline method for comparative analysis. For all the models mentioned above, we use the default settings.

In objective evaluation, we employ GPT-4 to assess the interactions between the GLM-4-simulated clients and the evaluated systems. Notably, there are 148 PM+ intervention transcripts and corresponding client portraits, leading to the simulation of 148 clients. Consequently, GPT-4 rates a total of $148 \times 3 = 444$ dialogues conducted with these simulated clients. In each evaluation round, GPT-4 reviews the dialogues between the same client and each of the three evaluated systems.

For subjective evaluation, we recruited 20 college students to act as clients and engage in conversations with the evaluated systems. Each participant was asked to select a client portrait extracted from the total of 3,134 multi-turn consultation dialogues in CPsyCounD [10], and then to interact with each of the three evaluated systems. Following these interactions, each participant rated the three systems according to the same dimensions used by GPT-4. The web interface designed for this subjective evaluation is available on our open-source project.

Table 1. Objective evaluation results: average ratings given by GPT-4 based on generated dialogue history. Ratings are on an integer scale from 1 to 5, with higher values indicating better performance.

System	Coherence	Professionalism	Empathy	Authenticity
CPsyCounX	3.9	**4.5**	**4.4**	**3.8**
Qwen2-7B	3.8	3.7	4.2	**3.8**
SoDuSys	4	4.2	4.1	3.7

3.2 Results and Discussion

Objective Evaluation. As illustrated in Table 1, SuDoSys outperforms other systems in terms of coherence, demonstrating the efficacy of its stage-aware scheme. Notably, CPsyCounX achieves the highest overall rating, particularly excelling in professionalism and empathy, likely due to its fine-tuning on a substantial corpus of counseling data.

Subjective Evaluation. In the subjective evaluation Table 2, SuDoSys surpasses other models in coherence with even more pronounced differences than those observed in the automatic evaluation. Furthermore, SuDoSys outperforms CPsyCounX in authenticity. This superiority may be attributed to SuDoSys's ability to manage long-term memories through the incorporation of relevant topics, thereby enhancing its human-like interaction quality.

Overall, leveraging the PM+'s problem managing stages, SuDoSys exhibits a slight advantage in coherence and remains competitive in other dimensions when compared with existing fine-tuning-based counseling models. Moreover, since

Table 2. Subjective evaluation results: ratings given by the 20 students after their interaction with the systems. Ratings follow the same scale as defined in Table 1.

System	Coherence	Professionalism	Empathy	Authenticity
CPsyCounX	3.6	**3.7**	3.5	3.7
Qwen2-7B	3.4	3.2	**3.8**	3.5
SoDuSys	**3.8**	**3.7**	3.5	**3.8**

SuDoSys does not require data for fine-tuning the LLM, it demonstrates a cost-effective and scalable alternative that can potentially reduce the resource burden associated with developing and deploying counseling models while maintaining competitive performance.

4   Conclusion

In conclusion, the Structured Dialogue System (SuDoSys) demonstrates a significant improvement in the coherence of counseling dialogues when compared with existing fine-tuning-based models. By leveraging the structured stages outlined in the Problem Management Plus (PM+) guidelines, SuDoSys ensures that the conversations remain coherent and are guided effectively through the counseling process. The system shows competitive performance in professionalism, empathy, and authenticity, as evidenced by both automatic evaluations using GPT-4 and human assessments by college students. These findings highlight the potential of SuDoSys to serve as a valuable tool in bridging the gap in accessible mental health services, particularly in regions lacking specialized professionals. Future work could explore further enhancements to the system, including leveraging real-world counseling datasets to refine the system's performance under complex human-computer interactions.

Acknowledgments. This work was supported by National Natural Science Foundation of China (NSFC U23B2018, 62106255) and Shenzhen Science and Technology Program (No. KQTD2020 0820113106007), ShenZhen Fundamental Research Program (JCYJ20220818101411025), and Youth Innovation Promotion Association CAS Grant 2023119.

We would like to express our sincere gratitude to Rennan Wang for her invaluable assistance in revising and improving this manuscript. Her insightful feedback and suggestions significantly enhanced the quality of our work.

References

1. Prince, M., et al.: No health without mental health. The Lancet **370**(9590), 859–877 (2007). https://doi.org/10.1016/S0140-6736(07)61238-0. https://www.sciencedirect.com/science/article/pii/S0140673607612380
2. Zhao, W.X., et al.: A survey of large language models (2023). https://arxiv.org/abs/2303.18223

3. Touvron, H., et al.: LLaMA: open and efficient foundation language models (2023). https://arxiv.org/abs/2302.13971
4. Touvron, H., et al.: Llama 2: open foundation and fine-tuned chat models (2023). https://arxiv.org/abs/2307.09288
5. Zeng, A., et al.: ChatGLM: a family of large language models from GLM-130B to GLM-4 all tools (2024). https://arxiv.org/abs/2406.12793
6. Yang, A., et al.: Qwen2 technical report (2024). https://arxiv.org/abs/2407.10671
7. Zheng, Z., Liao, L., Deng, Y., Nie, L.: Building emotional support chatbots in the era of LLMs (2023). https://arxiv.org/abs/2308.11584
8. Qiu, H., He, H., Zhang, S., Li, A., Lan, Z.: SMILE: single-turn to multi-turn inclusive language expansion via ChatGPT for mental health support (2024). https://arxiv.org/abs/2305.00450
9. Chen, Y., et al.: SoulChat: improving LLMs' empathy, listening, and comfort abilities through fine-tuning with multi-turn empathy conversations. In: Bouamor, H., Pino, J., Bali, K. (eds.) Findings of the Association for Computational Linguistics: EMNLP 2023, pp. 1170–1183. Association for Computational Linguistics, Singapore (2023). https://doi.org/10.18653/v1/2023.findings-emnlp.83. https://aclanthology.org/2023.findings-emnlp.83
10. Zhang, C., et al.: CPsyCoun: a report-based multi-turn dialogue reconstruction and evaluation framework for Chinese psychological counseling. CoRR abs/2405.16433 (2024). https://doi.org/10.48550/ARXIV.2405.16433
11. Qiu, H., Li, A., Ma, L., Lan, Z.: PsyChat: a client-centric dialogue system for mental health support. In: 2024 27th International Conference on Computer Supported Cooperative Work in Design (CSCWD), pp. 2979–2984 (2024). https://doi.org/10.1109/CSCWD61410.2024.10580641
12. World Health Organization, et al.: Problem management plus (PM+): Individual psychological help for adults impaired by distress in communities exposed to adversity. Technical report, World Health Organization (2016)
13. Feng, Y., Lu, Z., Liu, B., Zhan, L., Wu, X.M.: Towards LLM-driven dialogue state tracking. In: Bouamor, H., Pino, J., Bali, K. (eds.) Proceedings of the 2023 Conference on Empirical Methods in Natural Language Processing, pp. 739–755. Association for Computational Linguistics, Singapore (2023). https://doi.org/10.18653/v1/2023.emnlp-main.48. https://aclanthology.org/2023.emnlp-main.48
14. Niu, C., Wang, X., Cheng, X., Song, J., Zhang, T.: Enhancing dialogue state tracking models through LLM-backed user-agents simulation. In: Ku, L.W., Martins, A., Srikumar, V. (eds.) Proceedings of the 62nd Annual Meeting of the Association for Computational Linguistics (Volume 1: Long Papers), pp. 8724–8741. Association for Computational Linguistics, Bangkok (2024). https://aclanthology.org/2024.acl-long.473
15. Yuan, H., Yuan, Z., Tan, C., Wang, W., Huang, S., Huang, F.: RRHF: rank responses to align language models with human feedback. In: Oh, A., Naumann, T., Globerson, A., Saenko, K., Hardt, M., Levine, S. (eds.) Advances in Neural Information Processing Systems, vol. 36, pp. 10935–10950. Curran Associates, Inc. (2023)
16. Ouyang, L., et al.: Training language models to follow instructions with human feedback (2022). https://arxiv.org/abs/2203.02155
17. Lin, Y.T., Chen, Y.N.: LLM-Eval: unified multi-dimensional automatic evaluation for open-domain conversations with large language models. In: Chen, Y.N., Rastogi, A. (eds.) Proceedings of the 5th Workshop on NLP for Conversational AI (NLP4ConvAI 2023), pp. 47–58. Association for Computational Linguis-

tics, Toronto (2023). https://doi.org/10.18653/v1/2023.nlp4convai-1.5. https://aclanthology.org/2023.nlp4convai-1.5

18. Liu, Y., Iter, D., Xu, Y., Wang, S., Xu, R., Zhu, C.: G-Eval: NLG evaluation using GPT-4 with better human alignment. In: Bouamor, H., Pino, J., Bali, K. (eds.) Proceedings of the 2023 Conference on Empirical Methods in Natural Language Processing, pp. 2511–2522. Association for Computational Linguistics, Singapore (2023). https://doi.org/10.18653/v1/2023.emnlp-main.153. https://aclanthology.org/2023.emnlp-main.153

19. Liu, J.M., Li, D., Cao, H., Ren, T., Liao, Z., Wu, J.: ChatCounselor: a large language models for mental health support (2023). https://arxiv.org/abs/2309.15461

Feature Extraction Method Based on Contrastive Learning for Dysarthria Detection

Yudong Yang[1], Xinyi Wu[1,2], Xiaokang Liu[1,2], Juan Liu[1,2], Jingdong Zhou[1,2], Rennan Wang[3], Xin Wang[4], Rongfeng Su[1(✉)], Nan Yan[1(✉)], and Lan Wang[1(✉)]

[1] Guangdong-HongKong-Macao Joint Laboratory of Human-Machine Intelligence-Synergy Systems, Shenzhen Institute of Advanced Technology, Chinese Academy of Sciences, Shenzhen, China
{yd.yang2,rf.su,nan.yan,lan.wang}@siat.ac.cn
[2] University of Chinese Academy of Sciences, Beijing, China
[3] University of British Columbia, Vancouver, Canada
[4] Shenzhen Institute, Peking University, Beijing, China

Abstract. Dysarthria detection is crucial for clinical diagnosis and treatment. However, existing methods predominantly rely on supervised learning, which requires extensive annotated data, resulting in high costs and inconsistent data quality. To address this issue, this paper proposes a feature extraction method for dysarthria detection based on contrastive learning, which does not require annotated data. This method investigates how to extract features from patients and normal individuals using different pre-trained acoustic models. By maximizing the differences in their acoustic feature spaces, this method enhances detection accuracy. Finally, multiple classification methods are employed to detect dysarthria using the extracted features, achieving significant improvements across various evaluation metrics.

Keywords: Dysarthria detection · Contrastive learning · Feature extraction

1 Introduction

Dysarthria is a motor speech disorder caused by neurological diseases. It is primarily characterized by unclear pronunciation, unstable speech rate, and abnormal prosody [1–3]. Individuals with dysarthria can form grammatically correct sentences, but their speech is often challenging to understand due to pronunciation difficulties. This significantly impacts their social interactions and quality of life [4–6].

In recent years, various methods have been employed to analyze the speech data of individuals with dysarthria to better understand and detect acoustic characteristics that distinguish them from normal individuals [7–10]. For

© The Author(s), under exclusive license to Springer Nature Singapore Pte Ltd. 2025
H. Li et al. (Eds.): ICSR + InnoBiz 2024, LNAI 15170, pp. 272–281, 2025.
https://doi.org/10.1007/978-981-96-1151-5_28

instance, traditional acoustic features often used in the early years and large-scale pre-trained models such as Wav2Vec 2.0, which are used to directly extract features [11,12], have both been utilized to detect dysarthria and have achieved notable success. However, existing methods primarily rely on supervised learning, which demands a substantial amount of annotated data for training. Due to the diversity and complexity of dysarthria, obtaining annotated data is challenging and costly. Moreover, the significant differences in speech characteristics between individuals with dysarthria and normal individuals make manual annotation time-consuming and prone to inconsistencies due to subjective judgments. Therefore, developing an unsupervised learning method that does not require extensive annotated data for dysarthria detection is of great significance [13,16,17].

Latent patterns and structures within the data can be discovered using self-supervised contrastive learning methods to detect dysarthria without labeled data. These methods enhance classification accuracy and reliability by analyzing and comparing the acoustic features of individuals with dysarthria to those of normal individuals, thereby maximizing the differences between the two groups. This approach can effectively distinguish between normal individuals and those with dysarthria, meeting clinical needs and improving treatment outcomes of dysarthria patients [14,15].

Therefore, our main contribution is the detection of dysarthria based on a contrastive learning feature extraction method for self-supervised pre-training [18–20]. First, we extract acoustic features from dysarthria patients and normal individuals using various pre-trained acoustic features. Then, we maximize the feature differences between patients and healthy individuals through contrastive learning strategies, mapping these differences into distinct feature spaces. Finally, we extract features and conduct dysarthria detection on the Mandarin Subacute Stroke Dysarthria Multimodal database. The results show that the proposed method achieves significant improvements across multiple evaluation metrics. This approach not only enhances the accuracy of dysarthria detection and diagnosis but also provides strong support for personalized treatment, thereby advancing research and clinical applications in the field of dysarthria [3,21].

2   Methods

In this section, we introduce a method for extracting features of speech articulation disorders using contrastive learning. This approach utilizes various large-scale pre-trained audio models as feature encoders and optimizes the feature space representation through the adjustment of loss functions.

2.1   Audio Pre-training Model

In this study, we propose a contrastive learning-based framework for dysarthria detection, utilizing three state-of-the-art self-supervised pre-trained models

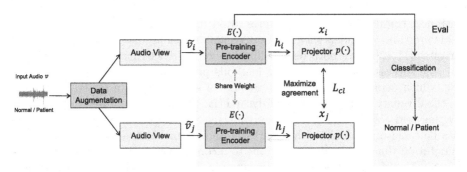

Fig. 1. The framework for dysarthria detection using contrastive learning. Input audio is augmented to create two views $\tilde{v}_i$ and $\tilde{v}_j$, processed by a shared pre-training encoder $E(\cdot)$ to extract features, and then projected to maximize agreement. Finally, the features are classified to determine if the audio is from a normal individual or a patient.

(Wav 2Vec 2.0 [22], HuBERT [23], and WavLM [24]) as feature extractors. These models, trained on large-scale unlabeled speech data, have demonstrated exceptional capability in capturing complex acoustic patterns and long-term dependencies. We hypothesize that the rich acoustic information obtained through this pre-training strategy holds significant potential for identifying speech abnormalities in dysarthric patients (Fig. 1).

To validate our hypothesis, we systematically evaluate the performance of these three pre-trained models in the dysarthria detection task. Specifically, we utilize the Wav2Vec2-XLSR-53 model, which is pre-trained on multilingual data, enhancing its adaptability to diverse speech patterns. The HuBERT-Large model, with its innovative masked prediction and clustering approach, is expected to capture more abstract and semantically relevant features, potentially aiding in the identification of subtle anomalies in dysarthric speech. The WavLM-Large model, through its unique pre-training strategy, demonstrates improved robustness to noise and diverse speech signals, which is particularly crucial for processing real-world dysarthric speech data.

By comparing the feature representations extracted from these different pre-trained models, our objective is to establish a robust feature foundation. The output dimensions of our three models are all uniformly averaged to 1024 dimensions to map into the feature space for subsequent contrastive learning and dysarthria detection tasks.

2.2   Feature Extraction Based on Contrastive Learning

Inspired by the SimCLR method [19,25], we explore the effectiveness of a contrastive learning framework in representing speech features for individuals with articulation disorders. Our approach utilizes several pre-trained models as encoders for feature extraction. Robust feature representations are learned through maximizing the consistency among different augmented audio samples of the same data instance through contrastive loss in the latent space.

The approach comprises four key components: a random data augmentation module, an encoder feature extraction module, a neural network projection module, and a contrastive loss function. Specifically, in the random data augmentation module, any given audio instance is transformed into two correlated audio samples $\tilde{v}_i$ and $\tilde{v}_j$, treated as a positive pair. Positive pairs, representing different augmented versions of the same audio instance, should exhibit high similarity in the feature space. Conversely, negative pairs, which are augmented samples from different audio instances, should exhibit low similarity in the feature space. By maximizing the similarity between positive pairs and minimizing the similarity between negative pairs, the model learns more robust and generalizable feature representations.

$$\mathbf{h}_i = E(\tilde{v}_i) \tag{1}$$

$$\mathbf{h}_j = E(\tilde{v}_j) \tag{2}$$

In the encoder feature extraction module, we utilize various pre-trained models such as WavLM, Hubert, and Wav2Vec2.0. These models have been pre-trained on large-scale audio datasets, enabling them to effectively capture complex features within audio signals. For audio of dysarthria patients with articulation disorders, these pre-trained models are particularly advantageous. Given that disordered speech may exhibit irregular pronunciations and other abnormal audio features, pre-trained models can leverage their extensive learned audio data to recognize these anomalies, thereby improving the accuracy and robustness of feature extraction.

$$\mathbf{x}_i = p(\mathbf{h}_i) \tag{3}$$

$$\mathbf{x}_j = p(\mathbf{h}_j) \tag{4}$$

Next, in the neural network projection module, we map the high-dimensional features extracted by the encoders into a lower-dimensional latent space. This process is accomplished through a small fully connected neural network, with the goal of further compressing the feature dimensions while preserving the most crucial information. The output of this projection network functions as the latent representation in contrastive learning to calculate the contrastive loss.

The contrastive loss function module is the core of the entire contrastive learning framework. We optimize the model by maximizing the similarity of positive pairs in the latent space while minimizing their similarity with other samples (negative pairs). Specifically, for each anchor-positive pair $(\mathbf{x}_i, \mathbf{x}_j)$, the cosine similarity is computed as:

$$sim(\mathbf{x}_i, \mathbf{x}_j) = \frac{\mathbf{x}_i \cdot \mathbf{x}_j}{\|\mathbf{x}_i\| \|\mathbf{x}_j\|} \tag{5}$$

The contrastive loss for a positive pair (i, j) and a set of negative samples is given by:

$$\mathcal{L}_{i,j} = -\log \frac{\exp(sim(\mathbf{x}_i, \mathbf{x}_j)/\tau)}{\sum_{k=1}^{2N} \mathbb{I}_{[k \neq i]} \exp(sim(\mathbf{x}_i, \mathbf{x}_k)/\tau)} \qquad (6)$$

In this context, $sim(\mathbf{x}_i, \mathbf{x}_j)$ represents the cosine similarity between the latent representations $\mathbf{x}_i$ and $\mathbf{x}_j$. The parameter τ is a temperature parameter that regulates the scaling of similarities. The indicator function $\mathbb{I}_{[k \neq i]}$ ensures that the sum excludes the anchor's similarity with itself. This formulation aims to maximize the similarity of positive pairs while minimizing the similarity with negative pairs.

The overall objective is to minimize the average contrastive loss across all positive pairs in the mini-batch:

$$\mathcal{L}_{cl} = \frac{1}{N} \sum_{i=1}^{N} \mathcal{L}_{i,j} \qquad (7)$$

Therefore, our contrastive learning-based feature representation method is particularly well-suited for capturing and enhancing the unique characteristics of speech with articulation disorders. Through data augmentation, we generate a more diverse range of audio samples, enhancing the model's robustness. The strong feature extraction capabilities provided by pre-trained models allow us to effectively extract features from disordered speech. The neural network projection module further optimizes feature representation, ensuring that contrastive loss in the latent space can more effectively learn the consistency between different augmented versions of the same audio instance. This enables us to obtain differential feature representations between disordered and normal speech, laying the groundwork for subsequent clinical research.

3   Experiment

3.1   Datasets

The database includes recordings and videos captured in a soundproof room. For this paper, we only use the audio data. The raw audio data were captured using a professional-grade microphone (MS400, Takstar), sampled at 16 kHz with 16-bit encoding and a single channel. The average signal-to-noise ratio (SNR) of the valid audio recordings is below 40 dB. The dataset contains a total of 17.05 h of synchronized audio-video data, with all silent segments removed.[1] It is divided into 13.69 h for the training set used during the model training phase and 3.36 h for the test set used for challenge scoring and ranking. The train and test sets consist of 87 unique speakers (58 male, 29 female) with balanced gender representation, including a training set of 73 participants and a test set of 14 participants (Table 1).

---

[1] https://huanraozhineng1.github.io/MSDM/.

Table 1. Details of the released Train and Test data.

	Utterance	Duration (h)	Audio Format	Video Formant
Train	61396	13.69	16 kHz, 16bit	30 f/s, 800 × 600
Test	13911	3.36	16 kHz, 16bit	30 f/s, 800 × 600

3.2 Experiments Setting

The model was trained on 4× NVIDIA A6000 GPUs, and we utilized various data augmentation techniques, such as polarity inversion, noise addition, gain variation, high-pass and low-pass filtering, delay, pitch shifting, and reverberation. The audio input was resampled to consistent 16 kHz and either padded or truncated to a fixed length of 36,000 samples. Training was conducted over 200 epochs with a batch size of 64, using the Adam optimizer with a learning rate of $1e-3$ and a weight decay of $1e-6$. The experimental results indicate that the combination of contrastive learning and data augmentation methods is highly effective in extracting distinct audio feature representations.

3.3 Evaluation Metrics

In our experiments, we utilized a comprehensive set of evaluation metrics to measure feature distinctiveness. Specifically, we employed two classification methods to assess the model's performance: KNN and logistic regression. During the testing phase, features were extracted using the KNN classifier, and cosine similarity was used to compute the similarity between each test sample and the samples in the memory bank, which were extracted from the training data. Additionally, logistic regression was used as a feature detection method, directly predicting the class of test samples by learning the relationship between features and labels from the training data, thereby validating the performance of different feature representations.

Furthermore, we used precision, recall, F1-score, and accuracy to evaluate the quality of the classification results. These metrics respectively measure the model's ability to correctly identify positive samples, recall positive samples, balance precision and recall, and predict correctly overall. These methods allowed us to comprehensively and accurately assess the performance of the extracted features in dysarthria detection.

3.4 Comparative Experiment

To validate the effectiveness of our extracted features, we first selected traditional eGeMAPS[2] features as a baseline for comparison. eGeMAPS is a widely used audio feature set designed to capture speech characteristic information by extracting a small but highly representative set of audio features. The results

---

[2] https://github.com/audeering/opensmile.

Table 2. Performance Metrics for Various Models

Model	Feature	Classification	Accuracy	Precision	Recall	F1-score
–	gGeMAPS	KNN	0.6754	0.6268	0.6162	0.6196
		Logistic Regression	0.8209	0.8029	0.7848	0.7924
ResNet	L_{cl}	KNN	0.8362	0.8367	0.7846	0.8018
		Logistic Regression	0.8596	0.8628	0.8146	0.8317
Hubert	×	KNN	0.9199	0.9215	0.8963	0.9071
		Logistic Regression	0.8944	0.9151	0.8496	0.8720
	L_{cl}	KNN	**0.9526**	0.9526	**0.9400**	**0.9459**
		Logistic Regression	0.9169	0.9050	0.9090	0.9069
WavLM	×	KNN	0.8790	0.8963	0.8312	0.8530
		Logistic Regression	0.9011	0.9147	0.8626	0.8819
	L_{cl}	KNN	0.9480	**0.9565**	0.9271	0.9397
		Logistic Regression	0.9120	0.9024	0.8988	0.9005
Wav2Vec2.0	×	KNN	0.8716	0.8949	0.8179	0.8418
		Logistic Regression	0.8925	0.9085	0.8497	0.8705
	L_{cl}	KNN	0.9272	0.9317	0.9034	0.9154
		Logistic Regression	0.9049	0.8948	0.8899	0.8923

showed that while these features could capture useful information from audio signals to some extent, their performance was significantly inferior to that of pre-trained models. For instance, a logistic regression model using eGeMAPS features achieved an accuracy of 0.8209, while a KNN model only reached 0.6754 (Table 2).

In recent years, pre-trained models have demonstrated their powerful feature extraction capabilities in computer vision and natural language processing. To further enhance the extraction and detection performance of audio features in speech articulation disorders, we introduced several pre-trained models, including HuBERT, WavLM, and Wav2Vec2.0. These models, pre-trained on large datasets, can capture richer and more meaningful features.

Quantitative experimental results further indicated that pre-trained models significantly outperformed non-pre-trained models across all evaluation metrics. For example, features extracted by the Wav2Vec2.0 model achieved an accuracy of 0.9049 on a logistic regression classifier, significantly higher than the 0.8209 accuracy of the logistic regression model using eGeMAPS features, also surpassing the 0.8596 accuracy of a ResNet model without pre-trained weights. This demonstrates that pre-trained models, as feature encoders, can extract more comprehensive information and significantly enhance detection performance.

The primary reason for selecting pre-trained models lies in their strong generalization and feature representation capabilities. By pre-training on large-scale datasets, these models learn rich feature representations that can be transferred to specific tasks, thereby improving task performance. Additionally, we introduced contrastive learning loss L_{cl}, aiming at enhancing feature discriminability by maximizing the similarity between similar samples and minimizing the similarity between different samples.

In our experiments, pre-trained models combined with contrastive learning loss exhibited outstanding performance across all evaluation metrics. For instance, a logistic regression classifier using Hubert combined with L_{cl} achieved an F1 score of 0.9069, compared to an F1 score of 0.8720 for the model without L_{cl}. This result validates the effectiveness of introducing contrastive learning in enhancing feature discrimination across different speakers.

Through comparative analysis of non-pre-trained and pre-trained models, we validated the significant advantages of pre-trained models in feature extraction and classification tasks. The integration of contrastive learning loss further improved the models' feature representation capabilities, leading to substantial performance enhancements in detection tasks. These results suggest that the pre-trained feature extraction method combined with contrastive learning has promising applications in the detection of dysarthria.

4   Conclusion

This paper proposes a feature extraction method based on contrastive learning and pre-trained models for detecting dysarthria. By leveraging various large-scale pre-trained audio models, we extract highly discriminative acoustic features without the need for annotated data. The contrastive learning approach significantly enhances detection accuracy by maximizing the differences in the acoustic feature spaces between dysarthric patients and normal individuals. Experimental results demonstrate that the feature extraction method, combined with contrastive learning and data augmentation, achieves significant improvements across multiple evaluation metrics. This method not only enhances the accuracy and diagnostic effectiveness of dysarthria detection but also provides strong support for personalized treatment, thereby advancing research and clinical applications in the field of dysarthria.

Acknowledgments. This work is supported by National Natural Science Foundation of China (U23B2018, NSFC 62271477), Shenzhen Science and Technology Program (JCYJ20220818101411025, JCYJ20220818102800001, JCYJ20220818101217037), and Shenzhen Peacock Team Project (KQTD20200820113106007).

Disclosure of Interests. The authors have no competing interests to declare that are relevant to the content of this article.

References

1. Spencer, K.A., Brown, K.A.: Dysarthria following stroke. In: Seminars in Speech and Language, vol. 39, no. 01, pp. 015–024. Thieme Medical Publishers (2018)
2. Tu, W.J., Hua, Y., Yan, F., et al.: Prevalence of stroke in China, 2013–2019: a population-based study. The Lancet Reg. Health West. Pac. **28** (2022)

3. Enderby, P.: Disorders of communication: dysarthria. Handb. Clin. Neurol. **110**, 273–281 (2013)
4. Mackenzie, C.: Dysarthria in stroke: a narrative review of its description and the outcome of intervention. Int. J. Speech Lang. Pathol. **13**(2), 125–136 (2011)
5. Liu, J., Du, X., Lu, S., et al.: Audio-video database from subacute stroke patients for dysarthric speech intelligence assessment and preliminary analysis. Biomed. Signal Process. Control **79**, 104161 (2023)
6. Rudzicz, F., Namasivayam, A.K., Wolff, T.: The TORGO database of acoustic and articulatory speech from speakers with dysarthria. Lang. Resour. Eval. **46**, 523–541 (2012)
7. Javanmardi, F., Kadiri, S.R., Alku, P.: Pre-trained models for detection and severity level classification of dysarthria from speech. Speech Commun. **158**, 103047 (2024)
8. Joshy, A.A., Rajan, R.: Automated dysarthria severity classification: a study on acoustic features and deep learning techniques. IEEE Trans. Neural Syst. Rehabil. Eng. **30**, 1147–1157 (2022). https://doi.org/10.1109/TNSRE.2022.3169814
9. Stipancic, K.L., Palmer, K.M., Rowe, H.P., et al.: "You say severe, i say mild": toward an empirical classification of dysarthria severity. J. Speech Lang. Hear. Res. **64**(12), 4718–4735 (2021)
10. Kumar, C.V.T., Bhattacharjee, T., Belur, Y., et al.: Classification of multi-class vowels and fricatives from patients having Amyotrophic Lateral Sclerosis with varied levels of dysarthria severity. In: Interspeech (2023)
11. Javanmardi, F., Tirronen, S., Kodali, M., et al.: Wav2vec-based detection and severity level classification of dysarthria from speech. In: ICASSP 2023-2023 IEEE International Conference on Acoustics, Speech and Signal Processing (ICASSP), pp. 1–5. IEEE (2023)
12. Wang, H., Jin, Z., Geng, M., et al.: Enhancing pre-trained ASR system fine-tuning for dysarthric speech recognition using adversarial data augmentation. In: ICASSP 2024-2024 IEEE International Conference on Acoustics, Speech and Signal Processing (ICASSP), pp. 12311–12315. IEEE (2024)
13. Kim, H., Hasegawa-Johnson, M., Perlman, A., et al.: Dysarthric speech database for universal access research. In: Interspeech 2008, pp. 1741–1744 (2008)
14. Hu, S., Xie, X., Jin, Z., et al.: Exploring self-supervised pre-trained ASR models for dysarthric and elderly speech recognition. In: ICASSP 2023-2023 IEEE International Conference on Acoustics, Speech and Signal Processing (ICASSP), pp. 1–5. IEEE (2023)
15. Hu, S., Xie, X., Geng, M., et al.: Self-supervised ASR models and features for dysarthric and elderly speech recognition. IEEE/ACM Trans. Audio Speech Lang. Process. **32**, 3561–3575 (2024)
16. Schu, G., Janbakhshi, P., Kodrasi, I.: On using the UA-Speech and TORGO databases to validate automatic dysarthric speech classification approaches. In: ICASSP 2023 - 2023 IEEE International Conference on Acoustics, Speech and Signal Processing (ICASSP), Rhodes Island, Greece, pp. 1–5 (2023). https://doi.org/10.1109/ICASSP49357.2023.10095981
17. Liu, X., Du, X., Liu, J., et al.: Automatic assessment of dysarthria using audio-visual vowel graph attention network. arXiv preprint arXiv:2405.03254 (2024)
18. Wu, L., Zong, D., Sun, S., Zhao, J.: A sequential contrastive learning framework for robust dysarthric speech recognition. In: ICASSP 2021 - 2021 IEEE International Conference on Acoustics, Speech and Signal Processing (ICASSP), Toronto, ON, Canada, pp. 7303–7307 (2021). https://doi.org/10.1109/ICASSP39728.2021.9415017

19. Chen, T., Kornblith, S., Norouzi, M., et al.: A simple framework for contrastive learning of visual representations. In: International Conference on Machine Learning, pp. 1597–1607. PMLR (2020)
20. Saeed, A., Grangier, D., Zeghidour, N.: Contrastive learning of general-purpose audio representations. In: ICASSP 2021 - 2021 IEEE International Conference on Acoustics, Speech and Signal Processing (ICASSP), Toronto, ON, Canada, pp. 3875–3879 (2021). https://doi.org/10.1109/ICASSP39728.2021.9413528
21. Yunusova, Y., Weismer, G., Westbury, J.R., et al.: Articulatory movements during vowels in speakers with dysarthria and healthy controls (2008)
22. Baevski, A., Zhou, Y., Mohamed, A., et al.: wav2vec 2.0: a framework for self-supervised learning of speech representations. In: Advances in Neural Information Processing Systems, vol. 33, pp. 12449–12460 (2020)
23. Hsu, W.N., Bolte, B., Tsai, Y.H.H., et al.: HuBERT: self-supervised speech representation learning by masked prediction of hidden units. IEEE/ACM Trans. Audio Speech Lang. Process. **29**, 3451–3460 (2021)
24. Chen, S., Wang, C., Chen, Z., et al.: WavLM: large-scale self-supervised pre-training for full stack speech processing. IEEE J. Sel. Top. Signal Process. **16**(6), 1505–1518 (2022)
25. Spijkervet, J., Burgoyne, J.A.: Contrastive learning of musical representations. arXiv preprint arXiv:2103.09410 (2021)

Flying Together with Audio and Video: Enhancing Communication for the Hearing-Impaired Through an Emerging Closed Captioning Standard

Luntian Mou[1,2]([✉]), Peize Li[1], Haiwu Zhao[3]([✉]), Qiang Fu[4], Hong Luo[5], Cong Liu[6], Nan Ma[1,2], Tiejun Huang[7], and Wen Gao[7,8]

[1] Beijing University of Technology, Beijing, China
[2] Beijing Institute of Artificial Intelligence, Beijing, China
ltmou@bjut.edu.cn
[3] Shanghai University of Engineering Science, Shanghai, China
zhao.hw@avsgm.com
[4] Photosynthetic AI Tech Co., Ltd., Hangzhou, China
[5] China Mobile Information Technology Co., Ltd., Hangzhou, China
[6] IFLYTEK Research, Hefei, China
[7] Peking University, Beijing, China
[8] Peng Cheng Laboratory, Shenzhen, China

Abstract. As the text-based visual representation of a program's audio elements, Closed Captioning primarily serves as a technology to enhance communication for the hearing impaired. Since text is much simpler than audio and video, Closed Captioning is traditionally transmitted as supplementary or auxiliary information as part of the image or in an extended or private data field of an encoded video bitstream called video elementary stream, usually accompanied by one or more audio elementary streams. Since Closed Captioning is extremely important for the accessibility of the audio content of a program to the hearing impaired, we propose to encode the closed caption into a bitstream called caption elementary stream, which can fly together with audio and video elementary streams. In other words, closed caption can be stored and transmitted in a manner similar to how audio and video are handled. We have drafted a national standard for Closed Captioning in China, which is now in its final stage of approval and publication. In this paper, the main technical content of the emerging Closed Captioning standard will be introduced. Specifically, the encoding, storage, and transmission of Closed Captioning will be described. Moreover, the decoding and presentation of Closed Captioning under the two scenarios of on demand streaming and live streaming will also be designed and discussed. The AI technology of Speech-to-Text enables Closed Captioning to be implemented efficiently with the help of manual proofreading. Positively, the emergence of the Closed Captioning standard will enhance accessibility to audio-visual programs on both the broadcasting network and the Internet for the hearing-impaired in China and worldwide.

H. Li et al. (Eds.): ICSR + InnoBiz 2024, LNAI 15170, pp. 282–292, 2025.
https://doi.org/10.1007/978-981-96-1151-5_29

Keywords: Closed Captioning · Caption Elementary Stream ·
Hearing Impaired

1 Introduction

Closed Captioning (CC) refers to displaying text on a television, video screen, or other visual display to provide interpretive information as the transcription of the audio content of a program, sometimes including descriptions of non-speech elements (such as door closing, car whistling, music playing, etc.) [1]. Typically, closed captions on a television set appear as white on a black background, locating on the top or bottom of the screen depending on the nature of the picture. The logo for CC and an example of CC on TV are shown in Fig. 1. CC is primarily a powerful tool to enhance accessibility for the deaf and hearing impaired audiences. Thus, CC can be turned on or off by pressing the CC button on a remote control or a menu, contrary to the caption embedded or burned-in to the video and cannot be turned off, which is called Open Captioning indicating visible to all viewers [2]. Additionally, CC can also provide a textual alternative language translation of a presentation's primary audio language, which is helpful for second language learners and foreign audiences. In Europe, CC is also equivalently referred to as captions for the hard of hearing [3].

(a)   (b)

Fig. 1. Logo and Example of Closed Captioning. (a) CC logo; (b) CC on TV.

CC was first demonstrated in the United States in 1971, and was successfully encoded and broadcast in 1973 with the cooperation of Public Broadcasting Service (PBS). In 1976, the US Federal Communications Commission (FCC) reserved Line 21 of the vertical blanking interval (VBI) for transmitting closed captions. BBC was the first broadcaster to include closed captions (called captions in the UK) in 1979 for pre-recorded programming. For real-time captioning of live broadcasts, it was developed by the National Captioning Institute in 1982, which depended on transcribers who can type at speeds of over 225 words per minute. Nowadays, advancements in speech recognition technology enables live captioning to be fully or partially automated [4].

According to the Television Decoder Circuitry Act, FCC required all analog television receivers 13 in. or larger to have the ability of displaying closed caption after July 1, 1993. For digital television receivers, they were also required by the Telecommunications Act of 1996 to provide closed captioning after July 1, 2002. As required by the Twenty-First Century Communications and Video Accessibility Act [5] passed in 2010, the Advanced Television Systems Committee (ATSC) set-top box remotes shall have a button to turn on or off the closed captioning in the output signal, and the broadcasters to provide captioning for television programs redistributed on the Internet.

Generally speaking, there are two types of captioning [6], namely, on demand (or post-production) captioning, and live (or real time) captioning. The primary advantage of on demand captioning is accuracy – a real human has prepared the captions and can therefore edit for polished captions, which can indicate environmental sounds and auditory events (e.g., "door slams") besides speech. However, on demand captioning can be expensive and time consuming. On the contrast, live captioning is needed on the spot in real time, such as at a sports game or a conference. In the past, live captioning required someone to re-speak what was said. With the rising of speech recognition technology, this duty is more and more taken by machine with satisfying accuracies. For example, the leading speech-to-text technology provider iFlytek can provide speech recognition and transcription services up to 11 languages, with accuracy of 98% for clear Chinese speech in quiet environment and 97% for clear English speech in general environment [7].

For accessibility and interoperability, open standards for Closed Captioning are extremely important. While CEA-608 uses VBI of the analog video signal to transmit caption data, CEA-708 is designed for digital television broadcasts, using the MPEG-2 Transport Stream (TS) [8] to transmit the caption data as a private data stream. Similarly, DVB Subtitling, also known as DVB Teletext or DVB Subtitling Service (DVB-SUB), is transmitted through the MPEG-2 TS using a specific type of Ancillary Data Service. What is special for DVB-SUB is that it supports both bitmap-based captions and text-based captions. Web Video Text Tracks (Web-VTT) is recognized as a closed captioning standard and is widely used in practice due to its transmission through the HTML5 <track> element, browser compatibility, flexibility, and interoperability with other standards. Timed Text Markup Language (TTML) is similarly supported by HTML5 [9,10], but with an XML-based data format and advanced styling options. And the Society of Motion Picture and Television Engineers Timed Text (SMPTE-TT) is a profile of TTML tailored for professional media production and distribution by SMPTE. On the 67th Annual Technology & Engineering Emmy Awards held by the National Academy of Television Arts & Sciences, the SMPTE and the World Wide Web Consortium (W3C), were recognized for their pioneering development of industry standards enabling closed captions on Internet video. The two freely available standards of W3C TTML and the SMPTE-TT enable audio-visual content to be closed-captioned when offered via the Internet [11].

According to existing standards, closed captions are either transmitted as an auxiliary/private data stream or as a text/XML track. Currently, there is no encoded bitstream of closed captions that is compatible with audio and video bitstreams in theoretical or practical terms [12]. Therefore, for the first time, we propose to encode closed captions into a caption elementary stream and transmit it together with audio and video elementary streams. This has two advantages. First, caption is now logically at the same level as audio and video, which will draw more attention to its significance and enhance accessibility for the hearing impaired. Second, the mechanisms for handling audio and video can be smoothly transferred to caption, improving the flexibility in processing caption information.

The rest of the paper is organized as follows. The encoding of CC is specified in Sect. 2. Section 3 introduces the storage and transmission of CC. And the decoding and presentation of CC is shown in Sect. 4. Finally, Sect. 5 concludes the paper with future work.

2 Encoding of Closed Captioning as a Caption Elementary Stream

2.1 Architecture of the Closed Captioning Standard

The architecture of the closed captioning standard is shown in Fig. 2 and mainly includes the following components: 1) The encoding of CC presents the syntax and semantics of the caption stream. 2) The storage of CC specifies the file formats for closed captions, including independent file format of Closed Caption File (CCF) and extension based on ISO Base Media File Format (ISO BMFF). 3) The transmission of closed captioning describes the formats for transmitting the caption elementary stream in MPEG-2 Transport Stream (MPEG-2 TS). The transmission formats for Real-time Transport Protocol (RTP), Adaptive Streaming (AS), and Smart Media Transport (SMT) protocols need to meet certain requirements, which are given in the normative Annex A of the standard.

2.2 Syntax and Semantics of Caption Elementary Stream

Structure of Caption Sequence and Caption Sample. The CC sequence consists of several CC samples, as shown in Syntax 1, starting with the CC sample start code and ending with the CC sequence end code. The start code is a specific bit string that should not appear in any other context in the bitstream conforming to the final draft national standard on CC. The start code consists of a start code prefix and a start code value. The start code prefix is the bit string 0000 0000 0000 0000 0000 0001, and all start codes should be byte-aligned. The CC_sample_start_code value is an 8-bit unsigned integer used to indicate the type of start code, as shown in Table 1. The CC_sequence_end_code is the bit string 0x000001C1, which marks the end of the CC sequence. To avoid the occurrence of false start code, a mask bit is set to a fixed value of 1.

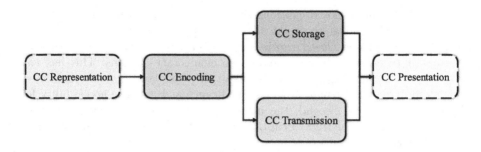

Fig. 2. The Architecture of the Closed Captioning Standard.

The definition of the CC Sample is shown in Syntax 2. The variable i is the loop index variable used to iterate through the user data bytes, and N represents the total number of user data bytes in the sample. The `CC_sample_start_code` is the bit string 0x000001C0, which marks the beginning of a CC sample. The Closed Captioning Type (CC_type) is an 8-bit unsigned integer, and the CC_type value assignments are shown in Table 2. The field language is represented by a 24-bit string. Terminals compliant with this final draft national standard on CC should at least support Chinese and English. The field of `CC_string_offset` indicates the caption string offset. And the field of `picture_data_byte` indicates the picture data byte bytes contained when CC_type takes the value of 2.

Important Caption Information. The caption sample defined in Syntax 2 includes descriptions of time, location, display, color, font, and style, as well as the caption string. Time details specify the start and end times of the caption's visibility on the screen, ensuring synchronization with the corresponding audiovisual content. The location is determined by coordinates that define the caption's position on the screen. Display characteristics describe the behavior of the caption, such as whether it remains static or scrolls across the screen. Color settings allow for customization of text and background colors. Font descriptions cover the selection of typefaces, which should at least support Chinese

---

Syntax 1. CC Sequence

```
CC_sequence() {
  do {
    while (next_bits(32) == CC_sample_start_code) {
      CC_sample() }
  } while (next_bits(32) != CC_sequence_end_code)
  CC_sequence_end_code
}
```

Table 1. Start Code Values

Start Code Type	Start Code Value (Hexadecimal)
CC Sample Start Code	C0
CC Sequence End Code	C1
Reserved	C2–C7
User Defined Start Codes	C8–FF, 00–BF

Table 2. The CC Type Values

The CC Type Values	Meaning
0	Forbidden
1	Plain Text
2	Image
3	Sign Language Glossing
4	Live Captioning
5... 254	Reserved
255	Emergency Broadcast

or English. Style elements include text attributes like bold, italic, or underline. These crucial caption details enhance the viewing experience for the audience.

Syntax 2. CC Sample

```
CC_sample()
{
  CC_sample_start_code
  CC_type
  language
  CC_string_offset
  if (CC_type != 4 && CC_type != 255) {
    time_information() }
  if (CC_type != 255) {
    position_description()
    display_description()
    color_description()
    font_description()
    style_description() }
  for i = 0 to N
    user_data_byte
  if (CC_type != 2) {
    CC_string() }
  else {
    picture_data_byte }
}
```

3   Storage and Transmission of Closed Captioning

3.1   Storage of Closed Captioning

Separate Caption File. To support offline editing of closed captions, a CCF format is defined. A CCF is a text file composed of several caption entries. The definition of a caption entry is provided in Syntax 3.

A caption entry consists of several note lines, several format lines, a counter line, a time line, several caption lines, and a blank line. A note line, denoted as `note_line()`, starts with a '#' and may contain any displayable characters until the end of the line. A format line, denoted as `format_line()`, contains a '#' in the middle, with the format name following the '#' and the format value preceding it. A counter line, denoted as `counter_line()`, contains only an integer. The number in the counter line of the first caption entry in the current caption file should be 0, and the number should increase by 1 for each subsequent counter line. A time line, denoted as `time_line()`, contains time information in two formats. When the second time represents the end time, it should be consistent with the SRT file format. A caption line, denoted as `caption_line()`, is a line of captions displayed on the screen and may contain any displayable characters. A caption entry may contain multiple caption lines. A blank line, denoted as `blank_line()`, signifies the end of a caption entry. Note lines may be absent in a caption entry. The first caption entry in a CCF should contain complete format lines to fully define the caption format. Subsequent caption entries may omit format lines or include only some format lines to redefine part of the format, with unchanged formats remaining the same.

Encapsulation Based on ISO BMFF. When using ISO/IEC 14496.12, the CC stream is encapsulated as a file track with the handler type 'subt' and included in the media box. The media info box should contain a caption header, and Decoding Time Stamp (DTS) and Composition Time Stamp (CTS) info should comply with the time-to-sample and composition offset specifications.

Syntax 3. Caption Entry

```
caption()
{
  for i = 0 to N {
    note_line() }
  for i = 0 to N {
    format_line() }
  counter_line()
  time_line()
  for i = 0 to N {
    caption_line() }
  blank_line()
}
```

Each sample should contain a `CC_sample()` without a sequence end code. The sample entry type should be 'avcc', with at least one 'avcc' sample entry in the track.

3.2 Transmission of Closed Captioning

Transmission over MPEG-2 TS. MPEG-2 TS defines how to use Packetized Elementary Stream (PES) to encapsulate and transmit audio and video data. The syntax for encapsulating the CC elementary stream in the PES of GB/T 17975.1 or ISO/IEC 13818.1 is shown in Syntax 4.

Syntax 4. PES Packet

```
PES_packet()
{
   packet_start_code_prefix
   stream_id
   PES_packet_length
   CC_start_code_value
   if stream_id == 0xFD {
     if CC_start_code_value == 0xC0 {
        CC_sample_without_startcode() }
     for i = 0 to N {
        stuffing_byte }
   }
}
```

The `packet_start_code_prefix` is used to identify the start of a PES packet. The `stream_id` is the stream identifier field, with a value of 0xFD (extended_stream_id). The `PES_packet_length` is the PES packet length field, which should equal the number of bytes in the caption sample minus the start code prefix plus the number of stuffing bytes. The `CC_start_code_value`, which should be 0xC0 (caption sample start code) or 0xC1 (caption sample end code).

Transmission over Other Protocols. In addition to MPEG-2 TS protocols, closed captions can also be transmitted over RTP, AS, and SMT protocols. For RTP, the format complies with IETF RFC 3550, supporting single and compound packets. For AS, it addresses continuous media and Media Presentation Description (MPD) structures, supporting synchronized interleaving with video and audio streams. For SMT, CC data is encapsulated as payload data, with defined data types and payload values.

4 Decoding and Presentation of Closed Captioning

4.1 On Demand Streaming Scenario

In the on demand scenario, the process of applying closed captions to playback terminals is depicted in Fig. 3. For each frame of the displayed video, existing

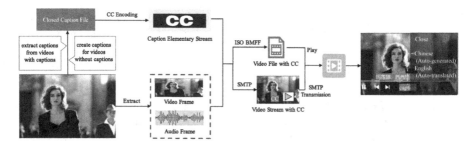

Fig. 3. On Demand Streaming Scenario for CC.

captions are extracted as CCF; if none are present, captions are generated using AI-based speech-to-text technology. The generated CCF can support offline editing, including the integration of onomatopoeic words into captions. Through CC encoding, a basic caption stream is created. This stream, along with video and audio frames, can be encapsulated offline using the ISO BMFF standard to produce a video file with embedded closed captions. Alternatively, by employing the SMTP standard for online encapsulation, an online video stream with independent closed captions can be formed. The terminal player extracts and decodes the CC stream data from the local video files or online video, audio, and caption streams for playback. Ultimately, users can see the captions on the playing video and have the option to turn on or off, and switch the caption language as needed.

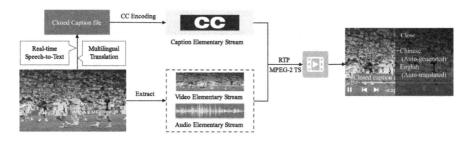

Fig. 4. Live Streaming Scenario for CC.

4.2 Live Streaming Scenario

In the live streaming scenario, the application of captions to playback terminals is illustrated in Fig. 4. For each frame of the live broadcast, CCF is created using AI-based technologies such as real-time speech-to-text and multilingual translation. The CCF is processed through CC encoding to form a caption elementary stream, which is synchronized with the video and audio elementary streams. The combined streams are encapsulated and transmitted to the terminal player using protocols such as RTP or MPEG-2 TS. Viewers can see the captions on the played video and have the option to enable or disable the captions and switch the caption language as required.

5 Conclusion

The proposed closed captioning standard in audiovisual content represents a significant technological advancement in aiding individuals with hearing impairments. By encoding closed captions as a caption elementary stream transmitted alongside the audio and video elementary streams, this standard ensures that captions are treated with equal importance and efficiency as other media components. Supported by iFlytek's speech-to-text technology and supplemented by human proofreading, the generation of captions for both on-demand and live content is accurate and timely. Additionally, the caption location is designed not to obstruct essential visual elements. The adoption of this standard enhances the accessibility of broadcast and internet-based audiovisual programs for individuals with hearing impairments, providing a more inclusive viewing experience both in China and globally. Moving forward, our focus is on further improving the quality of closed captions and considering the development of accessible technologies for individuals with other types of sensory impairments, thereby enhancing overall information accessibility. As this standard approaches final approval and publication, it sets a new benchmark in the field of accessibility technology.

References

1. "Closed Captioning." Wikipedia, The Free Encyclopedia. Wikimedia Foundation. https://en.wikipedia.org/wiki/Closed_captioning. Accessed 10 July 2024
2. Xu, W., Yu, J., Miao, Z., et al.: Deep reinforcement polishing network for video captioning. IEEE Trans. Multimedia **23**, 1772–1784 (2020)
3. Jelinek Lewis, M.S., Jackson, D.W.: Television literacy: comprehension of program content using closed captions for the deaf. J. Deaf Stud. Deaf Educ. **6**(1), 43–53 (2001)
4. Ding, N., Deng, C., Tan, M., et al.: Image captioning with controllable and adaptive length levels. IEEE Trans. Pattern Anal. Mach. Intell. (2023)
5. Burks, C.L.: Improving access to commercial websites under the Americans with disabilities act and the twenty-first century communications and video accessibility act. Iowa Law Rev. **99**, 363 (2013)
6. Song, P., Guo, D., Cheng, J., et al.: Contextual attention network for emotional video captioning. IEEE Trans. Multimedia **25**, 1858–1867 (2022)
7. Zhang, W., Zhang, H., Liu, C., et al.: Pre-trained acoustic-and-textual modeling for end-to-end speech-to-text translation. In: ICASSP 2024-2024 IEEE International Conference on Acoustics, Speech and Signal Processing, pp. 11451–11455 (2024)
8. "EIA-608." Wikipedia, The Free Encyclopedia. Wikimedia Foundation. https://en.wikipedia.org/wiki/EIA-608. Accessed 10 July 2024

9. Mou, L., Chen, X., Huang, T., et al.: Overview of IEEE 1857.3: systems of advanced audio and video coding. In: IEEE International Conference on Multimedia and Expo Workshops, pp. 1–4 (2014)
10. Amirpour, H., Zhu, J., Le Callet, P., et al.: A real-time video quality metric for HTTP adaptive streaming. In: ICASSP 2024-2024 IEEE International Conference on Acoustics, Speech and Signal Processing, pp. 3810–3814 (2024)
11. "Timed Text Markup Language." Wikipedia, The Free Encyclopedia. Wikimedia Foundation. https://en.wikipedia.org/wiki/Timed_Text_Markup_Language. Accessed 10 July 2024
12. Chang, Y., Zhang, W., Wang, H., et al.: Blind recognition of BCH and RS codes with small samples intercepted bitstream. IEEE Trans. Commun. (2023)

FARD: Fully Automated Railway Anomaly Detection System

Yichen Gao[1], Taocun Yang[2], and Wei Wang[1]($\boxtimes$)

[1] Beijing Jiaotong University, Beijing, China
wei.wang@bjtu.edu.cn
[2] Institute of Computing Technology, China Academy of Railway Sciences
Corporation Limited, Beijing, China

Abstract. Foreign object detection is crucial for railway safety, preventing accidents and ensuring smooth operations. Current railway foreign object detection methods face two significant challenges: the scarcity of annotated real-world data and the inability to adapt to complex scenarios. This paper proposes a novel FARD (Fully Automated Railway Anomaly Detection System) approach to address these issues. FARD incorporates two key components: (i) A Diffusion model with inpainting technique to generate a diverse and realistic auxiliary dataset of railway anomalies, effectively representing real-world outliers. (ii) An integrated framework combining traditional object detection pipeline with reconstruction-based anomaly detection module for robust foreign object detection in railway environments. Experimental results demonstrate that FRAD outperforms traditional object detection methods in identifying anomalies on rail tracks by a large margin. This research offers a robust, data-efficient solution for railway foreign object detection that works well even with limited initial data.

Keywords: Anomaly Detection · Railway Safety · Diffusion Models

1 Introduction

The safety and efficiency of railway systems are critical components of modern transportation infrastructure. With the increasing complexity and scale of the railway networks, the demand for reliable and accurate foreign object detection mechanisms has become increasingly urgent. Anomalies on rail tracks, ranging from Unexpected pedestrian and debris to more subtle irregularities, can lead to severe accidents, service disruptions, and significant economic losses. Traditional methods of track inspection and maintenance, while essential, are often time-consuming, labor-intensive, and prone to human error, especially when dealing with extensive railway networks.

Recent advancements in computer vision and machine learning offer promising new approaches for foreign object detection in railway systems [5,11,15,23]. However, these methods face two significant challenges in real-world railway

H. Li et al. (Eds.): ICSR + InnoBiz 2024, LNAI 15170, pp. 293–302, 2025.
https://doi.org/10.1007/978-981-96-1151-5_30

scenarios: 1) Limited Dataset Availability: Comprehensive and diverse datasets of railway anomalies are scarce, primarily due to the rarity of certain types of anomalies on the rail track. 2) Complexity of Real-World Scenarios: Railway environments contain a multitude of complex scenarios, including varying lighting conditions, diverse weather patterns, and the presence of shadows and reflections. Moreover, some reasonable anomalies (*e.g.* gravel under the railway track) introduce substantial interference to traditional object detection methods [7,9,22,27].

To address these issues, we propose FARD (Fully Automated Railway Anomaly Detection System). Our method consists of two key components: 1) Dataset Augmentation with Image Generation component: We leverage advanced AIGC techniques [6,8,19] to create a diverse dataset of railway anomalies. 2) Unsupervised Foreign Object Detection component in Complex Scenarios: We propose a novel hybrid framework that combines traditional object detection pipeline with unsupervised anomaly detection [12,14,25,26]. This integration leverages the strengths of both module: the ability of object detection to extract foreground objects and the capacity of unsupervised anomaly detection to capture abnormal changes.

2   Method

2.1   Dataset Augmentation with Image Generation

To overcome the scarcity of diverse railway anomaly data, we employ advanced diffusion model [17,18,21] to generate a rich dataset of synthetic anomalies.

Diffusion model inpainting [10,13] can be performed by sampling from the diffusion model as usual, but replacing the known region of the image with a sample from $q(x_t|x_0)$ after each sampling step. Here, $q(x_t|x_0)$ represents the conditional distribution of the noisy image x_t at diffusion timestep t, given the original image x_0.

We use the methodology and pre-trained model proposed by Glide [13] to perform inpainting on real-world images obtained from railway surveillance systems. Our objective was to generate a series of foreign objects within these images, simulating potential hazards in railway environments.

The pre-trained diffusion model builds upon the classifier guidance technique introduced by DrawBench [3], leveraging the CLIP [16] instead of a traditional classifier. CLIP provides a scalable method for learning joint representations between text and images, consisting of an image encoder $f(x)$ and a caption encoder $g(c)$. To perform inpainting, we perturb the reverse-process mean with the gradient of the dot product of the image and caption encodings with respect to the image:

$$\hat{\mu}_\theta(x_t|c) = \mu_\theta(x_t|c) + s \cdot \Sigma_\theta(x_t|c)\nabla_{x_t}(f(x_t) \cdot g(c)) \tag{1}$$

where c is the text prompt describing the desired anomaly.

This approach allows us to steer the diffusion model towards generating anomalies that align with the given text description, while maintaining the context of the railway surveillance image. The inpainting process involves identifying known regions within each input image and augmenting them with text prompts, which serve as conditional information to guide the generation of anomalies. The details are illustrated in Fig. 1.

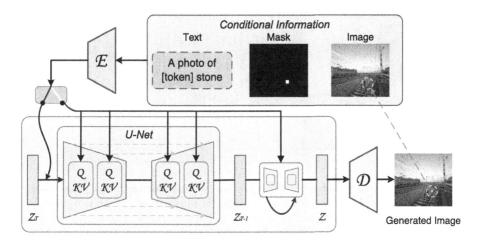

Fig. 1. Image Generation based Data Augmentation Framework. The framework consists of three main components: (i) Conditional Information (on the top), which includes a text prompt ("A photo of [token] stone"), a mask (black square with a small white area), and the original image of rail track. (ii) A U-Net architecture (on the bottom left) that processes the conditional information through multiple stages (Z_T to Z). (iii) The Generated Image (on the bottom right), which is the same as the input but with a stone edited onto the train tracks where the mask indicated. This system demonstrates how text prompts, masks, and original images can be combined to perform targeted, context-aware edits on specific areas of an image, enabling seamless integration of new elements like adding a stone to rail tracks.

By employing this text-guided inpainting technique, we synthesize a wide variety of contextually relevant anomalies, encompassing potential hazards such as unexpected pedestrians, debris, equipment malfunctions, and other obstacles that might pose risks in railway systems.

2.2 Unsupervised Foreign Object Detection for Complex Scenarios

In this section, we propose an innovative method for foreign object detection in railway systems, which consists of a specialized rail track locator and a reconstruction-based anomaly detector. This two-stage method aims to enhance the accuracy and efficiency of identifying foreign objects within railway environments. Our method is illustrated in Fig. 2.

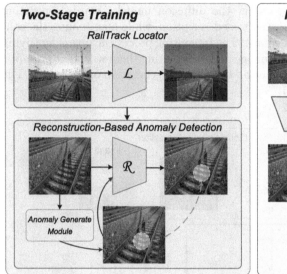 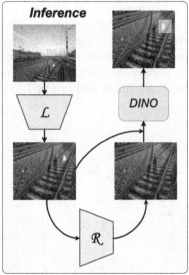

Fig. 2. The proposed two-stage method for Unsupervised Foreign Object Detection in Complex Scenarios. The left part illustrates the training process, which comprises two key components: (i) RailTrack Locator (L, in red), which learns to locate the rail track area, and (ii) Reconstruction-Based Anomaly Detection module (R, in red), which learns to reconstruct normal rail track images and detect anomalies. In the meanwhile, an Anomaly Generation Module simulates anomalous images in the training process. The right panel shows the inference process, where the trained L and R modules (now in blue, indicating frozen parameters) are applied sequentially. The pre-trained DINO [2], a detector, is employed to extract features which are then used to construct anomaly maps. The yellow box in output image indicates successful detection of foreign objects on the rail track. Note that red color indicates that the parameters in the module are updated during training process, blue color indicates that the parameters are frozen in the module. (Color figure online)

RailTrack Locator. We utilize YOLOv8[1] (You Only Look Once version 8), a state-of-the-art real-time object detection system, fine-tuned on our Rail Track Location Dataset. While its primary objective is to efficiently localize rail tracks within input images, it also serves to extract foreground information. Our experiments demonstrate that an effective rail track locator substantially enhances the performance of our railway foreign object detection framework (see Sect. 3.3 for detailed results).

Reconstruction-Based Anomaly Detection. We adopt the framework of GLAD [25], recognizing the critical importance of noise control in diffusion [8,20] model-based reconstruction. This approach addresses an inherent incompatibil-

---

[1] https://github.com/ultralytics/ultralytics

ity in the reconstruction process for anomaly detection, stemming from the principle that better reconstruction quality implies a lower value in our key equation:

$$\hat{x}_a - x \propto \sqrt{1 - \bar{\alpha}_t}(\varepsilon_a - \varepsilon) + \sqrt{\bar{\alpha}_t}n \to 0 \tag{2}$$

where $\bar{\alpha}_t$ is manually defined and negatively correlated with t, t represents the time step in the diffusion process; ε is a random noise; and n denotes the difference between x_a and x, i.e., $x_a = x + n$ (x represents the normal sample, x_a the abnormal sample).

Further analysis of this equation leads to a crucial insight:

$$\varepsilon_a \to \varepsilon - \frac{\sqrt{\bar{\alpha}_t}}{\sqrt{1 - \bar{\alpha}_t}}n \tag{3}$$

Given that $\varepsilon \sim \mathcal{N}(0, I)$ follows a standard Gaussian distribution, we can deduce that when anomalies exist (i.e., n is non-zero), ε_a necessarily deviates from the standard Gaussian distribution. This deviation presents a significant challenge for typical diffusion models (ε_θ) that are trained exclusively on normal samples and are thus constrained to predict noises following the standard Gaussian distribution.

To address this, we introduce anomalies during the training phase as well. This strategy enables our diffusion models to transcend the constraints of the standard Gaussian distribution and effectively fit the previous equation. Building upon this insight, the objective function is as follows:

$$L_{ATP} = E_{(x,x^a) \sim p_{data}, \epsilon \sim N(0,I), t}[(\epsilon - \frac{\sqrt{\alpha_t}}{\sqrt{1 - \alpha_t}}n) - \epsilon^a]_2]$$
$$= E_{(x,x^a) \sim p_{data}, \epsilon \sim N(0,I), t}[(\epsilon - \frac{\sqrt{\alpha_t}}{\sqrt{1 - \alpha_t}}(x^a - x)) - \epsilon_\theta(x_t^a, t)]_2] \tag{4}$$

To meet the requirement for corresponding normal samples for each anomaly in the learning objective, GLAD [25] adopt an innovative solution inspired by MemSeg [24] to synthesize abnormal samples from normal ones. This enables the training process to proceed in an unsupervised manner, addressing the data preparation challenge and enhancing the robustness and generalizability of our model.

Equation 4 generalizes the objective function of the original diffusion model. When dealing with normal regions, Eq. 4 degenerates to the original diffusion loss such that it maintains consistency with the original diffusion model. However, in abnormal regions, it predicts non-Gaussian noise, effectively reconstructing the corresponding normal regions.

3   Experiments

3.1   Experiments Set-Up

Dataset. Railway Surveillance Dataset: The Railway Surveillance Dataset consists of 1920×1080 color images of authentic surveillance images, which collectively spans diverse temporal and geographical settings, resulting in a total of 1,000 images.

Rail Track Location Dataset: The Railway Surveillance Dataset consists of 1920×1080 color images of authentic surveillance images, which collectively spans diverse temporal and geographical settings, each annotated with bounding boxes annotations of the rail location, resulting in a total of 891 images.

Model. Stable-Diffusion-Inpainting model: the model is initialized with the weights of Stable-Diffusion-v-1-2 [19]. The details are available at the url.[2]

Diffusion-Based Reconstruction Model: We use a pre-trained LDM [3] with a fine-tuned UNet [3] component for data reconstruction. For feature extraction, we employed DINO [2], a state-of-the-art vision transformer model with ViT-B/8 architecture. Specifically, we utilized features from layers 3, 6, 9, and 12 of the DINO model to construct comprehensive anomaly maps.

Evaluation Metrics. For anomaly detection, we utilize the image-level Area Under the Receiver Operating Characteristic curve (I-AUROC), and it is a widely used metric. To evaluate anomaly localization precision, we employ the pixel-level Area Under the Receiver Operating Characteristic curve (P-AUROC). Additionally, to facilitate comparison with traditional object detection methods, we introduce mean Average Precision at an Intersection over Union (IoU) threshold of 0.50 (mAP@0.50) and mean Average Precision across IoU thresholds from 0.50 to 0.95 (mAP@0.50:0.95).

3.2   Results

In this section, we present the performance comparison between traditional object detection models and our proposed method.

Table 1. Performance of FRAD. All values are reported in percentages.

Metric	I-AUROC	P-AUROC
FARD	100.0	78.1

The results of our reconstruction-based anomaly detection method are shown in Table 1. Our approach achieved an I-AUROC of 100.0% and an P-AUROC of

Table 2. Performance of Traditional Object Detection Models. All values are reported in percentages.

Model	mAP@0.50	mAP@0.50:0.95
Faster R-CNN [7]	79.3	36.3
Cascade R-CNN [1]	84.8	46.4
CenterNet [4]	59.1	18.3

78.1%, demonstrating superior performance of our approach in railway foreign object detection.

Table 2 illustrates the performance of traditional object detection models, namely RetinaNet and Faster R-CNN, on the same task. These results are presented using mean Average Precision (mAP) metrics at different IoU thresholds.

While the evaluation metrics differ between our method (AUROC) and traditional models (mAP), the magnitude of the difference in performance indicates the superior capability of our reconstruction-based approach. The high AUROC scores of our model suggest it can maintain high detection rates while minimizing false positives, even without any manually annotated images.

We can conclude that our FARD method outperforms traditional object detection models, especially in the challenging task of identifying small or unusual objects on rail tracks. This performance improvement holds great promise for enhancing safety and efficiency in railway operations.

3.3 Ablation Study

To thoroughly evaluate the effectiveness of our proposed framework, we conducted an ablation study focusing on the impact of the RailTrack Locator module as shown in Table 3.

Table 3. Ablation study results demonstrating the impact of the RailTrack Locator module. All values are reported in percentages.

Method	I-AUROC	P-AUROC
W/O RailTrack Locator	88.1	86.1
W RailTrack Locator	100.0	78.1

From Table 3, we can observe that with the integration of the RailTrack Locator module, a substantial improvement can be achieved. The remarkable improvement in I-AUROC (from 88.1% to 100.0%) underscores the RailTrack Locator module's critical role in enhancing the framework's ability to distinguish

---

[2] https://huggingface.co/runwayml/stable-diffusion-inpainting.

between normal and anomalous scenes. This demonstrates the importance of effectively isolating the rail track area for precise foreign object detection.

These results validate our hypothesis that combining specialized rail track localization with reconstruction-based anomaly detection enhances the overall performance of foreign object detection in railway environments.

4   Conclusion

This paper presents FARD, an efficient framework for foreign object detection in railway environments. Our experiments demonstrate that FARD outperforms traditional methods in detecting anomalies on rail tracks. The key contributions of our work include the novel use of image generation techniques for dataset augmentation and the integration of unsupervised anomaly detection with traditional object detection methods. While FARD has good performance in anomaly detection across various scenarios, there is still room for improvement in computational efficiency and precise object localization. Future work could focus on optimizing the model for real-time applications, enhancing its performance under extreme environmental conditions, and improving localization accuracy. By addressing these challenges, FARD has the potential to evolve into a more robust and practical tool for ensuring railway safety.

Funding Information. This study is supported by National NSF of China (No. 62372033), the Fundamental Research Funds for the Central Universities (No. 2022XKRC015) and China State Railway Group Co., Ltd. Science and Technology Research and Development Plan (No. P2023S001).

References

1. Cai, Z., Vasconcelos, N.: Cascade R-CNN: delving into high quality object detection. In: Proceedings of the IEEE Conference on Computer Vision and Pattern Recognition, pp. 6154–6162 (2018)
2. Caron, M., et al.: Emerging properties in self-supervised vision transformers. In: Proceedings of the IEEE/CVF International Conference on Computer Vision, pp. 9650–9660 (2021)
3. Dhariwal, P., Nichol, A.: Diffusion models beat GANs on image synthesis. In: Advances in Neural Information Processing Systems 34, pp. 8780–8794 (2021)
4. Duan, K., Bai, S., Xie, L., Qi, H., Huang, Q., Tian, Q.: CenterNet: keypoint triplets for object detection. In: Proceedings of the IEEE/CVF International Conference on Computer Vision, pp. 6569–6578 (2019)
5. Felzenszwalb, P.F., Girshick, R.B., McAllester, D., Ramanan, D.: Object detection with discriminatively trained part-based models. IEEE Trans. Pattern Anal. Mach. Intell. **32**(9), 1627–1645 (2009)
6. Gafni, O., Polyak, A., Ashual, O., Sheynin, S., Parikh, D., Taigman, Y.: Make-a-scene: scene-based text-to-image generation with human priors. In: European Conference on Computer Vision, pp. 89–106. Springer (2022)
7. Girshick, R.: Fast R-CNN. In: Proceedings of the IEEE International Conference on Computer Vision, pp. 1440–1448 (2015)

8. Ho, J., Jain, A., Abbeel, P.: Denoising diffusion probabilistic models. In: Advances in Neural Information Processing Systems 33, pp. 6840–6851 (2020)
9. Lin, T.Y., Goyal, P., Girshick, R., He, K., Dollár, P.: Focal loss for dense object detection. In: Proceedings of the IEEE international conference on computer vision. pp. 2980–2988 (2017)
10. Lugmayr, A., Danelljan, M., Romero, A., Yu, F., Timofte, R., Van Gool, L.: RePaint: inpainting using denoising diffusion probabilistic models. In: Proceedings of the IEEE/CVF Conference on Computer Vision and Pattern Recognition, pp. 11461–11471 (2022)
11. Mittal, S., Rao, D.: Vision based railway track monitoring using deep learning. arXiv preprint arXiv:1711.06423 (2017)
12. Mou, S., Gu, X., Cao, M., Bai, H., Huang, P., Shan, J., Shi, J.: Rgi: Robust gan-inversion for mask-free image inpainting and unsupervised pixel-wise anomaly detection. In: The Eleventh International Conference on Learning Representations (2023)
13. Nichol, A., et al.: GLIDE: towards photorealistic image generation and editing with text-guided diffusion models. arXiv preprint arXiv:2112.10741 (2021)
14. Pang, G., Shen, C., Cao, L., Hengel, A.V.D.: Deep learning for anomaly detection: a review. ACM Comput. Surv. (CSUR) 54(2), 1–38 (2021)
15. Pu, Y.R., Chen, L.W., Lee, S.H.: Study of moving obstacle detection at railway crossing by machine vision. Inf. Technol. J. 13(16), 2611–2618 (2014)
16. Radford, A., et al.: Learning transferable visual models from natural language supervision. In: International Conference on Machine Learning, pp. 8748–8763. PMLR (2021)
17. Ramesh, A., Dhariwal, P., Nichol, A., Chu, C., Chen, M.: Hierarchical text-conditional image generation with CLIP latents 1(2), 3. arXiv preprint arXiv:2204.06125 (2022)
18. Rombach, R., Blattmann, A., Lorenz, D., Esser, P., Ommer, B.: High-resolution image synthesis with latent diffusion models. In: Proceedings of the IEEE/CVF Conference on Computer Vision and Pattern Recognition, pp. 10684–10695 (2022)
19. Saharia, C., et al.: Photorealistic text-to-image diffusion models with deep language understanding. In: Advances in Neural Information Processing Systems 35, pp. 36479–36494 (2022)
20. Sohl-Dickstein, J., Weiss, E., Maheswaranathan, N., Ganguli, S.: Deep unsupervised learning using nonequilibrium thermodynamics. In: International Conference on Machine Learning, pp. 2256–2265. PMLR (2015)
21. Song, Y., Sohl-Dickstein, J., Kingma, D.P., Kumar, A., Ermon, S., Poole, B.: Score-based generative modeling through stochastic differential equations. arXiv preprint arXiv:2011.13456 (2020)
22. Viola, P., Jones, M.: Rapid object detection using a boosted cascade of simple features. In: Proceedings of the 2001 IEEE Computer Society Conference on Computer Vision and Pattern Recognition, CVPR 2001, vol. 1, p. I. IEEE (2001)
23. Wei, C.P., Huang, Y.M., Wang, Y.C.F., Shih, M.Y.: Background recovery in railroad crossing videos via incremental low-rank matrix decomposition. In: 2013 2nd IAPR Asian Conference on Pattern Recognition, pp. 702–706. IEEE (2013)
24. Yang, M., Wu, P., Feng, H.: MemSeg: a semi-supervised method for image surface defect detection using differences and commonalities. Eng. Appl. Artif. Intell. 119, 105835 (2023)
25. Yao, H., et al.: GLAD: towards better reconstruction with global and local adaptive diffusion models for unsupervised anomaly detection. arXiv preprint arXiv:2406.07487 (2024)

26. Zhang, X., Li, N., Li, J., Dai, T., Jiang, Y., Xia, S.T.: Unsupervised surface anomaly detection with diffusion probabilistic model. In: Proceedings of the IEEE/CVF International Conference on Computer Vision, pp. 6782–6791 (2023)
27. Zhao, Z.Q., Zheng, P., Xu, S.T., Wu, X.: Object detection with deep learning: a review. IEEE Trans. Neural Netw. Learn. Syst. **30**(11), 3212–3232 (2019)

M-Vec: Matryoshka Speaker Embeddings with Flexible Dimensions

Shuai Wang[1,2] , Pengcheng Zhu[3(✉)] , and Haizhou Li[1,2]

[1] Shenzhen Research Institute of Big Data, Shenzhen, China
{wangshuai,haizhouli}@cuhk.edu.cn
[2] School of Data Science, Chinese University of Hong Kong (Shenzhen), Shenzhen, India
[3] Fuxi AI Lab, NetEase Inc., Hangzhou, China
zhupengcheng@corp.netease.com

Abstract. Fixed-dimensional speaker embeddings have become the dominant approach in speaker modeling, typically spanning hundreds to thousands of dimensions. These dimensions are hyperparameters that are not specifically picked, nor are they hierarchically ordered in terms of importance. In large-scale speaker representation databases, reducing the dimensionality of embeddings can significantly lower storage and computational costs. However, directly training low-dimensional representations often yields suboptimal performance. In this paper, we introduce the Matryoshka speaker embedding, a method that allows dynamic extraction of sub-dimensions from the embedding while maintaining performance. Our approach is validated on the VoxCeleb dataset, demonstrating that it can achieve extremely low-dimensional embeddings, such as 8 dimensions, while preserving high speaker verification performance.

Keywords: Matryoshka representation learning · speaker embedding · low-dimensional · speaker verification

1 Introduction

1.1 Speaker Modeling for Human-Computer Interaction

Speech is one of the primary modalities for human-computer interaction and closely aligns with natural human-to-human communication methods. Voice interaction is suitable for various scenarios, including those where hands-free operation or visual impairment is necessary. Among the attributes of speech signals, the identity of the speaker is one of the most critical pieces of information. Preemptively identifying the speaker is a crucial step in delivering customized and personalized services. Speaker recognition in speech technology significantly enhances the intelligence, personalization, and security of human-computer interaction. Speaker recognition encompasses two tasks: speaker identification and speaker verification. Speaker identification selects the matching speaker from a list of candidates, while speaker verification determines if the registered and test voices are from the same person.

© The Author(s), under exclusive license to Springer Nature Singapore Pte Ltd. 2025
H. Li et al. (Eds.): ICSR + InnoBiz 2024, LNAI 15170, pp. 303–311, 2025.
https://doi.org/10.1007/978-981-96-1151-5_31

1.2   Background on Speaker Embedding Learning

Currently, speaker representation is primarily expressed using a fixed-dimensional embedding [10]. Before the advent of deep learning, this embedding was typically learned using factor analysis-based methods, with the corresponding representation known as the i-vector [5]. In the era of deep learning, neural networks are employed to compress the speech signal and extract speaker information. Generally, the entire neural network is trained with the optimization objective of speaker classification, ensuring that the extracted representation possesses sufficient speaker discriminability. Notable neural network frameworks include Time Delay Neural Networs (TDNN) [7,9], ResNet [6,8], and ECAPA-TDNN [11].

1.3   Extremely Low-Dimensional Embeddings

During large-scale database searches, the dimensionality of the representation directly influences the storage costs and is closely related to the efficiency of the search process. Consequently, many researchers are exploring ways to model information using the most compact vectors possible.

On the other hand, traditional i-vectors and subsequent deep speaker embeddings, such as i-vectors [5] with 400 or 600 dimensions, x-vectors [9] based on TDNN with 512 dimensions, or r-vectors [8] based on ResNet with 256 dimensions, are often set based on empirical values. Each dimension does not represent a specific meaning, and there is no distinction in importance, making it challenging to obtain low-dimensional representations by directly filtering the embedding dimensions. Li et al. [12] has trained an additional autoencoder for importance rearrangement to transform features, but this approach requires multiple stages in the extraction of speaker embeddings.

1.4   Contributions

In this paper, we introduce the concept of Matryoshka representation learning and apply it within the current mainstream AAM-loss learning framework. The main contribution can be sumarized as following,

1. We are the first to explore variable-dimensional speaker representations, where representations of different dimensions can be adapted to various related tasks.
2. We propose the training method Matryoshka Representation Learning (MRL), which enables simultaneous speaker discriminative training across multiple dimensions.
3. Our proposed structure significantly enhances the modeling capabilities of representations, even in extremely low-dimensional cases (e.g., 4-dimensional or 8-dimensional).

2 Matryoshka Embedding Learning

Traditional approaches typically employ fixed, full-sized embeddings for all tasks, disregarding the variations in resource constraints and requirements across different applications. This practice can result in computational inefficiency and poor scalability when dealing with the diverse resource availabilities in downstream scenarios. To address this challenge, Matryoshka Representation Learning (MRL) [1] introduces an innovative methodology: the concurrent training of multiple embeddings with nesting dimensions, thereby achieving scalable embedding sizes.

Inspired by Matryoshka dolls, where smaller dolls nest within larger ones, MRL similarly nests smaller embeddings within larger ones, enabling a single model to generate embeddings of varying sizes. This approach offers flexibility in computational resource utilization and adaptability to diverse application requirements.

2.1 Matryoshka Representation

The Matryoshka representation learning loss function for the first m dimensions is as follows:

$$\mathcal{L}_m = \min_{\{\mathbf{W}(m)\}_{m \in M}, \theta_F} \sum_{m \in M} c_m \cdot \mathcal{L}(\mathbf{W}(m) \cdot F(x; \theta_F)_{1:m}; y) \tag{1}$$

In this formula:

- $\mathbf{W}(m) \cdot F(x; \theta_F)_{1:m}$ represents feeding the first m dimensions of the embedding vector $F(x; \theta_F)_{1:m}$ to the linear classifier $\mathbf{W}(m)$ for classification.
- F is a feature extractor to transform input x to the embedding space.
- c_m is the loss weight for the first m dimensions.
- $\mathcal{L}$ is the multi-class cross-entropy loss function used to measure the difference between the classifier's output and the true label y.
- By minimizing this loss function, we can simultaneously optimize the neural network parameters θ_F and the weights of the linear classifiers $\{\mathbf{W}(m)\}_{m \in M}$ to ensure that the embedding vectors at different granularities have strong discriminative power.

2.2 MRL for Speaker Embedding Learning

In this work, we introduce the concept of Matryoshka Representation Learning (MRL) into the speaker embedding learning framework.

As shown in Fig. 1, the standard speaker representation extractor is illustrated in the left half of the figure. Frame-level features are extracted from wave files and encoded into frame-level deep features by a frame-level representation extractor, which maintains the temporal resolution. Next, a pooling layer is employed to aggregate frame-level features into segment-level features, which are subsequently projected to lower-dimensional speaker embeddings. The entire network is optimized for speaker classification loss, typically using functions from the softmax family, such as the original softmax or margin-based variants like AAM-softmax [13,14]. In this paper, we utilize AAM-Softmax.

In the improved system, by introducing the concept of MRL, we explicitly optimize the *nested sub-dimensions* of the entire speaker embedding. This approach allows for the flexible extraction of the first few dimensions as needed while maintaining performance. Specifically, we integrate the commonly employed AAM-Softmax loss function with the Matryoshka Representation Learning (MRL) framework. This novel loss function is then utilized to learn Matryoshka speaker embeddings.

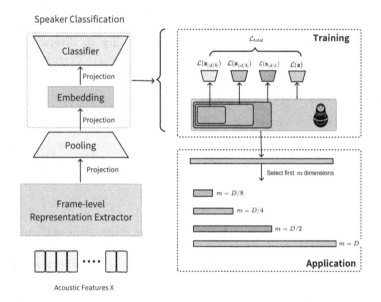

Fig. 1. Matryoshca Speaker Embedding Learning, we use 3 sub-dimensional embeddings as a illustration

AAM-Softmax (Additive Angular Margin Softmax) improves upon the standard Softmax loss by introducing an angular margin to enhance inter-class separation. The AAM-Softmax loss function with the embedding vector $\mathbf{e}$ and the margin k can be expressed as:

$$\mathcal{L}_{\text{AAM}} = -\frac{1}{N} \sum_{i=1}^{N} \log \frac{e^{s\left(\frac{\mathbf{w}_{y_i}^T \mathbf{e}_i}{\|\mathbf{w}_{y_i}\|\|\mathbf{e}_i\|} + k\right)}}{e^{s\left(\frac{\mathbf{w}_{y_i}^T \mathbf{e}_i}{\|\mathbf{w}_{y_i}\|\|\mathbf{e}_i\|} + k\right)} + \sum_{j \neq y_i} e^{s\frac{\mathbf{w}_j^T \mathbf{e}_i}{\|\mathbf{w}_j\|\|\mathbf{e}_i\|}}} \tag{2}$$

In this formula:

- $\mathbf{W}_{y_i}$ is the weight vector for the target class y_i.

- $\mathbf{W}_j$ are the weight vectors for the non-target classes.
- $\mathbf{e}_i$ is the embedding vector for the i-th sample.
- s is the scaling factor.
- k is the additive angular margin.

The MRL augmented version of AAM-softmax can be expressed as,

$$\mathcal{L}_m = \min_{\{\mathbf{W}(m)\}_{m \in M}, \theta_F} \sum_{m \in M} c_m \cdot \mathcal{L}_{\text{AAM}} \left(\mathbf{W}(m), \{\mathbf{e}_{i,1:m}\}_{i=1}^N, s, k \right) \tag{3}$$

where:

- $\mathcal{L}_{\text{AAM}} \left(\mathbf{W}(m), \{\mathbf{e}_{i,1:m}\}_{i=1}^N, s, k \right)$ is the AAM-Softmax loss function, which measures the difference between the classifier's output and the true label y. Specifically, the AAM-Softmax loss function is given by:

$$\mathcal{L}_{\text{AAM}} = -\frac{1}{N} \sum_{i=1}^N \log \frac{e^{s \left(\frac{\mathbf{W}_{y_i}(m)^T \mathbf{e}_{i,1:m}}{\|\mathbf{W}_{y_i}(m)\| \|\mathbf{e}_{i,1:m}\|} + k \right)}}{e^{s \left(\frac{\mathbf{W}_{y_i}(m)^T \mathbf{e}_{i,1:m}}{\|\mathbf{W}_{y_i}(m)\| \|\mathbf{e}_{i,1:m}\|} + k \right)} + \sum_{j \neq y_i} e^{s \frac{\mathbf{W}_j(m)^T \mathbf{e}_{i,1:m}}{\|\mathbf{W}_j(m)\| \|\mathbf{e}_{i,1:m}\|}}} \tag{4}$$

- $\mathbf{W}(m) \cdot \mathbf{e}_{i,1:m}$ represents feeding the first m dimensions of the embedding vector $\mathbf{e}_{i,1:m}$ to the linear classifier $\mathbf{W}(m)$ for classification.
- c_m is the loss weight for the first m dimensions.
- $\theta_{y_i}^m$ is the angle between the embedding $\mathbf{e}_{i,1:m}$ and the weight vector $\mathbf{W}_{y_i}(m)$ for the target class.
- θ_j^m are the angles between the embedding $\mathbf{e}_{i,1:m}$ and the weight vectors $\mathbf{W}_j(m)$ for all other classes.

3 Experiments

3.1 Dataset

The VoxCeleb dataset, introduced by Oxford University, has become one of the most extensively used text-independent speaker recognition datasets in the field. In this work, we adopt the "dev" partition of VoxCeleb2 as the training set and whole VoxCeleb1 as the test set. Equal error rate (EER) is used to evaluate the performance on the speaker verification task.

3.2 Experimental Setups

All experiments in this study were conducted using the `wespeaker` toolkit [2], adhering to the data preparation protocols outlined in its VoxCeleb recipe. Audio samples from the MUSAN dataset [4] served as additive noise sources, while simulated room impulse responses (RIRs)[1] were utilized to introduce reverberation effects. For each training set utterance, we applied either noise or reverberation

---

[1] https://www.openslr.org/28.

augmentation (but not both concurrently) with a probability of 0.6. Additionally, speed perturbation was performed by altering the speed of an utterance to 0.9x or 1.1x, with the resultant audio being treated as originating from new speakers due to the pitch shift caused by the augmentation.

Following data preparation, two baseline systems, TDNN and ResNet34 were implemented. Detailed optimization strategies for these systems can be found in the respective recipes provided by WeSpeaker[2].

For all experiments, we set c_m equally to 1, $M = \{8, 16, 32, 64, 128, 256\}$

3.3 Results and Analysis

The experimental results can be found in Table 2. As shown, the ResNet34 system significantly outperforms the TDNN system in full dimension scenarios. However, both systems exhibit similar performance when evaluated under extremely low-dimensional settings. We used the more powerful ResNet34 as main system for validate our algorithm, with the corresponding results represented by the "ResNet34-MRL".

Table 1. Performance Comparison Across Different Dimensions

Model	8	16	32	64	128	256
TDNN	18.99	10.59	7.526	4.971	3.068	2.579
ResNet34	18.78	10.41	5.733	2.499	1.420	**1.124**
ResNet34-MRL	**4.941**	**2.605**	**1.574**	**1.313**	**1.154**	1.153

To more intuitively demonstrate the performance of different systems at various embedding dimensions, we visualize the results from Table 1 in Fig. 2. It is evident that as the embedding dimension decreases, our proposed system, ResNet34-MRL, exhibits a significantly smoother performance curve.

Comparison of Embeddings with Different Dimensions. To more intuitively demonstrate the ability of the MRL method to preserve performance across different dimensions, we have visualized the results from Table 2 in Fig. 2. It is evident that, across all dimensions except the full-version, our proposed ResNet34-MRL method consistently outperforms the ResNet34 system. Particularly in low-dimensional scenarios, we do not observe the dramatic performance degradation seen in the baseline systems, further proving the effectiveness of our approach. For the full dimension of 256, we observe a slight performance degradation, with the EER increased from 1.124% to 1.153%

---

[2] https://github.com/wenet-e2e/wespeaker.

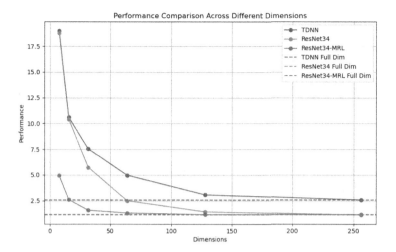

Fig. 2. Performance comparison of different systems using different dimensions

Extremely Low Dimensional Embeddings We would like to emphasize the relatively strong performance of dimensions lower than 32, highlighting the remarkable effectiveness of the MRL strategy in extremely low-dimensional settings. The 16-dimensional ResNet34-MRL embeddings achieve results comparable to the TDNN system using the full 256 dimensions, with an EER of 2.605%. Moreover, even in the extreme case of 8 dimensions, it achieves a relatively good performance with an EER of 4.941%.

3.4 Analysis on the Storage and Retivial Time

In the table below, we quantify the storage space usage and retrieval speed for different embedding dimensions. We utilized the Faiss library, a mature and widely adopted solution in many commercial systems, to demonstrate this point. The CPU version of Faiss[3] is used as the similarity-based search solution. The similarity measurement used is 'L2'[4] [5], and each time we retrieve the top 10 most similar entries for the given reference, from a database with *10 million* candidate embeddings. The CPU we used for running the Faiss tests is an 'Intel(R) Xeon(R) Silver 4210R CPU @ 2.40 GHz'.

By employing the Matryoshka speaker embedding strategy and selecting subdimensions, we can significantly reduce the demands on storage and computational resources. This approach not only helps lower storage costs but also enhances retrieval efficiency, making it highly valuable for constructing and querying large-scale speaker representation databases. The storage requirements

---

[3] https://github.com/facebookresearch/faiss.
[4] We first normalize all speaker embeddings and then do the L2 distance computation, which is equivalent to the cosine similarity.
[5] https://github.com/facebookresearch/faiss/wiki/MetricType-and-distances.

Table 2. Comparison of Storage and Retrieval Time under Different Dimensions

Dimension	Storage (MB)	Retrieval Time (ms)	Δ Storage (%)↓	Δ Retrieval Time (%)↓
256	9765.62	759.31	0.00	0.00
128	4882.81	377.42	50.00	50.29
64	2441.41	194.01	75.00	74.45
32	1220.70	115.18	87.50	84.83
16	610.35	76.86	93.75	89.88
8	305.18	47.46	96.88	93.75

are linearly related to the embedding dimensions, and retrieval efficiency based on similarity comparisons follows a similar linear relationship.

4 Conclusion

In this paper, we propose the Matryoshka speaker embedding learning strategy, which allows users to flexibly customize the embedding dimensions during inference without the need to retrain the model. We also ensure the discriminability of the representations at extremely low dimensions. On the VoxCeleb1 test set, using only an 8-dimensional embedding, we achieve an EER of 4.9%, and with a 16-dimensional embedding, we achieve an EER of 2.6%. This strategy can be extended to any speaker encoder. The extremely low-dimensional representations learned through our method can significantly reduce storage requirements and retrieval times.

Acknowledgments. This work is supported by Internal Project of Shenzhen Research Institute of Big Data under grant No. T00120220002 and No. J00220230014; and CCF-NetEase ThunderFire Innovation Research Funding (No. CCF-Netease 202302).

References

1. Kusupati, A., Bhatt, G., Rege, A., et al.: Matryoshka representation learning. Adv. Neural. Inf. Process. Syst. **35**, 30233–30249 (2022)
2. Wang, H., Liang, C., Wang, S., et al. Wespeaker: a research and production oriented speaker embedding learning toolkit. In: ICASSP 2023-2023 IEEE International Conference on Acoustics, Speech and Signal Processing (ICASSP), pp. 1–5. IEEE (2023)
3. Wang, S., Chen, Z., Han, B., et al. Advancing speaker embedding learning: wespeaker toolkit for research and production. Speech Commun. 103104 (2024)
4. Snyder, D., Chen, G., Povey, D.: Musan: a music, speech, and noise corpus. arXiv preprint arXiv:1510.08484 (2015)
5. Dehak, N., Kenny, P.J., Dehak, R., et al.: Front-end factor analysis for speaker verification. IEEE Trans. Audio Speech Lang. Process. **19**(4), 788–798 (2010)

6. He, K., Zhang, X., Ren, S., et al.: Deep residual learning for image recognition. In: Proceedings of the IEEE Conference on Computer Vision and Pattern Recognition, pp. 770-778 (2016)
7. Peddinti, V., Povey, D., Khudanpur, S.: A time delay neural network architecture for efficient modeling of long temporal contexts. Interspeech. 3214–3218 (2015)
8. Zeinali H, Wang S, Silnova A, et al.: But system description to voxceleb speaker recognition challenge 2019. arXiv preprint arXiv:1910.12592 (2019)
9. Snyder, D., Garcia-Romero, D., Sell, G., et al.: X-vectors: Robust dnn embeddings for speaker recognition. In: 2018 IEEE International Conference on Acoustics, Speech and Signal Processing (ICASSP), pp. 5329-5333. IEEE (2018)
10. Wang, S., Chen, Z., Lee, K.A., et al.: Overview of speaker modeling and its applications: from the lens of deep speaker representation learning. arXiv preprint arXiv:2407.15188 (2024)
11. Desplanques, B., Thienpondt, J., Demuynck, K.: Ecapa-tdnn: emphasized channel attention, propagation and aggregation in tdnn based speaker verification. arXiv preprint arXiv:2005.07143 (2020)
12. Li, L., Xing, C., Wang, D., et al.: Binary speaker embedding. In: 2016 10th International Symposium on Chinese Spoken Language Processing (ISCSLP), pp. 1–4. IEEE (2016)
13. Deng, J., Guo, J., Xue, N., et al.: Arcface: additive angular margin loss for deep face recognition. In: Proceedings of the IEEE/CVF Conference on Computer Vision and Pattern Recognition, pp. 4690–4699 (2019)
14. Xiang, X., Wang, S., Huang, H., et al.: Margin matters: Towards more discriminative deep neural network embeddings for speaker recognition. In: 2019 Asia-Pacific Signal and Information Processing Association Annual Summit and Conference (APSIPA ASC), pp. 1652–1656. IEEE (2019)

Complex Instruction Translation Using Fine-Tuned Large Language Models

Minhazul Arefin⬤, Dang Tran⬤, and Hongsheng He⁽✉⁾⬤

The University of Alabama, Tuscaloosa, AL 35487, USA
`hongsheng.he@ua.edu`

Abstract. Artificial Intelligence has made great progress in the area of Natural Language Processing, in the area of Human-Robot Interaction. The use of controlled robot language is an essential component in the process of enabling robots to comprehend and carry out human directions with pinpoint accuracy. The purpose of this work is to provide a framework that utilizes supervised fine-tuning of large language models in order to increase the accuracy of translation from natural language to Controlled Robot Language. This strategy considerably improves the dependability and effectiveness of human-robot interactions, as demonstrated by our extensive experimental investigation. The results of this study suggest that our methodology has the potential to result in more reliable robotic systems, which would be beneficial to the field of Human-Robot Interaction.

Keywords: Natural Language Processing · Human Robot Interaction · Machine Translation

1 Introduction

Natural Language Processing has become a foundational component of Artificial Intelligence. It enables machines to comprehend and interact effectively with human language. Over the past decade, significant strides have been made in natural language processing, enabling machines to perform complex tasks such as language translation, sentiment analysis, and conversational dialogue with unprecedented accuracy. Among these applications of natural language processing, the translation of natural language into Controlled Robot Language (CRL) stands out due to its potential to revolutionize human-robot interaction. Robots are increasingly becoming an integral part of various industries, including manufacturing, healthcare, logistics, and domestic services. For robots to function effectively in these diverse environments, they must be able to interpret and execute human commands accurately. This necessitates the development of a robust communication framework that bridges the gap between natural human language and the precise, unambiguous instructions required by robots. It will

This research was funded by NSF grant #2420355.

H. Li et al. (Eds.): ICSR + InnoBiz 2024, LNAI 15170, pp. 312–322, 2025.
https://doi.org/10.1007/978-981-96-1151-5_32

provide a formalized structure for translating human commands into executable robotic actions.

The Controlled Robot Language [1] is an efficient language to control robots more accurately. The base of the controlled robot language is the trustworthy robot commands followed by the semantic description. It will be used to command the robot to complete its task more efficiently and accurately. This formal grammar has the backbone of Attemptto Controlled English [2], which means it covers a variety of instructions. The controlled robot language grammar rigorously examines the syntax of commands and converts them into first-order logic, focusing on the semantic integrity of the human instructions. For that reason, the conversion helps humans command their natural language [3]. The robot can follow it accurately and reliably. This results in more dependable and efficient for human-robot interactions.

Several obstacles must be overcome to translate natural language into controlled robot language successfully. The main challenge is the use of natural language which is ambiguous, dependent on the surrounding context, and frequently imprecise. The execution of robotic commands, on the other hand, must be accurate, context-free, and explicit to guarantee dependable performance. Furthermore, a considerable obstacle is presented by the wide variety of expressions that are found in natural language. It is possible for humans to communicate the same directive in a variety of different ways, each of which has a little different meaning and context. In order for a translation system to be effective, it must be able to comprehend these changes and precisely generate the controlled robot language instructions that correspond to them. In order to accomplish this, it is necessary to make use of sophisticated machine learning models, in particular large language models, which have shown exceptional proficiency in comprehending and producing human language.

The purpose of this work is to solve the difficulty of translating commands from natural language into controlled robot language in order to increase the accuracy and dependability of interactions between humans and robots. Due to the fact that natural language is frequently imprecise and dependent on context, it is challenging for robots to accurately interpret and carry out commands. The authors offer an approach that makes use of supervised fine-tuning of large language models in order to improve the accuracy of these translations. This will ultimately result in an increase in the efficiency with which robotic systems comprehend and carry out human directions. The main contributions of this paper are:

1. We implemented a supervised fine-tuning algorithm to optimize language model performance for translating natural language to controlled robot language.
2. We enhanced the reliability and effectiveness of human-robot interaction by improving command translation accuracy.

By addressing the challenges of translating natural language into controlled robot language through the innovative application of supervised fine-tuning, this paper aims to enhance the accuracy and reliability of human-robot interactions, paving the way for more effective robotic systems.

2 Related Work

A new framework [4] was proposed that fine tuned the large language to improve the training efficiency of text-based reinforcement learning agents [5,6]. Aligning the semantic representations of the language models with the reward structure of the reinforcement learning environment helps the agent to better understand and respond to text-based inputs. Fine-tuning, can cause semantic degeneration— where the ability of the language model to generalize to fresh or changed text inputs is reduced. Their proposed system improved text-based reinforcement learning agent's task-specific performance and training efficiency. Semantic degeneration is a drawback, nevertheless, which can be resolved with the development of fine-tuning techniques preserving overall semantic knowledge.

An automatic translation framework [7] was proposed for the Spanish natural language to control robot commands [8]. The main backbone of this machine translation technique was the Long short-term memory-based neural network. Their proposed system magnificently applied Long short-term memory neural network for this task which improves its accuracy. One more reason for their higher accuracy is to use the attention mechanism. Their system has some limitations with limited data, artificial training corpus, and end-of-sentence identification. This problem leads their model to degrade the accuracy of the translation for complex sentences.

Robot Control Language [9] a new logic based control structure was suggest that can control robots more smoothly. This language is inspired by different types of task execution systems such as PRS [10], RPL [11], and GOLEX [12]. Robot control language used Lamba calculus often represented as a LISP-like format to execute the accurate instruction. It can handle complete control structures using probabilistic parsing such as Combinatory Categorial Grammars [13]. It has a limited language corpus that creates a problem for local error recovery.

Generative Adversarial Network [14] framework can enhance Grammatical Error Correction systems. A Transformer model is trained to generate syntactically accurate sentences from incorrect ones. At the same time, a deep neural network is trained to differentiate between phrases generated by humans and those generated by the model.

3 Complex Instruction Translation Framework

The Complex Instruction Translation Framework employs supervised fine-tuning of large language models to convert natural language instructions into controlled robotic language. For each batch of data, the model generates predictions, which are evaluated by the loss function. The framework for this fine-tuning process is illustrated in Fig. 1. This structured approach ensures fine-tuning techniques effectively supervise the model.

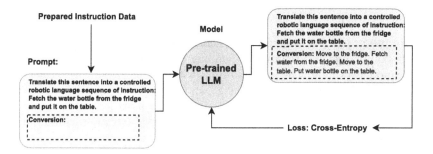

Fig. 1. Framework for the translation process.

This Algorithm 1 illustrates the supervised fine-tuning process of a large language model. It starts with data preprocessing. Then, it moves through the forward pass to compute predictions and the backward pass to update model parameters. Finally, the process ends with the creation of a fine-tuned model.

Algorithm 1. Supervised Fine-Tuning

```
 1: function SUPERVISED_FINE_TUNE(model, data, num_epochs)
 2:     for epoch = 1 to num_epochs do
 3:         for batch in data do
 4:             # Preprocess inputs and extract targets
 5:             inputs ← preprocess(batch.inputs)
 6:             targets ← batch.targets
 7:             # Forward pass: compute predictions and loss
 8:             predictions ← model(inputs)
 9:             loss ← compute_loss(predictions, targets)
10:             # Backward pass: compute gradients and update parameters
11:             loss.backward()
12:             optimizer.step()
13:             # Clear gradients for the next iteration
14:             optimizer.zero_grad()
15:         end for
16:     end for
17:     return model
18: end function
```

The Algorithm 1 uses *preprocess* function that handles the pre-processing of the input data. Before each batch is processed by the model, the inputs are passed through *preprocess* to ensure the correct batch format for the model. The rest of the process remains the same, ensuring that the model is trained with pre-processed data.

3.1   Data Pre-processing

The data pre-processing system is an essential step in preparing the raw natural language commands and their corresponding controlled robot language instructions for model training. The process begins with tokenization, where the Google T5 tokenizer converts the input text x_i and target text y_i into sequences of token IDs. Each sequence is then standardized to a fixed length L_{max} through padding and truncation, ensuring uniform input sizes by adding padding tokens to shorter sequences or truncating longer ones. Attention masks are generated to distinguish between actual data and padding within each sequence, guiding the model to focus on relevant tokens during training. This organized structure ensures that data is efficiently fed into the model in mini-batches, optimizing the training process and enhancing the overall effectiveness of the model fine-tuning.

3.2   Base Large Language Model

The model was initialized using pre-trained weights, denoted as θ_{pre}. These weights were derived from extensive training on large-scale text datasets, which allowed the model to capture rich linguistic patterns and general language knowledge. By leveraging these pre-trained weights, the model begins the fine-tuning process with a strong foundation, effectively utilizing the prior knowledge embedded in θ_{pre}. The primary objective during model initialization is to prepare the large language model to learn the specific translation task by minimizing a loss function that measures the discrepancy between the predicted controlled robot language sequence and the actual target sequence. According to the following lose function (1), the large language model is structured to minimize the pre-training loss,

$$\mathcal{L}_{pre}(\theta_{pre}) = -\sum_{t=1}^{T} \log P(y_t|y_{<t}, x; \theta_{pre}) \tag{1}$$

where, T represents the total length of the output sequence, i.e., the number of tokens in the controlled robot language instruction, y_t denotes the target token at the t-th position in the sequence and, $y_{<t}$ indicates all tokens before position t, which the model uses as context to predict y_t. The input sequence is x, which in this context is the natural language command provided to the model. The probability is $P(y_t|y_{<t}, x; \theta_{pre})$ assigned by the model to the target token y_t given the preceding tokens and the input sequence.

The loss function $\mathcal{L}_{pre}(\theta_{pre})$ thus quantifies how well the model's predicted sequence matches the target sequence. During training, the loss is minimized. This improves the model parameters (θ). As a result, the predictions become more accurate. It also ensures more reliable translations of natural language into controlled robotic language. The model is prepared for fine-tuning to improve its translation task performance after this initialization stage.

3.3   Model Fine Tuning

The fine-tuning process involves adjusting the pre-trained large language model's parameters θ to minimize the discrepancy between the predicted controlled robot language sequences and the actual target sequences. During fine-tuning, the model is trained on the specific dataset consisting of natural language commands paired with their corresponding controlled robot language instructions. As detailed in Eq. (2), the goal is to enhance the model's performance for this specific translation task, which is accomplished by minimizing the cross-entropy loss function:

$$\mathcal{L}(\theta) = \sum_{i=1}^{|D_{train}|} \sum_{t=1}^{T} \log P(y_t | y_{<t}, x; \theta) \tag{2}$$

where, D_{train} is the training dataset, T is the length of the controlled robot language sequence, y_t is the target token at position t, and $P(y_t | y_{<t}, x_i; \theta)$ represents the probability of the model predicting the correct token y_t given the preceding tokens and the input sequence x_i. The fine-tuning process is conducted over multiple epochs, with the model's performance evaluated on a validation set after each epoch. The learning process includes techniques such as gradient accumulation and mixed-precision training to enhance efficiency and manage computational resources effectively in the fine-tuning process. The final model parameters θ_{fine}, which have been optimized for the specific translation task. This involves saving both the fine-tuned model and the tokenizer, ensuring that the entire system can be reloaded and deployed for real-world applications without retraining. The saved model retains the ability to generalize from the fine-tuned dataset, making it capable of accurately translating new natural language commands into controlled robot language instructions.

4   Experiment

To evaluate the performance of the translation model, we conducted two experiments. The first experiment assessed the accuracy and generality of the fine-tuning method for the translation problem. The evaluation can determine whether the fine-tuned large language model could learn to translate natural language into controlled robot language. The experiment was developed and validated using a specially designed data, which is collected from real-world robotic planning scenarios. The second experiment evaluated the model's performance in a robotic environment, measuring the method's stability and practicality. Additionally, this second experiment provided insights into the operational effectiveness of the model under varying conditions and stress tests to simulate real-time decision-making by robots.

4.1   Experimental Setup

Experiment 1: To evaluate the accuracy of the translation method, we first train proposed large language models on our collected specific dataset, which was developed from real-world robotic planning scenarios. The dataset includes two features: 1) *input* based on natural language and 2) the appropriate *target* based on the controlled robot language grammar. The dataset consisted of 1,000 pairs of input and target texts and was split with a 70–30 training-to-validation ratio. To fine-tune large language models on the local machine, a finite maximum sentence length must be set. To identify this value, we conducted a statistical analysis on both the input and output of the dataset. Both the input and target text length distributions are shown in Fig. 2. The left histogram shows the distribution of input text lengths, which has a fairly symmetrical peak of around 55 characters. The right histogram depicts the distribution of target text lengths, also exhibiting symmetry and peaking at approximately 90 characters.

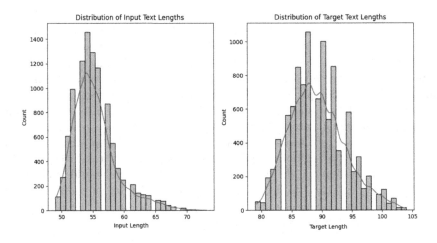

Fig. 2. Distribution of input and target text lengths.

In our experiments, we compared the performance of two large language models during the fine-tuning process: T5-base and LLaMA-2, both selected for their strong performance in natural language processing tasks. The fine-tuning was conducted over 10 epochs with an initial learning rate of $3e-5$, chosen based on preliminary tests that balanced effective learning with training stability. The model has a batch size of 8 for both training and evaluation. To manage the learning rate, 500 warmup steps are included, and a weight decay of 0.01 is applied to regularize the model. Logging and evaluation are performed every 500 steps and at the end of each epoch, respectively.

The accuracy performance of the trained large language models was evaluated using BERTScore [15]. BERTScore is an advanced statistic used to assess the quality of generated text by comparing it to a reference text. BERTScore utilizes the strength of deep contextual embeddings from models that depend on exact n-gram matches. BERTScore calculates the *cosine* similarity between the word embeddings of each word in the generated sentence $g = [g_1, g_2, \ldots, g_m]$ and the reference sentence $r = [r_1, r_2, \ldots, r_n]$. The precision (3), recall (4), and F1 score (5) for BERTScore are then computed.

$$P_{CRL} = \frac{1}{m} \cdot \sum_{g \in \mathbf{g}} \max_{r \in \mathbf{r}} \cos(E(g), E(r)) \tag{3}$$

$$R_{CRL} = \frac{1}{n} \cdot \sum_{r \in \mathbf{r}} \max_{g \in \mathbf{g}} \cos(E(r), E(g)) \tag{4}$$

$$F1 = \frac{2 \times P_{CRL} \times R_{CRL}}{P_{CRL} + R_{CRL}} \tag{5}$$

where, $E(x)$ denotes the process of embedding the word x. BERTScore is highly proficient in capturing both the syntactic structure and semantic substance of the text, rendering it a versatile metric for evaluating activities such as text production, where significance and fluency are paramount.

Experiment 2: To evaluate the model performance on the real robot system, we integrated the framework into a manipulation robot experiment. The robot system consists of a Rethink Sawyer robot equipped with a MagicHand [16]. The simulation of the system was developed in ROS Noetic and contains four executable actions: *move*, *grasp*, *release*, and *put*. These actions are triggered when users input the correct controlled robotic language commands we integrated the fine-tuned model into the controlled robot language framework [17], enabling users to provide instructions in natural language. The output from the translation model is sent to the controlled robotic language framework.

4.2   Results

Experiment 1: Table 1 represents the performance of fine-tuned models across various metrics. The $t5-base$ model consistently outperformed $Llama2$ across all metrics after fine-tuning, with higher precision, recall, and F1 scores. For example, $t5 - base$ achieved a BERTScore precision of 0.943 compared to $Llama2$'s 0.914. This suggests that $t5 - base$ was better at adhering to the controlled robot language grammar and producing accurate translations. The differences in performance could be attributed to the architectural strengths of $t5 - base$ in handling text-to-text tasks, which aligns well with the requirements of controlled robot language translation.

Experiment 2: The experiments depicted in the provided image demonstrate the system's capability to execute complex tasks based on natural language commands. For example, the command was to "Pick up the ball from the desk and put it left of the box." The robot successfully executed this instruction in a sequence of actions: initially positioning itself, grabbing the ball, moving towards the box, and finally placing the ball to the left of the box. In the simulation presented in Fig. 3, our robot could not move. So for that, we renamed any

Table 1. Comparison of different models.

Metric	Before Fine-Tuning		After Fine-Tuning	
	t5-base	Llama-2	t5-base	Llama-2
Precision	0.84	0.817	0.943	0.914
Recall	0.88	0.895	0.947	0.921
F1 Score	0.85	0.854	0.944	0.917

kind of movement command as the initial position. This adjustment in terminology was essential to maintain consistency in our testing protocol and ensure that each action could be distinctly identified and evaluated, particularly when movement capabilities were restricted due to simulation constraints. It also helped in aligning the programmed responses with the robot's current operational limits, providing a clear framework for future enhancements and troubleshooting.

Input (NL): Pick up the ball from the desk and put it left of the box
Output (CRL valid): Grasp the ball. Move to the box. Put the ball left of the box.

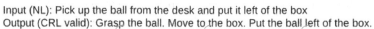
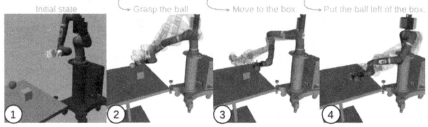

Fig. 3. Task Execution After the Translation Process.

The experimental results show that our system accurately translates natural language instructions into precise actions followed by controlled robot language. It maintains the correct sequence and spatial relations described by the user. Natural language processing enables the robot to interpret and execute complex instruction. This makes our approach suitable for real-world applications. Reliable and precise human-robot interaction is crucial in these scenarios.

5   Conclusion

The comparison of the models reveals that our model consistently performs better across different evaluation parameters. This methodology generates language that is more closely aligned with the reference material, both structurally and semantically. The proposed methodology has some limitations, including the quantity of the dataset. Furthermore, the dataset was based on specified activities. In the future, we plan to add more tasks and statements with it's real-world application. The model's improved performance in capturing the intended meaning while keeping the integrity of the original content demonstrates its usefulness in creating high-quality, trustworthy outputs. As a result, this model is better suited to tasks requiring precise and meaningful text creation, making it a better option for such applications.

References

1. Tran, D., Yan, F., Yihun, Y., Tan, J., He, H.: A framework of controlled robot language for reliable human-robot collaboration. In: Li, H., et al. (eds.) ICSR 2021. LNCS (LNAI), vol. 13086, pp. 339–349. Springer, Cham (2021). https://doi.org/10.1007/978-3-030-90525-5_29
2. Fuchs, N.E., Schwitter, R.: Attempto controlled English (ACE). arXiv preprint cmp-lg/9603003 (1996)
3. Bisk, Y., Yuret, D., Marcu, D.: Natural language communication with robots. In: Proceedings of the 2016 Conference of the North American Chapter of the Association for Computational Linguistics: Human Language Technologies, pp. 751–761 (2016)
4. Gruppi, M., et al.: On the effects of fine-tuning language models for text-based reinforcement learning. arXiv preprint arXiv:2404.10174 (2024)
5. Murugesan, K., et al.: Text-based RL agents with commonsense knowledge: new challenges, environments and baselines (2021a)
6. Ziegler, D.M., et al.: Fine-tuning language models from human preferences. arXiv preprint arXiv:1909.08593 (2019)
7. Suárez Bonilla, F., Ruiz Ugalde, F.: Automatic translation of Spanish natural language commands to control robot comands based on LSTM neural network. In: 2019 Third IEEE International Conference on Robotic Computing (IRC), Naples, Italy, pp. 125–131 (2019). https://doi.org/10.1109/IRC.2019.00026
8. Matuszek, C.: Learning to parse natural language commands to a robot control system. Int. Symp. Exp. Robot. (ISER) (2012)
9. Matuszek, C., et al.: Learning to parse natural language commands to a robot control system. In: Experimental robotics: the 13th International Symposium on Experimental Robotics. Springer International Publishing (2013)
10. Ingrand, F., Chatila, R., Alami, R., Robert, F.: PRS: a high level supervision and control language for autonomous mobile robots. In Proceedings of the IEEE International Conference on Robotics & Automation (ICRA) (1996)
11. Beetz, M., et al.: Integrated plan-based control of autonomous service robots in human environments. IEEE Intell. Syst. **16**(5) (2001)
12. Hähnel, D., Burgard, W., Lakemeyer, G.: GOLEX - bridging the gap between logic (GOLOG) and a real robot. In Proceedings of the German Conference on Artificial Intelligence (KI), Germany (1998)
13. Steedman, M., Baldridge, J.: Combinatory categorial grammar, pp. 181–224. Formal and Explicit Models of Grammar, Non-Transformational Syntax (2011)
14. Raheja, V., Alikaniotis, aD.: Adversarial grammatical error correction. arXiv preprint arXiv:2010.02407 (2020)
15. Zhang, T., Kishore, V., Wu, F., Weinberger, K.Q., Artzi, Y.: Bertscore: evaluating text generation with bert. arXiv preprint arXiv:1904.09675 (2019)

16. Li, H., Tan, J., He, H.: MagicHand: context-aware dexterous grasping using an anthropomorphic robotic hand. IN: 2020 IEEE International Conference on Robotics and Automation (ICRA), Paris, France, pp. 9895–9901 (2020). https://doi.org/10.1109/ICRA40945.2020.9196538
17. Tran, D., Li, H., He, H.: AI planning from natural-language instructions for trustworthy human-robot communication. In: Ali, A.A., et al. Social Robotics. ICSR 2023. Lecture Notes in Computer Science, vol. 14454. Springer, Singapore (2024). https://doi.org/10.1007/978-981-99-8718-4_22

Autonomous Multi-Robot Action Planning Through Controlled Robot Language

Dang Tran[1], Minhazul Arefin[1], Zhengchen Zhang[2],
and Hongsheng He[1(✉)]

[1] The University of Alabama, Tuscaloosa, AL 35487, USA
hongsheng.he@ua.edu
[2] Infocomm Technology Cluster, Singapore Institute of Technology, Singapore,
Singapore

Abstract. Interacting with multiple robots presents significant challenges for non-experts, especially in systems requiring concurrent behaviors. This paper introduces a plan generation method for multi-robot systems using Controlled Robot Language. The framework generates planning scripts with temporal constraints from large complex instructions, incorporating contextual awareness and resolving conflicts through mutual exclusivity expressions. Subjects, objects, and action parameters are extracted from the instructions and are grounded into robotic actions. Through linguistic evaluations and real-time experiments, the framework demonstrates its robustness in language comprehension and the ability to capture and provide temporal solutions for multi-robot planning. This work contributes to the accessibility and usability of multi-robot communication for non-experts using natural language.

Keywords: Planning · Natural Language Processing · Human Robot Interaction · Multiple Robot System

1 Introduction

Multiple robot planning, inspired by biological systems, addresses complex tasks beyond individual robot capabilities. However, interacting with these systems often requires expertise, limiting accessibility for non-experts. In this paper, we propose a communication framework using natural language commands to enable effective interaction with a multi-robot team. This approach aims to enhance accessibility for non-experts in multi-robot controls, bridging the gap between robotic teams and human operators.

Communicating with multi-robot teams using natural language presents challenges beyond typical linguistic platforms. Besides addressing language ambiguities, expressivity, and domain generality, multi-robot planning interfaces must

This work was supported by NSF 2327313 and Alabama EPSCoR Graduate Research Scholars Program Fellowship.

H. Li et al. (Eds.): ICSR + InnoBiz 2024, LNAI 15170, pp. 323–333, 2025.
https://doi.org/10.1007/978-981-96-1151-5_33

accommodate concurrency and mutual awareness. Concurrency allows simultaneous actions for complex operations, which enables multiple robots to collaborate. Mutual awareness, on the other hand, allows robots to understand the environment of itself and other robots, to avoid conflicts during planning and execution. These requirements significantly increase the complexity of multi-robot planning compared to single-robot domains.

While linguistic communication for individual robots has been explored [1,4], multi-robot communication remains a challenge. As the number of agents increases, the existing methods struggle to interpret instructions. This highlights the need for new approaches for multi-robot communication. Multi-robot communication was first addressed using the Generalized Grounding Graph approach, which can directly convert linguistic symbols into robotic actions [7]. However, the method primarily recognizes symbolic tokens, and overlooks syntactic and semantic structures, limiting its use in complex planning. To address this issue, a temporal logic framework for complex planning problems was proposed [6]. However, the method requires formal syntax inputs and a deep understanding of temporal logic. Additionally, temporal constraints are described in these methods using programming syntax, which is not intuitive for non-expert operators.

In this paper, we proposed a linguistic-based plan generation framework for multi-robot teams, using Controlled Robot Language (CRL). Extending from our prior work for individual robot platforms [8,9], this approach generates deterministic planning scripts from complex large-scale commands. The framework incorporates sophisticated capabilities to describe temporal constraints and mutual exclusivity (mutex) expressions. The generated plan is complete and comprehensible by temporal solvers, which eliminates the need for extensive postprocessing or human intervention. The contributions of this paper are:

1. We developed a CRL-based plan generation framework for multi-robot teams, which can comprehend complex, large-scale linguistic instructions. The proposed framework addresses critical requirements of concurrency and contextual awareness in multi-agent planning.
2. We demonstrated the robustness and applicability of the framework on real-time multi-robot simulation, emphasizing the need of context-aware communication methods for effective multi-robot navigation.

2 Plan-Generation for Multi-Robot Team

The general workflow of CRL-based framework for plan generation is visualized in Fig. 1. Given large contextual instructions in natural language, the framework returns deterministic semantics in the form of discourse representation structure (DRS). Information blocks are extracted from semantics, including temporal constraints and mutex expressions. The extract semantics are used to construct a complete Planning Domain Definition Language (PDDL) planning script, which is directly interpretable by the temporal solvers, and triggers the corresponding controls on each robot.

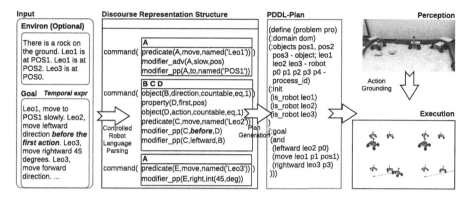

Fig. 1. CRL-based plan generation framework for multi-robot control.

2.1 Controlled Robot Language Parsing

A multi-layer CRL pipeline [8] is applied to construct semantics from the large-scale linguistic inputs. CRL can provide both syntactic and semantic analysis of the natural language. Developed using over 300 Context Free Grammar rules, CRL syntax covers lots of natural language expressions used in human-robot interaction. The CRL contains multiple preprocessing layers to analyze syntax, detect typographical errors, and automatically translate original instructions into a more suitable format that CRL semantic parser can understand. Given valid CRL-syntax instructions, CRL semantic parser generates a deterministic formal logic in linear DRS. Figure 2 illustrates the details of CRL, which contains seven layers: a tokenizer, lemmatizer, POS tagger, phrase chunker, syntactical parser, translator, and semantic parser.

Given the semantics in linear DRS, we extract core information using the Bottom-Up traversal algorithm. The linear DRS (Fig. 3a) is first translated into tree-like semantic structure (Fig. 3b) using a DRS parser. The Bottom-Up algorithm initiates at the root nonterminal and proceeds in a depth-first manner. During the iteration, symbolic tokens at specific nodes are captured locally and

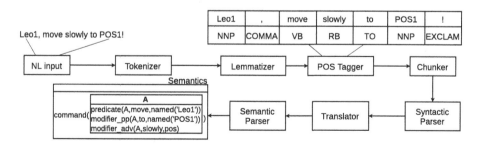

Fig. 2. Multi-layer CRL transformation: From natural language to formal semantic representation.

propagated back to their parents. The captured tokens are encapsulated with variable IDs and organized into information plates, representing partial data. Each information plate captures a specific property of an event. To capture the full context semantics, these plates are merged using ID cross-referencing.

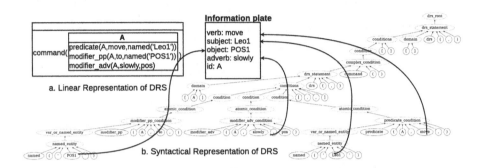

Fig. 3. Demonstration of semantics extraction from core statements.

2.2   Problem Formulation for Multi-Robot Planning

While single-agent planning problem can be described as classical planning, multi-robot planning requires a temporal model for concurrency and collaboration. Following the temporal reasoning framework [3], our framework accepts temporal constraints in the form of durative actions. Temporal constraints provide the requisite expressiveness to precisely model time, which enables concurrent activities and resource optimization in a multi-robot team.

Multi-agent temporal planning imposes unique challenges compared to single-agent planning, primarily due to resource conflicts. These conflicts, which can occur during planning or execution, arise from limited environmental perception and resource access among multiple robots. To prevent conflicts during planning, mutual awareness among robots is developed, to recognize each other's intentions and resource usage. We introduce the concept of mutual exclusivity (mutex) to describe mutual aware constraints. Events are considered mutually exclusive if they affect or rely on the same state variable assignment. More specifically, two events are considered to be mutex if they satisfy the following constraint

$$\text{mutex}(e_1, e_2) := (e_1 \rightarrow \neg e_2) \wedge (e_2 \rightarrow \neg e_1) \tag{1}$$

where e_1, e_2 are propositional events. The mutual exclusive concept is extendable for actions.

A planning problem for multi-robot team can be defined formally as follows

$$\mathcal{I} = \left(\mathcal{S}, s^i, \mathcal{S}^g, \mathcal{A}, \mathcal{O}, \mathcal{P}, \mathcal{T}, \mathcal{I} \right) \tag{2}$$

where S is a discrete set of problem states, $s^i \in S$ is the initial state, $S^g \subseteq S$ is a set of final states. Each action symbol $a \in \mathcal{A}$ corresponds to a primitive robotic motion. The terms $\mathcal{O}, \mathcal{P}$ are sets of object and predicate symbols. Each transition $t_a \in \mathcal{T}$ defines a transition from $s_i \in S$ to state $s_{i+1} \in S$ by applying an action $a \in A$. The term $\mathcal{I}$ is a set of temporal interval constraints where each $r_a \in \mathcal{I}$ is attached to an action transition t_a, describing the duration constraints of the action.

Multi-robot planning problem (2) can be described in PDDL [3] using two files: domain file $(S, \mathcal{A}, \mathcal{O}, \mathcal{P}, \mathcal{T}, \mathcal{I})$ and problem file (s^i, S^g). The domain file is typically predefined by the knowledge experts, which is based on planning scenario and the robots' capability. Additionally, the domain file contains temporal constraints and mutex expressions, enabling concurrent collaborating and task distribution for multi-agent planning. The problem file (s^i, S^g) defines the initial state and goal states of the planning problem. CRL-based plan generation algorithm provides a way to automatically construct $(s^i, S^g, \mathcal{T}, \mathcal{I})$ from complex linguistic instructions and temporal specifications.

2.3 Plan Generation Algorithm for Multi-robot Planning

To generate initial and goal states (s^i, S^g), the algorithm searches for command-type conditions within tree-DRS. Given a command-type DRS statement

$$\text{drs}(a) = \text{drs}([], \text{command}([X_1, X_2, ..., X_n, Y], $$
$$\text{predicate}(Y, a, X_1, X_2)))) \qquad (3)$$

the generation algorithm constructs a corresponding goal statement (a X_1 X_2), indicating an event a with two parameters X_1, X_2. For action signatures containing more than two parameters, additional information plates are extracted from other DRS conditions such as "object" and "adverbs". These plates are unified with the base goal statement and construct a complete action statement. The constructed action statements are aggregated and propagated back to the (: goal) section.

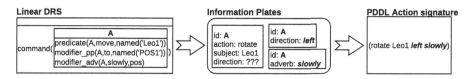

Fig. 4. Multi-parameter action statement construction from command-type DRS condition.

Figure 4 illustrates how an action signature with three arguments (`rotate`) is constructed. From command-type condition, only the action symbol and subject are obtainable. To identify the rotation direction and velocity, the framework searches all DRS adverbial-conditions matching the `rotate` verb ID. Partial information plates are extracted from these conditions, encapsulated by the same ID, and merged with the command-type plate through ID referencing. This process extends to additional arguments, ensuring the complete action statement.

Imperative sentences are commonly preferred for human instructions, but they often lack clarity about the actor in multi-robot team. For instance, the command "Please follow the first robot!" is valid in CRL [8] but not applicable in a multi-agent context. To address this issue, we designate one robot as the default actor to execute target actions when the subject is unspecified.

2.4 Temporal Constructions from Linguistic Descriptions

To generate temporal constraints from linguistic description, the framework focuses on preposition-condition DRS

$$\text{drs}_{\text{pp}}(q) = \text{drs}([X, Y], \text{modifier\_pp}(Y, q, X)) \tag{4}$$

Using Bottom-Up traversal algorithm, we can extract a corresponding temporal information plate $\langle \text{id} : Y, \text{duration} : X_1 \rangle$, where Y is the verb ID. Only preposition DRS statements with temporal lexicon – $q \in \{\text{during}, \text{within}, \text{in}\}$ – are iterated. From temporal information plate, we construct the corresponding temporal constraint $r_Y \in \mathscr{T}$ in PDDL syntax, using (: `duration`) section. The temporal constraint r_Y is updated directly into the domain file. The extracted duration X is converted into seconds. Figure 5 illustrates an example of how a temporal constraint is constructed from linguistic specifications. Due to the limitation of temporal model supported by PDDL, constraints in linear-time temporal logic (LTL) syntax are currently not feasible.

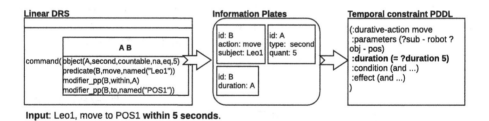

Input: Leo1, move to POS1 **within 5 seconds.**

Fig. 5. Temporal constraint construction from linguistic inputs.

2.5 Mutex Synthesis Algorithm

To manage concurrency, mutual exclusive operators are defined. There are two types of mutual exclusive expressions: property mutex and action mutex. Property mutex prevents simultaneous events during the planning phase. Meanwhile, action mutex prohibits incompatible actions during the execution phase, e.g., moving left and right at the same time. Describing mutex expression using CRL is challenging, due to its syntax limitation. Additionally, mutex expressions should be generalized as rules in the domain file, instead of being specified in the problem script. Therefore, instead of converting linguistic descriptions into mutex in PDDL, we developed a synthesis algorithm that automatically generates an updated domain file with mutex constraints. The algorithm handles property and action mutex separately.

To generate property mutex, the algorithm searches for all properties available in the (: predicates) section of the domain file. For each predicate $p \in \mathcal{P}$, we construct a new predicate negation $p_{\text{not}} \in \mathcal{P}$. A mutual exclusive relation between p and p_{not} is defined within (: derived) section, following (1). An example of property mutex generation is visualized in Fig. 6a. To handle action mutex, the logical relation (1) is defined within (: precondition) and (: effect) sections (Fig. 6b).

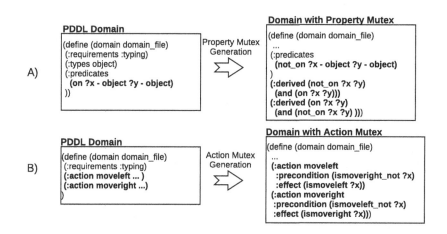

Fig. 6. Property mutex and Action mutex synthesis on the predefined PDDL domain.

After integrating temporal constraints and mutex expressions into the PDDL script, a temporal solver is applied to find suitable temporal plans [5]. In this paper, we utilize Partial Order Planning Forwards (POPF) [2] to find a concurrent solution for multi-robot team. Combining forward state-space search with partial-order planning techniques, POPF can effectively find temporal planning solutions by introducing minimal ordering constraints. POPF uses a Simple Temporal Network (STN) to represent durative action and temporal constraints. As actions are added to the plan, their start and end time points are incorporated into the STN with relevant ordering constraints. The final STN output provides a valid temporal solution that satisfies all temporal constraints. This solution is then dispatched to the multi-robot team, triggering appropriate actions on each robot. Each primitive action is associated with a Behavior Tree, allowing further decomposition into smaller modular actions, which enhances the system's flexibility and adaptability

3   Experiments

We evaluated the proposed method through two main experiments. The first experiment assessed the linguistic characteristics of the framework, aiming to demonstrate that key properties are preserved such as determinism, general domain applicability, and expressiveness from classical CRL [8]. The second experiment evaluated the method's stability of the method on a real-time multi-robot team in navigation missions.

3.1   Linguistic Model Evaluation

To compare this approach with classical CRL, we conducted an evaluation using the natural language instruction dataset [8]. This dataset was specifically developed for robotics and task-planning, comprising 335 planning scenarios and approximately 4,000 tokens. Each entry in the dataset represents a distinct planning scenario, and consists sequence of instructions, queries, and perception descriptions. The linguistic properties of the framework are evaluated on four core tasks: POS tagging, syntactic parsing, semantic parsing, and plan-generation. For POS tagging, we used multi-label accuracy. For syntactic parsing, semantic parsing, and plan-generation, we measured the framework' s feasibility in generating meaningful output, as used in [8].

Among 335 planning scenes, the proposed framework achieves 100% accuracy in POS tagging and syntax success rate, demonstrating the exceptional linguistic robustness and reliability of CRL-based method. Compared to the individual robot framework [9], we observe modest yet significant improvements: semantic parsing accuracy increased from 78% to 81%, while plan-generation success rate rose from 75% to 78%. These improvements can be attributed to the CRL's refined focus on subject identification and resource management in the multi-robot domain, highlighting the framework's adaptability to more complex scenarios.

3.2   Performance Evaluation

We integrated the framework into a real-time multi-robot system of three Leo Rovers. The linguistic framework was incorporated into the robot system via WebSocket communication. For each robot, we implemented five primitive executable actions: `moveto`, `moveforward`, `moveback`, `moveleft`, `moveright`. The `moveto` action requires two arguments (subject, object), while the other only requires one argument (subject). Temporal constraints were explicitly described by participants, while mutex expressions were carefully defined by knowledge experts. To find temporal solutions for the generated plans, we employed the

POPF planner, which efficiently dispatches concurrent actions to the robotic system when a viable solution is identified.

We conducted a study with five participants to evaluate the natural language control of our multi-robot team. Each participant was tasked with describing their desired goals using natural language given the available actions and robot identities within the system. The descriptions are requested to be complex, containing multiple actions, and involving all the robots. The participants were allowed to include temporal constraints. For each set of instructions, we performed 10 trials with varying initial robot states. After each execution, we observed the final state and verified the satisfaction of all the requirements in (:goal) section.

Input: There are 3 robots on the environment. Leo3, move to POS2 slowly. Leo1, move to POS1. Leo2, move to POS3 carefully. Leo3, rotate right after Leo1's first execution. Leo2, rotate left during Leo3's second action.	Output: define (problem demo_problem) (:domain demo_domain) (:objects pos1 pos2 pos3 - object; ldirect rdirect - direction; leo1 leo2 leo3 - robot; p1 p2 p3 p4 p5 p6 - pid; c - environment; g - execution; i - action; a - robot) (:init (after leo3 g) (during leo2 i) (on a c) (first g) (second i) (is_robot leo1) (is_robot leo2) (is_robot leo3)) (:goal (and (move leo3 p1 pos2) (move leo1 p2 pos1) (move leo2 p3 pos3) (rotate leo3 p4 rdirect) (rotate leo2 p5 ldirect))))
Input: There are 3 robots on the environment. Leo3, move to POS2 firstly. Leo1, move to POS1 afterward. Leo2, move to POS3 at the same time. Leo3, rotate right after Leo1's first execution. Leo2, rotate left during Leo3's second action. Leo3, move to POS4 after Leo2's second execution. Leo1, move to POS1 before Leo3's last execution.	Output: define (problem demo_problem) (:domain demo_domain) (:objects pos2 pos1 pos3 pos4 pos1 - object; ldirect rdirect - direction; leo1 leo2 leo3 - robot; p1 p2 p3 p4 p5 p6 p7 p8 - pid; c - environment; g - time; h l n - execution; a - robot; j - action) (:init (at leo2 g) (after leo3 h) (during leo2 j) (after leo3 l) (before leo1 n) (on a c) (same g) (first h) (second j) (second l) (last n) (is_robot leo1) (is_robot leo2) (is_robot leo3)) (:goal (and (move leo3 p1 pos2) (move leo1 p2 pos1) (move leo2 p3 pos3) (rotate leo3 p4 rdirect) (rotate leo2 p5 ldirect) (move leo3 p6 pos4) (move leo1 p7 pos1))))
Input: There are 3 robots on the environment. Leo1, move to POS2. Leo2, move to POS1 at the same time. Leo3, move to POS3 concurrently. Leo1, rotate left while Leo2's first exectetion.	Output: define (problem demo_problem) (:domain demo_domain) (:objects pos2 pos1 pos3 - object; ldirect rdirect - direction; leo1 leo2 leo3 - robot; p1 p2 p3 p4 p5 - pid; f - time; h - execution; c - environment; a - robot) (:init (at leo2 f) (while leo1 h) (on a c) (same f) (first h) (is_robot leo1) (is_robot leo2) (is_robot leo3)) (:goal (and (move leo1 p1 pos2) (move leo2 p2 pos1) (move leo3 p3 pos3) (rotate leo1 p4 ldirect))))

Fig. 7. Generated plans with temporal constraints from complex instructions for multi-robot team.

We evaluated the performance of the method on the real-time multi-robot system across various initial states. Each linguistic description contains both subject, object, and temporal expressions indicating the order of executions. Figure 7 showcases examples of these complex linguistic instructions alongside their corresponding generated plans. The outputs are complete and deterministic, and ready for direct interpretation by the POPF solver. These generated plans seamlessly integrate temporal conditions (e.g., after, during, before, while), precisely specifying the sequence of actions defined in the original inputs. This demonstrates the method's capability to handle sophisticated, time-sensitive multi-robot coordination tasks.

Input: There are 3 robots on the environment. Leo3, move to POS2 slowly. Leo1, move to POS1. Leo2, move to POS3 carefully. Leo3, rotate right after Leo1's first execution. Leo1, move to POS4 at the same time of Leo3. Leo2, move to POS1 after Leo3's second execution. Leo3, rotate right at the same time. Leo1, rotate left twice at the same time. Leo3, move to POS0, then move to POS3. Leo2, move to POS2 while Leo1 move to POS4.

Input: There are 3 robots on the environment. Leo1, move to POS3. Leo2, move to POS1 concurrently. Leo3, move to POS4 afterward. Leo1, rotate left after the first execution. Leo2 and Leo3, rotate left concurrently. Leo2, move to POS2. Leo1, move to POS4 concurrently. Leo3, move to POS1 at the same time. Leo2, move to POS0 afterward. Leo3, move to POS2 concurrently. Leo1, move to POS1 concurrently.

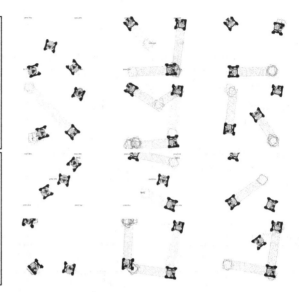

Fig. 8. Plan executions of multi-robot team using the generated temporal plan. The order of executions (left-right, top-down) is consistent with temporal constraints defined in commands.

The experiment demonstrated that multi-robot team consistently interpreted and executed temporal linguistic instructions across all trials, regardless of the initial states. Figure 8 illustrates different executions of the multi-robot at different time steps. The order of robot executions is defined by the temporal solver POPF, after considering all the temporal constraints declared in the generated plans.

4   Conclusion

This paper presents an enhanced Controlled Robot Language (CRL) based communication channel for multi-robot systems. Performance evaluations demonstrate improvements in semantic parsing and plan generation, which confirm the linguistic robustness of the CRL-based approach. Real-world experiments with Leo Rovers in complex planning scenarios further validated the reliability of the communication channel. In conclusion, this research underscores the potential of the CRL-based approach as an effective and user-friendly communication solution for multi-robot domains.

References

1. Beetz, M., et al.: Robosherlock: unstructured information processing for robot perception. In: 2015 IEEE International Conference on Robotics and Automation (ICRA), pp. 1549–1556 (2015)

2. Coles, A., Coles, A., Fox, M., Long, D.: Forward-chaining partial-order planning. In: Proceedings of the International Conference on Automated Planning and Scheduling, vol. 20, pp. 42–49 (2010)
3. Fox, M., Long, D.: Pddl2. 1: an extension to pddl for expressing temporal planning domains. J. Artif. Intell. Res. 61–124 (2003)
4. Liu, R., Guo, Y., Jin, R., Zhang, X.: A review of natural-language-instructed robot execution systems. AI 5, **3**, 948–989 (2024)
5. Mudrova, L., Lacerda, B., Hawes, N.: Partial order temporal plan merging for mobile robot tasks. In: European Conference on Artificial Intelligence (ECAI), pp. 1537–1545. IOS Press (2016)
6. Spencer, D.A., Wang, Y., Humphrey, L.R.: Trust-based human-robot interaction for multi-robot symbolic motion planning. In: IEEE/RSJ International Conference on Intelligent Robots and Systems (IROS), pp. 1443–1449. IEEE (2016)
7. Tellex, S., Knepper, R., Li, A., Rus, D., Roy, N.: Science and systems, asking for help using inverse semantics. In: Robotics: Science and Systems Foundation (2014)
8. Tran, D., Li, H., He, H.: Ai planning from natural-language instructions for trustworthy human-robot communication. In: International Conference on Social Robotics, pp. 254–265. Springer (2023)
9. Tran, D., Yan, F., Yihun, Y., Tan, J., He, H.: A framework of controlled robot language for reliable human-robot collaboration. In: International Conference on Social Robotics, pp. 339–349. Springer (2021)

Omnisurface: Common Reality for Intuitive Human-Robot Collaboration

Akhlak Uz Zaman[1] ![ORCID], Hui Li[1], Fujian Yan[2], Yinlong Zhang[3], and Hongsheng He[1(✉)] ![ORCID]

[1] The University of Alabama, Tuscaloosa, AL 35487, USA
hongsheng.he@ua.edu
[2] School of Computing, Wichita State University, Wichita, KS 67208, USA
[3] Shenyang Institute of Automation, Shenyang 110016, China

Abstract. Effective communication and information projection are essential for human-robot teaming. The projection of images on non-planar surfaces using a conventional projector is challenging due to the inherent problem of distortion. The projection distortion occurs due to the variations in depth across the surface of the teaming workspace. As a result, the projected image, information, or symbols lose their original shape and create confusion during human-robot teaming. In this paper, we presented an innovative approach to perform distortion-free projections in the teaming workspace. A pre-warped image is constructed based on the surface geometry that the projector displays and accurately replicates the original projection image. Beyond the technical achievement, this research highlights the social acceptance of improved spatial augmented reality in human-robot teams. It fosters better teamwork, trust, and efficiency by enabling more intuitive and reliable interactions.

Keywords: Human-Robot Teaming · Distortion Correction · RGB-D sensor · Common Reality

1 Introduction

Robots have been used as a tool for humankind for a long time. Gradually, they become like a human partner in terms of performing a common task. The incorporation of robots into collaborative human-robot teaming has become more widespread in recent years. It has led to a transformation in numerous industries due to the combination of the distinct capabilities of humans and robots [1,2]. Visualization approaches utilizing a projector can play a crucial role in improving the intuitiveness of human-robot collaboration by presenting cooperative instructions in the workspace. The visualization of images using a projector on real objects, also known as spatial augmented reality [3], can enhance coordination and team performance by enabling humans to monitor the actions of robots. It assures proper teamwork to gain more job satisfaction [4]. Projectors

This research was funded by NSF grants #2427895 and #2420355.

can be utilized to arrange a mixed-reality canvas in the physical work environment through a virtual visualization of the work plan. It can provide intuitive feelings for humans and improve collaborative team performance [5]. Traditional projectors cannot understand surface geometry and adjust images to account for non-flat projection surfaces. Consequently, ordinary projectors' cannot handle the depth variation at different points of a non-flat surface and make the projected image distorted [6]. The use of RGB-D sensors has become popular nowadays for 3D surface reconstructions and their utilization in different robotics and computer vision applications. It can provide the pixel-level depth of a particular surface with a very high frame rate. The depth data of RGB-D sensors can be utilized to understand surface geometry [7].

The projection distortion problem causes a change in the original shape of the object to be projected. It can mislead the human participants to understand robots' activities properly and seriously hamper the overall performance and intuition of human-robot teaming. The main focus of this study is to solve the distortion problem to facilitate quality human-robot teaming. This paper has the following contributions,

1. This paper proposes a new visualization-based interface for human-robot teaming in real-world scenarios, enhancing intuitive communication and collaboration between humans and robots.
2. This research proposes a unique method for correcting projection distortion on non-planar surfaces using RGB-D sensor data, significantly improving the accuracy and clarity of visual instructions in human-robot collaboration tasks.

2 Human-Robot Teaming

A robot was a helping hand to its operator (a human) from the beginning. It has become a partner or co-worker with the advancement of artificial intelligence and robotics. Human-robot teaming creates interdependence between the two entities through communication, collaboration, and coordination. A dual collaboration concept was proposed that guided the design of the components of the collaboration [2]. The proposed architecture suggests some factors that are useful for proper human-robot teaming. Figure 1 shows the basic components of human-robot teaming, where both humans and robots have their specific abilities. They are interdependent on one another in terms of collaboration factors such as context, environment, and task.

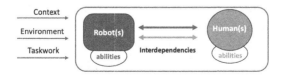

Fig. 1. Fundamental components responsible for Human-robot teaming.

2.1   Use of Visualization in Human-Robot Teaming

The concept of imaginary projection [4,8] in human-robot collaboration can potentially enhance team performance. Their main goal was to create a physical work environment using projectors and use this canvas as a friendly communication medium for collaborations. They proposed an object-tracking computer vision algorithm to recognize an object in the workspace and estimate the pose and state of the physical object. Their proposed method helps humans verify whether the alignment of the physical object with the robot's scope is perfect or not. They also initiated visual instructions to show the robot's intentions for the upcoming activities and warn humans if there were any safety issues. A projection-based communication channel was proposed that communicates between humans and robots to circulate necessary information using visual references [9]. A convolutional neural network architecture [10] was presented that transforms arbitrary surfaces into interactive touch interfaces. The architecture uses a CNN to detect fingertip touches on flat and curved surfaces with RGB-D sensor input, enabling intuitive human-robot interaction through touch gestures and reducing operator training time. The industrial scope of human-robot collaboration [11] was studied and showed some evidence that projector-based graphical visualization can improve industrial work efficiency and safety. The authors proposed a dynamic graphical user interface to interact with industrial robots and perform better human-robot interaction. A web-based interface [12] was designed to establish a dual communication system between robots and humans on the collaboration worktable. An augmented reality (AR) based collaboration framework [13] was proposed to establish better teamwork. They showed that AR-based visualization can have the potential for peer collaboration between humans and robots in unknown and instrument-less environments. The authors also proposed bidirectional communications between humans and autonomous robots to perform peer teamwork. Although image distortion can hamper the intuitiveness of the collaboration, none of the literature discussed above concentrated on image distortion problems.

2.2   Projector Distortion Correction

Image distortion occurs due to the improper geometry of the projection surfaces [14–16]. A novel system [14] was proposed to solve the image distortion problem by moving the projector direction from an uneven surface to an even surface. It does not work for our problem. Because, in most cases, human-robot teaming workplaces are non-plane. A distortion correction method [16] was suggested, utilizing the captured image from a camera attached to the projector. The system used an algorithm to correct the keystone distortion problem automatically. The authors considered the surface angle and computed a pre-warped trapezoid for keystone correction. The technique had no scope to capture non-plane surface geometry and correct distortion problems. A projector distortion correction-based system [17] was proposed for non-planner surfaces using a Kinect device as an RGB-D sensor. The authors implemented a 3D point cloud based on the non-planar surface data captured by Kinect. After that, the system performed geometric correction and generated a pre-warped image for distortion correction. The process utilized a projector to display the pre-warped image on the non-plane surface, minimizing the image distortion problem. The technique acknowledged that this method does not apply to real-time applications. This approach had a plan to reduce computation costs using GPUs so that their system could be used for real-time applications. According to the review, projector distortion correction on non-planar surfaces is a unique approach to initiating an intuitive interface for human-robot collaboration. None of this literature is directly aimed at this research goal. The literature mentioned above is really helpful in conceptualizing the background of our specific research goal.

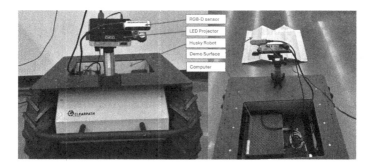

Fig. 2. Proposed distortion-free projection on omni-surface to facilitate human-robot teaming.

3   Projection Distortion Correction on Omnisurface

The proposed research initiates a visualization interface according to the following setup. The projector and the RGB-D sensor are fixed on top of the collaboration workspace. The target surface of the collaboration workspace is assumed to be a non-planner surface. Initially, the calibration method established the relationship between the projector and the depth camera (the extrinsic parameters). The depth sensor uses calculated calibration parameters and allows the projection of surface area by the projector. It determines the optimal correction area, which is the maximum rectangular region within the projection surface to perform the distortion correction. The original projection image is transformed into a pre-warped image to fit the effective correction area, removing any geometric distortion on the target surface. Finally, the projector outputs the corrected image. Figure 2 shows the hardware setup of our visualization-based collaboration framework for human-robot teaming. A projector and RGB-D sensor are attached above the collaboration surface on top of a robotic vehicle. The proposed method captures the 3D surface depth using an RGB-D sensor and visualizes a virtual object model onto the real-life object. This spatial augmented visualization helps humans monitor robot activity intuitively.

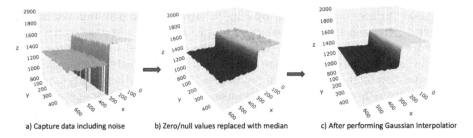

a) Capture data including noise   b) Zero/null values replaced with median   c) After performing Gaussian Interpolation

Fig. 3. 3D graphical representation of the Surface data a) captured using RGD-D sensor which includes noise, b) after replacing null/zero values with median, and c) after applying the Recursive Gaussian Interpolation.

3.1 Surface Data Acquisition and Refinement

It is imperative to extract noise from the depth data of the RGB-D sensor before initiating the distortion correction process. The presence of noise in the depth data can lead to a decrease in the surface smoothness and result in inaccurate distortion correction. At first, the system captures surface depth using an RGB-D sensor and then performs refinement. The proposed approach followed two steps to reduce noise: (i) replacing invalid null (practically zero) values with the median and (ii) performing the recursive Gaussian interpolation algorithm [18] to make a smoother surface. Figure 3 shows the progress of surface data refinement.

3.2 Inverse Projection Model

To project a 2D image onto a non-planar 3D surface using depth data, this approach must determine the inverse projection transformation. This involves first identifying the projection transformation equation, which generates the 2D image from 3D world coordinates using the pinhole camera model. Once this is established, the proposed technique can calculate the inverse projection transformation needed to project the 2D image onto the surface accurately as defined by its 3D world coordinates. The projection transformation equation from 3D world coordinates P_w to 2D image coordinates P_i, can be represented as

$$\mathbf{P}_i = \mathbf{K} \cdot \begin{bmatrix} \mathbf{R}\ \mathbf{t} \\ \mathbf{0}\ 1 \end{bmatrix} \cdot \mathbf{P}_w \tag{1}$$

where K, R, t, P_i, and P_w are denoted respectively as the camera intrinsic matrix, rotation matrix, translation vector, 2D image coordinates, and 3D world coordinates.

3.3 Pre-Warped Image Generation

To generate a pre-warped image, the proposed system needs to produce an equivalent opposite surface D'' of the given depth data D'. The proposed approach calculated the minimum depth $\mathbf{D}_{\min}$ and maximum depth $\mathbf{D}_{\max}$ for each of the depth values greater than zero. Then, prepare the equivalent opposite surface D'' using the following equation where every depth value $D''[i,j]$ is calculated from the original surface $D[i,j]$,

$$\mathbf{D}''[i,j] = \mathbf{D}_{\max} - (\mathbf{D}[i,j] - \mathbf{D}_{\min}) \tag{2}$$

To generate a pre-warped image, the opposite surface D'' is considered as coordinate depth data P_{w} and generates a 3D point-cloud using the pinhole camera model. The 2D view of this point-cloud is our expected pre-warped image P'_{i} which gives distortion-free projection on omni-surfaces.

4 Experiment

4.1 Experiment Setup

An "Intel RealSense D435" RGB-D sensor is used to capture non-planar surface depth. This sensor is small, lightweight, and low-cost. The "AAXM P300 Neo" is a small and lightweight LED projector. The proposed approach utilizes this projector to display the corrected image on the human-robot workspace (Fig. 4).

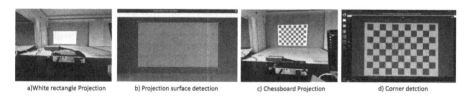

a)White rectangle Projection   b) Projection surface detection   c) Chessboard Projection   d) Corner detction

Fig. 4. Projection Surface Calculation and Calibration.

4.2 Projector and RGB-D Sensor Calibration

To perform the calibration between the projector and the RGB-D sensor, we first positioned both devices in a fixed setup with overlapping fields of view, aimed at a calibration surface. Using a checkerboard pattern, we captured multiple images from the RGB-D sensor in various orientations. We then calibrated the RGB-D sensor's RGB camera by detecting the corners of the checkerboard pattern and utilizing the OpenCV library [19] to estimate its intrinsic parameters. For the projector, we treated it as an inverse camera, projecting a known pattern and capturing it using the RGB-D sensor. This allowed us to calibrate the projector and determine its intrinsic parameters. Subsequently, we computed the extrinsic parameters by matching corresponding points from both the projector and the RGB-D sensor. This process enabled us to determine the spatial relationship between the two devices and align their coordinate systems. Finally, we validated the calibration by projecting patterns and confirming their alignment with the 3D depth data captured by the RGB-D sensor.

4.3   Projection Surface Calculation

The field of view (FOV) of the RGB-D sensor and the projector is not the
same. In practice, the RGB-D sensor covers more surface area than the projector
display. To ensure precise projection, we calculated the specific projection area
from the entire surface and used the depth array of this specific area to generate
a pre-warped image. We then placed a white rectangle on the surface, covering
the entire area of the projector display, and detected the coordinates of the four
corners of the rectangle.

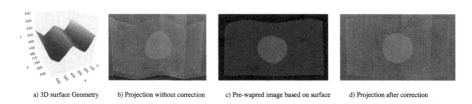

a) 3D surface Geometry   b) Projection without correction   c) Pre-wapred image based on surface   d) Projection after correction

Fig. 5. Major steps for distortion correction on a non-planner surface using RGB-D
sensor.

4.4   Distortion Correction and Projection

The proposed method requires to build a pre-warped image from the original
image. This pre-warped image is prepared based on the non-planner surface data
captured by the RGB-D sensor. Figure 5 presents the major steps for distortion
correction on a non-planner surface using an RGB-D sensor by our proposed
method. Here, Fig. 5 a) represents the 3D surface data captured using the RGB-
D sensor, (b) shows the projection without any correction, (c) represents the
pre-warped image generated using our proposed method, and (d) represents
the projection based on the proposed method. In order to test our distortion
correction method, we chose to project various symbols onto uneven surfaces such
as room corners, wavy walls, and wooden floors. These surfaces are not typically
suitable for projection using a regular projector due to their significant depth and
color variations. First, we captured the 3D depth of the surface and refined the
surface data to eliminate any noise. We then created pre-warped images using
the noise-free depth data based on our proposed distortion correction method.
Finally, we projected these pre-warped images onto the surfaces one by one.
The result we observed was extremely promising. Figure 6 shows three surfaces,
refined 3D depth data, and two corrected projection examples for each surface.

4.5   Performance and Accuracy

In order to evaluate the performance of our proposed model for point projections
accurately, we use the Root Mean Square Error, which is a standard statistical

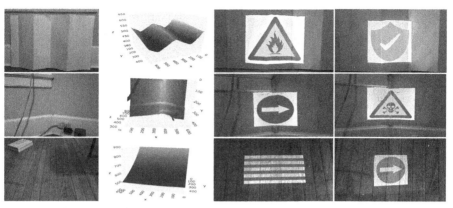

a) Rough/uneven surface images   b) 3D Surface data captured by RGB-sensor   c) Corrected projection examples

Fig. 6. Examples of Corrected projection on rough surfaces such as wavy walls, room corners, and floors.

metric for measuring average error magnitudes. It involves a series of mathematical operations to calculate, and here are the detailed equations used to represent error, $\mathbf{E} = \sqrt{\frac{1}{n}\sum_{i=1}^{n}(y_i - \hat{y}_i)^2}$. In this equation, the squared difference $(y_i - \hat{y}_i)^2$ represents the squared discrepancy between each target point, denoted as y_i , and its corresponding projected point, $\hat{y}_i$, for the i-th observation in a dataset where n represents the total number of pairs of points. To calculate the RMSE, we took 40 random (x,y) coordinates of target points, found the coordinates of the projected points, and calculated the errors between the target and projected points. We found the Root Mean Square Error value is as good as 3.34 mm, the average error is 3.13 mm, and the percentage of the error is 0.40%. Figure 7 presents the scatter plot illustrating the target points (in green) and projected points (in red) for each pair, with gray dashed lines connecting each target to its projected point. This visual helps you see the dispersion of the points in the 400 mm x 250 mm space and the error represented by the distance between corresponding points. Figure 8 shows a few examples of the projections, visually comparing ordinary and corrected projections using our proposed method.

4.6   Social Acceptance

In order to assess the social acceptance of our correction method for projection distortion on omni-surfaces to enhance human-robot collaboration, we have designed a survey with three evaluation criteria: originality, visibility, and understandability. We have assigned a weight to each criterion to calculate the final acceptance score for each perspective. The criteria are as follows: 1) Originality measures how closely the projection resembles the original image; 2) Visibility assesses whether the user can clearly see the robot's instructions; 3) Understandability gauges the extent to which the user can understand the robot's intention after viewing the projection. The final score across all criteria is 4.3

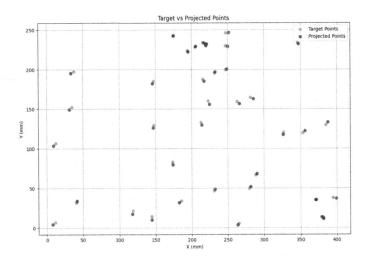

Fig. 7. Scatter Plot of Target and Projected Points with Error Visualization.

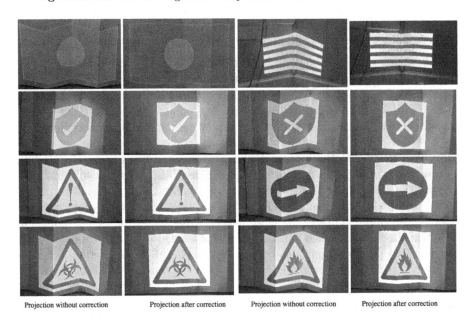

Projection without correction   Projection after correction   Projection without correction   Projection after correction

Fig. 8. Comparison between ordinary projection and corrected projection.

out of 5, and the visual representation of Fig. 9 allows us to compare the different aspects of evaluation. The result demonstrates how solving a technical issue can significantly improve the social acceptance of human-robot collaboration, thus advancing social robotics.

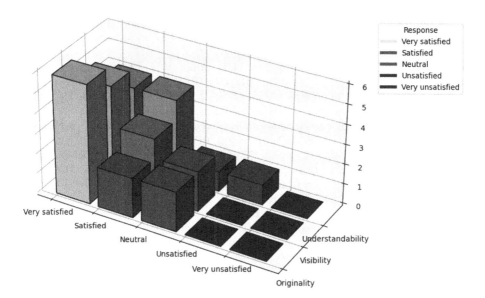

Fig. 9. User feedback distribution across criteria in evaluating projection distortion correction on omni-surfaces.

5   Conclusion

This research introduced an innovative approach to mitigate projection distortion on non-planar surfaces and improved human-robot collaboration. By leveraging an RGB-D sensor to capture surface geometry, the suggested system successfully corrects distortions in real time, thereby improving the accuracy and clarity of visual instructions in collaborative contexts. This innovation increased team trust and productivity while also enhancing the technical aspects of human-robot interaction. The technology has the potential to be widely applied in businesses that depend on human-robot cooperation, as demonstrated by its capacity to produce distortion-free projections on complicated surfaces. Further optimization for real-time processing and the application of this method to dynamic surfaces will be explored in future work.

References

1. Matheson, E., Minto, R., Zampieri, E.G., Faccio, M., Rosati, G.: Human-robot collaboration in manufacturing applications: a review. Robotics **8**(4), 100 (2019). https://doi.org/10.3390/robotics8040100
2. Mingyue Ma, L., Fong, T., Micire, M.J., Kim, Y.K., Feigh, K.: Human-robot teaming: concepts and components for design. In: Hutter, M., Siegwart, R. (eds.) Field and Service Robotics. SPAR, vol. 5, pp. 649–663. Springer, Cham (2018). https://doi.org/10.1007/978-3-319-67361-5_42
3. Casas, S., Gimeno, J., Casanova-Salas, P., Riera, J.V., Portalés, C.: Virtual and augmented reality for the visualization of summarized information in smart cities:

a use case for the city of Dubai. In: Smart Systems Design, Applications, and Challenges, pp. 299–325. IGI Global (2020). https://doi.org/10.4018/978-1-7998-2112-0.ch015

4. Andersen, R.S., Madsen, O., Moeslund, T.B., Amor, H.B.: Projecting robot intentions into human environments. In: 2016 25th IEEE International Symposium on Robot and Human Interactive Communication (RO-MAN), pp. 294–301. IEEE (2016). https://doi.org/10.1109/ROMAN.2016.7745145
5. Ganesan, R.K.: Mediating human-robot collaboration through mixed reality cues (Master's thesis, Arizona State University) (2017)
6. Boroomand, A., Sekkati, H., Lamm, M., Clausi, D.A., Wong, A.: Saliency-guided projection geometric correction using a projector-camera system. In: 2016 IEEE International Conference on Image Processing (ICIP), pp. 2951–2955. IEEE (2016). https://doi.org/10.1109/ICIP.2016.7532900
7. Jing, C., Potgieter, J., Noble, F., Wang, R.: A comparison and analysis of RGB-D cameras' depth performance for robotics application. In: 2017 24th International Conference on Mechatronics and Machine Vision in Practice (M2VIP), pp. 1–6. IEEE (2017). https://doi.org/10.1109/M2VIP.2017.8211432
8. Ganesan, R.K., Rathore, Y.K., Ross, H.M., Amor, H.B.: Better teaming through visual cues: how projecting imagery in a workspace can improve human-robot collaboration. IEEE Robot. Autom. Mag. 25(2), 59–71 (2018). https://doi.org/10.1109/MRA.2018.2815655
9. Weng, T., Perlmutter, L., Nikolaidis, S., Srinivasa, S., Cakmak, M.: Robot object referencing through legible situated projections. In: 2019 International Conference on Robotics and Automation (ICRA), pp. 8004–8010. IEEE (2019). https://doi.org/10.1109/ICRA.2019.8793638
10. Yan, F., Chavez, E., Yihun, Y.S., He, H.: Touch detection in augmented Omnisurface for human-robot teaming. J. Manag. Eng. Integr. 15(2), 92–99 (2022). https://doi.org/10.62704/10057/24828
11. Hietanen, A., et al.: Proof of concept of a projection-based safety system for human-robot collaborative engine assembly. In: 2019 28th IEEE International Conference on Robot and Human Interactive Communication (RO-MAN), pp. 1–7. IEEE (2019). https://doi.org/10.1109/RO-MAN46459.2019.8956446
12. David, J., Järvenpää, E., Lobov, A.: A web-based mixed reality interface facilitating explicit agent-oriented interactions for human-robot collaboration. In: 2022 8th International Conference on Mechatronics and Robotics Engineering (ICMRE), pp. 174–181. IEEE (2022). https://doi.org/10.1109/ICMRE54455.2022.9734094
13. Reardon, C., Lee, K., Rogers, J.G., Fink, J.: Communicating via augmented reality for human-robot teaming in field environments. In: 2019 IEEE International Symposium on Safety, Security, and Rescue Robotics (SSRR), pp. 94–101. IEEE (2019). https://doi.org/10.1109/SSRR.2019.8848971
14. Nakamura, N., Hiraike, R.: Active projector: image correction for moving image over uneven screens. In: Companion of the 15th Annual ACM Symposium on User Interface Software and Technology, pp. 1-2 (2002)
15. Han, D.: Real-time digital image warping for display distortion correction. In: Kamel, M., Campilho, A. (eds.) ICIAR 2005. LNCS, vol. 3656, pp. 1258–1265. Springer, Heidelberg (2005). https://doi.org/10.1007/11559573_152
16. Li, B., Sezan, I.: Automatic keystone correction for smart projectors with embedded camera. In: 2004 International Conference on Image Processing, 2004. ICIP 2004, vol. 4, pp. 2829–2832. IEEE (2004). https://doi.org/10.1109/ICIP.2004.1421693

17. Manevarthe, B., Kalpathi, R.: Geometric correction for projection on non planar surfaces using point clouds. In: Proceedings of the 12th International Conference on Distributed Smart Cameras, pp. 1–6 (2018). https://doi.org/10.1145/3243394.3243694

18. Wang, X., Liang, Y., Pan, Q., Yang, F.: A Gaussian approximation recursive filter for nonlinear systems with correlated noises. Automatica **48**(9), 2290–2297 (2012). https://doi.org/10.1016/j.automatica.2012.06.035

19. Camera Calibration and 3D Reconstruction (2024). OpenCV.org. https://docs.opencv.org/4.x/d9/d0c/group__calib3d.html. Accessed 25 July 2024

Grasp Intention Interpretation in Object Handover for Human-Robot Teaming

Hui Li, Akhlak Uz Zaman, and Hongsheng He[✉]

The University of Alabama, Tuscaloosa, AL 35487, USA
{hli98,azaman2}@crimson.ua.edu, hongsheng.he@ua.edu

Abstract. Effective human-robot collaboration requires social robots to adapt to individual human grasping habits to ensure smooth and safe object handovers. However, current robotic systems struggle to interpret diverse grasping behaviors, as individual habits can introduce variations even within the same grasp topology. This limitation affects the effectiveness of robotic systems in social contexts. This paper presents a grasp adaptation algorithm that enables robots to recognize and adjust to human grasping habits. The system identifies human grasping poses from RGB images and maps them to abstract representations consisting of 21 3D points each. These representations are then classified into one of six standard grasp topologies. Based on the identified topology, key points are selected from the abstract grasp to estimate the object's pose. A reinforcement learning model is subsequently employed to optimize the object handover process. Experimental results demonstrate that this approach significantly enhances both the fluidity and safety of human-robot object handovers.

Keywords: grasping habits adaptation · dexterous grasping · grasp topology · deep learning · reinforcement learning

1 Introduction

Human-robot collaboration, particularly in the context of object handovers, is essential for ensuring smooth and effective interactions in both structured and unstructured environments, such as healthcare and industrial settings [1,2,18]. For example, a robot delivering tools to a nurse or handing parts to a factory worker must adapt to the human's grasping preferences and workspace constraints to enhance both safety and efficiency. Extensive research has been conducted to address the handover task in human-robot collaboration. Studies have analyzed the trajectory and velocity of approach movements to ensure smooth transitions [9,13]. Additionally, object orientation and affordances have been optimized to make it easier for the receiver to grasp the object [4,15]. Some approaches also involve learning from human behavior to improve the naturalness and effectiveness of handovers [4]. However, less work has been done to

---

This research was funded by NSF grant #2420355 and #2402466.

adapt to the habits of the receiver, particularly the variability in human grasping behaviors, which are influenced by individual preferences and situational factors. Developing systems that can accurately recognize and adapt to these diverse human behaviors is crucial for making robots more intuitive and practical in real-world applications.

Grasp topology and taxonomy are key to understanding human grasping behaviors and robotic adaptation. Grasp topology describes the geometric configuration of the fingers or contact points with an object, such as pinching or cupping. Grasp taxonomy categorizes these topologies into structured classes based on factors like contact points and object shape. This classification aids in designing robots that can effectively recognize and adapt to human grasping behaviors in various tasks and environments. Previous research has shown that human grasp choices tend to cluster over a large set of objects, leading to the development of grasp taxonomies to simplify grasping choices. For example, Cutkosky's taxonomy identified 16 grasp types used by machinists [6], and Feix's taxonomy expanded this to 33 different grasp types [3,7].

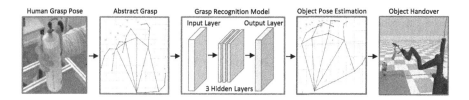

Fig. 1. Structure of the grasp adaptation system.

The FreiHAND dataset provides a large collection of annotated 3D hand poses, high-resolution RGB images, and key point annotations, which make it an invaluable resource for advancing research in hand tracking and grasp recognition [20]. In this paper, we extend the FreiHAND dataset to map individual grasping habits to a standard set of grasp topologies.

Reinforcement learning (RL) is a powerful approach for robot control, where robots learn to perform tasks through trial and error [8,16,19]. By receiving feedback in the form of rewards or penalties based on their actions, robots improve their behavior over time [17]. This method enables robots to develop adaptive and optimized control strategies for complex and dynamic environments. It enhances their ability to perform a wide range of tasks autonomously. In this paper, an RL model is designed to conduct the object handover task in a simulation environment, identical to the MagicHand system [10,11].

We propose a grasp adaptation algorithm, as illustrated in Fig. 1, that processes an RGB image of a human grasping pose, converts it into an abstract grasp representation, and classifies it into one of six standard grasp topologies. Key points are then selected from the abstract grasp, based on the identified grasp topology, to estimate the appropriate object pose. A reinforcement learning model is subsequently employed to optimize the object handover process. The contributions of this research include:

- We developed a grasp adaptation system that adjusts the robot's grasping strategy based on individual human grasping habits, enhancing the fluidity and safety of object handovers.
- We proposed a method for accurately estimating the appropriate object pose based on the identified grasp topology.
- We designed a reinforcement learning model to optimize the object handover process by learning adaptive strategies that align the object's position and orientation with the receiver's grasp pose while minimizing interaction errors

2   Human Grasping Habit Adaptation

To adapt to human grasping habits, three key challenges must be addressed: recognizing the human grasp, determining the object pose based on the grasp, and moving the object to the desired pose. The proposed system tackles these challenges through three integrated models: a grasp recognition model, an object pose estimation model, and a reinforcement learning model.

2.1   Recognition of Human Grasp Topology

Standard Grasp Topology. We classify grasp poses into six distinct grasp topologies [14], as illustrated in Fig. 2. The figure categorizes grasps into two main types: power grasps and precision grasps, based on object shapes and the involvement of virtual fingers (VF). Power grasps (e.g., circular or prismatic objects) prioritize security and stability, utilizing more virtual fingers and 3D wrapping. In contrast, precision grasps focus on dexterity and sensitivity, typically involving fewer virtual fingers and 2D wrapping.

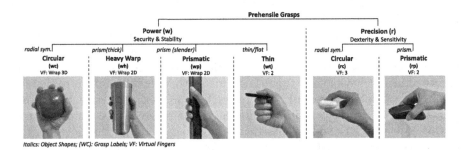

Fig. 2. The predefined grasp topology.

After establishing the grasp taxonomy, a standard grasp pose was selected for each topology by evaluating poses from the FreiHAND dataset. The evaluation was based on how well each pose matched the defined topologies. The pose that best fit each topology was chosen as the standard grasp pose. Figure 3 displays both the RGB image of the standard grasp pose and the corresponding grasp information, which includes abstract grasp key points (highlighted in green). The orange dotted axis represents the estimated object pose derived from the key points.

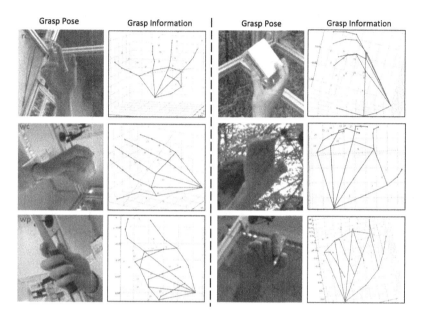

Fig. 3. Standard grasp topology: This figure displays images of the grasp topology, including the skeletons of each standard grasp topology and their corresponding key points, highlighted in green.

Grasp Topology Recognition. A multi-layer perceptron (MLP) deep neural network was developed to map abstract grasps to standard grasp topologies. Rectified Linear Units (ReLU) were used as activation functions in the input and hidden layers. The input layer comprises 63 neurons, corresponding to the 21 3D points in each abstract grasp. The network features three hidden layers with 1,024, 256, and 32 nodes, respectively. The output layer consists of six neurons with Softmax activation functions to classify the grasps. The model was trained using a refined FreiHAND dataset.

2.2 Object Pose Estimation

The pose of the object, including both position and orientation, is determined based on the key points associated with the standard grasp topology. For grasp topologies such as "wc", "wh", "wp", "rc", and "rp", the object should be positioned within the grasp's aperture, which is the space between the fingertips of the thumb and the fingers. The object position is defined as the midpoint between p_t, the point representing the tip of the thumb, and p_c, the closest fingertip to p_t. The object position is expressed as $p_m = 0.5[x_t + x_c, y_t + y_c, z_t + z_c]^T$. Since the orientation is typically aligned with the palm or fingers, two key points, p_s and p_e, are pre-selected from the abstract grasp to define the object's orientation. These points are usually located on the palm. The orientation of the object is expressed as

$$\mathbf{l}(t) = [x_m, y_m, z_m]^T + t \cdot [x_e - x_s, y_e - y_s, z_e - z_s]^T \tag{1}$$

where x, y, and z are coordinates of the point and t is a scalar parameter. The points p_s, p_e, p_c, and p_t, are specific to each grasp topology and serve as key points provided for analysis.

For the grasp topology "wt" the object should be positioned between the fingertip of the thumb and the side of the index finger, specifically at the key point p_{pip}, which corresponds to the PIP joint (Proximal Interphalangeal Joint) of the index finger. The object's position for this grasp topology is expressed as $p_m = 0.5[x_t + x_{\text{pip}}, y_t + y_{\text{pip}}, z_t + z_{\text{pip}}]^T$. The orientation of the object should be roughly parallel to the index finger. In this case, the key points p_s and p_e in (1) represent the PIP and MCP (Metacarpophalangeal) joints of the index finger, respectively.

2.3   Object Handover Using Reinforcement Learning

Once the object's pose is determined, the robot must adjust the object to the specified position and orientation. We designed and developed a reinforcement learning model to achieve this goal. A simulation environment mirroring the MagicHand platform, which supports a variety of manipulation tasks, has been established [10, 12].

The task is to handover the object to a human hand, simulated by a Schunk anthropomorphic robotic hand in a simulation environment, and positioning it at the target pose, represented by a green area. The action space of the proposed model is a six-dimensional vector, including movements and rotations of the robotic hand along the x, y, and z axes. The observation space consists of seven dimensions: the relative position and orientation between the object and the target, as well as the distance between them.

In this task, our goal is to position the object as close as possible to the target, defined as the center point of the green area, rewarding smaller distances between the object and the target. Additionally, we aim to align the object's orientation with the target's orientation, rewarding smaller differences in orientation along the x, y, and z axes. To ensure safe interaction, we impose penalties for collisions with the human hand. The reward function is expressed as

$$r = e^{-|d|} + e^{-|h|} + e^{-|l|} + e^{-|k|} - \alpha n_c \tag{2}$$

where d is the distance between the object and the target location, and h, l, and k represent the differences in orientation between the object and the target along the x, y, and z axes, respectively. The coefficient α is a constant, and n_c represents the number of contact points with the human hand. We chose an exponential function because its value changes more rapidly when the exponent is large and more slowly when the exponent is small. This approach encourages the robot to make larger adjustments when the current pose is far from the target, while allowing for more precise, gradual adjustments as the pose approaches the target.

The proximal policy optimization (PPO) algorithm is employed to train the model. PPO is a reinforcement learning algorithm designed to improve policy stability by limiting the size of policy updates. It uses a clipped objective function to ensure that the new policy does not deviate excessively from the old policy. The objective function is given by

$$J(\theta) = \mathbb{E}\left[\min\left(\frac{\pi_\theta(a|s)}{\pi_{\theta_{\text{old}}}(a|s)}\hat{A}(s,a), \text{clip}\left(\frac{\pi_\theta(a|s)}{\pi_{\theta_{\text{old}}}(a|s)}, 1-\epsilon, 1+\epsilon\right)\hat{A}(s,a)\right)\right]$$

where $\pi_\theta(a|s)$ and $\pi_{\theta_{\text{old}}}(a|s)$ are the probabilities of taking action a in state s under the new and old policies, respectively, and $\hat{A}(s,a)$ is the advantage function. The clipping function clip restricts the ratio of the new to old policy probabilities, with ϵ controlling the extent of the allowed change, thereby balancing exploration with stability.

3   Experiments

The proposed system was evaluated under different thresholds. The simulation environment was set up using PyBullet and Gym, and task simulations were conducted to test the final performance of the system.

3.1   Data Preparation

The FreiHAND dataset, comprising RGB images with 3D annotations, was refined by labeling each grasp pose with one of six predefined topologies. This updated dataset contains 600 annotated poses (100 per topology). Figure 4 illustrates sample images of these labeled poses alongside their abstract grasp representations.

3.2   Grasp Recognition

The revised dataset is divided into two parts: 540 grasp poses for training and validation, and 60 new grasp poses for testing. The proposed algorithm was evaluated using 4-fold cross-validation with hyperparameters of a batch size of 64, 500 epochs, and the Adam optimizer with a learning rate of 0.001. The training accuracy achieved 93.3% while the accuracy on testing set achieved 87.2%. The testing accuracy is relatively low because some of the grasp topologies are difficult to distinguish. For example, the "wh" and "rc" grasps have similar configurations, making them harder to recognize accurately.

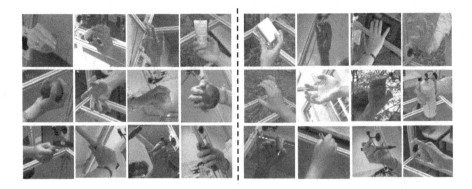

Fig. 4. The revised dataset consists of 600 grasp poses. Each pose is paired with a corresponding abstract grasp representation for each grasp topology.

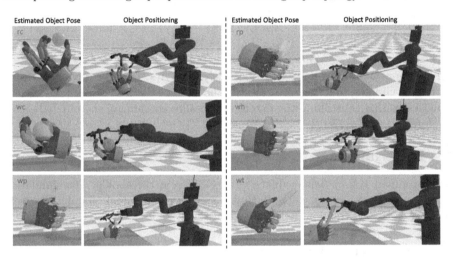

Fig. 5. Handover task for each grasp topology: In each task, the system first estimates the object pose based on the grasp pose of the simulated human hand. The model then attempts to place the object at the target pose.

3.3   Object Pose Estimation and Handover

The effectiveness and accuracy of an estimated object pose are evaluated through object-handover tasks in a simulation environment. An object pose is considered effective if the robot can successfully pass the object to the human hand, which should then be able to securely grasp it. For this evaluation, we used PyBullet [5] to simulate an AR10 robotic hand mounted on a Sawyer robot holding the object. The human hand, simulated by a Schunk robotic hand, positioned in front of the robot, performs a variant of one of the six grasp topologies. The system estimates the object pose based on the grasp pose of the simulated human hand and highlights the estimated pose as a green area. The handover task for each grasp topology is illustrated in Fig. 5, where the robot's goal is to position the object to align with the green area while avoiding collisions with the human hand.

The model was trained for 20,000 episodes with a learning rate of 1.6×10^{-6} and a batch size of 32, with varying target positions and orientations in each episode. Each grasp topology was tested 100 times achieving an overall success rate of 83%.

4 · Conclusions

In conclusion, this paper presents a robust approach to enhancing human-robot cooperation through the development of a grasp adaptation system. By accurately recognizing diverse human grasping habits and classifying them into standard grasp topologies, the system can determine optimal object handover strategies for smooth handovers. The use of deep learning for grasp pose recognition and reinforcement learning for strategy optimization demonstrated strong performance in experimental settings. Although challenges remain in distinguishing similar grasp configurations, the results underscore the potential of the proposed system to improve human-robot interaction by making robots more adaptable.

References

1. Ajoudani, A., Zanchettin, A.M., Ivaldi, S., Albu-Schäffer, A., Kosuge, K., Khatib, O.: Progress and prospects of the human-robot collaboration. Auton. Robot. **42**, 957–975 (2018)
2. Billard, A., Kragic, D.: Trends and challenges in robot manipulation. Science **364**(6446), eaat8414 (2019)
3. Bullock, I.M., Feix, T., Dollar, A.M.: The Yale human grasping dataset: grasp, object, and task data in household and machine shop environments. Int. J. Robot. Res. **34**(3), 251–255 (2015)
4. Cakmak, M., Srinivasa, S.S., Lee, M.K., Forlizzi, J., Kiesler, S.: Human preferences for robot-human hand-over configurations. In: 2011 IEEE/RSJ International Conference on Intelligent Robots and Systems, pp. 1986–1993. IEEE (2011)
5. Coumans, E., Bai, Y.: Pybullet, a python module for physics simulation for games, robotics and machine learning (2016–2019). http://pybullet.org
6. Cutkosky, M.R., et al.: On grasp choice, grasp models, and the design of hands for manufacturing tasks. IEEE Trans. Robot. Autom. **5**(3), 269–279 (1989)
7. Feix, T., Romero, J., Schmiedmayer, H.B., Dollar, A.M., Kragic, D.: The grasp taxonomy of human grasp types. IEEE Trans. Hum.-Mach. Syst. **46**(1), 66–77 (2015)
8. He, W., Gao, H., Zhou, C., Yang, C., Li, Z.: Reinforcement learning control of a flexible two-link manipulator: an experimental investigation. IEEE Trans. Syst., Man Cybern.: Syst. **51**(12), 7326–7336 (2020)
9. Huber, M., Rickert, M., Knoll, A., Brandt, T., Glasauer, S.: Human-robot interaction in handing-over tasks. In: RO-MAN 2008-the 17th IEEE International Symposium on Robot and Human Interactive Communication, pp. 107–112. IEEE (2008)

10. Li, H., Tan, J., He, H.: MagicHand: context-aware dexterous grasping using an anthropomorphic robotic hand. In: 2020 IEEE International Conference on Robotics and Automation (ICRA), pp. 9895–9901. IEEE (2020)
11. Li, H., Yihun, Y., He, H.: MagicHand: in-hand perception of object characteristics for dexterous manipulation. In: International Conference on Social Robotics, pp. 523–532. Springer (2018)
12. Li, H., Zhang, Y., Li, Y., He, H.: Learning task-oriented dexterous grasping from human knowledge. In: 2021 IEEE International Conference on Robotics and Automation (ICRA), pp. 6192–6198. IEEE (2021)
13. Mason, A.H., MacKenzie, C.L.: Grip forces when passing an object to a partner. Exp. Brain Res. **163**, 173–187 (2005)
14. Rao, B.: Learning robotic grasping strategy based on natural-language object descriptions (2018)
15. Strabala, K., et al.: Toward seamless human-robot handovers. J. Hum.-Robot Inter. **2**(1), 112–132 (2013)
16. Stulp, F., Theodorou, E.A., Schaal, S.: Reinforcement learning with sequences of motion primitives for robust manipulation. IEEE Trans. Rob. **28**(6), 1360–1370 (2012)
17. Sutton, R.S.: Reinforcement learning: an introduction (2018)
18. Tavakoli, M., Carriere, J., Torabi, A.: Robotics, smart wearable technologies, and autonomous intelligent systems for healthcare during the COVID-19 pandemic: an analysis of the state of the art and future vision. Adv. Intell. Syst. **2**(7), 2000071 (2020)
19. Thuruthel, T.G., Falotico, E., Renda, F., Laschi, C.: Model-based reinforcement learning for closed-loop dynamic control of soft robotic manipulators. IEEE Trans. Rob. **35**(1), 124–134 (2018)
20. Zimmermann, C., Ceylan, D., Yang, J., Russell, B., Argus, M., Brox, T.: FreiHand: a dataset for markerless capture of hand pose and shape from single RGB images. In: Proceedings of the IEEE/CVF International Conference on Computer Vision, pp. 813–822 (2019)

Leader-Follower Formation of a Car-Like Robot Using ROS and Trajectory Tracking

Faris Shahab[1][✉], Anas Dhahri[2], Adam Hamadi[3], Mohammed Noorizadeh[3], John-John Cabibihan[1], and Nader Meskin[4]

[1] Department of Mechanical and Industrial Engineering, Qatar University, Doha, Qatar
faris.shahab@yahoo.com, john.cabibihan@qu.edu.qa
[2] Private Higher School of Engineering and Technology (ESPRIT), Ariana, Tunisia
anesdhahri15@gmail.com
[3] Department of Computing, Qatar University, Doha, Qatar
{ah1705119,m.noorizadeh}@qu.edu.qa
[4] Department of Electrical Engineering,Qatar University, Doha, Qatar
nader.meskin@qu.edu.qa

Abstract. This paper explores the integration of the Robot Operating System (ROS) with human-robot interaction models for autonomous vehicle navigation in social robotics. Utilizing ROS as middleware, OptiTrack for positioning and localization, and MATLAB for control and ROS node deployment, this study investigates leader-follower formation dynamics in mixed environments. The leader vehicle is controlled using an RVIZ pointer, serving as a medium for human interaction, while both the leader and follower vehicles maintain safe distances using trajectory tracking methods. These methods are implemented and deployed to the robot cars as ROS nodes. The experiment involves a physical leader car and a virtual follower car, both tracked using OptiTrack. Numerical simulations and real-world experiments demonstrate ROS's role in enhancing coordination and interaction, providing insights into effective human-robot interaction and collision avoidance.

Keywords: robot operating system (ROS) · trajectory tracking · autonomous vehicle · human-robot interaction · social robotics · leader-follower formation

1 Introduction

Leader-follower dynamics are essential for coordinating autonomous systems where robots follow a leader to maintain formation, such as in convoys or industrial tasks. However, in social robotics, where robots must interact with humans in shared environments like hospitals, hotels, or public spaces. This challenge extends beyond simple coordination. Robots must not only maintain safe distances but also respect social norms, avoiding collisions and enhancing human comfort.

H. Li et al. (Eds.): ICSR + InnoBiz 2024, LNAI 15170, pp. 355–365, 2025.
https://doi.org/10.1007/978-981-96-1151-5_36

ROS, an open-source framework, facilitates structured communication among robotic components like sensors, actuators, and control algorithms [2]. Its modular architecture promotes collaboration and standardization across projects [15]. ROS enhances data processing and control in various applications, from industrial automation to autonomous vehicles [3,17]. In environments like hospitals and hotels, ROS enables seamless interaction between robots and humans, which is crucial where robots navigate crowds and complex spaces [1,7].

This research integrates a leader-follower dynamics with a concept similar to the Intelligent Driving Model (IDM) within a ROS framework for the interaction and coordination of autonomous robots. The study focuses on optimizing control algorithms to maintain safe distances between robots and humans, using two identical robot cars with Ackermann steering controllers to ensure smooth and collision-free operations in social settings.

2   Related Works

The importance of leader-follower formation in autonomous vehicles and social robots is well-documented. In such systems, a leading robot sets the pace while following robots adjust their movements to maintain formation, ensuring safe distances and speeds, particularly in dynamic environments. This concept is similar to the Intelligent Driving Model (IDM), which is used to ensure safe distances and speeds, making it suitable for dynamic environments [19].

These dynamics allow robots to interact with humans and other robots in shared spaces. For instance, service robots in hospitals or hotels may follow a human guide or another robot through crowds [16]. Shiomi et al. (2014) emphasized the need for socially acceptable collision avoidance, where robots respect personal space, enhancing comfort and safety in interactions [18].

ROS facilitates structured communication between system components such as sensors, actuators, and control algorithms through a modular architecture based on nodes and the publish/subscribe method [2,11]. This design supports the development of scalable and flexible systems, enabling efficient communication between nodes and the development of independent components. Rossi & Jokić (2023) highlight a ROS software package for modeling and simulating networks of dynamic systems, emphasizing its modular structure and easy implementation on physical systems [17]. Farzan (2023) highlights the improved learning outcomes of control engineering students when using ROS and Gazebo, demonstrating the central role of ROS in educational contexts and practical robotics applications [3].

Hussain et al. (2021) explore the safety perceptions of autonomous vehicles, emphasizing the importance of human-driven vehicle (HDV) and autonomous vehicle (AV) interactions. Their findings highlight that while there are positive perceptions regarding the elimination of human errors by AVs, there are significant concerns about interactions between HDVs and AVs in mixed traffic conditions [9].

This underscores the need for robust leader-follower formation to ensure safety and smooth interactions in both autonomous vehicles and social robotics.

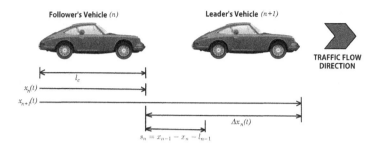

Fig. 1. Graphical Representation of Distance Keeping Between Cars [10]

Using IDM and ROS nodes helps achieve natural and intuitive interactions, crucial for the acceptance of robots in shared environments.

2.1 Safe Distance Model Interpretation

The Intelligent Driving Model (IDM) is a car-following model used to describe the behavior of a following vehicle based on the distance to the leading vehicle and the relative speed [6,10]. Figure 1 illustrates the IDM, formulated as:

$$\dot{v} = a_{max}\left(1 - \left(\frac{v}{v_0}\right)^{\delta} - \left(\frac{s^*}{s}\right)^2\right) \tag{1}$$

where $\dot{v}$ is the acceleration, a_{max} is the maximum acceleration, v is the current velocity, v_0 is the desired velocity, δ is the acceleration exponent, s is the actual gap to the leading vehicle, and s^* is the desired dynamic gap given by:

$$s^* = s_0 + \max\left(0, vT + \frac{v\Delta v}{2\sqrt{a_{max}b}}\right) \tag{2}$$

Here, s^* represents the desired dynamic gap. The term s_0 is the minimum gap maintained at a standstill, accounting for the physical space required to avoid a collision even at low speeds. The component vT represents the speed-dependent gap, where T is the time headway that ensures the following distance increases proportionally with speed, providing adequate reaction time. The term $\frac{v\Delta v}{2\sqrt{a_{max}b}}$ accounts for the relative speed (Δv) between the vehicles, where $\Delta v = v_{follower} - v_{leader}$, a_{max} is the maximum acceleration, and b is the comfortable deceleration. This ensures that the following vehicle decelerates appropriately when approaching the leading vehicle too quickly, maintaining a safe distance.

2.2 Bicycle Kinematic

The bicycle kinematic model simplifies the motion of a vehicle to that of a bicycle, where the front wheel handles steering and the rear wheel represents the drive mechanism. This model is particularly useful for understanding and controlling the motion of robots and vehicles in a planar environment.

The state of the vehicle is described by its position (x, y) and orientation (ϕ). The control inputs are the linear velocity (V) and the steering angle (ψ). The kinematic equations are:

$$\dot{x} = V \cos \phi$$
$$\dot{y} = V \sin \phi \qquad (3)$$
$$\dot{\phi} = V/l \cdot \tan \phi$$

The velocities in the x and y directions are represented as $\dot{x}$ and $\dot{y}$, respectively, while V denotes the linear velocity of the vehicle. The orientation angle is denoted by δ, the wheelbase by L, and the steering angle by δ.

2.3 The Trajectory Tracking & Dubins Curve

Various methods have been developed to address trajectory tracking challenges. One approach involves short-time and long-trajectory predictions, allowing the control system to adjust the vehicle's path more frequently for improved responsiveness and accuracy in dynamic environments [12].

In this project, trajectory tracking uses adaptive control gains within a backstepping technique that considers steering saturation [8]. This method enhances performance while maintaining input constraints. The backstepping approach adjusts control gains based on tracking error and desired vehicle speed, reducing tuning effort and improving convergence of tracking errors, especially for lateral deviations. The error pose $\mathbf{p}_e$ of the trajectory of the car $\mathbf{p}_c$ with respect to the reference pose $\mathbf{p}_r$ is:

$$\begin{bmatrix} x_e \\ y_e \\ \phi_e \end{bmatrix} = \begin{bmatrix} \cos \phi_c & \sin \phi_c & 0 \\ -\sin \phi_c & \cos \phi_c & 0 \\ 0 & 0 & 1 \end{bmatrix} \begin{bmatrix} x_e \\ y_e \\ \phi_e \end{bmatrix} \qquad (4)$$

Dubin's trajectory aims to find the shortest trajectory between two points while respecting curvature constraints [14]. The concept of Dubins paths, including the types LSR, RSL, LSL, RSR, LRL, and RLR, describes optimal trajectories for car-like robots when maneuvering in constrained environments. These paths are used for minimizing curvature and ensuring efficient movement between points. For a detailed visual representation see the original paper in Ref. [5].

Dubins' paths are used to connect field tracks, especially in headland areas and between distinct track blocks. The process begins with a geometric representation of the field, incorporating boundaries and obstacles as polygons. Tracks are generated within the minimum-bounding box, intersected with boundaries to retain feasible tracks, and clustered into blocks using the K-means algorithm. These blocks are connected using a permutation-based genetic algorithm, creating smooth trajectories that minimize operational time and fuel consumption, enhancing the efficiency and accuracy of autonomous robotic lawn mowers in agricultural settings [5].

3   Methodology

This section outlines the problem formulations addressed in this paper and the methods used to optimize the deceleration parameters to acceptable values within the control architecture. It also details the ROS communication setup, the integration with the ground station PC, the robot cars used in the experiment, and the array of OptiTrack cameras employed as the local positioning system.

3.1   Problem Formulation

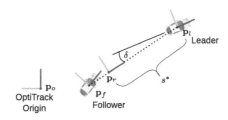

Fig. 2. Leader-Follower Formation Illustrating the Relationship between the Positions $\mathbf{p}_o$, $\mathbf{p}_f$, $\mathbf{p}_l$, and $\mathbf{p}_r$.

This research implements a concept similar to distance-keeping to address leader-follower formation in autonomous vehicles or social robotics, aiming to maintain safe distances efficiently. This experiment uses adaptive trajectory tracking from Ref. [8] and Dubins curve for trajectory, combined with the bicycle kinematic model, to achieve smooth navigation in shared environments with minimal collisions. The trajectory tracking is created in Simulink and deployed as C++ code to the QCar by Quanser as a ROS node for improved performance. By optimizing parameters related to distance, velocity, and time headway, the method ensures that the resulting distance (s) remains close to the desired gap (s^*) while maintaining safety as seen in Fig. 2. The following equation is used to maintain the safe distance between the leader and the follower:

$$s \geq s^* = s_0 + V_{lead}\tau \tag{5}$$

where τ is the time headway. The acceleration $\dot{V}$ are constrained to the maximum acceleration a_{max} and comfortable deceleration b.

The experiment uses a physical leader car, controlled using an RVIZ pointer, and a virtual follower car, tracked using OptiTrack. OptiTrack captures 3D motion data, which broadcasts the robots' position under OptiTrack's frame reference for real-time localization. This precise localization allows the follower to maintain a safe distance from the leader. Given the positions $\mathbf{p}_f = [x_f, y_f, \phi_f]$, $\mathbf{p}_l = [x_l, y_l, \phi_l]$, and $\mathbf{p}_o = [x_o, y_o, \phi_o]$ (origin, usually $[0, 0, 0]$), we aim to find p_r with respect to these known values. Here, s^* is the relative distance from the follower to the reference point in the follower's local frame.

First, we compute the angle δ between the follower and the leader:

$$\delta = \arctan 2(y_l - y_f, x_l - x_f) - \phi_f \tag{6}$$

Next, we compute $\mathbf{p}_r$ in the follower's frame:

$$\mathbf{p}'_r = \begin{bmatrix} x'_r \\ y'_r \end{bmatrix} = \begin{bmatrix} s^* \cos(\delta) \\ s^* \sin(\delta) \end{bmatrix} \tag{7}$$

Then, we transform $\mathbf{p}'_r$ to the global frame:

$$\begin{bmatrix} x_r \\ y_r \end{bmatrix} = \begin{bmatrix} x_l \\ y_l \end{bmatrix} - \begin{bmatrix} \cos(\phi_f) & -\sin(\phi_f) \\ \sin(\phi_f) & \cos(\phi_f) \end{bmatrix} \begin{bmatrix} x'_r \\ y'_r \end{bmatrix} \tag{8}$$

Finally, we compute ϕ_r:

$$\phi_r = \phi_f + \delta \tag{9}$$

This results in the final representation:

$$\mathbf{p}_r = \begin{bmatrix} x_l - s^* \cos(\delta + \phi_f) \\ y_l - s^* \sin(\delta + \phi_f) \\ \phi_f + \delta \end{bmatrix} \tag{10}$$

The reference of the follower's trajectory with respect to OptiTrack's coordinate system is crucial for maintaining the desired formation.

3.2 ROS Communication System

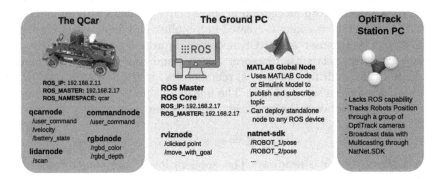

Fig. 3. ROS Connectivity Diagram

The Robot Operating System (ROS) is crucial for managing communication and coordination between devices in the leader-follower formation experiment, providing a framework for integrations of sensors, actuators, and control algorithms. The communication system facilitates data exchange between the ground station PC, the two identical robot car (QCar by Quanser) as the leader and follower, as illustrated in Fig. 3.

Key components include the ground station PC, which serves as the central node and the ROS Master, handles data processing, control execution, and user interaction. This also include RVIZ which serves as visualization of transforms in different fixed frames and controller of the leader, serving a medium of human-robot interaction.

Additionally, MATLAB which can be in separate PC or in the main ground station, allows publishing and subscribing to ROS topics, and applying transformation between points, under its global node. Additionally, this is where control nodes are developed, debugged and deployed as a form of C++ code, namely the trajectory tracking and the leader-follower formation, to the QCars as C++ code.

The leader vehicle is controlled using an RVIZ pose goal, which acts as a proxy for human commands, allowing the robot to follow waypoints in real-time. By using RVIZ, a widely-used visualization tool in the Robot Operating System (ROS), this setup enables the user to manually select and modify the leader's target position through a graphical interface. This mimics human decision-making in dynamic environments, making it possible to test how robots respond to real-time human input. The pose goal function, which allows setting specific positions and orientations, provides a flexible and intuitive method for controlling the robot in leader-follower formations. This approach enhances human-robot interaction, particularly in social robotics settings, by simulating human control in a way that robots can interpret and act upon, improving their ability to navigate shared environments safely and smoothly.

In this setup, OptiTrack data localizes both the physical leader car and the virtual follower car. Figure 4 shows how OptiTrack's data broadcasts from motion capture to ROS with multicasting through NatNet node in the main ground station PC. ROS uses a Z-up coordinate system, while OptiTrack uses a Y-up system [13]. To ensure compatibility, coordinate transformation is necessary, converting OptiTrack's Y-up coordinates to ROS's Z-up coordinates using the following transformation matrix:

$$\begin{bmatrix} x_{ros} \\ y_{ros} \\ z_{ros} \end{bmatrix} = \begin{bmatrix} 1 & 0 & 0 \\ 0 & 0 & 1 \\ 0 & -1 & 0 \end{bmatrix} \begin{bmatrix} x_{opti} \\ y_{opti} \\ z_{opti} \end{bmatrix} \tag{11}$$

Additionally, the quaternion orientation data from OptiTrack needs to be transformed into Euler angles for use in ROS. The conversion from quaternion (q_w, q_x, q_y, q_z) to Euler angles (ϕ, θ, ψ) can be done using the following equations:

$$\phi = \arctan 2 \left(2(q_w q_x + q_y q_z), 1 - 2(q_x^2 + q_y^2) \right)$$
$$\theta = \arcsin \left(2(q_w q_y - q_z q_x) \right) \tag{12}$$
$$\psi = \arctan 2 \left(2(q_w q_z + q_x q_y), 1 - 2(q_y^2 + q_z^2) \right)$$

Quaternions are particularly useful for interpolating angles and resolving the wrapping issues that Euler angles face, ensuring smooth and continuous rotation representation [4].

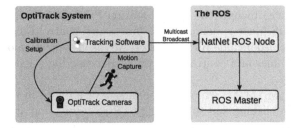

Fig. 4. OptiTrack to ROS System for Real-Time Localization

4   Results

This section presents the analysis of leader-follower formation based on the generated figures, focusing on key parameters: distance between leader and follower, velocities of the leader and follower, acceleration of the follower, and steering settings for both vehicles. In this experiment, a time headway of 0.5 and s_0 of 0.66 were used. The leader is manually controlled by publishing points on RVIZ, and the follower is a numerical model with pose based on OptiTrack's localization.

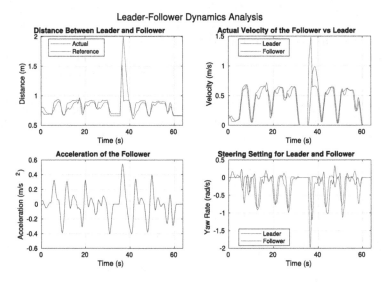

Fig. 5. Leader-Follower Formation Analysis illustrating distance between leader and follower, velocities, acceleration of the follower, and steering settings.

Distance Between Leader and Follower. The first subplot in Fig. 5 shows the actual and reference distances between the leader and follower over time. The actual distance closely follows the reference distance with some fluctuations, particularly around the 40-second mark due to sudden changes in the leader's speed or sharp turns.

Velocity of the Leader and Follower. The second subplot in Fig. 5 compares the velocities of the leader and follower. Both velocities show a similar pattern, indicating that the follower mirrors the leader's speed changes. Instances where the follower's velocity lags behind the leader's during rapid acceleration or deceleration can be attributed to the control system's response time.

Acceleration of the Follower. The third subplot in Fig. 5 illustrates the acceleration of the follower. The frequent peaks and troughs correspond to its attempts to match the leader's speed, indicating a responsive control system continuously correcting the follower's trajectory.

Steering Settings for Leader and Follower. The fourth subplot in Fig. 5 displays the steering settings for both the leader and follower as yaw rates. The yaw rates closely follow each other, demonstrating synchronized steering behavior. Occasional deviations may result from slight differences in the control algorithms or response times.

Summary. The follower vehicle effectively mirrors the leader's movements, maintaining a close match in distance, velocity, acceleration, and steering settings. However, some discrepancies, particularly in velocity response times and occasional deviations in steering, suggest areas for improvement in the control system. These findings highlight the need for refining control algorithms to enhance synchronization and reduce errors in leader-follower formation.

5   Conclusion and Future Work

The analysis of the leader-follower formation demonstrates that while the follower vehicle effectively mirrors the leader's movements, there are areas for improvement in the control system, particularly in addressing discrepancies between velocity measurements. Future work should focus on refining the velocity synchronization mechanisms and enhancing the control algorithms to reduce trajectory errors, ensuring smoother and more accurate navigation in dynamic environments.

Future work will explore the integration of multiple robot cars with different types of drives, such as differential drive and Ackermann steering, to study complex formation leader-follower formation. The focus will be on optimizing coordination among various robot types, improving formation control algorithms, and ensuring robust communication protocols. Additionally, the potential use of AprilTag for enhanced tracking accuracy will be considered, but the primary emphasis will be on refining existing control systems to improve trajectory adherence and reduce positional errors.

Acknowledgments. Special thanks to Mohammed Noorizadeh for his expertise and guidance on autonomous vehicles from his previous research. We would also like to thank Prof. Nader Meskin for providing lab facilities such as the QCar and the Opti-Track, and for keeping track of our ROS learning progress. Additionally, we extend our gratitude to Prof. John-John Cabibihan for his review and insightful feedback.

Disclosure of Interests. The authors have no competing interests to declare that are relevant to the content of this article.

References

1. Baek, E.T., Im, D.Y.: ROS-based unmanned mobile robot platform for agriculture. Appl. Sci. **12**(9) (2022). https://doi.org/10.3390/app12094335
2. Chen, Z., Albonico, M., Malavolta, I.: Automatic extraction of time-windowed ROS computation graphs from ROS bag files (2023). https://doi.org/10.48550/ARXIV.2305.16405
3. Farzan, S.: Project-based learning for robot control theory: a robot operating system (ROS) based approach. arXiv.org**abs/2305.11279** (2023)
4. Fossen, T.I.: Kinematics, chap. 2, pp. 15–44. John Wiley & Sons, Ltd (2011). https://doi.org/10.1002/9781119994138.ch2
5. Hameed, I.A.: Coverage path planning software for autonomous robotic lawn mower using Dubins' curve. In: 2017 IEEE International Conference on Real-time Computing and Robotics (RCAR). IEEE (2017). https://doi.org/10.1109/rcar.2017.8311915
6. Holley, D., D'sa, J., Mahjoub, H.N., Ali, G., Chalaki, B., Moradi-Pari, E.: MR-IDM – merge reactive intelligent driver model: towards enhancing laterally aware car-following models (2023). https://doi.org/10.48550/arXiv.2305.12014
7. Horelican, T.: Utilizability of navigation2/ROS2 in highly automated and distributed multi-robotic systems for industrial facilities. IFAC-PapersOnLine **55**(4), 109–114 (2022). https://doi.org/10.1016/j.ifacol.2022.06.018. 17th IFAC Conference on Programmable Devices and Embedded Systems PDES 2022 — Sarajevo, Bosnia and Herzegovina, 17–19 May 2022
8. Hu, J., Zhang, Y., Rakheja, S.: Adaptive trajectory tracking for car-like vehicles with input constraints. IEEE Trans. Industr. Electron. **69**(3), 2801–2810 (2022). https://doi.org/10.1109/tie.2021.3068672
9. Hussain, Q., Alhajyaseen, W.K., Adnan, M., Almallah, M., Almukdad, A., Alqaradawi, M.: Autonomous vehicles between anticipation and apprehension: investigations through safety and security perceptions. Transp. Policy **110**, 440–451 (2021). https://doi.org/10.1016/j.tranpol.2021.07.001
10. Islam, M.R.: Comparison of vehicle dynamics of microscopic car following models: optimal velocity and intelligent driver model. Master's thesis, Clemson University (2014). https://doi.org/10.13140/RG.2.2.22003.22564
11. Janavi, K., Teja, A.R.: Robot operating systems (ROS): the fundamentals of ROS and its remarkable performances in the world of drones. Int. J. Res. Appl. Sci. Eng. Technol. **10**(9), 1844–1849 (2022). https://doi.org/10.22214/ijraset.2022.46938
12. Kaixuan, C., Tianqing, C., Liyang, Z., Jie, Z., Xiaodong, Y.: Trajectory tracking method with short time step and long trajectory prediction. In: 2022 International Conference on Innovations and Development of Information Technologies and Robotics (IDITR). IEEE (2022). https://doi.org/10.1109/iditr54676.2022.9796480

13. Leong, X.W.J., Hesse, H.: Vision-based navigation for control of micro aerial vehicles. In: Guo, H., Ren, H., Bandla, A. (eds.) IRC-SET 2018, pp. 413–427. Springer, Singapore (2019). https://doi.org/10.1007/978-981-32-9828-6_33
14. Liang, T.C., Liu, J.S., Hung, G.T., Chang, Y.Z.: Practical and flexible path planning for car-like mobile robot using maximal-curvature cubic spiral. Robot. Auton. Syst. **52**(4), 312–335 (2005). https://doi.org/10.1016/j.robot.2005.05.001
15. Munera, E., Poza-Lujan, J.-L., Posadas-Yagüe, J.-L., Simó-Ten, J.-E., Blanes, F.: Smart resource integration on ROS-based systems: highly decoupled resources for a modular and scalable robot development. In: Distributed Computing and Artificial Intelligence, 13th International Conference. AISC, vol. 474, pp. 331–338. Springer, Cham (2016). https://doi.org/10.1007/978-3-319-40162-1_36
16. Mutlu, B., Forlizzi, J.: Robots in organizations: the role of workflow, social, and environmental factors in human-robot interaction. In: Proceedings of the 3rd ACM/IEEE International Conference On Human Robot Interaction. HRI 2008, ACM (2008). https://doi.org/10.1145/1349822.1349860
17. Rossi, M., Jokić, A.: ROS framework for distributed control of networks of dynamical systems. In: 2023 46th MIPRO ICT and Electronics Convention (MIPRO), pp. 356–362 (2023). https://doi.org/10.23919/MIPRO57284.2023.10159798
18. Shiomi, M., Zanlungo, F., Hayashi, K., Kanda, T.: Towards a socially acceptable collision avoidance for a mobile robot navigating among pedestrians using a pedestrian model. Int. J. Soc. Robot. **6**(3), 443–455 (2014). https://doi.org/10.1007/s12369-014-0238-y
19. Treiber, M., Hennecke, A., Helbing, D.: Congested traffic states in empirical observations and microscopic simulations (2000). https://doi.org/10.48550/ARXIV.COND-MAT/0002177

Author Index

Printed in the United States
by Baker & Taylor Publisher Services